Acting Out

Acting Out:
Feminist Performances

Lynda Hart and Peggy Phelan, Editors

Ann Arbor

THE UNIVERSITY OF MICHIGAN PRESS

For Madeline

Copyright © by the University of Michigan 1993
All rights reserved
Published in the United States of America by
The University of Michigan Press
Manufactured in the United States of America

1999   1998   1997   1996   7   6   5   4

A CIP catalog record for this book is available from the British Library.

Library of Congress Cataloging-in-Publication Data

Acting out : feminist performances / Lynda Hart and Peggy Phelan,
   editors.
      p.   cm.
   Includes bibliographical references.
      ISBN 0-472-09479-3 (alk. paper). — ISBN 0-472-06479-7 (pbk. :
   alk. paper)
      1. Feminist theater. 2. Performance art. 3. Feminism and
   theater.   I. Hart, Lynda, 1953–   .   II. Phelan, Peggy.
   PN1590.W64A38   1993
   792'.082—dc20   93-16280
                                                                   CIP

*Grateful acknowledgment is made to the following authors, publishers,
and journals for permission to reprint previously published materials.*
"Telling the Awfullest Truth: An Interview with Karen Finley"
by C. Carr, *ArtVu Magazine,* Fall, 1991. Reprinted by permission.
"Unspeakable Practices, Unnatural Acts," by C. Carr, *Village
Voice,* June 24, 1986. Reprinted by permission of the author and
The Village Voice. "Split Britches in *Split Britches:* Performing
History, Vaudeville, and the Everyday" by Vivian M. Patraka,
Women and Performance 4, no. 2, Issue 8, 1989. Reprinted by
permission. "Desire Cloaked in a Trenchcoat," by Jill Dolan,
reprinted from *The Drama Review* 33, no. 1 (Spring 1989) by
permission of The MIT Press, Cambridge, Massachusetts, Copy-
right © 1989 by The MIT Press. "Mimesis, Mimicry, and the
'True-Real'" by Elin Diamond, *Modern Drama* 32, no. 1 (1989).
Reprinted by permission of *Modern Drama.* "White Men and Pregnancy: Discovering the Body to Be Rescued" by Peggy Phelan,
reprinted from *Unmarked: The Politics of Performance* (London:
Routledge, 1993), copyright © 1993 by Peggy Phelan.

Contents

Introduction

Lynda Hart

I got the kind of madness Socrates talked about, "A divine release of the soul from the yoke of custom and convention." I refuse to be intimidated by reality anymore. After all, what is reality anyway? Nothin' but a collective hunch.
—Jane Wagner, *The Search for Signs of Intelligent Life in the Universe*

"Reality" is a fantasy-construction which enables us to mask the Real of our desire.
—Jacques Lacan

Jane Wagner's "bag lady" Trudy speaks her subjectivity from the far margins of the social order as well as the borderlands of psychic space. Wagner thus neatly connects the material circumstances of her heroine with her psychic determination. Lily Tomlin's one-woman performance processes a series of rapidly mutating personae, all traversed by the consciousness of Trudy, whose madness affords her a motility that might be read as evidence of the primordial splitting of the antihumanistic subject. Trudy inhabits a spatiotemporal order— the spaced-out time of her extraterrestrial chums—disconsonant with the linear time of humanistic narrative. Miming the unconscious, where the subject is not consonant with the self, where the "I" is multiple, shifting, and subject and object positions are endlessly mutable, this subject-without-a-fixed-identity created in the fissure of a radical split would be in need of a therapeutic restoration of wholeness for the humanist spectator. Trudy is "acting out," transgressing the boundary between the imaginary and the real. Catherine Clément points out that acting out, "however dangerous it might be, is also therapeutic, monstrously so."[1] Wagner both calls attention to and reinforces the impossibility of her female speaker's rejection of the symbolic as Trudy reports: "I never could've done stuff like that when I was in my *right* mind. I'd be worried people would think I was *crazy*."[2]

By translating her madness into divinity, Trudy attempts to make the best of a bad situation. Her dilemma is not unlike that of women in general. If "there can be nothing *human* that pre-exists or exists outside the law represented by the father; [if] there is only either its denial (psychosis) or the fortunes and misfortunes ('normality' and neurosis) of its terms,"[3] then we can better understand why *Search for Signs,* a materialist-feminist performance that satirizes the misfortunes of women caught within the sociosymbolic order dominated by the law of the Father, seeks escape in madness and communion with extrahuman space chums. Wagner and Tomlin deviously address the problem but nonetheless appeal to the model. There is no easy way out for Trudy and her multiple incarnations. She attempts to manipulate her world, but, Cassandra-like, no one will believe her. Her madness relegates her to an aberrant individuality; thus isolated, she cannot speak for a credible community. It is nonetheless in these moments of "acting out" that the "factitious identity of the subject disappears."[4] Clément speaks of identity as a prosthesis or an armor that one must wear in order to be understood. Identities are necessary if we are to live in reality, but they mask our desire. Feminist identities embrace the monstrous possibilities of acting out. Cutting ourselves off from "reality" can be a way to escape our inundation in *a* masculine imaginary that passes as *the* symbolic order.

If *Search for Signs* managed to squeak some subversive moments past the patriarchal censors and still gain wide popularity as well as commercial success, what the theatrical establishment usually authorizes under the name "women's," and occasionally even "feminist," theater is recently best represented by Wendy Wasserstein's *Heidi Chronicles.* Wasserstein herself as well as her main character, Heidi Holland, eschew a feminist identity in deference to a humanist one, and thereby become spokeswomen for a feminism that failed, that left women like Heidi "stranded." The play's most highly charged moment occurs when Dr. Heidi Holland is invited to address Miss Crain's School East Coast Alumnae Association as a distinguished alumna. Her topic is "Women, Where Are We Going?" "Nowhere" is her answer. She sums up the history of the feminist movement in an iconic aerobics class locker room scene, in which she finds herself alienated from, envious of, and superior to the young women wearing purple and green leather who bring their own heavier weights, the mothers with pressed blue jeans who know where to purchase Zeus sneakers, the gray-haired woman who talks about brown rice and women's fiction, and whom Heidi imagines is having "a bisexual relationship with a female dock worker."[5] Heidi realizes at this moment that she is not happy and hasn't been for a long time. Her speech ends with this spontaneous, nostalgic lament: "I don't blame the ladies in the locker room for how I feel. I don't blame any of us. We're all concerned, intelligent, good women. (Pause). It's just that I feel stranded. And I thought the whole point was that I wouldn't feel stranded. I thought the point was we were all in this together. Thank you. (She walks off.)"[6]

The Heidi Chronicles is a valuable commodity in this increasingly conservative political climate. Feminism, it insists, has woefully failed "women." The play's realism offers nothing in the way of commentary on the fact that the conceptual space it carves out for "women" is occupied by a white, middle-class, heterosexual woman who finds her fulfillment in motherhood and considers herself a humanist. For those women who have contributed to the demise of such a monolithic feminism, Heidi's "failure" is our triumph. This play fulfills the fantasy that the divisions within contemporary feminism signal a dissolve, rather than productive disassembling.

It is the "somewhere else" of feminisms that *The Heidi Chronicles* refuses to historicize. It is to these other places where feminism is performed that this book attends. No homage is paid here to an imaginary canon; no illusions are held that one book can contain the field of feminist performance. Collections like these always presuppose some unifying principle; reviewers almost always look for order, coherency, categories, concepts that in a number of ways this book presses against. We have grouped these articles into three sections, which, nonetheless, we hope will be read intertextually. Discrete identities are inadequate ground for coalition. This work thus mingles rather promiscuously. Like the performances they are speaking of and with, these writings have little respect for boundaries. Consequently, we have tried to resist the urge to strive too hard for that elusive "sameness" that feminist theory seems so unable to do without. This project is in part motivated by the desire to displace the dominance of text-based work in theater studies, to value the ephemerality of performance.

We have, however, as something of a general organizing principle, focused primarily on collective work and performance art. There is a moment in the U.S. lesbian-feminist Split Britches and London's gay duo Bloolips collaboration, *Belle Reprieve,* that addresses this emphasis. Frustrated with this postmodern pastiche of Tennessee Williams's *A Streetcar Named Desire,* Bloolips Bette (Blanche) demands a story. Stamping his feet and whining his complaints with hyperbolic distress, Bette insists that the cast stop all this "romping about in the avant-garde and I don't know what else,"[7] and allow him to memorize his lines, don a pair of pretty pumps, and play a real part, a part his seventy-three-year-old mother, who is still hoping to see him play Romeo one day, can understand. Lois Weaver (Stella) menacingly challenges Bette to a realistic scene. Peggy Shaw (Stanley) attempts to play it with him—straight—from *A Streetcar Named Desire:*

> *Blanche:* "Just let me get by you."
> *Stanley:* "Get by me? Sure, go ahead."
> *Blanche:* "You stand over there."
> *Stanley:* "You got plenty of room, go ahead."
> *Blanche:* "Not with you there! I've got to get by somehow!"

Bette is a drag queen, which offers him a way out of sliding too easily into patriarchal womanhood, and he refuses to play the scene. When he realizes what is about to happen to him, he interrupts the action by reminding Stanley that he is not a real man. No, Shaw admits, if I were a real man I would say: "Come to think of it, maybe you wouldn't be so bad to interfere with. . . . If you want to play a woman, the woman in this play gets raped and goes crazy."[8] Bette says that he didn't plan on getting raped and going crazy; he only wanted a chance to wear a nice frock. This is one moment in which the "reprieve," a temporary escape from pain or trouble, occurs. This performance of bodies and drives and violence upends any expectation for realism. If spectators are frustrated in their desire for identification, Bette (Blanche) finally gives them the moment described above in which they might enter this show. Laura Mulvey's claim that "sadism demands a story" has never seemed so incandescent.[9] Getting raped, going crazy, and, of course, dying—this is what women appear to do most often in realistic theater. The recurrence of these actions is often enough thematic, but it also indicates the space of representation for the feminine subject position. Within the psychosemiotics of theatrical realism, the "death-space," space of absence, negativity, unrepresentability, is where femininity most often takes a place. Realism, like/as ideology, needs subjects, and subjects are constituted through divisions and losses that are always already gendered.

One response to the impossibility of the feminine taking a place within the symbolic has been an effort to recover, or postulate, a prediscursive body, a critical effort to free the female body from its overdeterminations as a body saturated with sex, site of pleasure for (an)other, subjected and devoid of subjectivity. This issue has a particular valence in performance studies, where the female body on stage is easily received as iconic, seemingly less arbitrary than a linguistic sign, and even more so than photographic or televisual images, exceptionally susceptible to naturalization. Indeed, the female body on stage appears to be the "thing itself," incapable of mimesis, afforded not only no distance between sign and referent but, indeed, taken for the referent.

In his discussion of the reception of televisual broadcasts Stuart Hall retains the distinction "denotation/connotation"—a conceptual pairing that he recognizes as rather outmoded in linguistic theory—but which continues to hold a certain "analytic value." The distinction is useful for thinking about the female body in performance, for, as Hall outlines it, the connotative level of the sign is the site where "'meanings' are *not* apparently fixed in natural perception (that is, they are not fully naturalized), and their fluidity of meaning and association can be more fully exploited and transformed."[10] By contrast the denotative level of the sign (understood here as an analytic category and not a literal transcription) is the site where "its ideological value is strongly *fixed*—because it has become so fully universal and 'natural.'"[11] Elin Diamond has cautioned us against "leap[ing] to examples of performance art where, supposedly, the body's texts displace the conventional mimesis of the text-performance structure."[12] Certainly the work represented here does not simply and effortlessly evade the body/text conflation of conventional mimesis,

but I do envision this collection as an antidote to the virtual hegemony of realism in Anglo-American theater.

Most of the performance texts under discussion in this collection
do not have the status of "plays," nor do they aspire to such categorization. They do not, however, by virtue of operating on the level of
the connotative sign—where, according to Hall's schema, "situational ideologies alter and transform signification"—produce meanings that are *outside* of ideology. But perhaps they could be said to
have a certain advantage that is produced alongside their marginalized
status. In that sense they are in limited but important ways "unbound," achieving a fluidity of movement simultaneously inside and
outside dominant discourses. Although some of the articles are more
obviously historical as they record the trajectory of feminist performance collectives, this is not a book that pretends to retrieve a past
in feminist performance. The histories discussed here are useful documents in that they trace and locate the work of companies that might
otherwise become lost to future cultural workers, but they are also
self-consciously *making* these "histories" as strategical interventions
in the discourse of performance studies.

Collective authorship was an extremely important concept in
early feminist companies of the 1970s and 1980s. As the utopian
fervor of such collectivities gave way to a realization that they were,
to some extent, based on a vision of feminist homogeneity that could
not fully take into account the divisions and productive conflicts between and among feminists, the "idea" of a collective suffered frag-
mentations, largely in response to women of color and lesbians, who
began calling attention to the inadequacies of the model. Nevertheless, today we may yet have something to learn from the history of
these collectives; certainly the problem of authorship and textual
ownership has become even more pressing in the last few decades.
Julie Malnig and Judy Rosenthal map the history of the Women's
Experimental Theatre Company (WET), an emblematic company
founded in 1975. The optimism of the 1970s, in which feminist theater companies were operating with the idea that presenting "positive" images of women could counteract the misogyny of masculinist
representations of women, gave way to the realization that differences between, among, and within women precluded any direct access to what constitutes "positivity." WET dissolved in 1985, but its
ten-year history is marked with the conflicts that many women in

performance grappled with during this period. In the histories of these collectives we can observe the process of feminists wrestling with what Derrida has called "women as truth" and "women as untruth," both remaining "within the economy of truth's system, in the phallogocentric space."[13] Such oscillation between competing claims for a definition of "women," raises the problem of essentialism and the necessity of performing gender and sexuality in a register that disrupts a metaphysics of presence.

Janelle Reinelt's materialist analysis of England's Monstrous Regiment Company emphasizes the ideological consequences for feminist collectives who struggle to continue operating under the pressure of a conservative government. Issues of casting, collectivity, and feminist content cannot be adjudicated in isolation from questions of subsidy. Thus, Reinelt locates this company's fifteen-year history in its struggle to resist commodification and in the grip of a repressive government's resistance to feminist work.

Joyce Devlin demonstrates the effect of the fracturing of England's women's liberation movement on the work of the lesbian-feminist collective Siren Theatre Company. In its thirteen years of production an early lesbian-separatist position has undergone numerous transformations as issues of class and race have pressed heavily on their notion of a collectivity grounded in a homogeneous notion of lesbian identity. As feminism has become feminisms, the very notion of collectivity has been the site of heated debates. Nonetheless, feminist theater workers continue to struggle to theorize a way of working together that does not simply resort to the humanist model of the isolated artist, the author in possession of the text as property, the very (author)ity of textual production.

The three-woman troupe Split Britches has been one of the most influential groups in feminist performance. Its productions have been the subject of excitement, controversy, and much provocative writing in feminist performance studies. We reprint Vicki Patraka's essay, which discusses the group's eponymous debut "Split Britches," to record and contextualize the origins of this groundbreaking company's work. As a single feminist performance artist, Karen Finley probably has the highest profile of any woman working in the field today. Her notoriety as centerpiece for the National Endowment for the Arts (NEA) controversies has propelled her into a refractive and projective spotlight, which, as the interview with C. Carr reveals, has taken quite a toll on her. Long before the NEA debates began, however, Finley's performances elicited heated reactions. By reprinting Carr's article on one of her earliest and most controversial performances, we reclaim Finley's history and assert her presence in the field as an artist whose daring performances have always been located on the margins that constitute "the front" of feminist politics. Finley's work excites a multiplicity of spectatorial identifications that illuminate the complexities of seeing. She is both susceptible to assimilation and co-optation by the dominant gaze that decries her representations and a model for subversive transgressions.[14]

The question of identity formations is crucial to feminist theorizing. As the work of the collectives exemplifies, the last decade has been one of struggle between competing identities. Whereas earlier feminist theorists were enabled by constituting "women" as a group opposed to a dominant patriarchy, they also came to realize that such a position presumed a hegemonic Other that was by no means monolithic. Such an "us-them" stance was not only reductive, but it also precluded making coalitions across gender, race, and sexual borders. It relegated "us" to victims and gave "them" a hegemonic power that left no way out for feminist subjectivities. And, most important, it erased the differences between, among, and within "women," who presumably constituted the category. This has been a central issue in feminist theory for some time now, and its ongoing political importance is addressed by many writers in this collection. Yvonne Yarbro-Bejarano evokes the Chicana "speaking for ourselves" but is quick to problematize the expression in Cherríe Moraga's work that permits no simplistic access to a unified Chicana identity or experience. Moraga is one of the leading figures in representing and historicizing the imbrication of gender, race, and sexuality as both multiple sites of oppression and spaces of contradiction in which different subjectivities can be constructed. Yarbro-Bejarano shows that the "familia" is a crucial concept to maintain for Chicano/a ethnic identity—but it must be refigured by ending the social construct of "man." Her careful reading of Moraga's *Shadow of a Man* exemplifies this strategy.

Anna Deavere Smith's one-woman "On the Road" performances make patent the way in which feminist poststructuralists theorize formations of subjectivity. I particularly like Sandra Richard's description of Smith's work as "solo carnival," a provocative paradox that neatly captures Smith's "imitations" of her interviewees. If the "selves" that Smith performs are a series of ego identifications, she shows that these are dialogic formations that constantly mutate. Smith does not simply capture the people she interviews and reproduce their images; she also shows us the more unsettling process of their subjectivities being formed in the act of exchange with her, then among the spectators who witness the multiple incarnations. Such a "kaleidoscope of often contradictory positions" both addresses the problematics of community building and, ironically perhaps, facilitates their formation.

Kate Davy's essay demonstrates the problematics of "identity" and the necessity for keeping vigilance on shifting historical moments through her analysis of Holly Hughes's work. Davy is concerned with the politics of Hughes's location in the NEA controversies. By the time conservatives got around to targeting an overtly "lesbian" performance, Hughes was defunded for a show, *World without End,* which Davy argues was the *least* "lesbian" of all her work. This ironic moment raises again the clash between identity politics and the semiotics of subjectivity. What constituted the "content" that a subcultural group recognized as "lesbian," which, according to Davy, became "evacuated"? How do we resist reifying a metaphysical core without eliminating politically constructed identities?

Jill Dolan's "Desire Cloaked in a Trenchcoat" is reprinted here with a new, and second, epilogue. Her palimpestic text neatly encapsulates a historical trajectory of theoretical positions, demonstrating some of the movement that this book is about as well as further troubling the stability of a position from which one looks and is looked at. How we are all always already in the gaze becomes clearer as we read Dolan's thinking on these issues over a five-year period. If the "trenchcoat" can undergo a transformation from sadistic object to "efficacious political metaphor," perhaps the point is that the object is never either/or. Roland Barthes defines the essence of Western eroticism as "the intermittence of skin flashing between two articles of clothing . . . it is this flash itself which seduces or rather: the staging of appearance as disappearance."[15] We can give up the concept of identity as a metaphysical category, but, if the historicity of identity formations goes out with it, can we still then ask the question: Who's flashing whom?

When we began assembling this collection, Thurgood Marshall had just resigned from the Supreme Court of the United States. I read

Nat Hentoff in the *Village Voice* taking advantage of these ideological shifts to chide feminists for supporting abortion clinics, where women are "killed" and "babies" are mutilated.[16] Such reprehensible scare tactics are designed to tame feminism by widening our divisions. A *New York Times* story says that Marshall "could only watch as the ideological ground shifted inexorably away, leaving him isolated on most of the issues that imbue people with passion."[17] Now Clarence Thomas has taken Marshall's place; and Anita Hill is saying that the "verdict is still out." She closed a recent speech with the story of Celia, a slave who killed her master after he repeatedly raped her. Under Missouri law a woman had the right to defend herself by any means necessary during a sexual assault, but, for a slave woman, the owner's previous "accustomed" sexual intercourse with her caused the law to be overruled. Hill pointed out that technically the jury had no legal choice but to convict Celia of murder. She was hanged on 21 December 1855.

Hill implicitly made an analogy with her "jury," some of whom did perhaps "wince" as they enacted and perpetuated an oppressive system. Hill was surprisingly optimistic; throughout her lecture she seemed convinced of the inherent goodness of most people and of the power of working within the system. I found her optimism unsettling, even depressing. Her argument that sexual harassment needs to be understood as "an abuse of power," and not a sexual issue, repeats the early feminist attempt to define rape as violence, not sex. Most of the essays in this collection are about sex and power and their inescapable imbrication. The "truth" is not going to set us free— unless perhaps we understand that the truth is always structured like a fiction and that it arises from misrecognition. The trick is to *premeditate* the misrecognitions, to interpret before, not after, the event.

I am concerned that feminists will retreat in the face of the deeply reactionary times in which we are mired. Will the progress we have made in fracturing monumental, exclusionary, totalizing constructs of women lose its force as we seek ways to mobilize our defenses? This seems to me to be a most urgent threat. Is greater visibility our best offense and defense? Acting out, acting up, coming out—these have been the strategies most frequently deployed to resist the swell of the New Right's agenda. They have produced some astonishing successes but have also been compromising in complex ways that bear close scrutiny.

Reproduction, representation, and the visibility/invisibility axis are the focus of Peggy Phelan's article, which urges us to reconsider the import of visibility politics. If we find ourselves wondering how this article on paternity and the theatrics of Operation Rescue takes a space in a book on feminism and performance, then we must consider how we are still bound to old paradigms, those disciplinary mechanisms that I mentioned earlier. It is time perhaps to rethink Audre Lorde's mantra for feminist praxis: "the master's tools will never dismantle the master's house."[18] Technology and ideology change the function of tools, which in any case have no inherent instrumental function. Phelan subtly reconsiders how an old tool, such as Freud's theory of paternal anxiety and the resulting hierarchy of abstract (invisible) masculinity, can be redeployed with new meanings in a time like ours, when technology has rendered paternity knowable. Scientifically verifiable paternity is no less a discourse by and about men than is unmarked masculinity, but Phelan describes how the means and methods of representing them have changed significantly. Opening up a new direction for feminist inquiry, she asks us to think again about what these developments signal to feminists who are devoted to visibility politics. What are the costs? Who pays and with what currency? Certainly we cannot afford to relax our vigilance in monitoring the ways in which we are—and are not—represented.

NOTES

1. Catherine Clément, *The Lives and Legends of Jacques Lacan,* trans. Arthur Goldhammer (New York: Columbia University Press, 1983), 71.

2. Jane Wagner, *The Search for Signs of Intelligent Life in the Universe* (New York: Harper and Row, 1986), 18.

3. Juliet Mitchell, "Introduction—I," *Feminine Sexuality: Jacques Lacan and the école freudienne,* trans. Jacqueline Rose (New York: W. W. Norton, 1985), 23.

4. Clément, *Lives and Legends,* 92.

5 Wendy Wasserstein, *The Heidi Chronicles* (New York: Dramatists Play Services, 1990), 61. *The Heidi Chronicles* won not only the 1989 Pulitzer prize for drama but also the 1989 best play distinction from the Drama Desk, the New York Drama Critics' Circle, the Outer Critics' Circle, as well as the Dramatists Guild's Hull Warriner Award and the Susan Smith Blackburn Prize.

6. Ibid., 62.

7. *Belle Reprieve* is a collaborative work by Split Britches and Bloolips. It will be published in *Gay and Lesbian Plays Today,* ed. Terry Helbing (Portsmouth, N.H.: Heinemann). My quotations are taken from proof pages.

8. Ibid.

9. Laura Mulvey, "Visual Pleasure and Narrative Cinema," *Visual and Other Pleasures* (Bloomington: Indiana University Press, 1989), 22.

10. Stuart Hall, "Encoding/decoding," *Culture, Media, Language,* ed. Stuart Hall (London: Hutchinson, 1980), 133.

11. Ibid.

12. Elin Diamond, "Mimesis, Mimicry, and the 'True-Real,'" *Modern Drama* 32, no. 1 (March 1989): 68; reprinted in this volume.

13. Jacques Derrida, *Spurs: Nietzsche's Styles,* trans. Barbara Harlow (Chicago: University of Chicago Press, 1978), 97 and passim.

14. I have discussed Finley's work at length elsewhere. See Lynda Hart, "Motherhood according to Karen Finley: *The Theory of Total Blame,*" *Drama Review* 36, no. 1 (Spring 1992): 124–34; and "Karen Finley's Dirty Work: Homophobia, Censorship, and the NEA," *Genders* 14 (Fall 1992): 1–15.

15. Roland Barthes, *The Pleasure of the Text* (New York: Hill and Wang, 1975), 10.

16. Nat Hentoff, "Since Abortions Are Legal, Why Can't They Be Safe?" *Village Voice,* 2 July 1991, 22.

17. Andrew Rosenthal, "Only Black Justice, after 24-Year Tenure, Leaves in Frustration," *New York Times,* 27 June 1991.

18. Audre Lorde, "The Master's Tools Will Never Dismantle the Master's House," *Sister Outsider* (New York: Crossing Press, 1984), 110–13.

Reciting the Citation of Others; or, A Second Introduction

Peggy Phelan

Like most writers, I harbor fantasies of the perfect reader. One of these continues to be related to my dream of a phantasmatic mother— a fantastic woman who loved me before I did or was anything. It returns every time I face the empty screen, the blank paper. This unformed, uninformed fantasy is called True Love. We expect it to be playing at theaters near us—but it surprises us when it turns up in the collaborative art of feminist critical anthologies devoted to performance. Most of the artists here probably harbor fantasies of the perfect spectator, and most of the authors probably dream of the perfect editor. Alas, there are two of us, thus making it more difficult to sustain the illusion of (singular) perfect Being. *Acting Out* is set on a stage that taps the dream of True Love—but spends all its time dramatizing Real Love.

Shortly after I began teaching in the Performance Studies Department at New York University my friends, who were a bit mystified by what I was doing, called me up, elated. They had just seen *Legal Eagles* (1986) and were thrilled to have at last seen some "performance art." Daryl Hannah, playing a character who is a cross between a pyromaniac and an orphan, installs various electrical coils across the floor of her large loft, lights them, recites a passionately fiery text, and christens herself a performance artist. More recently, Steve Martin, roller-skating across the floors of the Los Angeles County Museum of Art while his best friend uses her camcorder to track his pirouettes, turns, and counterturns in front of Van Gogh's *Sunflowers* (with stick-on flowers that stand up as Martin whizzes

13

by), declares himself a performance artist in *L.A. Story* (1990). The distance between Hannah's version of performance art, all angst and fire, and Martin's, all smirk and smile, is as good a yardstick to measure the sea change in the U.S. mainstream perception of what performance art is as any other I can think of.

The comic domestication of performance art has been helped considerably by the National Endowment for the Arts (NEA) fiasco.[1] Conservative attacks on the "NEA Four"—Tim Miller, John Fleck, Holly Hughes, and Karen Finley—put performance art into the minds of the "decent taxpayer" as something potentially obscene but actually closer to the absurd.[2] Posturing politicians in tight re-election campaigns took up the role of art commentator with that peculiarly American combination of brashness and ignorance. Denouncing art that offended their narrow idea of beauty, Senators Jesse Helms and Alfonse D'Amato turned art into an arena of crude literalism and offensively linear logic. (If a man saw a Mapplethorpe photograph of two men kissing, he would be tempted to rush up to the nearest man and kiss him because Mapplethorpe makes it all seem, literally, irresistible.) The powerful legislative and financial threats to the Endowment launched by Helms framed John Frohnmayer's decision to deny NEA funding to four performance artists in 1990. The stinging tongues of late-night television comics, seeking to puncture the inflated rhetoric of the senators, quickly trivialized and mocked the performance art that motivated that rhetoric. Televangelists' warnings of moral corruption lurking in art like a dangerous virus gave the whole discussion of federal arts funding a macabre feel.

Karen Finley, it was widely reported, smeared chocolate all over her naked body and called it art. Finley said that this description was initiated in an editorial by Robert Novak and Roland Evans; she also claimed that neither man ever saw her work (see C. Carr's interview with Finley "Telling the Awfullest Truth," in this volume). Finley's fury was the same as any artist who is reviewed without being seen, but the particular force of her rage is worth considering in detail. Her specific complaint was that these editorials took her work out of context and thereby allowed other people to use it for their own political ends. In this part of her argument Finley pinpointed one of the dilemmas of and for performance art: the problem of citationality, documentation, and context.

I want to examine this problem at some length, for it points to

one of the most vexing and challenging issues in performance scholarship today. The essays collected here offer an opportunity to think
again about the dense political and psychic relations between writing
and performance, to reconsider the political and psychic currencies
that mediate the exchanges between artists and their critics, and to
reconsider two different notions of performance currently invoked
by artists and scholars on the Left.

As expressive systems in repressive cultures (I take as axiomatic
the Freudian contention that cultures always function to repress and
refashion libidinal energy), feminist writing and performance refuse
to accept the idea that what is "real" is only that which is visible.
Feminist writing and performance resist and supplement what is usually given to be seen, read, performed. The forceful intersection of
performance and feminist writing was manifest in the NEA controversy and the ensuing commentaries; it is not accidental that many
of the most passionate defenses of Andres Serrano, Mapplethorpe,
and the NEA Four were written by feminist critics.[3] Not accidental
either is the recent interest in performance and performativity on the
part of progressive literary critics, feminist cultural theorists, and
psychoanalytically inclined philosophers—Eve Sedgwick, Tania
Modleski, and Judith Butler among them. To date, however, there
has been little attempt to bring together the specific epistemological
and political possibilities of performance as it is enacted in what are
still known, for better or for worse, as "theater events" and the
epistemological and political openings enabled by the "performative"
invoked by contemporary theory. Each has much to learn from the
other.

With a broad stroke it can be said that for feminist theorists
concerned primarily with theatrical performance the living performing body is the center of semiotic crossings, which allows one to
perceive, interpret and document the performance event; while, for
feminists interested in the discursive performative, the acts of signifying systems themselves (language and the codes of textuality) are the
center of interpretive analyses. Like all broad strokes, this one is
incomplete and might lead one to the false assumption that "the living
performing body" is somehow outside of signifying systems or to
forget that signifying systems are always already embodied. By
thinking about both notions of the performative we can see how
thoroughly bodies inhabit signifying systems *and* how signifying sys-

tems are always organized as bodies. These are useful notions for people interested in reading how women are read *as* bodies and how most performing bodies are read as feminine—which is usually to say degraded—as any dance scholar or theorist working in the United States will quickly attest.[4]

Virtually all of the essays here concern performers working within a "theater event" idea of performance, however distinctly inflected the political frame for that event. Operation Rescue, for example, employs theatrical devices in service of a singular politics of the reproductive body, while Robbie McCauley explores the multiple ideologies of race and reproduction within a singular theatrical frame. The discursive performative at play in contemporary theory, however, is derived from a particular reading of linguistics. It is helpful, therefore, to rehearse briefly the epistemological history of the linguistic performative.

Tania Modleski, for example, has recently argued that feminist critical writing is itself performative.[5] She uses performative in the sense that J. L. Austin meant when he delivered the William James Lectures at Harvard University in 1955.[6] Austin distinguishes speech acts into two separate categories: constatives and performatives. Constatives describe events; performatives enact them. The performative is linguistically distinguished from the constative because within the former the signifier and the referent are mutually enfolded within one another: the signifier performs the referent within the performative *because* the referent *is* the speech act itself.

"The sun came up today" is a constative; "I worry she won't come up today" is a performative in which the act of saying "I worry" *is* part of the activity of worrying (and, no doubt for the one who hasn't shown up, a worrying activity). For Modleski feminist writing is performative because it *promises and, in the act of promising, brings a feminist future closer*—rather than, as most criticism seems to be, a constative, reliable description of what the sun/son did in the morning. Modleski sees feminist writing as utopian and the performative speech act itself as expressive of utopian vision.

Behind Modleski's complex and in many ways persuasive argument is a belief in reliable indexes of locations, clearly marked political affinities, and mutual understanding of the goals and aims of a feminist future. Writing, she implies, relies on the affective force and shared clarity of words. She is a writer who believes she is understood by her readers. I myself cannot believe this—although I'd like to. I can't quite make the leap of faith necessary to believe my words express my meaning; I cannot believe I am the word I name or am named by. You can call me Ishmael. Or you can call me Betty. Or Al. Or Peggy. I do not, in other words, believe that my writing from a feminist perspective toward a feminist future will necessarily be recognized as such, despite the repetitious marks of such a perspective enacted on my writing by editors, title givers, publishers. They need to repeat these signs precisely because they are not certain. And I need continually to rewrite my essay, repeat my desire to say it right, because I recognize the pervasive force of misrecognition, doubt, mistake, uncertainty at the level of the signifier, at the bonds and boundaries of location. My understanding of the unavoidability of misunderstanding leads me to believe this mistaking *is* history, the history in front of us no less than the history behind us. This is the history we recite and always rewrite.

Both of us, you and I, mistake what I think I am trying to say as I type the particular letters of this sentence in the here and now. After a friend's warning commentary about some of my mistakes and my many fantasies of a projected future reader's misreadings, I sit down again and rewrite. (What version of this sentence are you reading, am I writing? What event in the future will intervene between my here and now and yours and reframe these remarks? Misfires. Misinvocations. Infelicitous events spilling across different trajectories, trajectories that will allow us to meet, hand to eye, in some future time I cannot now see.) The lack in the signifier, the leak in the body: words and futures come together and fall apart across these thresholds.[7]

Derrida's well-known critique of Austin is a rigorous demonstration of the doubt engendered by the performative.[8] Austin believes that performative speech acts can be evaluated according to their success or failure; he uses various terminologies to describe these effects—misfires, felicitous or infelicitous performances, misinvocations, flaws, hitches. (There are many flowering phrases for flaws—just "plain speech" for successes.) These evaluative possibilities emerge from the assumption that speech acts *can* (although sometimes they *may* not) convey their full contexts transparently. But Derrida argues such transparent reproduction is impossible. For him every speech act both conveys and represses multiple "signatures, events, and contexts." These "supplements" *defer* (and make impossible) the exact match between signifier and referent, between meaning and Being.

To return: "I worry she won't come" seems to imply that my worry is about her. Is she there, not here? My psychic worry troubles the signs themselves—or, rather, the worry within the letters corresponds with my psychic doubt. Each mimes the other; each expresses, conveys, and represses the other precisely because each displaces the other. I mime the gesture of handing you a flower (Christopher Smart—"for elegant phrases are nothing but flowers") and register my desire to please you. You receive my substance-less gesture and smile. We toss gestures back and forth because the thing itself has fallen out.[9] (And behind my gesture is the compressed signification in which flowers are phrases, in which flowers are hearts, in which hearts are emotions. . . .)

Is she (not) her(e)?: the double parentheses allow us to *not/e* the knot between here and there, between me and her. Am I, in the act of worrying, expressing the profundity of my in/her/ent doubt *in her ent*/ity? By failing to appear does she generate my very worrying Being—that which is so (worryingly) here—in the very signifiers declaring me as the one worried over her(e). It becomes impossible to distinguish the object from the subject, the form of the conveyance from what is conveyed. Each reflects the same doubt; each can fill the other because it is empty. We position ourselves in relation to what we miss (True Love), not in relation to what we "have" (Real Love). This filling up and emptying out is the (nervous) digestive system of the linguistic, psychic, economic body. The linguistic economy of the performative speech act reproduces the signifier and the referent as the same. The performative speech act short-circuits the projected future (the other in the future) and lives only in the "Self-Same" present in which it is articulated. The linguistic performative, then, like performance art, cannot be exactly repeated or reproduced.[10]

Performatives make visible the linguistic economy of the Self-Same. In making this economy visible performative utterances display the failure of signifiers to signify "real" difference—including, of course, sexual difference. This is why the linguistic economy of the Self-Same is, in Irigaray's term, "hom(m)osexual."[11] The function of metaphor, whereby two different terms become one, is to reproduce the same signs. The performative utterance's repetitious exposure of the economy of the Self-Same leads Eve Sedgwick to claim that performance and performativity are queer.[12] While this claim might be vulnerable to the false notion that same-sex sexuality elides the problem of "the other," it also, more helpfully, enables the suggestion that the nonreproductive consequence of homosexuality forces (or allows, depending on one's perspective) same-sex lovers to live in the present (rather than take stock of one's reproductive legacy—turning two people into one child who will carry one name, his name, into the future). For the performative utterance, like the live performance event and the sexual union of two same-sex people, cannot be repeated or reproduced.

Thus, within the tight logic of the linguistic economy of the Self-Same the problem of citation, finding the "original" source of words whose meanings can be established only through repetition and reproduction, becomes exceedingly complex. I cite a line from a poem by Robert Lowell, "My eye has seen what my hand did." But the line comes from a poem called "The Dolphin," which is the title of a volume of his poems, poems that are largely made up of his rearrangements of his estranged wife's letters. These letters, her signature, remains unmarked (and I will not name her here) in his volume. Her letters are repetitions of words they said to each other in anguished contexts. She learned those words in contexts in which she lived before she lived with Lowell.

Derrida demonstrates that even at the seemingly simple level of the *linguistic* sign it is impossible for writers to convey the complete context in which a speech act occurs. (How much more difficult it is, then, to cite a performative event.) To report it back, to record and repeat it, is at once to transform it *and* to fuel the desire for its mimetic return. Writing is a substitute for the failure of this return—which is why "theater history" frequently contains a twist of nostalgia. *Nostalgia's* etymological history reveals other ways of writing "the wound of wishing to return." The desire to perform etymological histories is itself a nostalgic gesture, an attempt to return to the origin of a specific word. The nostalgia that motivates the etymological search (re)writes nostalgia itself: the search deepens the wound inflicted by nostalgia even as it seeks a cure in the wish, the (failed) attempt, to return.[13] The failure secures the return of the wish.

Come again? Yes, but only in other words: the performative speech act is what Dr. Seuss was after with his *Green Eggs and Ham*.

"I am Sam" becomes "Sam-I-am" because the reversible sign inscribed on the third page indicates the same Sam.[14]

Critical writing is an exercise in rewriting and repetition—or, as Derrida puts it, "As soon as a sign emerges, it begins by repeating itself."[15] This condition of (re)writing is linked to the nature of psychic-sexual desire in which, as Freud put it, "the finding of an object is in fact a refinding of it."[16] What changes over time—what makes history—is the mobile contexts in which a subject finds (and loses) objects. More than merely saying here that writing is a libidinal project, which Roland Barthes has already said in *The Pleasure of the Text,* I am trying to say that the failure to see, to properly cite/sight the "object" of one's writing, is precisely what allows us to see our desire for that object's return. (Our desire for the object's return constitutes our subjectivity.) But we content ourselves with seeing our desire, rather than securing the return that motivated the writing.

Critical writing about performance comes after the event and traces the impression left by its disappearing absence. The link between performance and critical writing, then, is psychic-sexual: it reveals itself at the site of failure. Like all erotic relations, the commingling of performance and critical writing can be *interpreted* precisely because it fails. Psychoanalysis is the rigorous interpretation of the repetition of erotic failure. Critical writing is the interpretation of the repetitious failure to secure a return (a return to the object toward which the writer writes). The reader, who has also lost the "original" object, the performance, contents herself with reading the observations of someone who (also) watched it disappear. The writer's loss mirrors yours but usually more intently, for, in attempting to write about it, she acquires some intimacy with it—if only an intimacy that is fractured by her struggle to retrieve it. And the record of that awkward and failed intimacy is the writing, the *essai,* itself.

Every writing of a word is a rewriting of it. Every finding of an object is a refinding because we are always losing sight of the object; the sign repeats itself because it cannot remain attached to the referent—it must function as a substitute for it. Disappearing performances, then, are the paradigmatic events of speech itself. Our critical eyes watch the failure of the attachment between the referent and the sign, between the critic and the performance, and attempt to compensate for this failure by performing other activities of documentation, research, citation. The consolation of (in)adequate compensation—the writer's loss of the performer's presence mimics the loss of the reader's loss of the writer's presence. The writer embraces, however earnestly or ironically, the possibility that maybe I am who I can say I am. Maybe I can see who I am. Sam-I-am. This I, this Peggy/Betty/Al, can merely say I am the one who doubts the maybe.

Modleski is absolutely correct when she claims that feminist critical writing is performative. But I come to this conclusion from the opposite direction. What makes feminist criticism performative is not its utopian pitch toward a better future but, rather, the "intimate dissonance" inspired by the recognition of mutual failure, in the here and now—the failure to enact what one can barely glimpse, can only imagine, and cannot reproduce.[17] The failure of this secure reproduction offers us the solace of repetitions and revisions. The solace comes because the supplement in repetition guarantees the (re)generation of Hope. Hope turns us toward the genre of Comedy, the confusing drama of Real Love, and away from Utopia, the ideal Romance of True Love.

Criticism, R. P. Blackmur wrote, "is the formal discourse of the amateur. When there is enough love and enough knowledge represented in the discourse it is a self-sufficient but by no means an isolated art."[18] I do not believe there ever is enough love or enough knowledge, and thus far, I have never encountered a self-sufficient person, idea, or art. In/formal amateurs: almost auteurs who lose their "am(s)." Sam-I-am. Lost i-ambs trying to find u. The first limb lost from that other body: ma falls out when the amateur revises herself and signs her name—"auteur."

Much of the writing in this volume is a record of a living relation between the writer and the artists she tries to see. This seeing is, necessarily, a distortion, a dream, a hallucination; writing rights it back toward reason by creating enabling fictions called clarity, history, intent, political ideology, or artistic plot, which function as "stable" frames of vision. The effort to "cite" the performance that interests us even as it disappears is much like the effort to find the word to say what we mean. It can't be done, but the futile looking attaches us again to Hope. It's impossible to succeed, but writing's supplement traces the architecture of the ruin's Hope (endlessly to return, reconstruct, represent, remember).

The performativity of feminist critical writing lies in its reimagining of the social bond, its refiguration of the binary and the dyad, the internal and external double. It makes two non-(re)citable contexts come together—the context of the performance and the context of the writing. Two signatures, then, to introduce eighteen auteurs. Criticism is the formal discourse of an amateur. When there's enough love within the discourse it stops. When Sam-I-am's resistant interlocutor discovers he loves green eggs and ham, the story ends. But unlike poetry or children's fairy tales, criticism is never self-sufficient; it never discovers "enough" love. So we continue—by returning. This time to the problem of citation in performance.

Concurrent with the NEA scandal, David Wojnarowicz sued Reverend Donald Wildmon, head of the American Family Association, for libel and copyright infringement. Wildmon cut fourteen images from the catalogue for Wojnarowicz's show, "Tongues of Flame," originally mounted at Illinois State University (and funded by the NEA), put them in a pamphlet denouncing the Endowment, and mailed six thousand copies of it to potential contributors and friends to the American Family Association. Wojnarowicz contended that Wildmon took his visual art out of context, infringed copyright law, and distorted his work for Wildmon's own political ends (ends that were diametrically opposed to Wojnarowicz's own artwork). Wojnarowicz won the case. (He was unable to prove financial damages, so Wildmon was required to pay Wojnarowicz only one dollar.) Wojnarowicz's case rested on two distinct documents that could be easily displayed to the judge. One was Wildmon's pamphlet, and one was the catalogue for "Tongues of Flame." The book and the pamphlet were read as stable referents capable of securely documenting Wildmon's citation of Wojnarowicz's work.

The Law overlooks the fact that the catalogue itself distorts the experience of seeing the work in a gallery or a studio and that seeing the work distorts the contextual motivation—Rimbaud, the politics of AIDS, the circulating dollar bill—that Wojnarowicz's artwork both conveys and represses. Each "citation" frames a previous set of citations, compressions, expansions.

Wildmon attempted to label Wojnarowicz pornographic and obscene, but to do so he had to reframe Wojnarowicz's own "context"—the work as a whole and the work in relation to

Wojnarowicz's increasingly weighted signature of rage. Wildmon's pamphlet was clearly a violation of Wojnarowicz's "signature, event, context," which Law could redress. But it is necessary to remember that Wojnarowicz's own manipulation of signature, event, context is licensed by Art. Wojnarowicz's deliberate distortion of citation can be made the legitimate and generative foundation of his artistic in/sight; Wildmon's deliberate and calculated distortion of Wojnarowicz's insights can be said to be "libelous."

In Finley's argument with Evans and Novak, however, not even the illusionary security of the document (Wojnarowicz's catalogue) can be had. As performance, Finley's work itself eludes representational economies that rely on secure reproductions. It might be objected that Finley could provide Evans and Novak with a script of her work, but to do so would leave out the performative dimension of it—which is to say, it would leave the "art" out of consideration. One might object that Finley could provide a video recording of the performance, but to do so would be to provide a pre-framed citation of her performance. (Shot selection, editing, lighting and so on would necessarily pre-frame Finley's performance.) Short of inviting every politician and (armchair) juror to her performances, Finley must confront the fact that her work will, inevitably, be distorted by writers, critics, and political ideologues.[19]

But Finley's point raises another question, one that highlights the unequal economy of power-knowledge in which performers and writers find themselves. For the writer's work can be reproduced, circulated, given a kind of (temporary) permanence that performance art itself lacks. Enfolded within an economy of power-knowledge, in which value is accorded to things that last and things that don't are routinely trashed, writers can and do have a large impact on the reception of performance artists' work.

Citation is always already an operation of power. To pretend otherwise is to proclaim a false innocence. Within the political and theoretical economy of performance, writing is always on the side of the Law, performance on the side of the Outlaw. Critical writing, "the good review," is the imprimatur of legitimacy, of grant funds, of containment and expansion for the performer. And yet for the academic feminist critic such writing rarely (if ever) *feels* like an operation of power. It feels doubtful, insubstantial, tentative, precari-

ous. Partially this is because we lack a history of models: there simply
is not a "canon" of great feminist critics of performance art through
the centuries (there is not a singular "origin" to which one can long
to return). But it is also due to an acute ontological mismatch: writing
seeks to preserve, record, and remember, and performance resists
documentation and reproduction. This brave insistence on the power
and fullness of the present as such is, for me, finally the beautiful folly
of performance—and it is this folly that critical writing must learn to
celebrate, not incarcerate.

How, then, might a performative critical writing begin to be
written? This seems to me to be a central question for contemporary
theory in the United States for the next decade. Within most universities performance art has little academic credibility. Relatively few
people know what we are on about, fewer still care. (Sam-I-am and
J. L. Austin, *Legal Eagles* and Lacan?) This inscrutability and perception of worthlessness is part of the appeal of the performative and
performance generally for theorists and artists anxious to inhabit a
politically subversive, but shielded, ideological and linguistic field.
As Judith Butler succinctly points out in relation to the embattled
field of contemporary identity and sexual/ity politics, it may now be
a matter of "letting that which cannot fully appear in any performance persist in its disruptive promise."[20]

Women remain that which cannot fully appear within the logic
of phallocentric representation, a logic whose metaphors reproduce
men as singular subjects. The various sightings of feminist appearances that are recorded in most of these essays promise not a fulsome
visibility for women in the specular economy but, rather, a different
way of reading appearance itself. The sometimes explicitly outlawed
performances discussed here will persist in their disruptive promises.
Like all promises, these won't be kept. And that's the point. For by
not keeping them these artists allow us to be loosened from our
enthrallment with the future they promise (a future itself enfolded
and articulated within a narrow narrative model), and, more important, the failure of these promises allows us to disengage from a
particular romance with our future selves—the perfect person who
we are always promising ourselves will write our next essay, perform
in our next show. True Love becomes less heroic and Real Love
more palpable. Performance can't rely on the future: it lives and loves
and fails and wins and whines in the pressing present.

The essays collected under the subtitle "The Reproduction of Visibility" interrogate the political and psychic negotiation of visibility across art forms, races, and sexualities. Rebecca Schneider begins her essay on Spiderwoman Theatre by recounting a dream that makes the opening pages of her essay resemble a ghost story. The reverberation from the dream punctuates her sojourn with Spiderwoman, whose performance work, as Schneider notes, both invites and is fittingly wry about the mythic dimensions of such "white" dreamings.

The hallucination of an ancestor as inspiration haunts the performance work of Spiderwoman and Robbie McCauley. As Raewyn Whyte demonstrates, "Sally's Rape" is a lamentation, an exorcism, a revision of the history of slavery, rape, and reproduction, performed by a black woman and a white woman for audiences of mixed races in a form that reenacts but never rights that history. McCauley's sustained meditation on this material—part autobiographical, part "objective" history, part performative recreation—is like a musical composition that repeats the same themes in order to explore and elaborate the variations that derive from these repetitions.

Elin Diamond's essay, "Mimesis, Mimicry, and the 'True-Real,'" which originally appeared in *Modern Drama,* is an inspired series of readings of the epistemological constructions of origins. She argues that there can be no notion of an origin/al that does not entail a notion of mimesis. Concentrating on Irigaray's reading of Plato's cave, Diamond deconstructs and reframes the dense relation between Platonic philosophy's interest in the original and the copy in terms of mimesis and feminist truth-telling. Diamond has added a brief discussion of Omaha Magic Theatre's performance of Megan Terry's *Body Leaks* to her previous analyses of Rachel Rosenthal, Adrienne Kennedy, Franca Rame, and Lois Weaver. These readings acutely demonstrate that the "place of play" imagined in and by these women's work "can be played not only again, but differently." That place of play includes the performativity of feminist critical writing.

Diamond's meditation on origins allows us to see how thoroughly saturated the real is with conceptions of the double. This doubling is part of the "mimicry" and "mimesis" Lynda Hill analyzes in Zora Neale Hurston's work. As contemporary theater seeks to find the "authentic" Hurston by staging and restaging her life and work, one begins to recognize that such a pursuit must always be doubled and redoubled. The very fantasy of recovery is hinged upon the fact of loss. Hurston herself fades in the repeated attempts to fix her. Lynn Whitfield and Ruby Dee can "split" Hurston in two in an effort to mime her as accurately as possible as she aged, but the very pitch toward resemblance requires a double body: the actor's body is doubled by the "real character" of Hurston and is redoubled by the bodies of Whitfield and Dee.

Theoretically, feminist theories' relation to the double may be best seen in relation to "the sex-gender system," which Hilary Harris vigorously deconstructs. In calling for a more powerful conception of gender Harris attempts to undo the intellectual fantasy of the (symmetrical) double. Harris argues that gender and sexuality are distinct terms with different discursive powers and histories. Insofar as some feminist theory has conflated sex and gender, the result has been to genderize sex, rather than to sexualize gender. Harris's argument usefully highlights the way in which binaries and hierarchies operate within and without feminist theory and theater.

Philip Auslander suggests a different way of thinking about traditional binaries between comedy and rage. For him feminist performance art suggests new modes of linking old categories. The "performative" part of the comics he studies comes not, as conventional wisdom would have it, when rage is tamed into comedy but, rather, when comedy exposes the rage that motivates it. Misogyny names one of the motivations for the rage he reads in Roseanne Barr (now renamed Roseanne Arnold). In Auslander's reading misogyny becomes comedic not by stripping it of rage but precisely by revealing the expectation that such hostility would not (re)produce outrage, acting out. Barr makes it apparent that complicity, silence, and inward acting are not logical for her—even though this is what she, as a woman, is expected continually to perform.

Amy Robinson's essay on Madonna returns us to a consideration of performance and Hollywood. Madonna, like Finley, seems at times to provoke controversy no matter what she does or says. Robinson's careful tracing of Madonna's political and aesthetic metamorphoses reveals the shifting boundaries of "private" identity in a performative world. Never able to name oneself, one steals the names of others. Who Madonna wants to be when changes; the Madonna-wanna-bes also revise their costumes and choreographies. As Robinson herself ruminates over *Rolling Stone* in one paragraph and legal briefs in the next, she mimes Madonna's fluid passing from Monroe to monarch. Madonna's identities, like the critics', are seductive in part because they so easily provoke identifications. They do so precisely because identities themselves are expressions of previous identifications. Madonna loved Monroe and reassigned her image as her own signature.

Lynda Hart points out that within the economy of lesbian desire identifications rather than identities are erotically compelling. Such identifications are compressed interpretations of a political, aesthetic, linguistic, erotic, and market economy. This economy is what Lacan called the Symbolic. Since lesbians themselves only appear *as* hallucinations within the Symbolic, Hart argues, citing/sighting them necessarily exposes the Symbolic as the male Imaginary. What is so intriguing to me about Hart's argument is the possibility that these things called lesbians continue to appear within a visual field that, by logical definition, cannot reproduce them. The (in)security of this reproductive alchemy may have something to do with the drama of Real Love enacted on these pages. The performance fades, and the writer tries to reproduce it. Like women who supposedly cannot be reproduced within the economy of the Self-Same and yet who, nonetheless, continue to appear, Hart's lesbian suggests a different relation to the standard reproductive cycle. She doubles everything that isn't there. She acts out what they almost always cease to see. These essays try to trace her as she falls away from our eyes. Is she her/e or theirs? These essays then function as perform/orials, as witnesses to her vanishing. For her disappearance summons and allows other (re)appearances. Maybe they will come again in these other words.

Late August: So to return once more to (re)citation. This is a postscript, added because an event "in the future" of this "original" writing has now happened and merits remarking.

In Sandra Richards's opening essay about Anna Deavere Smith, Richards documents the method Smith uses to create her extraordinary *On the Road* performances. The overwhelming success of Smith's most recent show, *Fires in the Mirror: Crown Heights, Brooklyn, and Other Identities,* which ran at the Joseph Papp Public Theater in New York from 14 May to 16 August 1992, signals a defining moment in the history and reception of performance art. *Fires,* like the work Richards so eloquently discusses here, was constructed based on interviews with members of the community who are both the subject of and an integral part of the intended audience for Smith's performance.

What is so remarkable about Smith's work is that she brings together within her own body and voice people who quite often are unaccustomed to speaking to one another. Smith uses the tragedy of Gavin Cato's and Yankel Rosenbaum's deaths in Crown Heights to create one of the densest meditations on race, violence, misunderstanding, love, grief, and Hope we are ever likely to see in the theater.[21] As the ninety-minute performance progresses and more and more voices are heard, one realizes that Smith is enacting a dramatic conversation between interlocutors who have never actually heard one another speak in quite this way before. What is required for the conversation to take place is Smith's intimate listening and reciting: the assurance that one is heard makes it easier to listen to someone else. Working with tapes and a Walkman, Smith takes the words of her "characters" into her body—introjects them, as Freud might say—and then repeats those words so that everyone else (including the person who spoke them) can hear them as if for the first time.

While much has been written already about the power of Smith's *Fires,* Richards's essay provides an invaluable discussion of the historical, political, and technical development that led to and in every way informs Smith's most successful work. Appearing on television shows as diverse in style and aim as "Arsenio" and the "MacNeil/ Lehrer Newshour," Smith has chartered a new "mainstream" position for politically progressive performers, one quite different from the fractious space Holly Hughes and Karen Finley have been forced (or allowed, depending on one's perspective) to take as a response to the NEA scandal.

Smith's method of performance composition remembers difference at the level of breath and word; her dogged rehearsal and recitation of each person's speech registers what is required to speak and live with and through difference. Her performance insists that such living is possible—although exhausting, humbling, and, like Real Love, endlessly demanding and fraught with the tears and terrors of misunderstanding.

The various identities Smith borrows and shakes in *Fires in the Mirror* are like the concatenation of our own several selves' partial introjections of one another. Smith's ongoing conversation with these "other identities" throughout the nine years she has been making *On the Road* exemplifies the transformative power of listening again and, this time, in other words. Anna Deavere Smith's work reminds us that if we are to create the woof of a different social fabric, we must remember to finger and test, not hide and repress, the knots that define our precarious weight/wait.

NOTES

1. See my articles "Money Talks," *Drama Review* 34, no. 1 (Spring 1990): 4–15; and "Money Talks, Again," *TDR* 35 (Fall 1991): 131–42, for a full discussion of the NEA scandal.

2. Carol Vance has persuasively argued that the construction of the "decent taxpayer" began with the Meese Commission Report on Pornography and blossomed during the attacks on the NEA. She made this argument at a conference held at New York University in January 1992 entitled "Explicit Sex." See also her earlier essay, "The Meese Commission on the Road," *Nation,* 2–9 August 1986.

3. For an assessment of the gender politics of the NEA debates, see my articles "Money Talks" and "Money Talks, Again."

4. The most obvious exception to this claim is the body of the professional male athlete—which is usually celebrated, worried over, and paid handsomely. Once that body is injured, however, a whole other set of discursive operations occur, and that body also becomes feminized.

5. Tania Modleski, "Some Functions of Feminist Criticism, or the Scandal of the Mute Body," *October,* no. 49 (Summer 1989): 3–24.

6. These lectures, edited from Austin's lecture notes by J. O. Urmson and Marina Sbisa, are published under the title *How to Do Things with Words,* 2d ed. (Cambridge, Mass.: Harvard University Press, 1975).

7. For a fuller discussion of the relation between the lack in the signifier and the leak in the body, see my article "Thirteen Ways of Looking at Choreographing Writing," in *Choreographing History,* ed. Susan Foster (Bloomington: Indiana University Press, forthcoming).

8. Jacques Derrida, "Signature, Event, Context," *Glyph,* nos. 1 and 2 (1977): 172–97.

9. Whether or not it was ever there is an open question. Language always expresses a longing to return to someplace where language is not needed. Lancanian psychoanalysis and the story of the Garden of Eden are alike in that the Imaginary Paradise they each posit as "origin" lacks linguistic *and* visual distinctions between who one is and what one sees. After what the Bible calls the Fall and Lacan calls the Mirror Stage, the eyes of everyone open, difference is discovered, and the fighting (for) words begin(s).

10. If performative speech acts are repeated, they become constatives. ("I told her I promised I would come" is a constative description of an event in the past; "I bet she won't" is a performative reply in the present. If I change it to "Yester-

day I had bet against her coming," I am describing, not enacting.) For a fuller discussion of the nonreproductive aspect of performance, see my chapter "The Ontology of Performance: Representation without Reproduction," in *Unmarked* (New York and London: Routledge, 1993), 146–66. Video documents of performances are constatives; so too are most critical essays about performances. The challenge of the performative for critics is to create a writing in which the present matters as much as, or more than, the future.

11. See her brilliant meditation on the Self-Same in *Speculum of the Other Woman,* trans. Gillian C. Gill (Ithaca, N.Y.: Cornell University Press, 1985).

12. "The course will make use of both the theatrical and the Austinian/deconstructive traditions of meaning for the verb 'perform'—meanings that I would suggest intersect, when they do at all, at a very odd angle somewhere in a neighborhood called queer." Eve Sedgwick, course description for "Queer Performativity: Across Genres, Across 'Perversions,'" School of Criticism and Theory, Summer 1992.

13. Perhaps, as Dorothy Chansky has argued, theater history may itself be an impossible enterprise. If so, we may do well to pursue the reconstruction of "theater myth" rather than "theater history." And by myth I mean what Roland Barthes means in "Myth Today," in *Mythologies:* a surface reading of complex cultural meanings—but with the proviso that the surface is precisely what motivates theater itself to appear and disappear. For an important discussion of the political stakes involved in preferring history over myth and vice versa, see Michele Wallace, *Invisibility Blues* (London and New York: Verso, 1990), 213–40.

14. This is not an exact reverse. If it were, Seuss would have to write "Sam-am-I" (and thus ruin the rhyme). The slight flaw is part of the appeal of the rhyme itself—the distorting dissonance of assonance rather than the rigid rules of rhyme (Real Love not True Love). Moreover, in the alteration between the positions of the *I* and the *S* one reads *is* and *si(ghs)* over the awed recognition of the exuberant Being that Seuss enacts with *Green Eggs and Ham.*

15. Jacques Derrida, "The Theatre of Cruelty," *Writing and Difference,* trans. Alan Bass (Chicago: University of Chicago Press, 1978), 297.

16. Sigmund Freud, *Three Essays on the Theory of Sexuality,* trans. James Strachey (New York: Basic Books, 1962), 88.

17. Eve Sedgwick, "intimate dissonance," *Epistemology of the Closet* (Berkeley: University of California Press, 1990), 61.

18. R. P. Blackmur, "A Critic's Job of Work," *The Double Agent: Essays in Craft and Elucidation* (Gloucester, Mass.: Peter Smith, 1962), 269.

19. Finley did issue repeated invitations to John Frohnmayer, former director of the NEA, to her performances throughout the two-year controversy, but he never appeared.

20. Judith Butler, "Imitation and Gender Insubordination," in *Inside/Out: Lesbian Theories, Gay Theories,* ed. Diana Fuss (New York and London: Routledge, 1992), 29.

21. Gavin Cato was a seven-year-old African-American boy who was fatally struck by a car in a motorcade of the Crown Heights' Lubavitch community's

spiritual leader on 19 August 1991. Witnesses at the scene suggested that the car in Rebbe Menachem M. Schneerson's motorcade, driven by Yosef Lifsh, ran a red light; some complained that the private ambulance for the Lubavitch community arrived before the city ambulance and that its medical personnel did not treat the injured children (Gavin's seven-year-old cousin, Angela Cato, was also struck and seriously injured by Lifsh's car). Other witnesses denied this. The incident set off four days of riots. Yankel Rosenbaum, a twenty-eight-year-old Hasidic scholar from Australia studying in New York for the summer, was stabbed by some member(s) of a group of twenty African-American teenagers during the ensuing riots. He later died at Kings County Hospital. In addition to members of the Crown Heights neighborhood, Smith also includes segments of interviews from Angela Davis, Leonard Jefferies, and Letty Cottin Pogrebin, among others, whose voices outline the larger issues of race, power, and history, which the particularities of Crown Heights vividly illuminate.

Politics of Identities

Chapter 1

Caught in the Act of Social Definition: On the Road with Anna Deavere Smith

Sandra L. Richards

Barefoot, yet dressed in a scooped-neck, 1950s purple taffeta dress with black tights and stiff crinoline slips visible underneath, Anna Deavere Smith strides down through the audience onto the stage of a Princeton lecture hall. Donning some fake pearls and picking up one of the many phones scattered about, she then launches into a fifty-minute monologue in which she performs some twenty-five men and women, many of whom are now sitting in her audience. They have been selected out of a pool of fifty people primarily associated with Princeton University and interviewed on such subjects as the university's exclusively male eating clubs, assault against women and "sex-role strain" among female undergraduates, color consciousness among black students, and the paradoxical relationship between hard-line ideologies and the absence of women's girdles in some contemporary societies. When finished Smith has offered this community of students, faculty, and staff a comic, provocative image of itself as it struggles to negotiate differences of gender, race, and class.

Performed interviews. Enacted oral history. A linguistic near-image. A solo carnival. Postmodern theater for development. These are some of the descriptive terms that may be applied to *On the Road,* the one-woman shows that Smith has been researching, scripting, and performing since 1982. As their juxtaposition and the Princeton performance synopsis suggest, Smith's artistry unsettles while it delights: it challenges viewers to locate—and relocate—themselves within a kaleidoscope of oftentimes contradictory positions. It presumes and speaks to a desire for community even while dramatizing the fractured quality of contemporary social networks.

To date, this American Conservatory Theatre (A.C.T.)-trained actress, playwright, and Stanford University professor has constructed some twenty performances. Generally, Smith is commissioned by a community interested in self-reflexively exploring a given topic. Working from a list of names and telephone numbers provided by the producer and following up leads suggested by the subjects themselves, Smith conducts taped telephone interviews, amassing on the average some seventy hours of information, which is then edited, memorized, and presented at a sixty-minute performance, which the interviewees are invited to attend.

In 1987, for example, she interviewed San Francisco–Bay Area women for the symposium "Bay Area Women in Theater"; in 1988 and 1989 she prepared pieces reviewing the history and ideological debates of the Women and Theater Program (WTP) of the Association for Theater in Higher Education (ATHE).[1] With the University of Pennsylvania and the Five Colleges at Amherst, Smith explored issues related to feminism and racism. Crossroads Theatre in New Brunswick commissioned a show on black theater and black identity, while San Francisco's Eureka Theatre wanted to probe realities behind the public mystique of "the city by the Bay." More recently, Smith has taken her *On the Road* into an international arena, having constructed a performance for a Rockefeller Foundation conference on interculturalism, which capitalized upon the exchange begun on the pages of *Performing Arts Journal* by bringing together such critics and artists as Gayatri Spivak, Eugenio Barba, Richard Schechner, and Folabo Ajayi in Bellagio, Italy.[2]

Generally, Smith's performances occur in such nontheatrical environments as hotel conference rooms, lecture halls, or rehearsal rooms, which seem to reflect not only the limited resources of her sponsors but also a Brechtian approach wherein the social constructedness of art remains undisguised.[3] Two or three chairs and a variety of telephones indicate different locations and characters; occasionally, coffee cups, eyeglasses, or shoes are used to further differentiate one person from the next. The actress's presentation follows a format wherein contextual remarks provide a frame for a series of close-up, medium, and panoramic shots of a given community and its relationship to a larger pattern of events. Narratives of no longer than two or three minutes are offered in rapid succession; their progression is nonlinear so that, while at times they clearly critique each other, at other points the relationship among voices is not immediately apparent. Because many of the people represented are personally known to viewers, audiences often greet these episodes with uproarious delight at the accuracy of Smith's rendition of speech patterns. Yet, because she is replaying volatile issues that have threatened to rupture their semblance of community, they also get caught in their own laughter, suddenly shocked or hurt by what this near-image reveals of their individual and collective shortcomings. Embedding her politics in the selection and structuring of episodes, Smith usually ends her oral history abruptly, with the audience left to impose some interpretive closure.

In the Princeton show entitled *Gender Bending* the actress begins with reminiscences of how women from the Seven Sisters colleges had historically been imported to the campus to provide weekend entertainment for fraternity men; then Charlayne Hunter-Gault's harrowing experience in integrating the University of Georgia provides a tighter focus for Sally Frank's account of the harassment she encountered in seeking to join the all-male Cottage Club. Information about male power projected from photographs lining eating club walls or about blacks employed at Princeton almost solely as low-paid, service personnel alternates with opinions on feminist definitions of the body or on the relationship of modern, literary representations of homosexuality to the AIDS crisis.

Similarly, Smith's San Francisco piece, *From the Outside Looking In,* begins predictably with stories of the reasons different ethnic groups settled in the Bay Area. Next follows a number of narratives attesting to the glories of the region—that is, its natural resources and varied cultural options—as represented by the Fleishackers' tradition of civic philanthropy, the political antics of the Mime Troupe, or the upbeat attitude of the Giants baseball manager. But, even in this reiteration of so much of what Bay Area residents hold dear, cultural critic Anna Smith has included what many would rather forget: early in the piece sculptor Ruth Asawa recounts memories of being herded off into World War II internment camps for Japanese Americans. A seemingly jarring note, it forewarns the audience of the disturbing quality of much that is to follow: Angela Davis talking of drugs being used by the power structure to criminalize the entire black community or Eric Jazmen struggling through the effects of dementia to insist upon respect for AIDS patients. Offered throughout is a series

Anna Deavere Smith in *On the Road*. Photo by Mary Ann Halpin.

Anna Deavere Smith in *Fires in the Mirror: Crown Heights, Brooklyn and Other Identities*. Photo by Martha Swope Studios/William Gibson.

of oppositions, so that, while a picture of entrenched racism comes
across strongly in an episode concerning black firefighters, one sees
working-class solidarity among female hotel workers in a context in
which the various minority communities are presumed to be fiercely
competitive, or one hears a cabaret singer talking of San Francisco as
a contemporary Camelot. The last voice Smith presents is that of the
director of Emergency Services reminding residents not to be caught
unprepared for an earthquake. His matter-of-fact observation that
"the most dangerous place to be [during an earthquake] is just outside . . . where things are falling" seems like a terribly unsatisfying
ending until the viewer begins to suspect that the artist is signifyin',
or slyly commenting on the viewer's position vis-à-vis the performance.[4] Having just witnessed an ill-defined "inside" in which a po-
lyphony of voices seems to agree on little more than the vitality of
the city or the human waste of drug and AIDS-induced death, how
will one recognize an even more perilous "outside"? What protective
steps can be taken against a danger as yet unknown?

Smith relates that she first started research that would take shape
as *On the Road* in 1982 when she was directing Adrienne Kennedy's *A
Movie Star Has to Star in Black and White* at Carnegie-Mellon University.[5] Because Kennedy constructs a black female protagonist who
often allows movie stars like Bette Davis and Montgomery Clift to
speak her narrative, which is virtually unconnected to their cinematic
identities, Smith's student actors were having difficulty establishing
character. Clearly, an approach other than the psychological
identification of method training was needed. Remembering her
mother's observation that in movies of the 1940s and 1950s each actor
had a distinctive vocal sound, Smith began watching television talk
shows. A Johnny Carson interview with Sophia Loren proved critical,
because, through Loren's subversion of Carson's innuendo-laden, fast-
paced rhythms, Smith realized that one's presence or identity is revealed to the extent that one establishes her/his vocal rhythms as the
norm for conversing parties. From staging talk shows Smith moved
to test her hypothesis further by approaching strangers on the streets
of New York; she would offer them an opportunity to see themselves
performed by look-alike actors, provided they first granted her an
interview that would serve as a text. Working with a linguist, she
devised questions such as "Have you ever been falsely accused? Or,

close to death? How would you describe your first sexual experience?" in order to find those moments when the interviewee became so engaged that a controlled, social identity was superseded by something more raw, distinct, and performable, something that seemed to constitute that person's self. From this prototypical situation of utilizing twenty actors to reproduce excerpts from the interviews (she conducted with twenty strangers), Smith has developed a methodology whereby she performs the interviewees herself.

Whereas in the earliest pieces Smith attempted to elicit from her speakers those moments when language breaks down into vocal utterances, lapses in syntax, markedly altered rhythms, or repetitions that betray the individual's great investment in what is being said, now her focus has shifted more to moments when her subjects are self-consciously devoted to conveying a particular point. This shift is partially a function of the expertise of the interviewees. In that her performances are commissioned, she is usually dealing with privileged communities, many of whose members—whether they be academics, politicians, or union organizers—are accustomed to authoritatively addressing a given public. Thus, Smith now attempts to structure sessions so as to elicit commentary on topics about which they are likely to have already spoken or written. She finds in such instances that subjects talk until they experience themselves as having spoken with clarity. Even with these polished speakers, the desire for clarity will often result in vocal markers similar to those deployed by earlier subjects, "betrayed" into revelation.

The excitement of experiencing one's own play of ideas registers as a linguistic distinctiveness that constitutes character. For Smith as an actor and playwright, the "how" of speaking is important. She states that sound, or the musicality of language, is one criteria by which she structures her shows. Yet for Smith as an editor and cultural critic, the "what" of speaking is, obviously, equally significant; as she explains in relation to her San Francisco *On the Road:*

> I try to understand, whenever I can, how power works: Who is powerful? Who is not? How [do] people use their power? How [do] powerful people behave when they are interviewed? How [do] disenfranchised people behave and how [do] they become empowered during the interview?[6]

Though her accomplished speakers may be accustomed to having the authority of their pronouncements acknowledged in most of their daily encounters, as the time of Smith's performance nears, that sense of empowerment vanishes. In its place is a host of anxieties: What excerpt from the interview will Smith choose? Will she represent opinions fairly? Will "I" appear appropriately insightful—to myself? to my colleagues, who may also have been subjected to Smith's scrutiny? How will the audience judge "me" in relation to the other presentations? Has Smith discovered some (small) idiosyncrasy that, when reproduced onstage, will trigger gleeful recognition from the others and pronounce me—the real me sitting in the audience—foolish? In trusting Smith during the interview did I unwittingly reveal something that I now wish had remained hidden? If she chooses not to include me in the presentation, how will I feel—relieved? Or proven inadequate to the task of producing some pithy, profound statement?

These were some of my concerns when invited to see "myself" in the 1987 "Bay Area Women in Theater" performance. In a postperformance discussion following Smith's most recent *On the Road,* Bellagio interculturalism conferees spoke of both titillation and dread at the prospect of being displayed.[7] Eugenio Barba linked Smith's dramaturgy to a tradition of political clowning that has largely been lost in the United States, while New York University's Richard Schechner described its theatricality in terms of a "fit that doesn't fit," thereby opening an arena of knowledge. The speaker is given back his or her own words and rhythms in a body that is clearly Other. In that a female body is seen at times executing "male" movements, gesture becomes paradigmatic of gendered, social constructions.

Within this uncanny doubling resides comic delight: for the person being represented, the experience may constitute a magical return to the mirror stage of development, where one first discovers his or her corporal distinctness and derives narcissistic pleasure from the gaze upon the self. For those viewers who know the individual, delight may arise from seeing the familiar emptied of a measure of self-importance. Laughter focuses not only on this alienating near-image but also targets both what has and has not been said.

That laughter is potentially therapeutic. Its kinesthetic, infectious quality means that all can unite and magnify its effect. Equally, it has the capacity to divide, as some in-group members may feel their persons or positions unfairly stigmatized. In the chuckle of recognition is the possibility of self-criticism, as observers acknowledge the extent to which they agree with the person or position being parodied. Like the age-grade festivals of West Africa, Smith's *On the Road* serves the ideological function of reaffirming the group's sense of itself while simultaneously allowing it a socially sanctioned mechanism for critique.

But for viewers unfamiliar with the interviewees being depicted, the others' voluble recognition may enforce a sense of exclusion from the in-group. Certainly, some episodes, in which a persona struggles to achieve clarity, will still be read as comic, but for these outsiders the more visceral component may quickly drop away, leaving a more cerebral experience in which critical, interpretive cues are sometimes missing. In being tempted to fill the void the viewer is also being subtly challenged to reexamine the cultural bases upon which interpretation is made.

Consider, for example, the "No Means No" sequence in the Princeton *Gender Bending* piece. Whereas someone observing Smith's performance in the campus lecture hall would presumably have a program indicating the name and position of the speaker, in watching the videotape one lacks this information and can only assume from the comments offered that the speaker is an advocate for or director of some interpersonal relations–rape prevention and counseling service. Given human services staffing patterns, the videotape viewer may also assume that the speaker is female, but nothing in Smith's performance has authorized that assumption. The performer stands, speaking on a phone while slightly leaning against a lecture hall lectern that has seemingly become a part of the set. She suppresses all gendered body gestures and vocal intonations, offering instead a crystalline image of an articulate person. Thus, the question arises: Upon what basis does one decide that the speaker is female? Equally important, how would present social relations in the United States have to change so that this insistence upon respect for a woman's wishes might as easily be read as emanating from a man?

In commenting on her work, Smith has indicated that she does not want audiences to engage in guessing games.[8] Considering the volatility of some of the subjects with which she is dealing, one easily understands the importance of speakers retaining ownership of their words and acknowledging the consequences those words engender. Yet, for those at a distance from the local events that have occasioned an *On the Road,* the identificational tags, provided in a printed program or through slides edited into a videotaped performance, limit the interpretive and social revisioning that the text seems to aim for.

The segment "Is Race a Trope?" offers a parallel example of the way in which the absence of cues may productively complicate audience response. In a small, fast-paced voice, with polysyllabic words practically tripping over one another, Smith represents an American academic who asks whether race is an objective fact or, rather, a social construction by means of which the dominant class maintains its hegemony over people who share certain economic interests. The comic potential of the segment is immediately apparent and was, in fact, realized when Smith presented it as part of evening performances for the "Cultural Diversity in American Theater" conference.[9] Smith's rapid delivery of the speaker's ponderous vocabulary makes it difficult to absorb the question posed, "Is race a trope?" Only when the sheet of sound comes to a halt is the audience able to step back and reflect upon content. In performance Smith in fact inserted a brief freeze-frame seemingly in order to allow space for a shift from a comic to a more reflexive reading.

Distance, defined here both as the viewer's lack of specific knowledge of the speaker and as an absence of a sense of communal gathering for self-reflection, has positive effect. It is worthwhile to recall here—and to paraphrase—Lynda Hart's comments concerning the performance of lesbian texts before pluralistic audiences,[10] namely, that, rather than reopen at this point the essentialist/constructionist debate in order to determine truth claims, one might more efficiently deploy resources by focusing on the effect that the discourse on race produces, particularly on the material lives of those who are identified as being other than the (white) norm. The reception accorded the unraveling of the presumed essentialism of race differs according to the "race," nationality, class, and gender of both speaker and listener. The more both speaker and listener seem to share an identity of experience, the more the listener may be willing to scrutinize the argument without being apprehensive about its political ramifications.

In the absence of contrary information the viewer assumes that this academic is white, primarily because women of color constitute an extremely small percentage of the American professorate. However true, her insights are likely to be considered offensive because she is fatefully implicated within her own discourse. Delivered from a position of authority to minorities, her words replicate the social processes by which a privileged class defines and constructs reality to the material detriment of minorities.

Were a program to signal, via name or organizational affiliation, that the speaker is a woman of color, Latino, African-American, or Asian-American audience members might be willing to entertain the validity of the argument for a little while longer than in the case of a white academic. Yet it is also likely that this discourse may ultimately meet with a similar hostility—witness the enraged pain that greeted Anthony Appiah's writings on the subject.[11] It will do so for two reasons. First, this line of reasoning fails to alter power relations, because the norm misnames itself and deploys an ideological apparatus to mask that apprehension and contain all murmurings of counterarguments on its borders. Consider, for example, the term *feminism* as well as the need for women of color to deploy such terms as *black* or *Third World* in order to register their conceptions. Or former *Theatre Journal* editor Sue-Ellen Case's reminder to readers of the "Theatre of Color" issue that all along, when the journal's pages were filled with articles on European or American theater, they had been reading issues related to race. Thus, the argument that race is a trope seems to demand that Others give up their misconceptions about the reality of "race" and attempt to conform to the standards set by the norm.

There is a second, and perhaps even more powerful, reason why among peoples of color this argument is likely to engender not only anger but also terror when advanced by one who shares a nonwhite identity. (Here, of course, the truth claims of the constructionist/essentialist debates reenter the discussion.) As JoAnne Cornwell-Giles notes, even though this marginalized identity has become the symbol of an otherness despised by the dominant group, it also functions as a means by which the marginalized individual and group frame a concept of the self whose very difference is understood as a positive value.[12] Thus, when a critic like Appiah makes this argument, using DuBois as his evidence, it is as though a family member has dared to desecrate the lines of lineage. If "robbed" of that nurturing definition, in what categories does one think oneself?[13] To that question I will attempt a partial return in the final pages of this chapter.

But let us consider now how the fact that one is actually seeing an African-American woman affects a reading of this sequence. Smith has put on and discarded racial and gendered identities several times before arriving at this sequence,[14] so that the racial identity of the character or fictional construct becomes blurred, lost somewhere on the radioactive American terrain between the likelihood of the original and the actuality of the visible. This blurring has potentially created a space in which the listener is afforded no easy way out; deprived of cues concerning the speaker's identity and location, she or he cannot focus solely on political ramifications. In such an instance a curious estrangement is at work in the theater: thought has become separated from its material, that is, racial embodiment. Like the videotaped "No Means No" sequence, this episode frees some segments of an audience from fixed perimeters, releasing them onto the difficult territory of contemplating methods of engineering a more effective equation between intellectual perceptions and sociopolitical relations.

Obviously, those who have personal knowledge or immediate investment in the people and issues under theatrical scrutiny read such sequences quite differently. The character of their interpretations addresses the seeming intentionality of Smith's project, which I am describing as a postmodern theater for development. Referring to the overt deployment of art for social purposes, the term *theater for development* is generally used in relation to Third World countries where governmental agencies are endeavoring to introduce technologies related, for example, to agriculture or health, to largely rural, more traditionally oriented populations.[15] But the concept can also have validity for elite Western settings where the problem is not technological but social underdevelopment.

Issuing a commission to Anna Smith most often constitutes an intervention into a volatile situation that a community is struggling to understand and ameliorate: at the University of Pennsylvania, for example, local feminist bashing, which occurred shortly after the violent antifeminist attack in Montreal, was the immediate occasion for Smith's performance; in contrast, the consortium of Five Colleges, Amherst contracted the artist as part of a long-range process addressing issues ranging from the appearance of racist graffiti on campus buildings to curriculum review and institutional relationships between traditionally oriented theater departments and cultural production by people of color.[16] Commenting on her experiences at the Five Colleges, where she was given a list of people to interview concerning cultural diversity, Smith confesses to a certain amount of surprise concerning the kinds of deeply felt opinions people are willing to share with an outsider even when they know that some of the conversation may be repeated before people with whom they apparently cannot or will not speak in such direct terms.[17] What is fascinating—and painful—for Smith is to experience the volatility present on all sides of an issue. Those who have organized the commission very often are attempting to self-consciously reexamine hierarchies of difference in which they are implicated; those who are disenfranchised often engage in verbal histrionics as part of a process of arriving at some authorship over their thoughts and lives; those who are hostile to changes in sociopolitical privilege strive, nonetheless, to project a personable, tolerant image to this black woman whose agenda they suspect. Once Anna Smith represents these interviewees onstage the provocative nature of the performance threatens to reify the community's fissures, even while it validates the existence of previously marginal or silenced positions. Factions have now been clearly identified, and the difficulty of speaking to each other can no longer be denied. Everyone—organizers, speakers, other community members, and performer as well—has been caught in an act whose high stakes leave no one unscathed.

Race, rather than gender, seems to be the point around which much of the controversy arising from Smith's work has coalesced. To paraphrase Hart yet again, thanks to feminism, we have apparently come to understand that gender is performative. However, race—or, more properly stated, visible difference in skin color—remains tied to a metaphysics of substance. Whether it functions as an absolute or potential sign of difference is open to debate, based in part, again, upon one's relationship to the community under theatrical review. My comments here are taken from the published accounts of proceedings of the Women and Theatre Program, which exhibits the paradoxical virtue of a willingness to subject the contradictory praxis of its members to public, ideological, and theoretical critique, despite considerable risk of personal, emotional distress and organizational dysfunction; again, my position is that of an outsider, one whose knowledge of the principals and specific performances is limited.

At issue are two conflated questions: When does race read—or not read—as a sign of difference? What constitutes an appropriate next step, what is a suitable plan for development, after the community has viewed Smith's portrait of itself? The public record of Smith's 1988 and 1989 WTP performances documents three gradations of response. Judith L. Stephens alludes simply to Smith's piece as "a gut-wrenching rehashing of familiar conflicts and a tearing open of old wounds,"[18] without specifying the nature of the controversy. Sue-Ellen Case notes that, when Smith switched from representing a black woman to representing a white one confronting the issue of color,

> her [Smith's] own color became part of the perspective. This was apparent not only on stage, but in her relative isolation in the theatre. The only other women of color appeared specifically for Smith's performance and absented themselves from the rest of the preconvention.

And she wonders, "How could we, as primarily white women, better organize with women of color? What was Smith literally showing us?"[19] Jill Dolan seems to argue both that the performance maintained a mimetic function and that, in refusing to build character around psychological, empathetic techniques, Smith glossed over members' personal attributes, so that,

> if she provided a mirror, it was distorted by her presence as a Black woman, which conveyed an editorial comment in the personalities and issues she interwove. The performance was not an objective history of the WTP, but a Black, female performer's perspective on the preoccupations of a predominantly white women's organization.[20]

Disallowing the possibility of any person's delivering an "objective" history, one can advance a more complex argument. Members of different racial groups read race onstage differently, and in an episodic piece such as Smith's the reading any person does may change in response to a given segment. Whereas Dolan apparently saw a performer whose race was always a sign of difference,[21] I wonder whether the fact of race becomes immaterial at certain points in the text. That is, given the subject matter, the history of a predominantly white organization, for much of the performance Smith is playing characters whose race is different from her own. It is as though she were playing *Three Sisters* at A.C.T. or some other regional theater: at the outset one may remark upon the discrepancy between the race of the character and that of the actress, but, as the performance progresses, that disbelief, along with a host of others, is suspended, provided the actress satisfies basic textual demands, which include conformity to the cultural universe stipulated by the production. For the duration of that performance an African-American actress has become a (white) Russian character. Similarly, in those pieces constructed for predominantly white institutions, for most of the performance Smith has become white. An audience member may be inclined to "remember" the performer's race only when it is clear from diction or situation that the speaker is also black.

Certainly, as Case contends, at those points at which the racial identities of Smith's characters have switched in rapid progression *and* racial issues are part of the content of their speech, the performer's own race can become an alienating sign, offering its own editorial comment to members of the audience. What, perhaps, should be of equal notice are those places where Smith has presented people of different racial backgrounds and their experiences share certain commonalities. To cite the Princeton *Gender Bending* performance again, the narratives of Charlayne Hunter-Gault, who integrated the University of Georgia, and of Sally Frank, who sought to integrate male eating clubs, are illustrative of this point. Smith plays them almost back to back, separating them only by one speaker whose gender she signals by donning a pair of men's shoes. What seems most remarkable about both women's stories is their utter innocence and vulnerability in the face of ugly hostility. Hunter-Gault remembers worrying that the debris from dormitory windows, shattered by a howling mob, might ruin her new college clothes; Frank, having had a pitcher of beer dumped on her head, recalls wondering, in response to male threats to throw her in, whether there was water in the pool. Given the juxtaposition of these memories, racial difference momentarily ceases to have meaning. Seemingly, that moment needs to be cher-

ished as a community struggles to negotiate its divisions, for it offers
a hope of eventual unity.

Earlier I argued that dismantling the essentialism of race is likely
to strike terror in the hearts of minority peoples. Dolan's comments
seem to suggest that, given a metaphysics of substance, essentialism
is operative for some whites as well. How, then, do we think ourselves anew? Humanists and scientists seeking to articulate a "new
science of the human" have argued that human species survival depends upon our being socialized through the "enchantment" of symbolic discourse into desiring a particular mode of being; thus, each
culture must create, as it were, necessary lies or an order of discourse
that presents itself as the true narrative in opposition to all others in
order to function systematically as a behavior regulatory mechanism.[22] By beginning to understand how we are necessarily seduced
into thinking and feeling certain aspects of identity as an irreducible
category of existence, we become aware of the limits of our own
discourse and may be more open to entertaining different modes of
being that address some of those limitations. Theater, because it deploys multiple sign systems within a public arena, can serve as a
particularly powerful realm for the renegotiation of identity(ies).
Certainly, the Hunter-Gault and Frank segments of *Gender Bending*
hint at that possibility, but the various controversies surrounding
both Smith's performances and Appiah's writings register the
difficulties.

Theater for development is successful seemingly in those cases
in which objectives—teaching the value of child immunization, for
example—are clearly defined and progress easily measured. If the
goals are more ambitious—for instance, empowering people who
have grown resigned to their disenfranchisement—then it is arduous,
messy work. Outsiders may be brought in to gather information
concerning a community's perceptions of its problems. That some
may be angry or hurt by the resultant, unpleasant reflections is to be
expected. And, as Michael Etherton reports in describing such efforts
in Africa, often community people complain that they already know
their problems; what they want from artist-activators is help in effect-
ing solutions.[23] On the African continent Ngugi wa Thiong'o and
Ngugi wa Mirii pioneered one of the most stunning examples of a
theater for development project, which did, in fact, empower its host
community. By writing down the oral history given them by rural

Kenyans, by casting informants and rehearsal onlookers as actors, these men used the stage to better understand and critique their post-colonial predicament.[24] But the coda to this success story is that the Kenyan government destroyed the theater project and forced Ngugi wa Thiong'o into exile.

The Ngugi example demonstrates that a community must find its solutions from within. Undoubtedly Anna Smith has crafted a powerful, disturbing performance mode that can potentially serve a positive, interventionist function. But her "On the Road" snapshots of America are only one part of a long process. Having caught sight of our beauty and ugliness, having laughed and despaired at our reflections in her alienating mirror, we have to be about the business of constructing our own, indigenous theaters for development, where we can explore difference and attempt to eradicate its invidiousness.

NOTES

1. Three commentaries, along with a partial text of one of those performances, are offered in *Women & Performance* 4, no. 8 (1989); see Judith L. Stephens, "Women and Theatre Program: Reactions and Reflections"; Sue-Ellen Case, "Introduction to 'Chlorophyll Postmodernism and the Mother Goddess/A Conversation'"; and Jill Dolan, "Staking Claims and Positions: The Women and Theatre Program, San Diego, and the Danger Zone." Other commissions have included the University of Nevada, Las Vegas; the National Conference on Women and the Law; and Minority Claims Association.

2. *Performing Arts Journal* 33–34, 11, no. 3; 12, no. 1 (1989).

3. My analysis of the form is based primarily upon review of videotapes of the 1989 Princeton University and 1990 Eureka Theatre productions.

4. I use the term *signifyin'* in the Black English sense of commenting via metaphor and indirection. See, for example, Geneva Smitherman, *Talkin and Testifyin: The Language of Black America* (Detroit: Wayne State University Press, 1977); and Henry Louis Gates, Jr., "The Blackness of Blackness: A Critique of the Sign and the Signifying Monkey," in *Black Literature and Literary Theory*, ed. Henry Louis Gates, Jr. (New York: Methuen, 1984), 287–90.

5. Interview with Anna Deavere Smith, 11 May 1990.

6. Interview with Smith, 11 May 1990.

7. An audiotape of the 19 February 1991 postperformance discussion was made available to me by Anna Smith. Discussion participants included Folabo Ajayi, Eugenio Barba, Jean Franco, Barbara Kirshenblatt-Gimblett, Yamaguchi Masao, Margaret Phelan, Richard Schechner, and Gayatri Spivak. Trin Minh-Ha and Sun Huizhu were among the other participants; apparently, Homi

Bhabha "appeared" in Smith's performance piece, but given tensions arising from the Persian Gulf War, did not actually attend the conference.

8. Bellagio audiotape, 19 February 1991.

9. This segment was originally presented as part of a 1990 performance at the University of Pennsylvania. My remarks are based on a conference performance sponsored by the Black Arts Program of University of California, San Diego, in November 1990. In that the conference on diversity in theater was part of a program of events celebrating the twentieth anniversary of the establishment of Third College, most attendees were people of color. Though I have not been able to review this segment on videotape, I have discussed the episode with Smith sufficiently to feel certain that recall of this performance is accurate. The final interpretation is, of course, my own.

10. Lynda Hart, "Identity and Seduction: Lesbians in the Mainstream," in this volume.

11. Appiah's original article, "The Uncompleted Argument: DuBois and the Illusion of Race," in *"Race," Writing, and Difference,* ed. Henry Louis Gates, Jr. (Chicago: University of Chicago Press, 1986), 21–37, initially appeared in the first of two *Critical Inquiry* issues (12, no. 1 [Autumn 1985] and 13, no. 1 [Autumn 1986]) devoted, as the title indicates, to race and writing. These volumes represented a significant moment, for contemporary critical theory was being brought to bear on ideas of race. Appiah's essay met with a storm of protests from critics such as Houston Baker and Joyce Joyce. See, for example, Houston A. Baker, Jr., "Caliban's Triple Play," in Gates, *"Race"*; and Joyce A. Joyce, " 'Who the Cap Fit': Unconsciousness and Unconscionableness in the Criticism of Houston A. Baker, Jr., and Henry Louis Gates, Jr.," *New Literary History* 18 (1986): 371–84. Seemingly, the hostile response of these critics and others occasioned a second Appiah article, "The Conservation of 'Race,' " *Black American Literature Forum* 23, no. 1 (Spring 1989): 37–60.

12. JoAnne Cornwell-Giles, "Afro-American Criticism and Western Consciousness: The Politics of Knowing," *Black American Literature Forum* 24, no. 1 (Spring 1990): 87, 91.

13. In fact, Appiah acknowledges as much when he suggests that the astute DuBois—and later critics following in his wake—never accepted what he intellectually recognized because "the absence [of an essential notion of race] simply threatens to leave too vast a discursive void." "The Conservation of 'Race,' " 41.

14. Here I should admit the possibility that a viewer's sense of the ease with which Smith has switched racial identities is aided by the fact that she is a light-skinned African-American woman.

15. For an introduction to the field of theater for development in Africa, see such works as Michael Etherton, *The Development of African Drama* (London: Hutchinson University Library for Africa, 1982), 314–57; Oga Abah and Michael Etherton, "The Samaru Projects: Street Theatre in Northern Nigeria," *Theatre Research International* 7, no. 2 (1982): 222–34; and Christopher Kamlongera, "Theatre for Development: The Case of Malawi," *Theatre Research International* 7, no. 2 (1982): 207–22.

16. Telephone interviews with Smith, March 1990 and 4 April 1991.

17. Telephone interview, 21 March 1991.

18. Stephens, 14.

19. Case, "Introduction," 23.

20. Dolan, "Staking Claims," 52.

21. Note that earlier in the article Dolan remarks: "But her presence as a Black woman performer—the only Black woman of the 100 women attending the conference—was continually foregrounded through the piece, since the personae she assumed were often non-coincident with her race," 52.

22. With these few words I am, of course, violently flattening the complexity of this research. For a more adequate representation, see, for example, Sylvia Wynter, "On Disenchanting Discourse: 'Minority' Literary Criticism and Beyond," *Cultural Critique* 7 (Fall 1987): 207–44.

23. Etherton, *Development,* 27.

24. Accounts of the Kamiriithu theater project are numerous. See, for example, Ngugi wa Thiong'o, "Women in Cultural Work: The Fate of Kamiriithu People's Theater in Kenya," *Barrel of a Pen: Resistance to Repression in Neo-Colonial Kenya* (Trenton, N.J.: Africa World Press, 1983); Ngugi wa Thiong'o, "The Language of African Theatre," *Decolonising the Mind: The Politics of Language in African Literature* (London: James Currey, 1986); and Ingrid Bjorkman, *"Mother, Sing for Me": People's Theatre in Kenya* (London: Zed Books, 1989).

Chapter 2

From *Lady Dick* to Ladylike:
The Work of Holly Hughes

Kate Davy

In the last decade no figure in lesbian theater and performance art has been more contentious, more contested, and at the same time more celebrated than Holly Hughes. As one of four artists "defunded" by the National Endowment for the Arts (NEA) in the summer of 1990, Hughes became a central player in a debate that began in the summer of 1989 and focused on issues regarding public funding of art deemed obscene, a debate played out in the disparate if not divergent spheres of the Congress, the academy, and the art world. Chronicled nationally in arts publications, academic journals, and alternative presses and "covered" by mainstream news venues, this censorship-in-general debate was ignited initially by a very specific desire to suppress any depiction of homoeroticism in art production.[1] Indeed, while the larger issue of freedom of speech and artistic expression defined the terms of the debate, homoeroticism (read: homophobia) remained visible as the issue fanning the fire.

The profound irony of this homoerotic-art-panic with regard to the stage it set for Hughes's voice as a writer of works described as lesbian[2] lies in the narrative trajectory and performative strategies of the piece she was performing at the moment when the NEA debacle involved her directly; during the furor surrounding then NEA chairman John Frohnmayer's move to rescind her funding, Hughes was performing her fourth major effort, a piece she describes as "not very homoerotic." Naysayers looking for the lesbianism in this particular specimen of nominally lesbian work would instead find a piece permeated with tropes of heterosexuality that remain largely undisturbed. In a short article she wrote just before the NEA decision and published subsequently Hughes describes a trip home to her alma mater, Kalamazoo College, where she had been invited to perform her latest work. She writes, "I was sorry the piece I was to perform, *World without End,* was not very homoerotic, and that those who were coming to be either offended or inspired might feel short changed. On the plane I tried to think of ways I could inject all the pussy juice into the spectacle."[3]

Even before the NEA decision against her brought nationwide attention to her work, Hughes's reputation as a lesbian artist preceded her at Kalamazoo, so much so that she posits a potentially disappointed audience if the performance is not homoerotic enough. "Pussy juice" presumably signifies the "lesbianness" and, concomitantly, disruptiveness missing from *World without End.* Hughes ponders how to recuperate that discursive and performative space for an expectant audience and, perhaps, realizes that lesbian "identity" does not automatically imbue a piece with a readable lesbian discourse and aesthetic by virtue of some ontological status. The juice is crucial, not merely the scent (read: essence). Lesbian is not a state of being that a priori inscribes cultural products made by the hands of women who identify as lesbian and participate in lesbian discourses, cultures, and practices. Far from ontology, lesbian in, for example, Irigaray's image of the "goods that refuse to go to market," marks an alternative, disruptive discursive space in the *performance* of that refusal.[4] Lesbian is located, in part, in a performative resistance to a phallic regime whose operating principles underpin and drive (at least Western) hegemonic cultures, a regime in which, as suggested by the salvation history its title invokes, *World without End* is firmly embedded.

Writing about the NEA controversy and the intense hatred gay men elicit because they "implicitly 'feminize' all men," Peggy Phelan states, "Lesbians are not as overtly hated because they are so locked out of the visible, so far from the minds of the N.E.A and the New Right, that they are not acknowledged as a threat." (14) This notion of being "locked out" is a compelling one; it signals the lesbian's sociosymbolic status as one of not being in the game or even in the room where the game repeatedly and perpetually plays itself out. The lesbian's distance from the symbolic order is so great, her status as empty signifier so decisive, that she is effectively erased in the psychosocial register of the visible. This is both her oppression and her promise as a destabilizing force. While notoriety as an individual artist who publicly identifies as lesbian certainly has its political effects, it does little in itself "to produce the conditions of visibility for a different social subject"—a move Teresa de Lauretis identified in 1984 as a kind of bottom line feminist project.[5]

Hughes was targeted by the NEA primarily on the basis of her previous work in which she aggressively pushed at the symbolic and conventional boundaries of performance as a meaning-making apparatus to challenge and eschew male sexuality as a universal norm and to produce a theater that both responds to and engenders lesbian subjectivities, a theater with the potential to create a representational space for lesbians—as constitutive of a sexual minority—to engage as speaking, desiring agents. When the production of her play *The Lady Dick* opened at the WOW Cafe in New York City in 1985 it represented a radical and significant shift in the tenor of much Anglo-American lesbian and feminist theater. Even when addressed to lesbian spectators, most plays by Anglo-American lesbian authors about lesbians typically carried either a direct or surreptitious request for acceptance from heterosexual society. Lesbians were more often than not portrayed as ordinary, innocuous people, no more neurotic than heterosexuals, and grappling with the same mundane life, love, and career problems.[6]

The lesbians who people *Lady Dick* are not nice girls. There is no subterranean appeal to dominant culture for understanding. Instead, Hughes explores lesbian sexuality through (homo)gender play in a production that drops heterosexuals from the performative address altogether. The characters are bawdy, sinister and sinful, aggressive, sexy, and dangerous—no nurturing types here. At *Lady Dick* the lesbian spectator who looked into the "mirror" of the production in search of "positive images" and politically correct role models was thwarted. In a sense Hughes's *Lady Dick* liberated lesbian and feminist theater from the "good-girl syndrome" in its many dominant discourse guises as well as its feminist ones. Women in the world of *Lady Dick* are overtly sexual and on the prowl—for other women.[7]

When the NEA debate, as productive of a particular historical moment, got around to interrogating an Anglo-American lesbian's performance work, the lesbian had been virtually evacuated from the

Early staged reading of *Dress Suits to Hire* with Peggy Shaw and Lois Weaver. Photo by Dona Ann McAdams.

Sharon Jane Smith and Holly Hughes in Holly Hughes's *Lady Dick*.
Photo by Dona Ann McAdams.

theatrical sign. This is not to suggest that the burden for lesbian representation rests solely with Holly Hughes nor that the evacuation from a fledgling lesbian sign of the specificity of its referent is unique to her work. A number of recent productions at WOW—the women's theater collective in New York, where Hughes got her start—reflect similar moves, moves Hughes's work foreshadows and, perhaps, influences.[8]

Given this turn in her work, combined with her "bad-girl attitude" with regard to producing positive images of women and lesbians, it should not be surprising that Hughes is not only under attack from the Right but that she has squared off against a number of feminists as well. Since *Lady Dick,* her work has shifted in its production context, content, performative style, and address, igniting heated debates, especially among feminist lesbian critics, and raising nearly every issue relevant to feminist theater practice and criticism today. This essay examines the nature of the shift in Hughes's work in light of some of these debates and explores the implications for feminist lesbian theater as cultural production. While I argue that Hughes's earlier productions perform a homoerotically specific and, consequently, more lethally resistant threat to hegemonic signifying systems and practices than her later pieces, I do so because I recognize the aesthetic, political, and cultural importance of her work. Holly Hughes is clearly one of the most compelling and significant writers to emerge in the last decade.

In a piece that ostensibly sets out to hypostatize *lesbian* for purposes of determining what constitutes a lesbian play, Lynda Hart explores a range of dramatic literature labeled "lesbian" according to a variety of discrete and competing ideological frameworks. On the way to pinpointing a working definition of *lesbian,* Hart problematizes the entire endeavor and instead locates lesbian sexuality in its definitional interstice, that is, in its very resistance to coherent definition and identification. By the end of this cogent analysis of lesbian dramatic literature Holly Hughes's first play, *The Well of Horniness,* becomes paradigmatic for Hart of the disruptive strategies theorized by the feminist lesbian critics she engages. Hart writes that it "is both transgressive and *aggressive*—it assaults the audience with barrages of signs that insist on disrupting heterosexist conceptions of lesbian desire."[9]

The Well of Horniness began as a kind of mini-one-act spoof based very loosely on Radclyffe Hall's classic novel of lesbian sexuality, *The Well of Loneliness,* and was performed in a number of small, underground nightclubs in Manhattan's East Village.[10] The parody's success inspired two sequels, which appear in the final version as "Part II: Victim Victoria" and "Part III: In the Realm of the Senseless."[11] What little plot exists is broken repeatedly by a narrator's commentary, mock commercials, announcements, and a plethora of sound effects, all of which conspire to keep spectators firmly in the realm of the (re)presentational. In an apparent send-up of *Our Town* style the Narrator establishes the scene for part 1:

> The setting, a peaceful New England town, just a town like many others . . . where every winter day is a white Christmas *(humming "White Christmas")*. . . . But beneath the apparently serene breast of new-fallen snow, a whirlpool rages . . . *(sucking noises)* sucking the weak, the infirm, the original and all others who don't wear beige down . . . down, down. As carrots in the Cuisinart . . . *(blender)* so are souls in the Well *(scream)* of Horniness! Meet Georgette. (225–26)

Georgette, a "well-groomed word-processing trainee" and one-time member of the "Tridelta Tribads"[12] sorority (also referred to in the text as the "sisterhood of sin"), meets her brother, Rod (in the sexual sense of "packing a rod"), and his wife-to-be, Vicki, at a restaurant only to discover that Vicki is someone she knows from her past in the "sisterhood." They are introduced and, according to the stage direction, "stand frozen . . . in near-embrace." Georgette orders dinner, but Vicki does not; instead, she stares longingly at Georgette, prompting the following lines:

> *Georgette:* Whatsamatter honey? You sit in a puddle, or are you just glad to see me?
> *Waitress:* Excuse me, Miss, are you gonna order anything or are you just gonna eat hers?

The last line, delivered to Vicki, foreshadows and frames the scene that follows:

> *Narrator:* As Vicki's fork clatters to the ground, something darker than etiquette draws Vicki down. . . . What began inno-

cently enough, takes a turn for the worse underneath the table. Vicki finds no cutlery, but Georgette's legs, two succulent rainbows leading to the same pot of gold. (228–29)

As Rod delivers a lengthy monologue in which he ponders the itinerary of his coming honeymoon, his fiancée is under the table with her head between his sister's legs. In Hughes's many productions of the play around the East Village this scene was staged explicitly with Georgette responding elaborately while Rod prattled on obliviously about honeymoon hideaways. As "the rod" reproduces and reinscribes the patriarchal construction of marriage, his fiancée busily disrupts it through her sexuality.

Vicki emerges from under the table, announces that she is feeling "a little hot," and heads for the restroom. Rod turns to Georgette and says—in the context of a play permeated with references to fish that signify lesbian sex—"Something's fishy, I can't quite put my finger on it, can you?" Georgette replies, "I'm working on it." Only four pages into the script lesbian sexuality is established not merely as theme but as the raison d'être for whatever else transpires in the representational economy of *The Well of Horniness*. As the play proceeds, it abounds with references to fish, muff-divers, bush leagues, eager beavers, tribads, bosom buddies, and the Stowed Finger Lodge where two girls meet for a tryst.

Hart concludes her essay with the following assessment:

Any play that effectively challenges the hegemony of heterosexuality and the tenacity of sexual difference offers a hopeful new space of visibility for feminists. *The Well of Horniness* presents such possibilities. At this historical moment, it is located on the borderline, a place both there and not there. It is a delicate balance to maintain, but as long as it holds itself tautly in that tension, deferring totalization, elusively in motion, poised in a position of aggressive resistance, I would name that play lesbian. (289)

My point in quoting Hughes's script at length is not only to support Hart's conclusions but also to make explicit the ways in which *The Well of Horniness* achieves its status as a lesbian play. Eking out a space in which the staging of alternative desire(s), gender(s), and sexualities can occur on their own terms is crucial to the project of creating a representational currency that circulates in contradistinction to hegemonic cum phallic representational economies. Somehow the seemingly forever devalued notion of "content" becomes salient again in the context of representation that would call itself lesbian. The sum total of Hart's description of *The Well*'s plot is the following: "When Hughes's lesbian character, Georgette, lasciviously goes on the prowl for the newest girl in town and seduces her under a restaurant table where she is having dinner with her fiance [*sic*],[13] heterosexist misperceptions of lesbians as male-identified sex maniacs suffer a parodic disruption" (288). While "seduction under the table" has great metaphoric potential for lesbian existence in homophobic culture, it hardly adequately expresses the pussy-eating Hughes put in her text and on the stage. I contend that the scene's address is to lesbians in a performative image that lived on notoriously and juicily in the lesbian community long after the play had ceased to be performed.

I unreservedly agree with Hart that, when it comes to lesbians, "their elusiveness is their strength, indicating that they are somewhere else . . ." (288) and that "the overwhelming ambiguity of lesbian sexuality, its resistance to coherent identification, its radical contingencies, propose a site from which this elsewhere might be constructed most productively" (287). At the same time I want to be careful that all this elusiveness and ambiguity does not once again push lesbians off the sexual map. When it comes to lesbians both meaning *and* its means of production are relevant. De-eroticising lesbian is a wholly unproductive project, and I am not suggesting that Hart engages in it. But, as we describe lesbian resistance, the multiple and heterogeneous possibilities her narrative spaces, positionalities, and subjectivities present, it is imperative to inscribe the ways in which these possibilities are enacted or performed so as to retain the specificity of that refusal/resistance lesbians perform—the specificity of, if not lesbian desire, then lesbians desiring; if not lesbian sexuality, then lesbians as sexual.[14] In the introduction to the published version of *The Well of Horniness* Hughes suggests the following for those who wish to produce her play: "Occasionally the cast should break into frenetic sexual activity. . . ." (221). Hughes's lesbians are sexual; their desire for each other is palpable.

C. Carr, who has followed Hughes's productions from the be-

ginning and written about them in the *Village Voice,* recalls the pre-
miere of *The Well,* before its two sequels, "at the tiny Limbo Lounge
on Tompkins Square, [where] a cast member ended up on an audience member's lap during one cramped scene." Writing about the
experience nearly five years later, Carr captures the disruptive performative dimension of the play in an especially "dyky" image. She
remembers the performance as ending "dramatically that first night
when the door to the Limbo banged open and a woman stepped in
off 10th Street, announcing, 'Stella Bruce. Lesbian detective.'"[15] Perhaps this striking image was the impulse behind Carr's inspired and
enormously productive notion of *dyke noir,* the term she coined to
describe Hughes's work. In appropriating the characteristics of *film
noir* as a genre, Hughes created a vehicle in her subsequent venture,
The Lady Dick, for realizing what *The Well* had been only sporadi-
cally and partially able to accomplish. Unlike *The Well,* in which a
detective is introduced in part 2 to solve a murder that takes place in
part 1, *Lady Dick* drops crime *as an event* from a narrative in which
lesbians are the crime—a crime against nature. The detective who
appears in *The Well* as "a gorgeous gendarme who loves girls almost
as much as she loves murder" (231) reappears in *Lady Dick* as "a
woman who likes having a mystery around more than she likes solv-
ing them. The woman is Garnet McClit, Lady Dick."[16]

A book entitled *Women in Film Noir* appeared in 1978 in which
essays by eight critics demonstrate the singular iconographic and narrative terrain of film noir as especially productive ground for exploring and exposing the construction and position of "woman" in phallocratic systems of representation.[17] The central figure in film noir is
the now classic stereotype of the sensual and dangerous femme fatale.
Although she is finally defeated, abandoned, recuperated, or destroyed in what are ultimately male worldview "pictures," her importance for feminist inquiry derives from what she accomplishes
before her literal or symbolic demise. Janey Place argues that, whatever the form of that demise, femme fatales are remembered far less
for their tragic ends than for their exciting—because initially virtually
uncontained—sexuality. "Visually, film noir is fluid, sensual, extraor-
dinarily expressive, making the sexually expressive woman, which
is its dominant image of woman, extremely powerful" (36). A number of feminist film critics point to film noir, certainly not as a form
to be exemplified and celebrated but, rather, because—however brief

its moments and however truncated—film noir allows female sexuality to be expressed as having agency. And, while this agency is manifestly articulated within a (hetero)gendered representational economy, female sexuality in film noir is expressed not solely in one's ability to attract men—with its attendant presumed willingness to assume the missionary position—but, coincidentally, in terms of intelligence, ambition, independence, gumption, and guile. Indeed, the reason the sexually aggressive femme fatale must be punished so severely, utterly recuperated, or destroyed is because of the power she garners as a result of the access she has to her own sexuality—even if glimpsed only when her influence over camera movement, her visually dominant position within the frame, and her discursive voice converge.

Moreover, the milieu Place articulates as integral to film noir is set against Sylvia Harvey's contention that film noir is "structured around the destruction or absence of [unrestored] romantic love and the family" (25). Place writes: "The dominant world view expressed in film noir is paranoid, claustrophobic, hopeless, doomed, predetermined by the past, *without clear moral or personal identity*" (41; my emphasis). Hence, a genre—for which Harvey uses the words *abnormal, dissonant, disoriented, unease, disequilibrium,* and *disturbing* (22) to describe; which Christine Gledhill calls "tangibly artificial" with a frequently "incomprehensible plot structure" (6) that produces "female representations outside family definition and dependency" (15); and which Richard Dyer contends is marked by "anxiety over the existence and definition of masculinity and normality" (91)—is the site where a fatal female discourse of sexuality is articulated and circulates vis-à-vis the absence or ambiguity of a "clear [read: male] moral or personal identity." What better representational playground of conventions could there be for a romp with variations on lesbian desire and sexuality? Of the heroines of film noir Gledhill writes that "their *performance* of the roles accorded them in this form of male story-telling foregrounds the fact of their image as an artifice and suggests another place behind the image where the woman might be" (17). Or another place behind the woman where the lesbian might be. Or, simply, another *place* where there are no "beings" but only performances of sexualities through a reconfigured notion of gender(s).[18]

Genres, according to Fredric Jameson, are not only particular

conglomerates of aesthetic characteristics and production conventions, but even more they are "essentially literary *institutions,* or social
contracts between a writer and a specific public, whose function is to
specify the proper use of a particular cultural artifact."[19] With this
definition of genre in mind it is interesting to note the debate with
regard to film noir as constitutive of genre at all; it is sometimes
described as a subgenre, one derived from gangster and thriller films.
While the reasons for this classification quandary revolve around aesthetic and structural criteria in film theory and historiography, it is
also possible to understand it as stemming, in part, from film noir's
inability to maintain the social contract Jameson suggests, its inability
to satisfactorily fulfill its social pact on the terms of the foundational
social covenant, the heterosexual contract, the contract that under-
girds all others.[20]

The productive, disruptive potential of film noir for the project
of dyke noir lies beyond a mere appropriation of its themes, iconography, and style. More than these salient features, Hughes appropriates the operating principles that drive film noir and, taken together,
force a wedge or open a gap in a social contract that both determines
and is determined by an imperative heterosexuality. The position of
"woman" in any classic genre film, or any other narrative structure,
as (back)ground for the real work of the film, is challenged in film
noir—in which "real work" is the ideological metadiscourse of normality, as synonomous with heterosexual masculinity and its phallocratic sociosymbolic regime and which is carried out discursively
through men as speaking subjects. The discursive position available
to women through their fixed roles as always-already-in-relation
(wives, whores, mothers, daughters, lovers, mistresses) is defied in
the displaced figure of the femme fatale. E. Ann Kaplan writes,
"Thus the film noir *expresses* alienation, locates its cause squarely in
the excesses of female sexuality ('natural' consequences of women's
independence), and punishes that excess in order to re-place it within
the patriarchal order" (3). The enactment of this excess of female
sexuality, however, the femme fatale's displacement through deviance, is so overwhelming that "where there is a metadiscourse . . . it
exists at great cost, through considerable narrative and visual contor-
tion" (2).

Hence, film noir's conventions are themselves profoundly
skewed precisely in relation to the threat of the femme fatale's dis-

placement in, and challenge to, the phallocratic order. The distorted machinations of film noir's narrative trajectory open to interrogation the perennial metadiscourse of heterosexual normalcy and its concomitant heterogendered binary positions of male-privileged dominance and all-that-is-not-white-male submission. An implicit chink in the armor of the heterosexual contract is thus rendered visible in the gaps and fissures of an ultimately less than monolithic heterosexual configuration. The way in which the femme fatale's visual and narrative position is inhabited (that is, female sexuality as independent, sensual/sexual, aggressive, and ambitious) undermines a reductive reading of her status as always already and only an object of (male) desire.

The gap or rupture engendered by film noir's inability to comply unproblematically with the dictates of a foundational (hetero)socio-sexual contract cannot be explored within film noir's own terrain, as the exceedingly telling *but* in the following sentence marks: of the femme fatale, Place writes, "Independence is her goal, but her nature is fundamentally and irredeemably sexual in film noir" (46). *Lady Dick* rewrites the sentence thus: "Independence is her [femme, butch, kiki, dyke, lesbian] modus operandi, *and* her context is fundamentally and irredeemably sexual in dyke noir."

In the final moments of *Lady Dick* the actors—as actors, not characters—stand together on the set. They pass the lady dick's Bogey-like hat around to one another. As each actor receives the hat, she tells a piece of a story about becoming "woman" and watching and making movies. I quote it at length because, with the exception of a few lines, the entire hat-passing, movie-making ending that follows does not appear in the published version of the play. Even so, it appears here in significantly reduced form.

The first actor tells about going fishing every morning with her father and sharing fully in the rites of his (male homosocial) culture until one day:

> Poppa don't wake me up to go fishing. Later in the day he's looking funny at me, like he don't know me. Didn't know what to do with me. Too big to sit in his lap, too little to give away. He picks me up and carries me down to the water. But he don't take me to the boat. . . . he gets into the boat and disappears. For a long time I sit there, pretending I'm going somewhere. Then

the snakes come out of the woods. . . . I'm screaming til I lose my voice. Lucky for me I get a new voice. . . .

The hat is passed to another actor:

> I see my daddy no more. . . . Stay up late as I want with mama now. . . . We watch the movies. And this guy comes in [into the movie]. . . . he's the guy you watch. He's the one. I thought when I grow up I'm going to be like that man. Know all the side streets. Gonna get the girl. But this movie is crazy. Can't figure out what's going on. Somebody got shot early on, but nobody even cries. Momma said they need some place to start a movie. And a dead man is as good as any. They need a movie so the guy can get the girl.

The hat is passed again:

> This is the part I like. When he meets the girl. And you can't decide to like her or hate her. Some of both. So I'm thinking this is a real good movie. When all of a sudden my mother starts saying: "She's gonna get it." I thought you hadn't seen this movie before, Mom. That don't matter. You can tell she's gonna get it. . . . And I say what the hell kind of movie is this? My momma . . . says "It's a mystery."

Again:

> Like hell it's a mystery. We stay up to watch another movie, so I can get the bad taste of the last one outta my mouth. In this movie there's this lady singer. . . . She's got this boyfriend. She sings a song about her boyfriend and . . . he hits her. Then she sings another song. And he hits her again . . . My momma says she loves a love story. She loves a movie.

Another actor gets the hat:

> Well I love a movie too, I'm gonna live my whole life like a movie only this time the girl's not gonna get it. . . . One thing's for sure: This girl don't get it.

The hat is returned to the actor who had it first:

> I got it in an alley between a pizzeria and a Catholic Church. It was during a folk mass. The whole time I'm thinking, on one side of me is people believing they're eating the body of god, on the other is people pretending they're eating the genuine cuisine of Italy. I wonder who is getting ripped off the most. I try to think I'm gonna have a future. In the future, in my movie, I'm gonna cut out the scene where the girl gets it. . . .

The lady dick takes the hat:

> That's about it. There's a lot of people promising to clean up this town but in my movie I'm fighting to make sure there's always a wrong side of town. My side of town. . . . When you're in trouble or just looking for it, you'll look me up. . . .
>
> I'll show you a card trick. Anybody got a dollar?
>
> *(Takes dollar from audience member.)*
>
> Thanks. *(Pockets the dollar.)* Goodnight.

This final scene is paradigmatic of the ways in which *Lady Dick* transforms film noir into dyke noir. Like the discursive movement of a single monologue as articulated through a number of different performers above, the discourse of the femme fatale cum lady dick is not embodied in a single actor but, rather, articulated through a number of different discursive and performative tropes.

The Lady Dick is a detective story without a plot. Rather than the traditional configuration of "character/action," *Lady Dick* constructs its (re)presentational world in terms of "location/acts." The setting is the underground world of a lesbian bar called "The Pit." Described as "a dumpster for love's leftovers" it is also a site for something else: "They call it 'Show biz.'" The bar in *Lady Dick* functions as both a gathering place for social outcasts and as a stage, a site for a series of "acts," or "turns." Gledhill points to a generic feature of film noir in the construction of femme fatales as "strong women in image-producing roles—nightclub singers, hostesses, models etc." (17). In dropping the crime out of the detective story film noir's setting for an unfolding plot becomes, in dyke noir, solely an arena for "image-producing roles." There are no fully developed characters in *Lady*

Dick, no individuals striving toward a particular end. Image production in *Lady Dick* is accomplished by performers who intermittently assume certain show biz personas or character types through which they deliver monologues, give commercials, make announcements, and sing songs; there are a dozen songs in *Lady Dick,* a show with a running time under ninety minutes. In short, the femme fatale cum lady dick discourse emerges as a result of the interaction of different theatrical and noir iconographic, performative, and narrative conventions, not through a struggle among discretely drawn characters.

Unlike *The Well,* in which lesbians are contextualized in familial relationships and surface as desiring and sexual according to the dictates of a plot, *Lady Dick* is permeated with signifiers of desire that circulate among "drifters," itinerants who undermine the totalizing characteristics of identity and, at the same time, perform a resistant stance that is manifestly homoerotic. *Lady Dick* can be understood not only as a series of resistant discursive stances but as a repetition of resistant performative stances as well—resistant to the dictates of the heterosexual contract, with its requisite and asymmetrical dynamics of sexual difference.

Played by Sharon Jane Smith, *The Lady Dick*'s detective begins the play wearing a green strapless cocktail dress circa the end of the noir era. In this getup she spars verbally with Mickey Paramus, a circuit performer played by Peggy Shaw as a kind of lounge lizard, lady-killer. In their exchange of caustic sexual remarks Shaw's Paramus character "comes on" in sleazy, smarmy fashion to Smith's lady. Embedded in this come-on is an articulation of the anxiety and insecurities of masculinity that underlie film noir's excess of female sexuality.

The lady momentarily suspends the seduction-in-progress ostensibly to change into something more comfortable. Thwarting expectations of the femme fatale's classic negligee, Smith instead holds a man's suit from the noir era on a hanger in front of her. Stroking the suit, she sings:

> A butch is a woman
> Who looks like a man
> Depending how close you look

> A femme is a female
> Sometimes she may be male
> Sometimes she don't want to cook
>
> A femme can be fatal
> A butch be prenatal
> But everyone knows a dick
>
> Some walk like their moms
> Some walk like their dads
> It's never too late to switch.

Using her hand and finger to mime the action of a gun, the lady shoots Paramus, who grabs "his" groin and dies elaborately. Then, as the onstage piano player strikes up a rendition of "Pistol-Packin Mama," Paramus gets up to sing a song that begins:

> Never flirt with a girl
> who's been down old Lesbos way

and ends:

> Listen to my story of a green-eyed dick named Clit
> She shot her pistol in the air
> And she hit me in the *[lights out]*.

Although Mickey Paramus leaves the play forever, Shaw reappears throughout the performance in a number of different guises.[21] With the suggestive, boozy sound of an onstage saxophone as background, Smith delivers a monologue about growing up queer in a town that never changes while she puts on each piece of the dick costume over the green cocktail dress.[22]

The entire opening sequence is significant in that the lady-killer (performed in a fiercely heteropatriarchal manner) is killed off by the lady, who promises and posits the butch as an alternative performative space. Just as the song that precedes the kill makes the butch explicit, lest there be any confusion about the lady becoming or simulating a man, the lounge lizard's postmortem song makes lesbian explicit as the agent of "his" demise. That Smith wears the lady's dress underneath the man's suit throughout the production signals a transgression that gestures toward, if not supersedes, an alternative to the dynamics of heterogender's unremittingly polarized roles.

Such a reading, however, may be too facile, a sleight of hand. After all, if Smith's "lady" represents the femme fatale, that representation could be understood as swallowed up, covered over, by "the suit" when she dons the outfit, attitude, and stance of the dick figure, echoing precisely the configuration of desire in film noir. But there is no femme fatale in dyke noir, nor a lady dick for that matter. Because in a heterosexual representational economy the operating principle is the phallus, the first terms (femme/lady) of the equation femme/fatale = lady/dick are subsumed by their second terms. In a phallocratic representational economy *lady dick* can be understood as any such combination in, for example, the strong independent "career girl" films of Katherine Hepburn or Rosalind Russell, inhabited by "lady lawyers" and "lady reporters."

Contrary to what the line from the Mickey Paramus song might suggest, the green-eyed dick cannot simply be (re)named Clit. When Hughes privileges "lady dick" within a dyke noir, homoerotic circulation of desire, it is not played out by way of a figure who merely fills the shoes of a phallic second term; instead, the equation becomes lady/dick = femme/butch. Whereas in the first equation fatale = dick = phallus (the principle that recuperates the femme fatale's excess of sexuality), in the second equation dick ($\neq$ fatale $\neq$ phallus) = butch, which is not butch, per se, but always already the discourse of butch/femme, what Sue-Ellen Case has articulated as the subject position of a "dynamic duo."[23] If the film noir notion of plot is gone, if the femme fatale is gone, then what is left is the excess of sexuality, which in dyke noir is performed through a restructured and reassigned notion of *lady dick,* a neologism articulated in the discourse and dynamic of butch/femme desire and (homo)gender play. The sign butch/femme initially resides in the figure of Garnet McClit when she literally wears two gender-marked costumes simultaneously, while the dynamics of butch/femme discourse are played out, not in a single couple, not among fully formed characters, essences, or identities, but, instead, by actors who play variations on a number of homoerotic and (homo)gender themes, picking up and then discarding roles, stereotypes, attitudes, and stances as well as the style, conventions, and mise-en-scène of popular culture forms like film noir. The disjunctive nature of these performative and discursive strategies, when conjoined to address imagined alternative subjectivities, resonates with what Donna Haraway might call a "coalition of affinities,"[24] a configuration that gestures toward the notion of a collective subject position.[25]

While descriptions of moments from *Lady Dick* inadequately capture the resistant and (homo)erotic *movement* of the whole, perhaps the following excerpt from one much longer monologue will suffice to give a feeling for the erotic content with which *Lady Dick* is saturated.

> So I told my tale to the girl down at the pump. She's a fixit girl and mighty good with her hands in general, so I thought she could fix me up but good. She offered to fill me up for nothing. Then she said slide over sweetheart, you and me and this tin chariot are making a run for it. Once we get outta town I'm gonna buy you a red dress and take you out for a real chicken dinner. I must have passed out from the excitement. When I came to, we were already in St. Louis. They were outta chicken cuz the chickens were laying but not hatching. Seems like the hens had all flown the coop. The waiter tried to slip us a breaded veal cutlet when we weren't looking, but I can't look at beef when I've got a taste for girls. The fixit girl said she'd make it up to me, give me a tour of Missouri. Well, I was in quite a state. The "show me" state. But she drove me to the zoo. And I said: Hold on. You think I came all this way to see a pair of toothless tabbies in a box. You want wild pussy. I'll show you wild pussy. And I'll do better than that. This pussy's not in chains. It was her turn to pass out. When she came to, we were already in the motel. But she didn't know what to say. Then I'll say it. Just three little words. Do it, baby, do it.[26]

The sense of sexual agency articulated discursively here is manifest performatively as well in erotically charged dance numbers, songs, riffs of dialogue, and sensual stage kisses.

The excess of sexuality that comes under the scrutiny of a controlling male gaze and desire in film noir is recuperated in dyke noir and performed extravagantly. In the context of a lesbian production/ spectatorial space it circulates within a reconfigured representational economy, one that allows for what Jill Dolan has identified as a kind of "recognition of mutual subjectivity" among performers and spectators.[27]

Lady Dick is a far cry from the "not very homoerotic" *World without End* as well as from Hughes's subsequent solo piece, *Dead Meat*. Laurel Paley describes the ending of this work in her review of the performance for *Art Week:*

> Flesh finally becomes abhorrent in the last moments of *Dead Meat*. Healthy sexuality is repressed, lesbianism veiled, food made inedible, rage deepened. Waitresses, nurturers, lesbians, women are still filled with anger, are still powerless, are still bystanders. They are guns that cannot shoot.
>
> Hughes explains languidly and without emotion, in the performance's last metaphor and moment. "I'm a gun, but I'm not dangerous. My bullets can't kill—can't even kill me. I want to be a gun. I dream of someday becoming something beautiful and dangerous."[28]

This mapping of Lacanian lack and dispirited call for agency in some dreamed-of future is utterly antithetical to the discursive and performative potency of *The Lady Dick,* in which the gun-wielding dick is a butch cum femme whose shot is sure, where the only victim is heterosexuality and the only crime "beautiful and dangerous" lesbians.

Hughes's work has been a site of controversy for a number of lesbian critics ever since her dyke noir piece *Dress Suits to Hire*—on which she collaborated with Peggy Shaw and Lois Weaver—was created to be performed in venues other than WOW, that is, in contexts other than those that are primarily for women or lesbians.[29] Sue-Ellen Case argued that ultimately the "lesbian text" of *Dress Suits* resided in the performances of Shaw and Weaver, which, when the piece was performed outside the context of a lesbian spectatorial community, resulted in its assimilation and co-optation by dominant culture vis-à-vis the sociosexual configuration of the audiences and an attendant "horizon of expectations."[30]

Case locates what she contends is an absence of a "lesbian text" in *Dress Suits* as residing, in part, in the "Shepard-like-style," images, and tropes she reads into the production. In this move toward a Shepardesque interpretation she misreads the lesbian cultural tropes of the Midwest, which pervade the text in regionalisms engendered by a homoerotic culture with which she is apparently not familiar; in so doing, she participates unwittingly in a project of American literati—hungry for canon fodder—to validate Hughes as an emerging American playwright by virtue of the mechanisms of literary "influence."[31]

Hughes maintains that she would have written the same play even if the goal had been to present it at WOW. But because the collaborative process of writing/making *Dress Suits* was rife with intense conversations and debates over what would be *said*, as well as performed, for "mixed audiences,"[32] I have argued that *Dress Suits* is not only the result of a struggle to maintain a resistant and specifically lesbian stance, it performs that struggle.

Significantly, by the time the production went on tour to a number of different cities across the country, Hughes was already performing *World without End* in New York and word of its notorious bisexual stance—articulated in lines such as "Do you have any idea who you're porking? I am the preeminent lesbian playwright of my generation"[33]—had been widely reported. My point here is that *Dress Suits* was in large part read back through the moves Hughes makes in *World without End;*[34] *Dress Suits* as dyke noir was arguably different from its *Lady Dick* version, but it was nonetheless a productive, disruptive representational site.

The solo work Hughes began to perform following *Dress Suits* shifts the terms of dyke noir radically. Jill Dolan not only reads this shift through the dynamic of an altered performance context but also marks additional contributing factors.

The mix of heterosexual and lesbian spectators might be the condition that allows Hughes to bring her bisexuality out of the closet in *World*. . . . Her usual maniacal, unpredictable stage presence is exchanged for the high-heeled, prettily dressed, lugubrious politeness of the family drama. Her adamant flaunting of her "polymorphous perversity" constructs her as sexually autono-

mous, but in the process, unmoors her from the lesbian community that fostered her early work. Hughes has been domesticated
by her own bisexual, bourgeois narrative. (1990: 40 n.4)

The renegade lesbian stance of *The Well of Horniness, The Lady Dick,*
and *Dress Suits to Hire* is indeed tamed, domesticated and, ultimately,
recuperated in works Hughes would call *queer* even when those
works do not "perform" in manifestly homoerotic or homogendered
ways. While the issues raised by Hughes's current work are numerous and complex, this notion of "queer"—itself an enormously complex concept—is worth examining briefly for insight into what I perceive as a kind of general impasse in the project of creating lesbian
representation,[35] or "its condition of possibility," as de Lauretis puts
it (1988, 159).

Since her work first garnered attention in the form of reviews
and interviews, Holly Hughes has maintained, in her public discourse
with the press, that she prefers the word *queer* over *gay* to describe
herself. The following example, quoted from Harriet Swift's article
in the *Oakland Tribune,* echoes dozens of others over several years:

> "I don't like the term 'gay playwright,'" she says. "I really prefer
> 'queer.' Gay is a word invented to make straight people like us,"
> she plows on. "I am anti-assimilation. I say go out there and be
> as weird as you are."[36]

For Hughes queer signifies the we-are-*not*-just-like-everybody-else
stance that resists assimilation into a hetero-socio-sexual world order.
At the same time queer is a particular style of "weirdness," a kind of
"trashy," kitschy way of constructing and performing the self; it's the
camp sensibility of the outsider, exaggerating and ironizing the seemingly commonsense notions of hegemonic cultures.

Hughes locates the queer theatrical tradition in the gay male drag
performances of Charles Ludlam, Jack Smith, and Ethyl Eichelberger
and, of them, states, "The permission to invent yourself as a new
person beyond male and female is something that I really got from
gay theatre of that era."[37] Camp, of course, is the most salient feature
of these performances and one that has received growing attention
as a subversive strategy that wittily exploits the ironies of artifice.
But, as I have argued elsewhere, camp does not function in the same

ways in lesbian representation—it *could,* but not as the sociosymbolic apparatus of representation is currently constructed.[38] In Phelan's formulation, cited at the beginning of this essay, of the relative visibility of gay men in comparison with lesbians, the difference could be understood as owing, in part, to the inability of camp to garner visibility for lesbians in the ways it has for gay men. To think or feel intensely about gay men for supposedly "feminizing all men," as Phelan suggests is the case, is to be able to imagine the site of that alleged feminization. The making visible of homoerotic desire signals homosexual practice, the subversive site of all that phallocratic culture attempts to suppress, contain, and eradicate. If lesbians, too, are targets of homophobia, and they are, why aren't they visible in Phelan's formulation? Because, like woman, they continue to be constructed, not on their own terms but in terms of what they are not—summarized most succinctly perhaps in a line delivered to one of the lesbians in the Donna Deitch film *Desert Hearts* by a ranch hand as he watches a woman leave her cottage one morning. He says, "How you get all that traffic with no equipment is beyond me." As Marilyn Frye has written, "There is nothing women could do in the absence of men that could, without semantic oddity, be called 'having sex.'"[39]

I contend that Hughes's earlier work performed lesbian homoeroticism(s) in ways that signaled a plethora of lesbian sexual practices. Many would argue that her *World without End* opens up the range of possible sexualities in its move to bisexuality. But bisexuality is all about heterosexuality in *World.* The question posed in the text is not "Do you have any idea who is fucking you? I am the preeminent lesbian playwright of my generation." Instead, it asks, "Do you have any idea who you are porking?" Lesbian sexual practices are subsumed in relationship to the active male sexual agent implicit and naturalized in the question's heterosexually inflected syntax. Not only is "porking" configured as a practice that always involves a man, but the "lesbian" is not the one doing the fucking; she is always already the one getting porked.

Moreover, speaking of the same constellation of gay male theater practitioners Hughes cites above, C. Carr points out that "'Queerness' was never really about sexual preference. Certainly not all gays are 'queer'" (32). Queerness becomes an ever-expanding site for the notion of outsiderness. As Hughes states: "A lot of people have experienced being an outsider. Everybody feels queer in some sense of the word" (176). In her later work Hughes seems to have maintained, ironically, a queer stance, if not a lesbian one.

This is not to suggest that a notion of queer is not a productive site for significant work resonant with "coalitions of affinities." But it is to suggest, paradoxically, that in the trajectory of current performance, as exemplified by the work of Holly Hughes, queer is not always lesbian, or even homosexual, while for Hughes lesbian was once always queer.[40] Queer's inclusive, universalizing move vis-à-vis fellow-traveling outsiders tends to, once again, ensure that lesbian sexuality will remain *locked out of the visible*. As Jameson puts it, "Every universalizing approach, whether the phenomenological or the semiotic, will from the dialectical point of view be found to conceal its own contradictions and repress its own historicity by strategically framing its perspective so as to omit the negative, absence, contradiction, repression, the *non-dit,* or the *impense"* (109–10).

At the time of this writing a play by Sharon Jane Smith—the original lady dick—entitled *Of Men and Steamboat Men* is being performed at WOW; it is a production not atypical of the kind of work currently being produced there. In it Smith reminisces about her experiences working the *Delta Queen* steamboat on the Mississippi River. She is surrounded by a cast of lesbians who represent the *Delta Queen* crew. Some play male characters; others play women. If homosexuality exists, it is not a structuring strategy, and heterosexuality is wholly uninterrogated. The production's central feature is Smith's description of slipping into the captain's quarters to perform sympathy blow-jobs on the near-retirement and romanticized, if not eroticized, man. What is being performed in *Of Men and Steamboat Men?* What is the impotent gun being performed at the end of Hughes's *Dead Meat?*

In 1989, following what one critic called Holly Hughes's "first brush with commercial success" and my observations regarding the pending move at WOW to perform "straight" male drag, I posed the question, "What would it mean for the project of feminism if the next wave of lesbian performance were to enter the mainstream in drag?"[41] Lesbian performance remains light-years away from entering the mainstream, but it had not occurred to me in 1989 that the drag being performed at WOW, and by artists like Holly Hughes, would be "woman."

NOTES

1. The debate did not begin with homoerotic art, but, rather, the controversy surrounding Andres Serrano's piece *Piss Christ* created the context for the cancellation of an exhibition of Robert Mapplethorpe's photographs, some of which were not only homoerotic but employed the paraphernalia and imagery of sadomasochism. It was, however, the reason for the Corcoran Gallery's cancellation of the Mapplethorpe exhibit—i.e., homoerotic content—that proved incendiary and propelled the debate to the national level. For an early account of the events and their implications, see Peggy Phelan's excellent commentary, "Serrano, Mapplethorpe, the NEA and You: 'Money Talks'," *TDR* 34, no. 1 (Spring 1990): 4–15. *Art in America* published articles related to the growing controversy nearly continuously. See especially Carole Vance's pieces: "The War on Culture," September 1989, 39–45; "Misunderstanding Obscenity," May 1990, 49–55; and "Reagan's Revenge: Restructuring the NEA," November 1990, 49–55. With regard to the NEA's action involving Hughes, Karen Finley, Tim Miller, and John Fleck, see Doug Sadownick's interview "The NEA's Latest Bout of Homophobia: Four Rejected Artists Talk Queer," *Advocate*, 14 August 1990, 50–53; and Laura Shapiro's article on Finley (the only heterosexual among the four), "A One-Woman Tour of Hell," *Newsweek*, 6 August 1990, 60–61.

2. The definition of *lesbian,* as this essay will suggest, is not transparent. The following questions, posed by Judith Butler in *Gender Trouble: Feminism and the Subversion of Identity* (New York: Routledge, 1990), 127–28, indicate some of the term's contested ground as a practice underpinning an "identity." (An ever-expanding list of questions can be posed regarding lesbian as constitutive of certain positionalities and discourses.) "If to become a lesbian is an *act,* a leave-taking of heterosexuality, a self-naming that contests the compulsory meanings of heterosexuality's *women* and *men,* what is to keep the name lesbian from becoming an equally compulsory category. What qualifies as lesbian? . . . if it is an "act" that founds the identity as a performative accomplishment of sexuality, are there certain kinds of acts that qualify over others as foundational?"

Teresa de Lauretis has suggested in "Sexual Indifference and Lesbian Representation," *Theatre Journal* 40, no. 2 (1988): 170–71, that "the difficulty in defining an autonomous form of female sexuality and desire . . . is perhaps even greater than the difficulty in devising strategies of representation which will . . . alter the standard of vision, the frame of reference of visibility, of *what can be seen.*" This essay concerns itself with both projects.

3. Hughes wrote "You Have a Gal in Kalamazoo," for the fifteen-page inaugural issue of *Performance Journal* (published by Movement Research, Inc.) in 1990, 10. The article included the following editor's note: "Since this article was written, Holly Hughes's NEA fellowship for solo theatre artists, which had been recommended by a peer panel, was overturned by the chairman of the NEA."

4. Luce Irigaray, "When the Goods Get Together," in *New French Feminisms: An Anthology,* ed. Elaine Marks and Isabelle de Courtivron (New York: Schocken Books, 1981), 110.

5. Teresa de Lauretis, *Alice Doesn't: Feminism, Semiotics, Cinema* (Blooming-ton: Indiana University Press, 1984), 9.

6. See my article "Constructing the Spectator: Reception, Context, and Ad-dress in Lesbian Performance," *Performing Arts Journal* 10, no. 2 (1986): 43–52, in which I discuss the lesbian couple in Jane Wagner's and Lily Tomlin's *Search for Signs of Intelligent Life in the Universe* as representative of this "lesbians-as-just-like-everyone-else" phenomenon. I also discuss Hughes's *Lady Dick* in the same article but in quite different terms. See also Jill Dolan, "'Lesbian' Subjectivity in Realism: Dragging at the Margins of Structure and Ideology," in *Performing Feminisms: Feminist Critical Theory and Theatre,* ed. Sue-Ellen Case (Baltimore: Johns Hopkins University Press, 1990), 40–53.

7. At the same time there are *no* women in *Lady Dick* if, as Monique Wittig suggests, in "One Is Not Born a Woman," *Feminist Issues* 1, no. 2 (1981): 47–54, lesbian is located outside the heterosexual gender binary man/woman; for Wittig woman can be located only in socioeconomic, political, and ideological relation to (the term) man.

8. See my essay "Fe/male Impersonation: The Discourse of Camp," in *Criti-cal Theory and Performance,* ed. Janelle Reinelt and Joseph Roach (Ann Arbor: University of Michigan Press, 1992) in which I not only lay out the basic charac-teristics of WOW performances but also discuss the recent shift in the nature of those performances in relation to the performative strategies of camp.

9. Lynda Hart, "Canonizing Lesbians?" in *Modern American Drama: The Fe-male Canon,* ed. June Schlueter (Cranbury, N.J.: Associated University Presses, 1990), 289.

10. See the East Village Performance issue of *Drama Review* 29, no. 1 (1985), which covers the club scene extensively and in which Alisa Solomon's article on "The Wow Cafe" appears (92–101), as well as other pieces on the work of WOW artists and part 1 of *The Well of Horniness* (102–7). All three parts of *The Well* were performed at the WOW Cafe on 3 March 1983.

11. Holly Hughes, *The Well of Horniness,* in *Out Front: Contemporary Gay and Lesbian Plays,* ed. Don Shewey (New York: Grove Press, 1988), 221–51. Hughes's text opens up production possibilities for aggressive resistance both in terms of foregrounding gender as a representational apparatus and in terms of staging alternative sexualities. In her introduction to the play in this volume Hughes gives the following directive with regard to gender in the original pro-duction's casting: "All of the performers were, and still are as far as I know, women. I'm pretty tough about this part. No men in *The Well,* okay? I don't care if you're doing a staged reading in Crib Death, Iowa—no men" (222).

12. A pun on *tribadism,* which by dictionary definition means homosexuality between women, lesbianism. It is also a term, however, for the only kind of sex two women were thought to be able to have—i.e., rubbing genitals together.

13. Hart is right in naming Georgette the play's lesbian-on-the-prowl, but it is Vicki who seduces Georgette under a restaurant table.

14. This, of course, once again begs the question of what constitutes "les-bian." Rather than engage the debate over fraught categories of identity, I want instead to invoke, by analogy, Tania Modleski's warning in her brilliant and

brave book *Feminism Without Women* (New York: Routledge, 1991). She argues that the urgency to get beyond gender and "woman" has tended to prematurely move us beyond women. So, too, the urgency to get beyond the gendered identifies of lesbian and gay to crucial issues of (homo)*sexuality* has moved us prematurely beyond lesbian.

15. C. Carr, "The Lady Is a Dick: The Dyke Noir Theater of Holly Hughes," *Village Voice*, 19 May 1987, 34.

16. This line is taken from the production script of Holly Hughes's play *The Lady Dick*. Although a version of the play was published in *TDR* 35, no. 3 (1991): 198–215, all subsequent references to *The Lady Dick* that appear in this essay are taken from the production script, which coincides with both the original production I saw at the WOW Cafe in 1985 and with the videotaped documentation of that production. Because the published version differs from the original in ways that are important to my argument, these differences are marked throughout the essay.

17. *Women in Film Noir*, ed. E. Ann Kaplan (London: British Film Institute, 1978). Essays referred to here include: Christine Gledhill, "Klute 1: A Contemporary Film Noir and Feminist Criticism," 6–21; Sylvia Harvey, "Woman's Place: The Absent Family of Film Noir," 22–34; Janey Place, "Women in Film Noir," 35–67; and Richard Dyer, "Resistance through Charisma: Rita Hayworth and *Gilda*," 91–99.

18. In her essay in this volume, "Toward a Lesbian Theory of Performance: Refunctioning Gender," Hilary Harris interrogates recent critical moves in what Eve Kosofsky Sedgwick calls "antihomophobic theory" to separate gender analysis from theories of sexuality. Engaging recent feminist/lesbian theory Harris makes a compelling argument for a refunctioned notion of gender as crucial to the project of theorizing lesbian sexuality. See Gayle Rubin, "Thinking Sex: Notes for a Radical Theory of the Politics of Sexuality," in *Pleasure and Danger: Exploring Female Sexuality*, ed. Carole S. Vance (Boston: Routledge and Kegan Paul, 1984), 267–319; Teresa de Lauretis, *Technologies of Gender: Essays on Theory, Film, and Fiction* (Bloomington: Indiana University Press, 1987), 1–30; and Judith Butler, *Gender Trouble: Feminism and the Subversion of Identity* (New York: Routledge, 1990).

19. Fredric Jameson, *The Political Unconscious: Narrative as a Socially Symbolic Act* (Ithaca, N.Y.: Cornell University Press, 1981), 106. What Jameson says about genre might also be said about gender, especially when taken in light of the sentence following the one quoted here: "The speech acts of daily life are themselves marked with indications and signals (intonation, gesturality, contextual deictics and pragmatics) which ensure their appropriate reception."

20. See Monique Wittig, "On the Sexual Contract," in *Homosexuality, Which Homosexuality?: International Conference on Gay and Lesbian Studies*, ed. Dennis Altman, Carole Vance, Martha Vicinus, and Jeffrey Weeks (London: GMP Publishers, 1989), 239–49. Teresa de Lauretis states, in *Technologies of Gender: Essays on Theory, Film, and Fiction* (Bloomington: Indiana University Press, 1987), 17, that "the heterosexual contract . . . is the very site in which the social relations of gender and thus gender ideology are reproduced in everyday life."

21. In the *TDR* version of the play (see n. 16) every incarnation of Peggy Shaw's performance is marked as "Mickey," lending a kind of structural coherence to the work that was utterly absent from the original. There was no hint of the Mickey Paramus character in any subsequent moment of Shaw's performance, which was the performative point—that is, "he" was "deep-sixed," as the lady dick puts it, early on.

22. A stage direction in the printed version of the play (see n. 16) states *"Garnet strips out of her prom dress . . ."* (201). A crucial feature of the production, for me, was a continuing consciousness—an awareness throughout the performance—of the femme-turned-dick's dress underneath the classic male detective garb. The published version also does not mention that she puts on a suit. Moreover, "prom dress" suggests a teenager on her way to a dance. The dress in the original production signaled an adult woman on her way, if anywhere, to a cocktail party.

23. Sue-Ellen Case, "Toward a Butch-Femme Aesthetic," in *Making a Spectacle: Feminist Essays on Contemporary Women's Theatre,* ed. Lynda Hart (Ann Arbor: University of Michigan Press, 1989): 282–99. The promise of Garnet McClit's status as prime mover of the evening's events is quickly diminished when, following her introduction, she takes a seat at the bar and basically participates—on a par with the other performers—in the emerging discourse of (excess/homo) sexuality through butch/femme (homo)gender play.

24. Donna Haraway, "A Manifesto for Cyborgs: Science, Technology, and Socialist Feminism in the 1980s," in *Feminism/Postmodernism,* ed. Linda J. Nicholson (New York: Routledge, 1990), 190–223. There is a way in which, I think, *lesbian* can be substituted productively for *cyborg* throughout this essay—not lesbian in the sense of an essence or identity, of course, but as always already located outside the realm of the natural—i.e., a crime against nature.

25. See Sue-Ellen Case's essay, "From Split Subject to Split Britches," in *Feminine Focus: The New Women Playwrights,* ed. Enoch Brater (New York: Oxford University Press, 1989), 126–46, in which she identifies and traces the emergence of three types of subject positions—split, metonymically displaced, and collective—in plays written by women over the last two decades. See also Jill Dolan's Brechtian reading of *Lady Dick* in her book *The Feminist Spectator as Critic* (1988; reprint, Ann Arbor: University of Michigan Press, 1991), 107, 117.

26. In the published version (see n. 16) the lines read: "You think I came all this way to see a show of wild pussy. And I'll do better than that" (206). The original is as follows: "You think I came all this way to see a pair of toothless tabbies in a box. You want wild pussy. I'll show you wild pussy. And I'll do better than that." In terms of erotic force it's quite a difference. Also, not all of the songs from the original production appear in the published text. There is no reference, for example, to a wickedly funny parody of the song "You Make Me Feel Like a Natural Woman," performed by the same actress who delivered the monologue cited above while wielding a butcher's cleaver over her head.

27. Jill Dolan, "Desire Cloaked in a Trenchcoat," *TDR* 33, no. 1 (1989): 64. See also Dolan's essay, "The Dynamics of Desire: Sexuality and Gender in Pornography and Performance," *Theatre Journal* 39, no. 2 (1987): 156–74.

28. Laurel Paley, "Looking Busy at the Red Onion: *Dead Meat*, Holly Hughes at Highways," *Art Week* 21, no. 1 (August 1990): 10.

29. See my piece "Reading Past the Heterosexual Imperative: *Dress Suits to Hire*," *TDR* 33, no. 1 (1989): 153–70; as well as Rebecca Schneider's interview, "Holly Hughes: Polymorphous Perversity and the Lesbian Scientist," published in the same issue (171–83), along with the text of Hughes's play *Dress Suits to Hire* (132–52).

30. Case's argument, articulated in an insightful but contentious letter to the editor of *TDR* 33, no. 4 (1989): 10–14, is a response to statements made by Hughes in the interview with Schneider cited above. Hughes's stinging response to Case also appears in this issue (14–17).

31. A "Shepardian" reading is a hegemonic one; the *New York Times* review of *Dress Suits* included four references to Sam Shepard to validate Hughes's play and, presumably, to explain why the *Times* would pay attention to it. Hughes brought the production to Milwaukee, Wisconsin, where its reception was as controlled as it could possibly be. There was no publicity for the performances outside of a single lesbian advertising venue. The local producer told me that she wasn't sure her audience would show up because her clientele did not ordinarily attend theater of any kind; they "come out" for women's music and stand-up comedy concerts. All the performances sold out to an audience that in all probability did not read the production through the imagery and dramatic tropes of Sam Shepard. Interestingly, a certain subcultural spectatorial presentation-of-self resonated with the midwestern imagery in *Dress Suits*, imagery that Case reads as belonging to Sam Shepard. See Stephen Holden, "Theatre: 'Dress Suits,'" *New York Times*, 3 February 1988.

32. I was in touch with Hughes, Shaw, and Weaver at various points during their collaborative rehearsal process. All expressed the enormous and ongoing difficulty of creating an explicitly homoerotic piece to be performed in front of mixed (both in gender and sexuality) audiences.

33. *World without End* appears in the collection *Out from Under: Texts by Women Performance Artists*, ed. Lenora Champagne (New York: Theatre Communications Group, 1990), 9–32. In this version the line reads: "Do you have any idea at all who you are porking? I'm the preeminent lesbian performance artist from southern Michigan" (31). I quote the line as it appears in a *TDR* interview with Hughes (see n. 29), which is how it was delivered in Hughes's original productions of the play.

34. In a similar vein it could be argued that Hughes reads her own *Lady Dick* back through the moves she makes in her later pieces in that the version of the play published in 1991 is different in some striking ways from its original production.

35. At this point is should be evident that I am not referring to *all* lesbian representation but specifically to lesbian representation in the form of dramatic literature, theater, and performance art that is primarily Anglo-American and located geographically in New York City.

36. Holly Hughes, as quoted by Harriet Swift, "To Playwright Hughes, Life

Is Meant to Glitter and Be Gay," *Tribune Calendar* (Oakland, Calif.), 2 October 1988, 5.

37. Holly Hughes, as quoted by Dennis Harvey, "Interview with a Pussy Pusher: 'Queer' Playwright Holly Hughes Redefines the Ambitions of Gay Theatre," *San Francisco Sentinel,* 7 October 1988, 22–24.

38. The analysis of camp as a productive strategy that I began in an earlier essay (see n. 8) is fleshed out in a subsequent paper of mine delivered on the "Performing Lesbian Theories" panel of the American Theatre in Higher Education (ATHE) Conference in Seattle, 8 August 1991. Following the lead of Andrew Ross in his book *No Respect: Intellectuals and Popular Culture* (New York: Routledge, 1989), in which he maintains that camp as a politics eschews the search for some dreamed-of utopian alternative and instead refuses to break completely with existing definitions and representations in a commitment to working with and through them (162), I suggest that the ways in which the materials of existing cultural representations can be deployed in the service of a social subject constituted in discourse *as* culture (i.e., male) are diametrically different from the ways they work in the service of a subject position discursively constituted *as* nature (i.e., female). Can women, as embodied on the stage, engender parody, or, as a function of gender, are they always already constituted as the material, or fodder, of parody? Many camp aficionados claim that there is no such thing as "lesbian camp"—this may be why.

39. Marilyn Frye, *The Politics of Reality: Essays in Feminist Theory* (Freedom, Calif.: Crossing Press, 1983), 157.

40. In an article on a group performance art show at the Brooklyn Museum entitled "Too Shocking to Show," Karin Lipson writes about the response of a spectator to a piece performed by Holly Hughes:

> Harriet Haritos of Brooklyn, who said she and her husband have conservative taste in the arts, was nevertheless taken by the gentleness of Hughes' performance. "She's sneaky, in that her demeanor is not at all off-putting," Haritos said. "I was thinking, 'There's a lesbian Garrison Keillor.'"

"'Too Shocking to Show' Shows Up in Brooklyn," *Los Angeles Times,* 24 June 1992, F10.

41. Swift, "To Playwright Hughes," 5; Davy, "Reading Past," 167.

Chapter 3

Cherríe Moraga's "Shadow of a Man": Touching the Wound in Order to Heal

Yvonne Yarbro-Bejarano

From 6 November to 9 December of 1990 Chicana writer Cherríe Moraga's second play, *Shadow of a Man,* enjoyed a five-week run at San Francisco's Eureka Theater (coproduced by Brava! for Women in the Arts).[1] The Eureka/Brava production broke ground for several reasons. As Sheila Wright pointed out in her review, it is unusual to see theater "generated almost solely by women."[2] Not only was it sponsored by an organization that promotes the work of women of color, headed by Ellen Gavin, but, as Gavin remarked, it also brought together two Latinas, playwright Moraga and director Irene Fornes, from different generations.[3]

Moraga dedicates *Shadow* to "las chicanas, that we may come downstage center and speak for ourselves."[4] "Speaking for ourselves" no longer means defining a unified "Chicano" identity in opposition to dominant groups. With its focus on controversial issues of sexuality and desire within a Chicano family Moraga continues the shift currently evident in the cultural production of people of color away from unifying notions of identity and experience. As Stuart Hall points out, in the new discourses on race and ethnicity "the point of contestation is . . . *inside* the concept of ethnicity itself."[5] Hall proclaims the "end of the innocent notion" of the essential black (or Chicano) subject, in the understanding that "black" (or "Chicano") is a politically and culturally constructed category, "which cannot be grounded in a set of fixed transcultural or transcendental racial categories and which therefore has no guarantees in Nature."

What Hall calls the new politics of representation creates a space for "the recognition of the extraordinary diversity of subject positions, social experiences and cultural identities which compose the category 'black.'" In a Chicano context, since the 1980s certain conceptions of masculinity and femininity have been put into question in an attempt to relate issues of race and ethnicity to gender and sexuality. With their emphasis on multiplicity and their refusal to choose between race and gender, sexual practice and culture, the contributors to *This Bridge Called My Back* and Chicana writers such as Moraga and Gloria Anzaldúa helped undermine the unifying concept of identity promulgated by the cultural nationalism of 1960s movements.[6] Moraga's writing has been in the forefront of the attempts of people of color and others to represent the manifold interrelations among multiple sites of oppression.

This interrogation of the concept of ethnicity *inside* the concept of ethnicity itself was palpable in Moraga's presentation at the recent "OutWrite '91: National Lesbian and Gay Writers Conference" in San Francisco. As in *Shadow,* rather than "explaining" Chicano reality to a white audience, she concentrated her remarks on the obstacles preventing unity among Chicana lesbians and Chicano gay men. Moraga called for a return to some of the valuable tenets of the Chicano movement, such as the connection with the indigenous movement and the validation of the Indian component of Chicano identity, but "with a difference" (for example, the inclusion of the leadership of women and an analysis of homophobia and heterosexism). In line with the current critique of exclusionary and homogenizing ideologies of "nation," Moraga jokingly envisioned the new movement to be a cross between cultural nationalism and Queer Nation.[7] In order for a positive reimagining of nation as a space of nonhierarchical diversity to emerge, it is necessary to conceptualize new social structures. Because *"familia"* has often been the site of the silencing of gays and lesbians and the abuse of women and children, an expanded notion of extended family must be conceived in which Chicana/o lesbians and gays could play a special role as "two-spirited" people.[8]

But before this kind of community building can happen, Moraga went on to say, Chicano gay men have to deal with their misogyny and male privilege, exploring their love for brown men as seriously as Chicana lesbians have explored their love for brown women. This means that the analysis of machismo is not by any means exclusively the task of Chicana lesbians. As Leo Bersani asserts, "sexual desire for men can't be merely a culturally neutral attraction to a Platonic Idea of the male body; the object of that desire necessarily includes a socially determined and socially pervasive definition of what it means to be a man."[9] For Moraga the kind of "familia" that embraces both men and women without privileging one over the other depends on the end of the social construct of "man."

It is the destructive privileging of "man" in the bosom of the unreconstructed family that her play *Shadow of a Man* explores, for part of the process of building nontoxic "familia" entails a compassionate yet unflinching analysis of this traditionally structured heterosexual Chicano family. As the epigraph of *Shadow* states:

> Family is the place
> where, for better or worse,
> we first learn to love.[10]

Using this epigraph as an interpretive guidepost leads us to consider with particular attention the fate of the daughters, those in the process of "learning how to love."[11]

The unrelenting focus on the lives of the members of a working-class Chicano family decentered (and disconcerted) non-Latino spectators. On the other hand, the play was difficult for some Latino spectators because of its treatment of gender roles and sexuality.

The bilingual voice of the play was a source of discomfort for non-Latino spectators. Some white male critics, bound by their race, gender, and class positions, spoke of the bilingual dialogue of the play as a "drawback"[12] or of the play's "frequent excursions into Spanish."[13] This perspective is shared by the interviewer in the *Open Window* video, who referred to the "novelty" of the script's mixing of Spanish and English. This novelty has a twenty-five-year history in Chicano theater. In the program of the Eureka/Brava production Moraga writes: "The blending of Spanish and English found in this work is very common among first-generation Chicanos/Latinos and those living in he barrios of the U.S. This is the 'natural voice' of the play and its characters."[14] Trinh T. Minh-ha comments that "woman as subject can only redefine while being defined by language."[15] Chi-

cana/o writers such as Moraga and Anzaldúa claim Chicano language
as a legitimate medium for discursive self-production as mestizas,
constituted by racial, cultural, *and* linguistic hybridity.

Yet *Shadow* is equally challenging to Latino audiences. While
Moraga aligns herself with the Chicano theater tradition in terms of
bilinguality, she is critical of its silences: "Latino and Chicano theaters
have been notoriously sexist and homophobic and have not shown a
great interest in doing women's work."[16] Moraga respects the political origins of Chicano theater and recognizes the need for outrage
and protest; her third play, *Heroes and Saints,* deals with the pesticide
poisoning of farmworkers while politicizing questions of subjectivity
and sexuality. *Shadow* critiques the intimate dynamics of gender production within the family from a perspective of solidarity:

> Traditionally, Chicano theater has not dealt with the condition
> of our families. . . . It tends to romanticize "la familia." I feel we
> need to kind of touch the wounds a little bit, look at the sore
> spots in us.[17]

Theater provides a forum for this kind of intracultural debate, while
also helping to bridge the gap between the educated playwright and
certain segments of her community. Her goal is to speak a language
that all classes understand but which at the same time captures both
the poetry and the complexity of working-class Chicano lives.

Set in the late 1960s in Los Angeles, the play tells the story of the
members of the Rodríguez family: the father, Manuel, in his early
fifties; the mother, Hortensia, mid-forties; Hortensia's sister Rosario,
mid-fifties; and the two daughters, twelve-year-old Lupe and Leticia,
seventeen. Moraga's previous writing focuses on Chicanas' negotiations of their culture's privileging of males; *Shadow* also explores the
harmful impact of machismo on Chicano men. The playwright states
that *Shadow* was born out of a

> fascination with how Latino men value each other so much.
> There's a certain way in which, in the face of that, women
> are . . . like functionaries, objects in the dealings of men's rela-
> tionships with themselves.[18]

The title's "shadow of a man" functions on multiple levels of the text in relationship to both male and female characters.

In Manuel's case it refers to the construction of masculinity that orders his self-perception. From the beginning of the play Manuel appears to be eaten away by some private misery. He is merely a shadow of a man, plagued by heart trouble and excessive drinking, which cause absenteeism at work; alternately abusive to and dependent on his family; and emotionally and sexually shut down to his wife. Gradually, it is revealed that Manuel is heavily invested in his relationship with his *compadre* Conrado.[19] When the latter's departure from Los Angeles was imminent some thirteen years ago Manuel gave up his place in Hortensia's bed for one night to Conrado. While this may seem like a classic example of male traffic in women in which two male subjects bond through the body of a woman, it backfires for Manuel when he is consumed by jealousy of Hortensia, who has come closer to Conrado than he ever can. He becomes obsessed by his sense of failure to live up to the masculine ideal that Conrado embodies for him. He wants to be Conrado at the same time that he desires him; both are impossible scenarios. In this sense he lives in Conrado's "shadow" and is eventually destroyed by a construct of masculinity that holds out the promise of wholeness in the love of men yet has not yielded that wholeness.[20] It is the twist that Moraga gives to the traditional erotic triangle in her focus on Manuel's love for Conrado that prompts Fornes to say: "all family plays, of course, are different, yet this play, to me, makes all other family plays seem the same."[21]

In spite of Manuel's strategy to convince him to stay Conrado did leave Los Angeles, and both Manuel and Hortensia have had to live with the repercussions of that night ever since. For Manuel it is both proof of his lack of manhood and emblem of his loss of Conrado; for Hortensia it is a constant source of shame and guilt. For both Lupe serves as a constant reminder, since she takes after Conrado, her biological father. Manuel has developed a special attachment to Lupita, not so much for any qualities of her own but because she is all of Conrado he has left.

The family has lived with this secret for thirteen years, yet the catalyst that brings the situation to a head is the son Rigo's decision to marry a gringa. The fact that he never appears on stage communicates his abandonment of home, class, and culture. The play's action opens a few days before Rigo's wedding and traces its aftermath through the following months.

The first time the audience sees Manuel he comes home drunk and mourns the loss of his son in a monologue. Manuel grieves for Rigo's rejection of Mexican-marked displays of affection between men in his process of assimilation (1.4). In the previous scene Hortensia described for Rosario how Rigo had pushed Manuel away when he tried to give him a welcome home embrace, preferring to shake hands.[22]

But Manuel also grieves for another kind of loss—that is, his need to see himself reflected in a brown man's eyes:

> You usetu sit and converse with me. Your eyes were so black, I forgot myself in there sometimes. I watched the little fold of indio skin above your eyes, and felt those eyes hold me to the ground. They saw. I know they saw that I am a weak man, but they did not judge me. Why do you judge me now, hijo? How does the eye turn like that so suddenly? (1.4)

This passage is useful in drawing the connection between Rigo's wedding, which stands for his rejection of the family, and the final festering of the wound inflicted by Conrado's departure. Manuel's comment about Rigo's gaze anchoring him to the ground, to his identity as a man, echoes in a later monologue remembering Conrado:

> I look across the table and my compadre's there y me siento bien. All I gotta do is sit in my own skin in the chair. . . . But he was leaving. I could smell it coming. I tried to make him stay. How did I let myself disappear like that? I became nothing, a ghost. . . . I floated into the room with him. In my mind, I was him. . . . And then, I was her, too. In my mind, I imagined their pleasure . . . and I turned to nothing. (2.2)

Only when he could see himself reflected in the mirror that is Conrado could Manuel feel content to be "in his own skin." The phrase "And then, I was her, too" is the closest Manuel can come to admitting not only his desire to be his friend but also his homoerotic desire for Conrado. Given the construction of masculinity under which he labors, this desire can only spell the dissolution of Manuel's identity as a man, just as the absence of a male figure onto which he can project his fantasies of the masculine ideal forces him to confront his own failure to live up to that ideal (". . . I am a weak man").

Other scenes allow glimpses of Manuel's subjectivity—for example, when he fantasizes Conrado's fulfillment of the "American success story" building swimming pools in Phoenix (1.5; 2.1) or summons adolescent memories of male homosocial pleasure untainted by adult desire or failure: "Sometimes you know you want to be a boy like that again. The rain was better then, it cleaned something" (1.5).

After the wedding Manuel deteriorates rapidly, talking of nothing but Conrado and withdrawing further from Hortensia, his heart closed as a fist (1.9). In a desperate attempt to recover the past Manuel writes to Conrado, inviting him to come back. For Hortensia this action is the equivalent of opening old wounds, an activity she refuses to participate in. But for Manuel Conrado's return clearly spells the opportunity to relive the past relationship, free of Hortensia's mediating role. Just as he blamed his son's desertion on Rigo's future wife, he now places the burden of his loss of Conrado squarely on Hortensia's shoulders. The night Manuel goes out to meet his *compadre* he dresses like Conrado in dark suit and hat (except that the crease refuses to stay in his pants). Just before he exits "he dips his hat slightly over one eye and runs his fingers over the rim of it. He imagines himself in Conrado's image, muy suave" (2.4).

But later that evening, when Conrado returns to their home before Manuel, Manuel arrives in time to witness the old attraction between him and Hortensia. His self-imposed isolation intensifies as he relives the consequences of that night thirteen years ago:

> She walked around the house like she was something special, like she got a piece of you. [He grabs Conrado by the balls, then slumps into the chair.] You know how that feels? To have your own wife holding something inside her that's not yours. She made me feel like I was nothing. [Turning to him.] I loved you, man. I gave you my woman. . . . What does that make me? (2.5)

By objectifying Conrado in the image of the masculine ideal (clearly it is Manuel who wanted a piece of him), Manuel has written himself

out of his own script ("How did I let myself disappear like that?").
Hortensia refuses to carry the blame for what happened, reminding
Manuel that it was what he wanted. After she sends Conrado away
and makes one last futile attempt to reach out to Manuel he orches-
trates his death with a combination of pills and tequila. His final
words are: "She took everything from me" (2.5).

This is a play about heterosexuality (pace Lupe's budding lesbian
sexuality), although the take on it is clearly not a traditional one. A
Chicana lesbian playwright is asking the Latino community to think
about sexuality and desire beyond rigid heterosexual roles. *Giving
Up the Ghost* already undertakes the project of understanding lesbian
desire by looking at heterosexuality—specifically, how the imposition of binary oppositions ("man"/"woman," "taker"/"taken," etc.)
damages and forms lesbian sexuality. At issue in *Shadow* is not
whether Manuel is gay or not; instead, the audience is invited to
consider sexuality along a continuum, to explore the intersections
between homosociality and homosexuality. Cultures that teach men
that they are more valuable than women and that they should reserve
their deepest love for men create the conditions in which they prefer
each other to women. Yet these same cultures that promote male
homosocial relations through the exchange of women prohibit geni-
tal sex. Luce Irigaray answers her own question: "why is masculine
homosexuality considered exceptional . . . when in fact the whole
economy as a whole is based upon it?":

> *Because they* [masculine homosexual relations] *openly interpret the
> law according to which society operates. . . .* Furthermore, they might
> lower the sublime value of the standard, the yardstick. Once the
> penis itself becomes merely a means to pleasure, pleasure among
> men, *the phallus loses its power.*[23]

The cultural dynamic that destroys Manuel has different consequences for women. The women in the family live in the shadow of
Manuel's failure, drunkenness, and violence, and eventually his self-
annihilation; they live in the shadow of the absent Conrado, who
nevertheless continues to affect their lives; and they live in the far-
reaching shadow of the "man" as construct, which teaches them their
own nonvalue. But they are also witnesses and survivors, deriving
strength and support from one another. Yet the conditioning that

teaches men's superiority has devastating repercussions for the ability of women to love themselves and other women. The myriad betrayals of self and other women that stem from women's internalization of this belief form a thematic cluster in Moraga's writing. In her first play, *Giving Up the Ghost,* Marisa says:

> What *is* betrayal?
> Let me tell you about it, it is not clean, nothing neat.
> It's about a battle I will never win and never stop fighting.
> The dick beats me every time.[24]

On one level this passage refers to Marisa's fear that the heterosexual woman she is involved with will leave her for a man, or the "ghost" of a man (the memory of her dead male lover or even patriarchy's prohibition of women loving women). On another level Marisa betrays herself. As a lover of women, she wants to heal their wounds but cannot heal them in herself because she does not love herself.

The essay "A Long Line of Vendidas" in Moraga's first book, *Loving in the War Years,* explores the paradigm in which mothers teach their daughters, first, that they are not as valuable as men and, second, that they are only valuable if they have one. This primary betrayal sets off the "long line" of betrayals among both heterosexual women and lesbians who do not value each other or themselves. As Anzaldúa and other Chicana/o writers and artists explore the concept of "borderlands" as both reality (United States/Mexico) and metaphor ("border" consciousness), Moraga uses sex both as sexual practice and as metaphorical vehicle to represent the intimate struggle to overcome this conditioning on the most vulnerable level.

The play's focus on betrayal among women prevents the female characters from appearing as victims of machismo. They are both complicitous and resistant in the construction of gender roles.

In spite of Hortensia's own experience of Manuel's alienation due to his overinvestment in a *machista* ideal, she reproduces values and attitudes within her family that subordinate women. When Lupe gets her period Hortensia tells her now she must behave differently (1.9). Hortensia's perpetuation of the double standard creates conflict between her and Leticia, since for Hortensia only a man can have the freedom that Leticia craves: "If God had wanted you to be a man, he would of given you somet'ing between your legs" (1.4). Leticia rejects this definition of woman as "lack" when she asserts, "I have something between my legs" (2.5).

Hortensia's phallocentric view is best dramatized in her proud display of her grandson's penis for her daughters to adore: "A sleeping mountain, with a little worm of life in it. Una joya" (1.4). In this scene Hortensia teaches her daughters, in an act of fundamental betrayal, that women's only access to value (the phallus, in her eyes) is bestowed through reproduction, through the birth of a *male* child. When Leticia comments that maybe she won't have children Hortensia responds, "Then you should have been born a man."

Frustrated in her relationship with Manuel, which fails to give her what she wants (fulfilled desire, value), Hortensia looks to her son to give her the kind of power or prestige her daughters never could. She then attempts to hand down this lesson to her daughters in the scene described above.[25] It is too early to know its affect on Lupe, but Leticia at this point resists the message that only the penis confers value at the same time as she recognizes her place in the world as female and powerless.

Responding to criticism that her work is male-identified because it gives the penis so much attention, Moraga states that she is merely calling power by its name. "The dick" in her writing does not represent biological superiority but the symbol of power; for women to write the vagina it is necessary to break down the violence done to us in the name of the phallus.[26] At the "OutWrite '91" conference Chicano poet Ronnie Burk commented on the slogan brandished on placards during protests against the Gulf War: "The war is a dick thing." Similarly, "the dick" referred to by Marisa in *Ghost* or the penis adored by Hortensia in *Shadow* are crucial components of the construct of "man" that must be eliminated.

Given the importance awarded the "son," Hortensia's verbal and emotional expressions of loss seem muted in the face of Rigo's class and cultural rejection. Perhaps she is unwilling to connect with the depth of her loss and, instead of blaming Rigo for his defection, blames first his *gabacha* wife-to-be (1.3) then Manuel, who has no trouble identifying the reason for Rigo's departure from the house: "Because he's a gabachero!" For Hortensia Rigo left out of shame for what Manuel has become (1.4). Although Hortensia ostensibly refers to Manuel's drinking, there is an undertone that insinuates Rigo's perception that his father is less than a "man." Manuel is sensitive to this nuance, as he immediate replies: "Soy hombre!"

Another silence in Hortensia's character centers around her loyalty to Manuel. Verbal expressions of love are absent, but caretaking actions and words abound. It is possible that Hortensia's decision to stay with Manuel in spite of the emotional and sexual estrangement between them has to do with yet another message inherited from mothers and passed down to daughters: the wife's obligation of staying in the marriage at all costs, subordinating her own needs to the supposed welfare of the family.

But Hortensia has not entirely sacrificed her needs in silence; in fact, it is her demand for recognition as a subject, and as a desiring subject, that leads to open conflict with Manuel. In a scene between Hortensia and Rosario it is revealed that Hortensia was more attracted to Conrado than to Manuel but married Manuel because, as Rosario puts it, "Conrado was not the kina man you marry" (1.9). Hortensia chose stability and tranquility, but she remembers the erotic tension around Conrado: "I've never felt that with Manuel." Rosario is an independent woman, and healthily in touch with her body, as when she declares that her "thing is still good 'n' hot" (1.3). But when she describes her independent life ("Ahora, tengo mi casita, mi jardin, my kids are grown. What more do I need?"), Hortensia rejects Rosario's implied celibacy ("I need more, Chayo"). The younger woman makes it clear that celibacy, whether inside or outside of marriage, is not enough for her, rejecting the idea of a marriage in which she is both invisible and unloved (1.9).

In the encounter with Manuel that follows this conversation Hortensia demands his touch and his recognition of her existence ("Touch me. Yo existo."). But the fact that Conrado, and not she, is the object of Manuel's desire redounds upon Hortensia's negative conception of her own desire. She reads his rejection of her as a result of her sexual needs, both now and in the past with Conrado. Her shame and guilt at having desires (both fulfilled and unfulfilled) take the form of self-hate as a woman. For Hortensia the desiring female body can only be filthy and in need of redemption and purification through sacrifice.

Like Hortensia, Leticia is both complicitous in and resistant to the socialization of her desire. From her first appearance she is identified with the Chicano movement and its race politics, both in her clothing (". . . late 60's Chicana 'radical' attire: tight jeans, large looped earrings, an army jacket with a UFW [United Farm Workers] insignia on it. . .") and Hortensia's words ("Alli viene la politica").[27] She criticizes the *telenovela* (Mexican soap opera) Hortensia, Rosario, and Lupe are watching for representing Mexicans as blonds; later, when the women look at pictures of Rigo's wedding, Leticia is acutely aware of the racist treatment of her family as well as her brother's attempts to "get over" (1.6). She avenges both by pointing up differences between European Americans and Chicanos and between Rigo's wedding and traditional Mexican ones. The bride's family had dis-invited Rosario and the rest of Rigo's extended family, pretending that it would be a small ceremony. Leticia comments: "They were afraid that if too many Mexicans got together, we'd take over the joint. Bring out the mariachis, spill guacamole over everything . . ." (1.6).

Immersed in the politicization of her culture as an activist Chicana, Leticia has become radicalized by both race and feminist politics. She has experienced the contradiction of fighting for justice around issues of race within the movement, while only the men, whom she refers to ironically as "Raza gods," have the power. This insight has enabled her to articulate the gender inequality reproduced in her own home, as in the earlier dialogues with Hortensia.

When a student at the University of Washington suggested that Leticia cut herself off from her family and culture because she had allied herself with white feminist values, Moraga was emphatic in her insistence that Leticia's feminism emerges fundamentally out of her specific experience of twofold oppression as a Chicana; she responds to white patriarchy as well as to Chicano machismo. Rather than being less Chicana for her feminist politics, Leticia is the most culturally identified of all the characters. As Moraga phrased it:

She is no less brown, she is too dark almost, darker than her family wants her to get. She reflects a changing culture, and that makes her la nueva Chicana. Her feminism has nothing to do with white women, who may superimpose that reading on the material because white women think they invented feminism. Emotionally, she has had to distance herself from her family, to avoid being swallowed up by it, but that doesn't make her any less Mexican.

Leticia seems to echo Hortensia's belief that women can come into power only through men when she tells her mother about her first sexual experience, with the difference that she is *aware* of the power structures behind male/female relationships: "It's not about love. It's power. Power we get to hold and caress and protect." When Hortensia asks why she gave away her virginity for nothing Leticia expresses her desire not to have her worth and her sexuality defined by men: "I wanted it to be worthless, Mamá. Don't you see? Not for me to be worthless, but to know my worth had nothing to do with it" (2.5).

Rosario, perhaps because by her mid-fifties she has organized her life independently of a man's desires, has the clearest and most pragmatic insights into the ways the "man" throws his shadow over women's lives. Justifying her life without a husband to her sister, Rosario says: "After you see the other side of a man, your heart changes. It's harder to love. I've seen that side too many times, mija" (1.9). The flipside of Rosario's analysis of marriage, in which the man doesn't "see" his wife and lives out of touch with his feelings, is her incisive perception of Manuel's homosocial desire and the way it affects marriage and family life:

> Sometimes a man thinks of another man before he thinks of nobody else. He don' think about his woman ni su madre ni los children, jus' what he gots in his head about that man. He closes his eyes and dreams, "If I could get inside that man's skin, then I'd really be somebody!" But when he opens his eyes and sees that he's as empty as he was before he curls his fingers into fists and knocks down whatever stands in his way. (2.4)

She is strong in her aversion to a mindset of suffering and sacrifice in both men and women. She cautions Lupe against her obsession with sin and the devil; when Lupe protests that she cannot control what she thinks her aunt disagrees. Yet she validates Lupe's road to self-understanding through wrestling her own private demons: "Only los estúpidos don't know enough to be afraid. The rest of us, we learn to live con nuestros diablitos. Tanto que if those little devils weren't around, we wouldn't know who we were" (1.2). Later she catches Manuel wallowing in self-pity before Rigo's wedding, drinking beer and listening to Mexican love songs, and warns him: "If you listen too much to that music, you start to believe there's something good about suffering" (1.6). When Lupe wonders if her father is a saint because he "suffers inside" Rosario makes it clear that she believes his suffering is self-inflicted (2.1).

Lupe, lacking Rosario's years and Leticia's politics, is much more vulnerable. Like Corky, the young lesbian in *Ghost,* Lupe embodies some autobiographical elements of Moraga's early struggles with Catholicism and sexuality. But, whereas the tough little Corky rebelliously confronts gender roles and rejects feminine socialization, Lupe is more fragile, more open, and more anxious to please. In the manner of dysfunctional families she tries to provide for the needs each parent finds unmet in the other. Most disturbing is Manuel's attachment to Lupe. When he comes home drunk and quarrels with Hortensia he seeks out Lupita as a special source of comfort. Although there is no textual evidence of actual incest, the inappropriateness and invasiveness of Manuel's actions imply a damaging blurring of boundaries for the young girl.

Hortensia's internalized shame also rebounds in intensely damaging actions for Lupe. The first occurrence in the play is the violent transfer of guilt from herself to the twelve-year-old Lupe in the reenactment of a scene from the girl's infancy, in which she almost drowned the baby, overcome by guilt at Lupe's resemblance to Conrado. The second, following fast on the heels of the first, mirrors the kind of role reversal that occurs with Manuel. After Manual rejects her demand for recognition as desiring subject she spills vinegar over herself in the bath in response to what she perceives as the stench of her body. Leticia and Lupe manage to calm her; as Lupe strokes her mother's hair and gently dabs at her bruises, Hortensia tells her: "Now, I'm your baby, no mija? Now you have to clean my nalguitas jus' like I wipe yours when you was a baby. . . . You girls are all I got in the world, you know" (1.9)—to which Lupe sadly replies, as before to Manuel, "Sí, mami. Sí."

Besides assigning Lupe the role of caretaker of adults who are not behaving like adults, the secret gnawing at the heart of this family manifests itself in Lupe's fascination with sin and the devil. The play opens with a striking image of the young girl:

> At rise, spot on Lupe, staring into the bathroom mirror. She wears a catholic school uniform. She holds a votive candle under her chin and a rosary crucifix in her hand. Her face is a circle of light in the darkness. The shadow of the crucifix looms over the back wall. (1.1)

In her monologue she speaks of her sin: "keeping secrets." Although Lupe is unaware of the relationship between her obsession with the devil and the problems in her family, the image of the shadow of the crucifix, and later the word *shadow,* with which she chooses to tell Rosario about the devil, reveal this thematic connection to the reader/spectator: "He's like a shadow. . . . I jus' feel the brush of his tail as he goes by me" (1.2). The connection is strengthened when she tells her aunt: "Sometimes I jus' feel like my eyes are too open. It's like the more I see, the more I got to be afraid of." In the way children have of "reading" situations correctly through nonverbal cues and other kinds of information Lupe "sees" more than she can express, understands the truth everything around her denies. This becomes a terrible burden for her, expressed in her childlike equation of suffering and saintliness in Manuel.

Lupe's fear of having eyes that are "too open" and "keeping secrets" in the context of a punitive religiosity are also connected to her developing sexuality. Act 1, scene 8, parallels the opening scene of the play in the repetition of the same image positioning Lupe's head encircled by light in front of the bathroom mirror, "inspecting the black holes of her eyes." But this time, in the shadow of the crucifix looming against the black wall, she speaks of her "ex-ray eyes" as she imagines Sister Genevieve naked under her habit. Her curiosity about sex makes her feel different from the other children, who "seem to be seeing things purty much like they are. I mean, not ex-ray or nut'ing."

This scene adds to the other meanings of the title's "shadow," that of the man on the crucifix, symbolizing the patriarchal collusion between the structures of the church and the family.[28] Catholicism in its institutionalized form not only indoctrinates women to accept

suffering and sacrifice as their lot but also inculcates in them the need
to sublimate the body and its desires, as captured in the image of
Lupe's disembodied head illuminated by a candle in the shadow of
the cross. In an interview Moraga acknowledged the link between
Lupe's "ex-ray eyes" and a passage in *Loving:* "The more potent my
dreams and fantasies became and the more I sensed my own explod-
ing sexual power, the more I retreated from my body's messages and
into the region of religion."[29] Another passage from *Loving* sheds
light on Lupe's refuge in the church in the face of familial and sexual
realities beyond her control: "The strange comfort that the church
would be standing there, just around the turn from the ceme-
tery. . . . That the end of mass would find a palm placed in my
hand. . . . The comfort and terror of powerlessness" (121). At the
crossroads of consciousness and sexual choice Lupe prefers the oddly
comforting disempowerment the church ensures, that frees her from
the necessity of thinking or choosing for herself.

Paradoxically, the church also offers outlets for sexuality and
subjectivity. Alongside the repression of the body and sexual desire,
Catholicism provides its followers with a peculiar brand of sensuality. Moraga's writing characteristically infuses Mexican and Catholic
archetypes with the "heat" of female desire.[30] Toying with the idea
of taking "Magdalene" as her confirmation name, Lupe uses the classic narrative of the sinner's repentance to safely indulge in a vol'uptu-
ous lesbian fantasy, while painting Leticia's toenails (2.1)! On another
level the rituals and the seasons of the church, designed to set up the
individual's relationship with God, facilitate the development of a
private, internal life.[31] Although it is ostensibly tied up with God,
this relationship is ultimately about the subject's own spirituality,
which can continue to exist in adult life independent of organized
religion. It is in the space of this interior world that Lupe expresses,
in her wonderful monologues, her desire for knowledge and the intimate connections between that desire, sexuality, and spirituality.

Lupe ends the play in front of the mirror, as she enters her
interior world once more to explore her feelings about Frances:

> I've decided my confirmation name will be Frances cuz that's
> what Frances Pacheco's name is and I wannu be in her
> body. . . . If I could, . . . I'd like to jus' unzip her chest and climb
> right inside there, next to her heart, to feel everyt'ing she's feel-

ing an' I could forget about me. It's okay if she doesn't feel the same way, . . . it's my secret. (2.6)

There is something alarming about the young girl's desire to get inside of someone else and forget about herself, recalling Marisa's self-betraying gesture of turning away from herself to another in *Ghost*. Closer to home, it recalls Manuel's intense desire, perceived by Rosario, to get inside Conrado's skin in order to "be" somebody, his need to see his identity simultaneously anchored and erased in the eyes of the other. Lupe's boundary confusion was apparent earlier in her fascination with her reflection in her own pupils, echoing Manuel's pondering the loss of his reflection in his son's eye: "You can see yourself in there . . . in the darkest part. . . . Two little faces, one in each eye. It's like you got other people living inside you. Maybe you're not really you. Maybe they're the real you and the big you, is just a dream-you" (1.5). Lupe's indecidability concerning her "real" identity is not surprising, considering that other people, especially Manuel, are attempting to live through her.

Yet Lupe's choice of a love object outside the family is progressive, doubly so in that, for a female, Frances is relatively free of feminine socialization. And, while looking away from herself may anticipate a series of problems in adult life, there is also something positive about Lupe's desires to enter someone's body, as an expression of the basic human need for communion, "to be relieved of oneself, to be loved."[32] In this sense Lupe expresses the fundamental theme of the play: desire. *Shadow* traces the erotic hunger for passion and wholeness of each of the members of this family, even to the youngest child, showing how they "subvert it or divert it" and otherwise strive to be met.[33]

Shadow's commitment to delve into these painful aspects of Chicano culture responds to Moraga's belief that a theater that does not provide the opportunity for self-criticism, for looking within in addition to externally oriented protest, does a fundamental disservice to the community it serves.[34] This self-criticism is part of the struggle to put into question the cultural construction of gender roles and to carve out a space within Chicano culture for the recognition of diverse racial and sexual identities. Moraga's writing fills the need for a "healing theater," a theater that extends the possibility of transformation by addressing Chicano subjects in all their complexity. Moraga's refusal to produce "positive images" prohibits a complacent spectator position for non-Latino and Latino viewers alike. Whether dealing with Chicana lesbian sexuality, as in *Ghost,* or the Chicano family in *Shadow,* Moraga examines the contradictions, the mixed messages, the positive as well as the negative. For Moraga criticizing her culture is an act of love.[35]

NOTES

1. "Shadow" is soon to be published by Arte Público Press in *Shattering the Myth,* a collection of works for the theater by Latinas edited by Denise Chávez. Quotations from the manuscript of the play will be followed by Act and Scene number in parentheses. For a discussion of Moraga's literary trajectory from poetry and essays to theater, see Yarbro-Bejarano, "Cherríe Moraga," *Dictionary of Literary Biography,* Vol. 82, *Chicano Writers First Series,* ed. F. A. Lomeli and C. R. Shirley (Detroit: Bruccoli Clark Layman, 1989), 165–77.

2. *Daily Ledger-Post Dispatch,* November 15, 1990.

3. *El Tecolote,* November, 1990.

4. "Who's Who," program, Eureka/Brava production.

5. "New Ethnicities," in *Black Film/British Cinema,* ed. Kobena Mercer (London: ICA Document 7, British Film Institute Production Special, 1988), 6.

6. See particularly the section "Between the Lines. On Culture, Class, and Homophobia" and Moraga's Introduction to this section in *This Bridge Called My Back. Writings by Radical Women of Color,* ed. Gloria Anzaldúa and Cherríe Moraga (1981; reprint, New York: Kitchen Table/Women of Color Press, 1983).

7. On "nation," see Paul Gilroy, *"There Ain't No Black in the Union Jack": The Cultural Politics of Race and Nation* (London: Hutchinson, 1987); and *Nation and Narration,* ed. Homi Bhabha (London and New York: Routledge, 1990), especially Bhabha's introduction and article "DissemiNation: Time, Narrative, and the Margins of the Modern Nation," 291–322. For articles on Queer Nation, see *Out/Look: National Lesbian and Gay Quarterly* 11 and 12 (Winter and Spring 1991), for a critique of its exclusionary ramifications for gays and lesbians of color by Charles Fernández, "Undocumented Aliens in the Queer Nation," 20–23.

8. With this term Moraga refers to the discussion of precolonization Native American views of gays and lesbians at the Native American Writers Panel, "OutWrite '91."

9. "Is the Rectum a Grave?" in *AIDS: Cultural Analysis, Cultural Activism,* ed. Douglas Crimp (Cambridge, Mass.: MIT Press, 1989), 208–9.

10. Moraga first referred to this notion of learning to love in the family in an interview with Luz Maria Umpierre, "With Cherríe Moraga," *Americas Review* 14, no. 2 (Summer 1986): 54–67.

11. On this theme, see Moraga's poem "La dulce culpa," *Loving in the War Years* (Boston: South End Press, 1983), 14–15; and Norma Alarcón's "What Kind of Lover Have You Made Me, Mother?" in *Women of Color: Perspectives on Feminism and Identity*, ed. Audrey T. McCluskey (Bloomington: Women Studies Press, Indiana University, 1985), 85–110.

12. Wright, *Daily-Ledger-Post Dispatch*.

13. Steven Winn, *San Francisco Chronicle*, 11 November 1990.

14. Program Eureka/Brava production.

15. *Woman, Native, Other: Writing, Postcoloniality and Feminism* (Bloomington: Indiana University Press, 1989), 44.

16. Andrea Lewis, *Mother Jones*, January–February 1991. See Yolanda Broyles, "Women in El Teatro Campesino: 'Apoco Estaba Molacha La Virgen de Guadalupe?'" in *Chicana Voices: Intersections of Class, Race, and Gender*, ed. Teresa Córdova et al. (Austin: University of Texas, CMAS Publications, 1986), 162–87; and "Toward a Re-Vision of Chicano Theatre History: The Women of El Teatro Campesino," in *Making a Spectacle: Feminist Essays on Contemporary Women's Theatre*, ed. Lynda Hart (Ann Arbor: University of Michigan Press, 1989), 209–38.

17. Roberto Lovato, "'Yo existo': The Woman of Color Breaks the Silence," *The City*, November 1990. In the same interview Moraga remarks, "My concern as a writer is to explore those things that I need to understand, and that I feel as a people we need to understand."

18. Lovato, *The City*.

19. From the program's "Note on Language": "'Compadre' refers to the relation of a Godfather to the parents of a child. In Mexican culture, it is a very special bond, akin to that of blood ties, sometimes stronger."

20. Katia Noyes, *San Francisco Sentinel*, 29 November 1990.

21. Matthew Barber, *San Francisco Independent* 35, no. 82 (November 1990).

22. Katia Noyes misses the culturally specific meaning of Rigo's refusal to embrace Manuel, explaining it "as a way of showing manliness" (*San Francisco Sentinel*, 29 November 1990). Rigo's words to Manuel—"No, Dad. I'm a man, now. We shake hands"—as reported by Hortensia, cancel out Manuel's Mexican/Chicano definition of manhood with a Euro-American one.

23. *This Sex Which Is Not One*, trans. Catherine Porter (Ithaca: Cornell University Press, 1985), 192–93.

24. *Giving Up the Ghost* (Los Angeles: West End Press, 1986), 7–8.

25. In a misreading of this scene that borders on the hilarious Scott Rosenberg described its thematic focus as "ruminations on time" (*Examiner*, 13 November 1990).

26. University of Washington lectures.

27. Later, when Hortensia tells Leticia how handsome Rigo looked in his uniform, Leticia groans: "The entire Raza's on the streets protesting the war and my brother's got to be strutting around in a uniform" (1.7).

28. One of the epigraphs of an earlier version of the play is the sign of the cross: "In the name of the Father, and of the Son and of the Holy Ghost."

29. Katia Noyes, *San Francisco Sentinel*, 8 November 1990, 119.

30. Noyes, *San Francisco Sentinel,* 3 November 1990. One example, among many, from *Loving:* "I dreamed of church and cunt. . . . The suffering and the thick musty mysticism of the catholic church fused with the sensation of entering the vagina—like that of a colored woman's—dark, rica, full-bodied. The heavy sensation of complexity. A journey I must unravel, work out for myself. I long to enter you like a temple" (90).

31. Moraga spoke of this secret interior life in her University of Washington lectures.

32. "Interview with Cherríe Moraga and Maria Irene Fornes." Moraga's third play, "Heroes and Saints," explores the complexities of this need for communion.

33. "Interview with Cherríe Moraga and Maria Irene Fornes."

34. "Interview with Cherríe Moraga and Maria Irene Fornes."

35. Lovato, "Notes from the Playwright" (program), Eureka/Brava production.

Chapter 4

Desire Cloaked in a Trenchcoat

Jill Dolan

"Desire Cloaked in a Trenchcoat" is maybe a corny image to inform an investigation of pornography, performance, and spectators. But the man sitting alone in a darkened theater masturbating under his coat while staring at the screen is an image engraved on our collective imagination. Male arousal by pictures is an accepted part of dominant cultural discourse.

The provocative relationship between sexuality and representation is revealed perhaps most blatantly in pornography. Pornography is an important locus for feminist critical thought because it provides a site for the intersection of feminist sexual politics and the politics of representation.

Whether you are for or against pornography, or straddle the anticensorship fence with "First Amendment" painted on it, pornography has to be dealt with as representation. As Susanne Kappeler points out in *The Pornography of Representation*, "Representation is not so much the means of representing an object through imitation (that is, matching contents) as a means of self-representation through authorship: The expression of subjectivity" (1986:53). Antiporn feminists condemning pornography as both image and educator of male violence against women look for a match of contents by equating pornography and reality.[1] But pornography is more than simple mimesis. As representation, it helps to construct subject positions that maintain the strict gender divisions on which the culture operates.

The subject/object relations delineated by pornography are also paradigmatic of those structured by representation in general. Feminist film and performance critics argue that representation is addressed to the gaze of the male spectator. He is invited to identify

105

with the active male protagonist portrayed in the narrative through voyeuristic and fetishistic viewing conventions. The male spectator shares in the pleasure of the hero's quest to fulfill his desire for the story's passively situated female (see de Lauretis 1984, Kaplan 1983, Mulvey 1975).

If all representation is structured by male desire, then sexuality is as integral a part of constructing spectator subjectivity in a Shakespeare production at Stratford as it is in live sex shows in Times Square. Any representation can be seen as essentially pornographic, since the structure of gendered relationships through which it operates is based on granting men subjectivity while denying it to women.

Kantian aesthetics propose that the only way to contemplate a work of art is through a certain detachment from reality. Disengagement allows the artwork a separate, "objective" existence and hides the fact of its authorship within a particular historical moment governed by cultural and economic considerations. Kappeler argues after Kant that the principles of aesthetic distance and disinterestedness motivate pornography as well as art. She suggests that in the peep shows where men masturbate while watching women perform behind glass windows, the goal is not actually to fuck women. Rather, the goal is what she calls the "feeling of life, the pleasure of the subject" derived from aesthetic distance (1986:49–62). Kappeler says that the pornographic representation is even preferable, because it allows the total assertion of a man's subjectivity. Since there is no intersubjective action, the image of the woman behind the glass becomes a screen for the projection of a fantasy over which the male viewer has total control.

In "Bar Wars," written for *Esquire* in November 1986, Bob Greene provides a succinct example of the intersection of sexuality, pornography, and spectatorship on the representational economy. A bar called B. T.'s in Dearborn, Michigan, which usually presents topless female dancing entertainment, also offers what it calls "Rambo Wet Panty Nights." Black plastic Uzi submachine water guns are handed out to the customers. Then a woman—sometimes a regular B. T.'s dancer, sometimes an "amateur" volunteer—mounts the stage dressed in a skimpy T-shirt and underwear and stands covering her eyes and face while the men shoot their water guns at her vagina. Six or seven women perform each evening, and cash prizes are given to the women who do the "best" job of being shot at according to the bar owner's subjective judgments. Greene doesn't describe the critical standards applied (1986:61–62).

This performative exchange is a cultural feminist's nightmare of the conflation of sexuality and violence. But, aside from this neat match of contents, it's an overt example of representation proceeding according to a pornographic model. The bar is packed with men drawn by a chance to become Rambo in the flesh. The elements of a prior representation, then, are mapped onto the performance at the bar. Sylvester Stallone and his Rambo movies are missing, but they're implied in the narrative.

In the Rambo films, as in most Vietnam films, the enemy—or the Other—is an Asian race. In the paramilitary ambience of B. T.'s bar the woman onstage becomes the alien enemy, the Other defined by her difference.[2] The floor manager at B. T.'s encourages the men with guns to think of the woman on stage as Vietnam, or Libya, or even Nicaragua. It's a neat way of eroticizing imperialism and keeping sexuality imperialist.

The men with the Uzis are implicitly identifying with Rambo as they aim, and they experience visual pleasure by projecting their subjective fantasies onto the passive women. One man tells Greene: "I got her. She's hot; I know she likes it. She likes it, and she knows that I know she likes it" (1986:62). But if the woman's eyes were covered, how could this man possibly think the performer was acknowledging and enjoying a spray from his gun, except by fantasizing because he wants it that way?

What do the performers at B. T.'s think about allowing their bodies to be used as substitutes for Third World nations and becoming screens for projections of male fantasy? One woman tells Greene that "it's a power game." Unlike most, she doesn't cover her eyes when she performs: "I try to look out into the audience and make eye contact with as many of the men with guns as I can. A lot of times, they'll turn away. If a woman looks them in the eye, they'll turn away" (1986:62). At issue here is the struggle for subjectivity. These men can't face the intersubjectivity of the woman's gaze. They must maintain the disengagement of desire inspired by the safe aesthetic distance of the representation.

Greene's article, of course, is governed by the exigencies of his own male gaze, and he doesn't mention whether there are women spectators in the bar. But, theoretically, where could a woman place herself in relation to this display? How could she position herself in front of a peep show window? The image of a woman sitting in a darkened theater wearing a trenchcoat is incongruous at best.

Whether or not female spectators can be placed in positions of power that might allow for the objectification of male performers or that might allow for the liberation of both gender classes from the oppressions of the representational gaze is an issue hotly debated in feminist theory. As Kappeler and others have pointed out, simply trading gender positions isn't as easy as it sounds. While women in representation usually signify their gender class, the culturally sanctioned power of male subjectivity makes a similar signification very difficult. Women cannot simply express their subjectivity by objectifying men. A nude male in an objectified position remains an individual man, not necessarily a representative of the male gender class.

For example, Richard Schechner, while pondering these issues, described the activity at several sex clubs in Montreal in which males danced for females as examples of women adopting the male gaze. Schechner says the male dancers

> stripped until fully naked. They played with their cocks and displayed the rest of their bodies in a way very parallel to what women do in strip clubs. . . . As a new male entered the stage, the dancer who was on stage went from table to table, and danced directly in front of women. The male dancer brought with him a little step stool so that his genitals were face level to the female spectator(s). The women tipped him. There was a lot of flirtation, kissing, and some genital playing. (Schechner 1987)

While this situation seems to reverse the traditional paradigm, male sexuality is still active, privileged, and displayed. The women spectators want the male performer to desire them. Similar conditions are implied by female dancers in clubs for male spectators. The female dancers aren't performing their own sexuality—their display implies penile satisfaction, their open legs and wet vaginas imply the possibility of penetration. In both situations the desire of women spectators or performers is subordinate to male desire.

According to the psychoanalytical model, since male desire drives representation, a female spectator is given two options. She can identify with the active male and symbolically participate in the female performer's objectification, or she can identify with the narrative's objectified female and position herself as an object.

I do not mean to propose a universalism when I use the term "female spectator." For the materialist feminist women are differentiated along class, race, and sexual orientation lines that make it impossible for them to respond to any image as a unit. Part of the problem with the psychoanalytical model of spectatorship is just this tendency to pose universal "male" and "female" spectators who respond only according to gender. Part of my project here is to suggest that sexuality is as large a part of spectator response as gender and that, by altering the assumed sexuality of spectators, the representational exchange can also be changed.

Mary Ann Doane in *The Desire to Desire* writes: "There is a certain naïveté assigned to women in relation to systems of signification, a tendency to deny the process of representation, to collapse the opposition between the sign (the image) and the real" (1987:1). Women remain part of Lacan's Imaginary realm, completely marginal to the signifying process. Since she cannot separate herself from the image, the female spectator cannot experience the mirror phase through which she might see herself reflected as a separate subject. Because Doane's psychoanalytic reading considers desire as a form of disengagement "crucial to the assumption of the position of the speaking subject" (1987:11), a woman cannot hope to articulate her desire in the representational space.

Since she can assume neither disengagement nor aesthetic distance from the image, she is denied the scopophilic pleasure of voyeurism. Fetishism—which also operates particularly in the cinematic apparatus to provide visual pleasure—is also unavailable to the female spectator, since her "originary" lack dictates that she already has nothing to lose.

Woman as a psychic subject, then, is unarticulated in representation. Doane goes on to propose that women as social subjects are constructed merely as passive consumers invited to buy the idealized, male-generated image of the female body as a commodity displayed in the representational frame.

If the female spectator chooses to accept this passively constructed consumer position, Doane writes, "The mirror/window takes on then the aspect of a trap whereby her subjectivity becomes synonymous with her objectification" (1987:33). Buying the idealized image of herself, she turns herself into a commodity to then be sold, as the performer already has. The positions of the female performer and the female spectator are collapsed into one; they become prostitutes who buy and sell their own image in a male-generated visual economy. They are goods in the representational marketplace, commodities in an exchange by means of which they are both objectified.[3]

The women performing at B. T.'s, for example, are sheer spectacle in a representational exchange constructed for the male gaze. Some of the women admit they do it for the money, prostituting their subjectivity to the demands of the representational space. The owner of B. T.'s, of course, doesn't see it in so mercenary a light. He romanticizes the women's involvement, speculating that they are willing to perform because they come from disturbed backgrounds and need attention—a variation on *A Chorus Line*'s "What I Did for Love."

The idea that specularized, objectified women do it for the love of the male gaze is a concept perpetuated by dominant cultural discourse. In "Confessions of a Feminist Porno Star," printed in a feminist anthology of personal narratives called *Sex Work,* Nina Hartley acquiesces to this view. She says she is an exhibitionist, a woman who is aroused by being looked at. But she also feels she has some control over the production of her image. "In choosing my roles and characterizations carefully," she writes, "I strive to show, always, women who thoroughly enjoy sex and are forceful, self-satisfying and guilt-free without also being neurotic, unhappy, or somehow unfulfilled" (1987:142). Hartley proposes that she can subvert the representational apparatus by adjusting the content of its images and giving the positive, active roles to women.

This is a kind of liberal feminist, matching-contents argument that has been used to justify generating feminist erotica. Some feminists think that, if women controlled the means of producing pornography, its representations would be different. But the genderized component of heterosexuality, with its inevitable constant of male desire, problematizes positioning women as the producers or subjects of heterosexual pornography. Heterosexual feminist erotica, such as the magazine *Eidos,* and much feminist performance art indicates that disarming male desire in the representational space requires "feminizing" the represented males or avoiding sexuality as an integral issue.

These attempts are for the most part either unsuccessful—since the erect male penis is still a power-filled image even if it's displayed in a feminine, "natural" context—or banal, as sexuality gives way to the obfuscating realm of spirituality (see Dolan 1987:157–61).

Debi Sundahl, in her *Sex Work* essay called "Stripper," acknowledges the subject/object problem inherent in heterosexual representation. Initially, she says,

> the hardest part of the job was dealing with my feminist principles concerning the objectification of women. Dancing nude is the epitome of woman as sex object. As the weeks passed, I found I liked being a sex object, because the context was appropriate. . . . I perform to turn you on, and if I fail, I feel I've done a poor job. Women who work in the sex industry are not responsible for, nor do they in any way perpetuate, the sexual oppression of women. In fact, to any enlightened observer, our very existence provides a distinction and a choice as to when a woman should be treated like a sex object and when she should not be. At the theatre, yes; on the street, no. (1987:176)

I find this a provocative statement. Sundahl suggests that subject positions onstage can be separated from those assumed in life. But she also suggests that bowing to the demands of objectification in theater is the only role a woman can play in the heterosexual representational space. Implicit in her argument is the idea that representation is driven by a kind of sexuality in which objectification is constantly assumed. But is all sexuality motivated by objectification? And if not, what might happen to representation if the sexual desire motivating it were different?

There's a twist to Sundahl's story. She is a lesbian; she publishes *On Our Backs,* a lesbian porn magazine; and she started a women-only strip show at Baybrick's, a now defunct lesbian bar in San Francisco. Sundahl herself makes a distinction between her performance spaces, pointing out that the different cultural mandates of the heterosexual and lesbian contexts make the terms of the performative exchange very different, even if the images used or roles played are the same. Describing the show at Baybrick's, for example, Sundahl writes, "The dancers loved performing for the all-female audiences because they had more freedom of expression. They were not limited to ultrafeminine acts only; they could be butch and dress in masculine attire" (1987:178). In other words, if they wanted to, the performers could assume the subject position rather than objectifying themselves. The butch/femme role play allowed the performers to seduce each other and the lesbian spectators through the constant of lesbian sexuality.

This context allows lesbian desire to circulate as the motivating representational term. The subject/object relations that trap women performers and spectators as commodities in a heterosexual context dissolve. The lesbian subject, according to Monique Wittig (1980, 1981) and others, has free range across a gender continuum, and, to paraphrase Sue-Ellen Case, her role-playing through a "strategy of appearances" (1987) disrupts the dominant cultural discourse representation mandates. Wittig says lesbians are "not women" and not men according to the way these gender roles are culturally constructed (1980:110). Since they are already outside a strictly dichotomized gender context, they are free to pick and choose from both extremes. There are no prostitutes on the lesbian representational economy because the goods have gotten together (see Irigaray 1981).

In *Upwardly Mobile Home,* a production by the lesbian performance troupe Split Britches, Peggy Shaw has a monologue describing her character's trip to see the fat lady at the circus. She says the lights and the posters promised her entertainment, but she got much, much more. When she entered the fat lady's tent, Shaw says: "She knew I had come to see her being fat. She looked at me and I looked at her. I loved that fat lady." Rather than the fight for subjectivity that takes place in B. T.'s heterosexual bar, Shaw's exchange with the fat woman seems paradigmatic of the lesbian viewing experience. The recognition of mutual subjectivity allows the gaze to be shared in a direct way. Shaw tells *Upwardly Mobile Home* spectators, "You have paid to see me"—but the visual economy is now under lesbian control.

Lesbians are appropriating the subject position of the male gaze by beginning to articulate the exchange of desire between women. Lesbian subjectivity creates a new economy of desire. To borrow from Irigaray once again, lesbians "go to the 'market' alone, to profit from their own value, to talk to each other, to desire each other, without the control of the selling-buying-consuming subjects" (1981:110). Rather than gazing through the representational window at their commodification as women, lesbians are generating and buying their own desire on a different representational economy. Perhaps the lesbian subject can offer a model for women spectators that will appropriate the male gaze. The aim is not to look like men, but to look at all.

Epilogue

Since reading Teresa de Lauretis's article on lesbian representation (1988), I've been rethinking the issue of desire, and with it, the whole of what Case calls the "psychosemiotic" theoretical endeavor (1988). When I attempt to wrench myself from the psychosemiotic subject considerations that have governed my work on the spectator, and that hinge on the question of desire in representation, I come to the notion of spectatorial communities. This is where de Lauretis, too, seems to arrive in her exploration of how to represent lesbian differences, how not to reify the lesbian spectator as some new, unbroken, unified idol.

The hint of utopianism that creeps into my thoughts when I write about changing the entrenched gender dynamics of representation comes from my conception of lesbian subjectivit(ies) as one of the most challenging, fruitful areas in this field of investigation. According to the psychosemiotic feminist critical model, of which my argument here makes use, male desire is the variable in the representational exchange that upsets the balance of power, reinforces the gender dichotomy in art and culture, and proscribes heterosexuality as compulsory (see Rich 1983). Male desire is not at all a factor in representations created by lesbians. As a result, the area of lesbian subjectivity seems a place to begin to envision new possibilities for representation.

Shifting my emphasis from the psychological construction of the individual spectator, however, brings me perhaps to a less utopian notion of lesbian spectatorial communities, separated and differentiated by class, race, and ideology. As de Lauretis chastises, changing the shape of desire from heterosexual to lesbian won't get the entire crisis of representation off our backs. There is no universal lesbian spectator to whom each lesbian representation will provide the embodiment of the same lesbian desire. Sexuality, and desire, and lesbian subjects are more complicated than that.

Although I might concede the utopianism of my writing on lesbian desire and am currently working to think within the contradictions, I can't concede or condone what some see as the necessity to "universalize" this model to heterosexual women and men. For instance, Linda Walsh Jenkins mistakenly suggests that "most of the leading [feminist theorists] in the middle 80s are lesbian" and complains that "the heterosexual female position has not been given much attention or articulation" (Chinoy and Jenkins 1987:373). Jenkins fails to acknowledge that heterosexual women are in a more visible, privileged position in the culture than lesbians and have in fact been given a great deal of attention. The history of theater and performance studies, as well as its criticism and theory, cloaks its heterosexuality in a universal guise that leaves lesbian subjects invisible in its discourse. I am, as Wittig suggests, shifting the axis of categorization (1983).

Placing the lesbian subject at the center of the debate, rescued from the invisible margins, illuminates aspects of the arguments about representation that were clouded or unexamined. But my argument also has a personal and political component that aims toward the liberation of a sexual minority. Heterosexual readers unsettled by their absence from this debate might have to confront their own homophobia, just as I, as a white reader grappling with work by racial and ethnic minorities, am forced to examine my own racism. As the postmodernists insist, the center is constantly shifting. The shock might be finding yourself on the margins.

Afterthoughts, 1992

From this remove—looking back on an article conceived nearly five years ago—"Desire Cloaked in a Trenchcoat" seems like a piece of theoretical history, a kind of Americana in the discourse about female spectatorship. Although I see glimmers of my own more recent thinking through the cracks of my argument here, the piece in many ways represents an earlier moment in feminist and lesbian discourse about spectatorship and "the gaze."

The recent theoretical move into cultural studies, for example, to supplement the critical paradigms of psychoanalytic research on the operation of desire, offers innumerable ways to reconceptualize the fraught exchanges between performers, spectators, and audiences in particular, historicized, localized contexts. In fact, the move into audience studies (described, in part, by Susan Bennett's recent *Theatre Audiences: A Theory of Production and Reception* [New York: Routledge, 1990]) reconfigures the concept of the spectator as a singular position interacting with a representational text into a community of viewers responding multivocally to multiply meaningful productions.

Whereas the female spectator in "Desire Cloaked in a Trenchcoat" seems bound to the limited options of identification with the narrative's active male or its objectified female, new research in media and film studies, just now being applied in theater studies, argues that spectators use representation in more active, complicated ways— that, even within the inequities of gendered viewing, resistance can be found and agency claimed. Such counterhegemonic practices now seem available to heterosexual female, as well as lesbian, spectators and audiences, in ways that the more singular, psychosemiotic explorations of desire once obscured.

Likewise, the eruption in the early 1990s of counterhegemonic lesbian discourse on sexual practice offers even more sites at which to look for alternatives to the "cultural" feminist representations of female desire than in 1987, when *On Our Backs* and the testimonies in *Sex Work* seemed indeed a brave new world. The new "economy of desire" has proven a legitimate capitalist one for lesbians as well, as publications such as the quarterly *Out/Look* and Susie Bright's now notorious *Susie Sexpert's Lesbian Sex World* (San Francisco: Cleis Press, 1990) have redefined the boundaries of the debate over lesbian and gay representation and sexual practice. The "pornography of capitalism" now proves lucrative in new and different ways, as lesbians across a range of political and identity affiliations have bought and sold a differently eroticized gaze.

If "Trenchcoat" ends with a mandate to "appropriate the male gaze . . . to look at all," the flourishing alternative visual culture in lesbian and gay publications, bars, and boutiques seems to indicate a liberation of the gaze not only in the theater but also in the performance of everyday life. But maybe I'm still waxing utopian, as I know that costs continue to be exacted for what appear to be these newfound freedoms to gaze.

My first epilogue in this now palimpsestic text challenges heterosexual readers to confront their own imminent panic at finding themselves on the margin of lesbian texts and suggests that efficacious political work in representation happens when the center continually shifts, across gender, race, sexuality, class, and other identity and community lines. If I were to rewrite this article today, I would attempt to trouble even further the binary of margin and center, inside and outside, that structures my ideas and my text. The concept of a discursive center, even when it's comprised of identity communities once "silenced," "oppressed," and "marginalized" by dominant discourse, seems less productive in 1992 than a less fixed, less stabilized, less monolithic concept of positionality, in which lesbians, too, can find their respective rugs continually pulled out from under them. Positionality moves us all around some other space than a center or a margin, through the complications of considering (and living) more crossed, intersected identities. Giving up the notion of a center, of a privileged, fixed position to which spectators might aspire, will have useful implications for reconsidering the focus and power of a unidirectional gaze.

My last thought—inspired in part by a lecture Peggy Phelan gave at the University of Wisconsin-Madison in March 1992 and in part by the new resonances rereading this article sounds for me—troubles the issue of visibility as a progressive, even transgressive value in representation, to which my work has been so attached. In her talk Peggy proposed a new model of political activism founded in undecidability, which would challenge what she called the impoverishment of the "economy of certainty." She pointed out that being able to see and to know and therefore provoke to action is a paradigm used to equal effect by the New Right, as well as feminists and the New, floundering Left. Peggy challenged her audience to confront the provocation of doubt, to resist a causal link between representation and the real that requires a deep, profound revision of an investment in visibility as politically radical.

While I remain hesitant to fully divest from "looking" or from "visibility" as desirable on a representational economy, I am provoked by Peggy's challenge to rethink the terms of political resistance. How, in the production/reception paradigm that structures performance, can we cast the "provocation of doubt" over how we look and what we see? How can we unmoor identity from visibility—in some ways the logical extension of deuniversalizing the lesbian spectator, as de Lauretis offered—without leaving desire cloaked in a trenchcoat? Or is the trenchcoat, with its enigmatic potential to flash the desire it hides, a most efficacious political metaphor?

NOTES

1. Antiporn feminism is very much in line with the cultural feminist politic, which maintains that the biological differences between men and women are the basis of their psychological and social differences. This stance translates into often prescriptive dichotomies that describe men's behavior as violent, women's as pacifist. Andrea Dworkin is the most vocal and visible antiporn cultural feminist; her book *Pornography: Men Possessing Women* (1979) is the bible of the movement. See Dolan (1987) for a further explication of antiporn feminism in terms of feminist performance and criticism.

2. For example, this link between the eroticization of imperialism and sexual imperialism is drawn in Stanley Kubrick's Vietnam film *Full Metal Jacket* (1987). When the American soldiers get to Vietnam in Kubrick's film, they are immediately initiated into an economy based on the exchange of Vietnamese prostitutes for American dollars. The soldiers' options in the war context are sex or fighting, and the two inevitably blur. The slow motion, orgasmic quality of blood capsules bursting all over soldiers falling in battle is unmistakably sexual. After a series of more or less faceless skirmishes with the Asian enemy, the film climaxes with the face-to-face murder of a sniper who, not accidentally, is a woman. Aggression toward an entire country is signified by what ends up as sexual aggression toward one alien woman, the dark territory incarnate. Substituting a woman for the alien Asian enemy cannot be coincidental. In Kubrick's film Vietnam is signified by a woman.

3. Gayle Rubin, in "The Traffic in Women" (1978) argues that women have been use-value in a male economy at least since the kinship systems studied by Lévi-Strauss. Luce Irigaray, in "When the Goods Get Together" (1981), suggests that, if women refused to "go to market," they could fundamentally disrupt the dominant culture's structure.

REFERENCES

Case, Sue-Ellen. 1987. "Toward a Butch Femme Aesthetic." Women and Theatre Conference keynote address. 2 August, Chicago, Il.

——. 1988. *Feminism and Theatre*. New York: Methuen.

Chinoy, Helen Krich, and Linda Walsh Jenkins. 1987. *Women in American Theatre*. New York: Theatre Communications Group.

de Lauretis, Teresa. 1984. "Desire in Narrative." In *Alice Doesn't*, 103–57. Bloomington: Indiana University Press.

——. 1988. "Sexual Indifference and Lesbian Representation." *Theatre Journal* 40 (no. 2): 155–77.

Doane, Mary Ann. 1987. *The Desire to Desire: The Woman's Film of the 1940's.* Bloomington: Indiana University Press.

Dolan, Jill. 1987. "The Dynamics of Desire: Sexuality and Gender in Pornography and Performance." *Theatre Journal* 30, no. 2 (May): 156–74.

Dworkin, Andrea. 1979. *Pornography: Men Possessing Women.* New York: Pedigree Books.

Greene, Bob. 1986. "Bar Wars," *Esquire,* November, 61–62.

Hartley, Nina. 1987. "Confessions of a Feminist Porno Star." In *Sex Work: Writings by Women in the Sex Industry,* edited by Frederique Delacoste and Priscilla Alexander, 142–44. San Francisco: Cleis Press.

Irigaray, Luce. 1981. "When the Goods Get Together." In *New French Feminisms,* edited by Elaine Marks and Isabelle de Courtivron, translated by Claudia Reeder, 107–10. New York: Schocken Books.

Kaplan, E. Ann. 1983. *Women & Film: Both Sides of the Camera.* New York: Methuen.

Kappeler, Susanne. 1986. *The Pornography of Representation.* Minneapolis: University of Minnesota Press.

Mulvey, Laura. 1975. "Visual Pleasure and Narrative Cinema." *Screen* 16 (no. 3): 6–18.

Rich, Adrienne. 1983. "Compulsory Heterosexuality and Lesbian Existence." In *Powers of Desire,* edited by Ann Snitow, Christine Stansell, and Sharon Thompson, 177–205. New York: Monthly Review Press.

Rubin, Gayle. 1978. "The Traffic in Women: Notes on the 'Political Economy' of Sex." In *Toward an Anthropology of Women,* edited by Rayna Reiter. New York: Monthly Review Press.

Schechner, Richard. 1987. Personal correspondence, 7 September.

Sundahl, Debi. 1987. "Stripper." In *Sex Work: Writings by Women in the Sex Industry,* edited by Frederique Delacoste and Priscilla Alexander, 175–80. San Francisco: Cleis Press.

Wittig, Monique. 1980. "The Straight Mind." *Feminist Issues,* Summer, 103–11.

———. 1981. "One is Not Born a Woman." *Feminist Issues,* Winter, 47–54.

———. 1983. "The Point of View: Universal or Particular?" *Feminist Issues,* Fall, 63–69.

Chapter 5

Identity and Seduction: Lesbians in the Mainstream

Lynda Hart

Sexual identities are, on the one hand, less stable "objects" than gender identities; on the other hand, they remain more wedded to a metaphysics of substance. The historical soldering of sexual subjectivities with object choices has produced a double bind that confounds adjudication. Deciding when and where to deploy a constructionist or essentialist account of "homosexuality" has taken on heightened political import. Giving credence to them both simultaneously is a necessarily anxious affair. The essentialist/constructionist debate is in some sense a red herring,[1] for it is not the "truth" of sexualities and their identities that we seek; rather, it is the *effects* of producing one discourse or the other in the material lives of those persons who identify themselves as members of a sexual minority that concerns us.

The last few decades have produced an abundance of historicizing discourse on sexual identities, most supporting a constructionist view. While one might fully concur with the constructionists in theory, the legitimacy of an essentialist rhetoric must be acknowledged, not as a claim to truth but in response to the political ramifications of an absolute constructionist position, which can be too easily appropriated to perform acts of violence against a minority population.

The performance of lesbian sexuality has found itself caught in this dilemma both textually and contextually. In her afterword to *The Feminist Spectator as Critic*, Jill Dolan presciently forecast that the pressing question for feminist performance criticism would focus on lesbian performance and its risks of assimilation as it moved into more mainstream performance venues.[2] This issue produced something of a crisis when Lois Weaver and Peggy Shaw, the butch-femme couple of the performance group Split Britches, performed Holly Hughes's *Dress Suits to Hire* at the University of Michigan. In response to this production lesbian-feminist theorist Sue-Ellen Case, who has written extensively about Split Britches, and lesbian performer/playwright Holly Hughes exchanged tendentious letters in an issue of *The Drama Review*. Case maintained that the disruptive strategies of Weaver and Shaw's lesbian performance were assimilated by an audience that was gleefully entertained, consuming and erasing the specificity of lesbian lives and desires. Weaver and Shaw, according to Case, were appropriated in this particular performance in ways that reflect a wider assimilation of gay and lesbian cultural performances: "we've barely begun to write or perform lesbian sexuality among/by/for ourselves when presses, ivy league schools, and regional theatres are already bedecking themselves with lesbian/gay themes and studies like wearing Liz Taylor's diamond...."[3] Case attributed her response to both the context of the performance at Michigan and to Hughes's text, with her emphasis falling heavily on the latter. Hughes responded by accusing Case of appointing herself an "authority on true Orthodox Lesbianism,...a woman with a mission, a born again lesbian, a Shiite lesbian."[4] Hughes took Case's critique of her text as an assault on her personal identity, and she shored up the integrity of that identity by evoking her female lover.

This debate once again publicly profiled the question that feminist and lesbian theorists cannot relinquish: When is a text a lesbian text?—a question that is inextricably bound to the issue of what constitutes, if anything, lesbian identity. The long tradition behind the Case/Hughes argument need not be reiterated here. As I have argued elsewhere, what is now generally referred to as the essentialist/constructionist debate has been present, though somewhat latent, in contestations over the sign "lesbian" in feminist theoretical projects at least since the early 1970s, when the Radicalesbians published their manifesto, "The Woman-Identified Woman."[5] One might expect that such debates would be obsolete in light of cultural theorists' radical destabilization of all identities and deconstruction of the homosexual/heterosexual binary. Nevertheless, it is clear that the stakes remain high for adjudicating lesbian identities, recognition of them as historical constructs notwithstanding.

The anxiety both reflected and produced by this debate between lesbians is indicative of what Eve Sedgwick refers to as an "intimate dissonance" that frequently emerges when feminists find themselves caught in the tension between the political motive of identifying with one another as women, or as the subjects of a particular sexuality, and the operation of identification itself, which always involves not only an identification *as* but an identification *with* and *as against*. Identifying as against is obviously fraught with tension, if not hostility. But, as Sedgwick points out, identification with is sufficient to produce an unnerving, painful situation, since, as psychoanalysis suggests, "the relations implicit in *identifying with* are . . . in themselves quite sufficiently fraught with intensities of incorporation, diminishment, inflation, threat, loss, reparation, and disavowal."[6] Identity politics are destined to remain with us for some time; feminist movement cannot seem to live with it or without it.

I want to enter into this debate by looking closely at one particular production, Weaver and Shaw's *Anniversary Waltz,* as it was performed at the University of Pennsylvania in February of 1990. Based on a performance of *Anniversary Waltz* that she saw in Milwaukee, Dolan argues that *Anniversary Waltz* is "ultimately an assimilationist lesbian text because of its emphasis on romance and familial relationships rather than sexual ones."[7] Thus, she takes a position similar to Case's response to *Dress Suits to Hire* but based on a text written and performed solely by Weaver and Shaw. As in Case's argument, Dolan attributes the ultimate culpability for assimilation to the text, backgrounding the context.

Highlighted copy from a local review of the Philadelphia production supported Dolan's reading of the text. "Split Britches presents universal tales of love and marriage," it read.[8] This response was by no means anomalous. Numerous spectators commented on the familiar themes and wide-based appeal of the performance. The audience was certainly not a heterogeneous one, even from a local perspective, but it was not the already tuned-in audiences that attend productions at the WOW cafe, or other East Village venues. Even so, how could they have missed the "lesbian difference" that this performance so obviously encoded? What I saw as I read the reviews, overheard spectators' comments, and listened to my students discuss the show was an almost seamless repudiation of any lesbian presence in this performance. This response was startling given the blatant mapping of a highly specific lesbian and gay history in *Anniversary Waltz*.

Employing the same performative styles that Split Britches uses in all of their work—monologues, role playing, song, dance, vaudeville routines—*Anniversary Waltz* tells the story of Weaver's and Shaw's ten-year lesbian relationship. As spectators entered the performing space, big band music was playing softly; pink napkins proclaiming "Happy Anniversary Peggy and Lois" were offered by the ushers along with a bite of anniversary cake. The cabaret tables were adorned with stand-up bride and groom paper dolls on which Lois's and Peggy's faces were superimposed; pink and lavendar balloons floated from under the stage into the audience space. People bought drinks at the bar, volleyed the balloons around, ate their cake, and enjoyed the music. As the lights began to dim, we heard the words of a wedding ceremony in progress—"Dearly beloved, we are gathered here together in the eyes of god to witness this man and this woman joined in the bond of holy matrimony"—as Weaver and Shaw emerged from behind the bright pink curtain in full wedding regalia, Weaver as bride, Shaw as groom, posing as the happy couple for postceremony photographs.

Although the performance announces itself as an anniversary celebration and sets up the performing space in minute detail as a realistic party/reception, Weaver and Shaw immediately upset expectations of conventional narrativity, linearity, or causality. They present themselves as perpetually frozen in the posture of bride and groom, static and excessive images of a heterosexual union. The time is out of joint, along with the sex/gender system. If any anniversary is a "turning back to the day," it is usually done in memory with perhaps a few material reminders of the original event present to evoke the past, such as a frozen piece of the cake or a dried corsage. Conventionally, anniversary celebrations might be thought of as hysterical occasions, dedicated as they are to reminiscences, in which partial objects are presented to evoke the past.

But this anniversary is more like a hallucination. Weaver and Shaw are not merely remembering; rather, they are conjuring up the past in all of its imaginary fullness, displaying it as spectacle, actively producing rather than reproducing the real. It is in this fantasy space that they situate their lesbian desire. And yet it seemed that the comfort of familiar iconicity overcame this deconstructive performance.

Lois Weaver and Peggy Shaw in *Anniversary Waltz*. Photo © by Amy Meadow.

For some spectators Weaver's and Shaw's performance "normalized" lesbianism; that is, they made it seem as familiar as a heterosexual relationship of a particular type—middle-class, monogamous with the exception of a few "mistakes," procreative, enduring 'til death do us part. A liberal gay rights agenda that proposes raising the consciousness of the American public to the sameness of homosexual and heterosexual life-styles might be pleased with these results. They are, of course, entirely unsatisfactory for lesbian feminists, who propose the lesbian subject position as a site for subverting gender.

According to such responses, Weaver and Shaw were unsuccessful in presenting themselves *as* lesbians. But what is this "something-to-be-seen" that is presumed to be so crucial to the political project? Why do we so often assume that visibility always and everywhere has a positive sociopolitical value? Visibility politics, the dominant agenda of gay and lesbian activism, clashes with psychoanalytic constructions of sexual subjectivities. The former's assertion of identity politics is unraveled by the latter's destabilizing identifications. Peggy Phelan has elaborated the "dangerous complicity between progressives dedicated to visibility politics and conservatives patrolling the borders of museums, movie houses, and mainstream broadcasting."[9] Her nuanced rethinking of the Left's position claims the power and value of that which cannot be represented—the "unmarked." Surely we must take as axiomatic her point that, "if representational visibility equals power then almost-naked young white women should be running Western culture"[10] Diana Fuss has also pointed out the paradox of the visibility/invisibility opposition: to be "out is really to be in—inside the realm of the visible, the culturally intelligible."[11] And Judith Butler raises the possibility that it is at the very site of our exclusions from ontology that a "rallying point for resistance" might be possible.[12]

Like any other identity formation, lesbian identities are constructed from a history of identifications, not only identifications as, but also identifications *with;* and not only *between* the signs heterosexual/homosexual, but also *within* the sign lesbian, which is all too often presumed to be a unified, coherent category. Perhaps, then, lesbians should not submit themselves at all to this "pluralistic" specular economy. In particular, the butch-femme couple is at high risk for assimilation precisely because of the duo's historical visibility. The butch-femme couple is charged with the double and precarious task of political affirmation for lesbians effected through visibility and the radical negative critique of humanistic binaries. If subculturally constructed butch-femme role playing is the most visible sign of lesbian, it would seem to be so precisely because it permits the spectator to read gender. Hence, it is particularly susceptible to reinscription of the heterosexual contract. Whereas heterosexual couples are presumed to have ontological status as men and women, the butch in the lesbian duo, unless she passes for a "man," is the most visible performance of gender. Therefore, within the terms of the specular economy only the butch is a "real" lesbian, but she paradoxically attains her status in the real through her consummate imitation. Her "reality" as a lesbian is based on her ability to foreground the counterfeiting of gender; "seeing" her thus points to the real as merely another formation of the imaginary. If sighting the butch produces a recognition of the instability of gender, this seeing nonetheless retains, indeed depends upon, the facticity of sex. As the figure who makes possible the entry of lesbians into the visible, the butch balances uneasily on the divide between disruption of rigid heterosexual sign systems and assimilation or reification of the heterosexual dyad.

Lesbian performers who appropriate representations of heterosexual romance, as Weaver and Shaw do in *Anniversary Waltz*, while simultaneously performing the subculturally constructed butch-femme roles, might be read as deploying a tactic similar to the "Principle of Reverse," which Tania Modleski describes as the mimicry of "oppressed groups, who often appear to acquiesce in the oppressor's ideas about it, thus producing a double meaning: the same language or act simultaneously confirms the oppressor's stereotypes of the oppressed and offers a dissenting and empowering view for those in the know."[13] This principle has its obvious limitations as a political and representational strategy, for it presumes a stable knowledge, experience, and identity for the group "in the know," as well as for the group of oppressors. And for the strategy to be effective it depends on the inability of members of the oppressor group to cross over into the marginalized group. Thus, while it effects a kind of subversive catharsis for the oppressed group, it reifies the dominant constructions of members of that group.

Another kind of parody appropriates not the dominant group's constructions of the subjected but, rather, the dominant group's self-generated images of itself. Weaver and Shaw's butch-femme role playing might be understood as the simultaneous deployment of *both* parodic strategies. From the dominant cultural perspective their enactment of butch-femme could be read as an example of Modleski's "principle of reverse." That is to say, they seem to acquiesce to the cultural construction of butch-femme as imitations, and thus reinscriptions of heterosexuality's signs, but offer a subversive reading for lesbians. On the other hand, stealing their images from popular heterosexual romance rituals could be read as a parodic assault on their value as well as their stability. In either case, however, the reception of their performance would still depend on the heterosexual/homosexual binary's rigidity. Reversal and parody do not offer ways past this impasse. What is seen remains their *difference* from heterosexuality, and it is a difference that is "othered," which is to say that they inhabit a negative semantic space. Within these strategies "lesbian" has no content outside the representation of heterosexuality, which remains the norm, the neutral, substantive position that makes the marginal position visible only as alterity. The heterosexually-positioned spectator is likely to see the butch as a cross-dressed female, missing the radically unsettling concept of drag, and the femme as a stable representation of the feminine woman. This is precisely the way that nineteenth-century sexologists constructed their distinctions between "true inverts" and "inverts" who were not essentially inverted but merely sometimes responsive to the seductions of the real inverts. Even Havelock Ellis, however, had to admit that there was some disturbing fluidity between these roles.[14]

Since Weaver and Shaw do not remain fixed within the femme and butch roles, but rather alternate between them, they could be seen as performing that fluidity. However, the neat conflation of sex and gender, which makes possible the spectatorial response that heterosexualizes these lesbian performers, is not easily undone through alternations. For, much like the principle of reverse, alternations still fail to interrogate the constitution of the group in the know. The question remains: What is it that those who presumably know, *know,* and does what they know constitute who they are, or does who they are constitute what they know? In other words, these performances and their reception in a variety of contexts produce another set of questions: Does identity get constructed from a shared body of knowledge? Or does identity produce a set of experiences that is then constituted as knowledge? More broadly, how does one come to claim a lesbian identity? Is it something that can be seen and thus identified by a spectator? Are there boundaries that surround the lesbian identity, and, if so, who possesses the specular ability to determine where those boundaries begin and end? It is precisely in and around these questions that the anxiety of identity and identifications arises. How can performers like Split Britches hold in tension the *performative* nature of lesbian identity (the constructionist perspective) without erasing the material and historical reality of lesbian lives?

Dolan's earlier argument that lesbian performers such as Weaver and Shaw successfully accomplish the disruption of sexual difference is based to a large extent on the performance of gender in excess. She contends, for example, that "exaggerating stereotypes in the lesbian context foregrounds gender as unnatural construction."[15] Dolan reminds her readers, however, that she is speaking, and spectating, from within a context that is primarily, if not exclusively, lesbian. Thus, she acknowledges that Lois Weaver's femme "sendup" Tammy Whynot depends largely on a shared perception of lesbians from the community, who know one another and who thus have an insider's view of Weaver's performance. "This intertextuality," Dolan writes, "helps to create the representation's shared meanings."[16] The "lesbian performative context" seems finally to depend largely, if not absolutely, upon lesbians constituting the audience. Thus, Dolan tacitly assumes a stable identity for lesbians, who recognize other lesbians and share an understanding of gender as role playing. Teresa de Lauretis has argued that Dolan's argument begs the question of lesbian desire as it is based on "the presumption of a unified lesbian viewer/reader, gifted with undivided and non-contradictory subjectivity."[17] Dolan's argument is grounded in a widely shared concern that the radical destabilization of the lesbian subject position effects an ontological purge that empties "lesbian" of all content. Case shares this concern when she writes:

> the revision of simpler terms into more complex, heterogeneous ones has caused the evacuation of key sites. At this point in time, some feminist theorists acknowledge the necessity for reinhabiting in some way, the term "women" for political praxis as well as terms such as "lesbian."[18]

Valid as this concern may be, it risks reinstating a metaphysics of substance in order to maintain a political perspective that can be referred to as lesbian. Weaver and Shaw's radical deconstruction of heterosexuality and its iconic rituals seems to me to challenge the construction of the heterosexual/homosexual binary, adulterating the first term and foregrounding the *production* of the second term. Thus, *both* categories are destabilized in this representation.

By now we are all familiar with the cultural critique of identity as a fiction. Following Foucault, many cultural theorists have accepted as axiomatic that the category of homosexuality is a recent phenomena, constructed by late nineteenth-century sexologists in an effort to shore up the coherency of heterosexual identity. The historicizing, or genealogical, approach permits us to understand how the primary term in a binary produces its secondary term as a supplement that is somewhat occluded but never erased, for the secondary term is necessary to maintain an illusion of the primary term's reality. To put it simply, without "homosexuality" there would be no "heterosexuality." Given that these categories have already been successfully deployed, however, gays and lesbians are caught in the dilemma of having to maintain a coherent, albeit fictive, identity, while simultaneously striving to undo the binary distinction. These two projects are obviously at cross-purposes, and the choice of which strategy to deploy must take into account a whole range of temporal and spatial differences as well as attuning political and rhetorical strategies to take into account race, sex, class, ethnic, age, and a host of other differences. A pure or absolute adherence to a constructionist theory cannot possibly be politically efficacious for everyone, everywhere.

Gayatri's Spivak's concept of "strategic essentialism" seemed to offer a productive solution to this dilemma,[19] but, as Judith Butler has pointed out, strategies are dangerously inclined to exceed their intentions.[20] In addition, lesbian and gay strategic essentialism is particularly difficult to constitute. Whereas political essentialisms of race and gender may resort to color or sex to ground their strategies (not, of course, without their attendant risks), sexual identities would seem to rely not on some presumably visible difference but, instead, on acts that cannot be marked. Lesbian and gay identities are thus more radically unstable than racial or gender identifies, and any effort to identify lesbians and gays would require a violent invasiveness. Naming oneself lesbian or gay remains not only an act of resistance, but also it would seem to carry a necessary authority. Challenging one's announced sexual positionality is, in Eve Sedgwick's words, "the most intimate violence possible" and "central to the modern history of homophobic oppression."[21]

By extension, universalizing, or "heterosexualizing," lesbian performers is also an act of intimate violence. The reviewer who could see no reason why Split Britches shouldn't be "booked on the next Bob Hope special" demonstrated the violent erasure of Weaver and Shaw's identities in a gesture that is representative of spectators' response to this performance.[22] In the name of "humanistic truth" about relationships the violence of liberalism becomes patent. Shaw and Weaver attempt to negotiate the treacherous crossroads between identity politics and destabilized identifications as they chart the history of their seductions. A key narrative in this mapping is the story of how they met, fell in love, and "married."

Shaw was traveling with "Hot Peaches," a gay theater group consisting mostly of drag queens. Weaver was traveling with the feminist theater group Spiderwoman. They met on tour in Berlin. Spiderwoman had arrived without their costumes; feminists at the time were busy, as Weaver says, "deconstructing the feminine image," hence they were accustomed to wearing old clothes, "rags with baby's toys tied around their belts."[23] That night, however, they went on stage wearing the resplendent gowns and sequined accessories of the drag queens, and Weaver "knew that somehow they would never be the same again." And, indeed, before the tour was over Weaver would be transformed from a drab feminist into a sexy femme, playing to Shaw's butch.

This representation points to sexual preference as a choice that is not bound to a gendered object. Although Shaw challenges Weaver, in the course of the seduction, to admit that she is "really a lesbian," Weaver insists on being persuaded rather than confessing, or "realizing," her desire. Shaw begins her seduction of Weaver by asking her a series of questions—Are you a vegetarian? Do you ever wear vests? Do you have cats—that parody the clichéd signifiers of "lesbian" from the 1970s and 1980s. And they nearly work to convince Weaver that she *is* a lesbian since she bears the cultural markings. Finally, however, this part of the seduction fails, for Weaver does not accept the cultural signs as the mark of identity. This rejection of an underlying identity exemplifies Case's argument that butch-femme role playing effects a seduction of the sign system.[24] This part of the seduction, however, does *not* win Weaver over to a lesbian identity. Rather, it is only when Shaw taps into one of Weaver's former identifications, her desire to *be* Katherine Hepburn, that she succumbs to Shaw's proposal and thus *becomes* "a lesbian." Notably, other formulations of famous butch-femme couples do not have the seductive appeal of the Katherine Hepburn–Spencer Tracy duo, which is based on Weaver's *identification,* not her *identity.* Weaver does not delight in the notion of playing Alice B. Toklas to Shaw's Gertrude Stein. Nor did Shaw's fantasy of playing James Dean work when she fell in love with a woman who thought she was Montgomery Clift.

The history of their failed seductions elicits tremendous laughter from the audience, probably due in part to the playful pathology of "becoming" a historical persona—but also, I think, it is a laughter that recognizes the mutability of identities in a history of identifications. In the first scenario Shaw won't play James Dean to a woman's Montgomery Clift. If her desire is to inhabit a female body with a male gender fantasy, she does not want her female lover to inhabit the same gender identity; her desire is not for symmetry. Nor does she desire a man who thinks he is Lauren Bacall, that is, a male sex with a female gender identity. In this scenario the biological sexes are different, but the gender identities remain symmetrical. Weaver and Shaw are struggling to locate a fantasy that will facilitate their mutual seduction, and it is when Shaw taps into Weaver's old identification, with her roommate, which seemed to be working just fine until the heterosexist censors stepped in, that they arrive at the right "formula." That is, they share the desire to inhabit female bodies with psychically fluid gender identities. Activating their sexual desire depends on a mutual recognition that gender is performance—seducing the sign system—but "becoming a lesbian" for Weaver is not the acquisition of an identity; rather, it is the accessing of a former identification that was suppressed by the dominant cultural censors. Rather than showing their lesbian "identities," they demonstrate the construction of their desires through the history of their identifications. Identity itself thus loses its meaning as a fixed construct, and sexuality is performed as a historical process that is both social and psychic. "Lesbian" retains its meaning in this context as a vantage point, a perspective, a desire that permits them to erase the margins of gender and evade the conflation of biological sex and gender. Identifications, not identities, constitute their seduction.

If lesbian identities are not necessary to the circulation of their desire, fantasy identifications that refuse modern constructions of same or opposite sex desire—that is, gendered object choices—*constitute* that desire. Consequently, the possibility is open for spectators to substitute their own identifications or to overlay them onto the performers, thus "universalizing" the performance. Identifications that are not wedded to modern constructs of sex and gender may also produce responses that are homophobic, when the reviewer assumes heterosexuality as normative. Thus, a reviewer for *Commonweal* found himself in the "minority of the enthusiastic spectators with whom [he] saw the piece." He was only "mildly interested" in the romance plot of the performance, not because the story was lesbian, he hastens to remind us, but because he simply has little taste for other people's sex lives in general.[25] Unusual as that may be—as he himself reminds us, most people have a very strong interest in other people's sex lives—I am certainly in no position to evaluate his sexual fantasies. Nonetheless, his reminder that his distaste for the performance has nothing to do with the "butch-femme relationship" would certainly sound like a gratuitous defense if he were reviewing a play about heterosexual romance. Given that much American theater is built around the romantic/sexual lives of heterosexual couples, this reviewer must have a difficult time finding anything to his taste in American theater. His closing sentence, however, tells us much more about his defensiveness: "[*Anniversary Waltz*] is a celebratory declaration in the face of an *essentially* homophobic society."[26]

Does he mean that American society is inherently, indispensably, requisitely homophobic, as in the ordinary dictionary definition of *essentially*? If so, then we must conclude that his response is also homophobic, since, minority member that he claims to be notwithstanding, one can scarcely attribute to him an absolute transcendence of this "essentially homophobic society." In strict usage that which is essential is necessary for something to exist; thus, following the syntactical logic of his sentence, homophobia is essential for society to exist. If that is the case, then everyone's response to *Anniversary Waltz* must have been homophobic.

Both official reviewers erased the specificity of the performance as lesbian, one in order to validate it, the other in order to defend himself against an anticipated charge of heterosexism, as did most of the unofficial responses. In both cases, however, their rhetoric betrays what can indeed be read as homophobic responses. While this is obviously not a politically desirable effect, it is, I think, the effect of a desire that is historically specific, that is, produced by the modern alignment of sexual desire with opposite sex/gender choice. Thus, the heterosexualizing rhetoric exceeds itself by evoking precisely that which it desires to erase: same-sex desire. While this does not take us past the impasse, it does permit the opening of a space in which we can read the ways in which differences get subsumed under sameness.

Split Britches not only challenges fixed identities; the group also disturbs the integrity of the rituals that underpin its performance. Weaver and Shaw throw their own party to surprise the invited guests, playing on the conventional actor/audience dynamic of realistic theater while reversing the expected setup for a "surprise party." Anniversaries, as celebrations of returns to origins, are exploded. The two are never sure exactly when they met, how long they have been together, or "which time to count" as the beginning. It's not that they can't remember when they first had sex, but that they don't know exactly what constitutes having had it. If they are here to celebrate anything, it is the deconstruction of the whole notion of origins, and most significant among them are the originary identities that conceal their own genealogy and reproduce oppressive categories like sex and gender. Heterosexuality and homosexuality are *both* historicized in moments like these; they are shown to have a set of signifiers that can be rearranged, redeployed, and thus rendered incoherent.

If some spectators did not *see* lesbians in this performance, it is because these lesbians resist and mock the permissible visibility of dominant sexual discourse. Shaw, in particular, as the butch, upsets mainstream specularity. In one scene in particular she calls attention to her "to-be-looked-at-ness" by recalling a childhood experience at a fair, where she went to see the fat lady. At this moment she emphasizes her desire "to be alone" while she changes from her suit to an evening gown. Her strip teases out the spectators' voyeuristic pleasure then disappoints it by reminding us that we are all always already objectified by the gaze. Like the fat lady who knew Shaw had come "to see her being fat," Shaw knows, and announces, that some spec-

tators have come to see her being a lesbian. As he puts *on* her stocking
and fastens the garters, a reversal of an iconic moment in traditional
striptease, she says to the audience: "You paid to see me. You won't
get your money back. Am I worth five dollars? I'm a mother. Are
you willing to pay to see a good lesbian mother?" The audience, of
course, cannot see a lesbian mother, no matter how much they pay.
Shaw doubly disrupts their expectations of looking at identifiable
objects. Indeed, the scopophilic gaze does not allow lesbian bodies *or*
maternal bodies into its field of vision. The dominant gaze in this
scene is Shaw's; like the fat lady, she looks back and knows that some
spectators have come to see her being a lesbian. But there is no
"being" to be seen, only a succession of fantasy formations. These
lesbians do not seek visibility among the negative semantic spaces and
cognitive gaps of the patriarchal unconscious; rather, they seize the
apparatus, distort its mirrors, and lead the audience into the intersti-
tial dancing space, where lesbian subjectivity refuses the dichotomy
of the revealed and the concealed.

In her article "Toward a Butch-Femme Aesthetic" Case proposes
that the first task necessary for the strong subject position of the
butch-femme duo to emerge is for "the lesbian subject of feminist
theory to come out of the closet."[27] But, if this task must be accomplished *before* the lesbian-feminist subject can emerge, then what happens when the butch-femme duo "comes out" in the performative
context itself, and before a dominant, rather than a subcultural, audience? In order to establish the textual or contextual situation in which
such an audience can recognize the performers *as* lesbian, without a
pre-performance identification *with* them, we would have to inquire
into the performative operation of "coming out." As the reception
of this performance demonstrates, and as any lesbian or gay person
knows, "coming out" is no simple operation. As lesbian comedian
Lisa Kron puts it in one of her monologues, "you might as well come
out, because no one will believe you anyway."[28] What Eve Sedgwick
has called the "epistemological privilege of unknowing"[29]—that is,
the way in which dominant cultural discourses advantage the interlocutor whose ignorance allows him to define the terms of exchange—is
bound to be powerfully operative in a performative context that
moves outside the subcultural security where groups like Split
Britches have hitherto performed. While I agree with Case that some
texts, like the plays of Jane Chambers, manage to remain "lesbian"

whenever and wherever they are performed,[30] I also find that Chambers's plays are not engaged in deconstructive analysis of gender or sexual identities. Groups like Split Britches are valued by lesbian feminist theorists precisely because they strive to negotiate the perilous project of undoing the conflation of sex/gender/sexuality by historicizing it. At the same time they are charged with the strategic project of making lesbians visible. Depending upon whether a spectator is invested in the production of visible identities or whether she is looking at the performance and making identifications, Split Britches is bound to be caught in the clash of conflicting desires.

Case has argued that the identifications in the butch/femme seduction are "camp assimilations of dominant culture" that play on, not to, the phallic economy.[31] Camp, however, has something in common with negation; it affirms what it denies. It is aggressive but not indifferent. The positions of "having" and "being" the phallus are ironized, reversed, alternated, but they are not undone, even when they are exchanged between women. This makes any logic of "twos," of coupling, problematic. If it takes two to make a lesbian, as Teresa de Lauretis has argued,[32] it's no simple matter to secure a reception context so that it's not one to have and one to be the phallus. Butler has suggested that the power of lesbian subjectivity may be not in appearance but in disappearance, in "letting that which cannot fully appear . . . persist in its disruptive promise."[33]

That which cannot fully appear, however, could too easily be read as a hysterical symptom that is permitted and recuperated through the discourse of bisexuality. Lesbian desire, on the other hand, is less like a hysterical symptom and more like a hallucination— "the return of the Real that has never been signified." *Anniversary Waltz* seems to play self-consciously with this difference. As I have said before, the anniversary is a hysterical occasion, "a turning back to the day," which is evoked through partial objects intended to summon a prior plenitude. Weaver and Shaw, however, are not remembering, Rather, they recreate the seduction as if it were happening in the present. In hysterical discourse the neurotic symptom interprets what has been repressed. But in the hallucination what cannot be signified in the symbolic nonetheless makes an appearance. Both signify gaps in the symbolic order that are, according to Lacan, "voids as significant as the plenums." In the hallucination, however, the spectator "halts before the strangeness of the signified" because it produces what "has been originally cut out of the Symbolic itself."[34] If spectators to this event could only see lesbians by incorporating them into their heterosexual logic, their response nonetheless made visible the heterosexual imperative of the specular economy. Only those whom Kate Davy calls the "literate perverts" were able to see the hallucination.[35]

Within the terms of the specular economy the lesbian can only call attention to herself as the "impossible-real."[36] But in this very impossibility lies the potency of her effects. For Split Britches lesbian subjectivity is that which refuses the dichotomy of the revealed and the concealed. Whereas the hysterical symptom signifies repression and bisexuality, the hallucination is the gaze at what is unseen, what never comes to light in the Symbolic but must logically appear in the Real. If the hallucination arises from the Real, the domain outside of symbolization, it also points to the incompleteness of the Symbolic. Unlike the "lack" that upholds the Symbolic order, the lesbian as the impossible-real is that before which the Imaginary falters and the Symbolic stumbles.

Lacan locates the possibility for a positive subjectivity outside the Other in fantasy identity. He tells the story of a man who dreamt of being a butterfly and upon awakening asked himself how he could know that he was not now a butterfly dreaming of being a man. He was not a fool—one who believes in his immediate identity with himself. Rather, he was a man in symbolic reality but a butterfly in the real of his desire.[37] If the symbolic order is the social order of a masculine imaginary, within its terms lesbian identities are hallucinations. When they nonetheless appear they indicate that the symbolic order is itself a fantasy construction. When Shaw says in *Anniversary Waltz*, "All my fantasies were becoming realities, so I went to see a shrink," she indicates that "awakening" to the reality of the Symbolic would be entering into a fantasy where the real of her lesbian desire could not take place.

NOTES

1. For an excellent discussion of essentialism as a "red flag (if not a red herring)" (50) see Naomi Schor, "This Essentialism Which Is Not One," *Differences* 1, no. 2 (Summer 1989): 38–58. She argues: "If we are to move beyond

the increasingly sterile conflict over essentialism, we must begin by deessentializing essentialism, for no more than deconstruction *essentialism is not one"* (41).

2. Jill Dolan, *The Feminist Spectator as Critic* (1988; reprint, Ann Arbor: University of Michigan Press, 1991), 119–21.

3. Sue-Ellen Case, "A Case concerning Hughes," *Drama Review* 33 (Winter 1989): 12.

4. Holly Hughes, "A Case concerning Hughes," *Drama Review* 33 (Winter 1989): 16.

4. Lynda Hart, "Canonizing Lesbians?" in *Modern American Drama: The Female Canon,* ed. June Schlueter (Madison, N.J.: Fairleigh Dickinson University Press, 1990), 275–92.

6. Eve Kosofsky Sedgwick, *Epistemology of the Closet* (Berkeley: University of California Press, 1990), 61.

7. Jill Dolan, "Practicing Cultural Disruptions: Gay and Lesbian Representation and Sexuality," in *Critical Theory and Performance,* ed. Janelle Reinelt and Joe Roach (Ann Arbor: University of Michigan Press, 1992).

8. Thea Diamond, "Two for the (Lesbian) Seesaw," *Welcomat/After Dark,* 28 February 1990.

9. Peggy Phelan, *Unmarked: The Politics of Performance* (New York and London: Routledge, 1993).

10. Phelan, intro., *Unmarked.*

11. Diana Fuss, intro., *inside/out: Lesbian Theories, Gay Theories,* ed. Diana Fuss (New York and London: Routledge, 1991), 4.

12. Judith Butler, "Imitation and Gender Insubordination," in *inside/out,* 20.

13. Tania Modleski, "Feminism and the Power of Interpretation: Some Critical Readings." *Feminist Studies/Critical Studies,* ed. Teresa de Lauretis (Bloomington: Indiana University Press, 1986), 129.

14. Havelock, Ellis, *Studies in the Psychology of Sex: Sexual Inversion,* vol. 2 (Philadelphia: F. A. Davis, 1904).

15. Dolan, *Feminist Spectator,* 70.

16. Ibid.

17. Teresa de Lauretis, "Sexual Indifference and Lesbian Representation," *Theatre Journal* 40, no. 2 (May 1988): 155–77.

18. Sue-Ellen Case, intro., *Performing Feminisms* (Baltimore: Johns Hopkins University Press, 1991).

19. Gayatri Spivak, "Subaltern Studies: Deconstructing Historiography," *In Other Worlds: Essays in Cultural Politics* (New York: Methuen, 1987).

20. Judith Butler, *Gender Trouble: Feminism and the Subversion of Identity* (New York: Routledge, 1990), 4.

21. Sedgwick, *Epistemology,* 26.

22. Diamond, "Two," 11.

23. *Anniversary Waltz* is unpublished. All quotations are taken from a tape of the performance in Philadelphia in February 1990.

24. Sue-Ellen Case, "Toward a Butch-Femme Aesthetic," in *Making a Spectacle: Feminist Essays on Contemporary Women's Theatre,* ed. Lynda Hart (Ann Arbor: University of Michigan Press, 1989), 282–99.

25. Gerald Weales, "Meeting and Melding: Three Couples," *Commonweal* 20 (April 1990): 259.

26. Ibid.

27. Case, "Butch-Femme," 283.

28. Lisa Kron's monologue was part of the same festival of plays. It is untitled and unpublished.

29. Sedgwick, *Epistemology,* 4–5.

30. Case, "Case concerning Hughes."

31. Case, "Butch-Femme," 291.

32. Teresa de Lauretis, "Film and the Primal Fantasy—One More Time: On Sheila McLaughlin's *She Must Be Seeing Things,*" Working Papers, Center for Twentieth Century Studies, University of Wisconsin, Milwaukee, 1990.

33. Butler, "Imitation and Gender," 29.

34. Anthony Wilden, "Lacan and the Discourse of the Other," in *Speech and Language in Psychoanalysis,* ed. Jacques Lacan, trans. Anthony Wilden (Baltimore: Johns Hopkins Press, 1968), 281.

35. Kate Davy, unpublished paper delivered at the American Theatre in Higher Education conference, seattle, August 1991.

36. The "real-impossible" is defined in the translator's note to Lacan's *Ecrits,* trans. Alan Sheridan (New York: W. W. Norton, 1977): "that which is lacking in the symbolic order, the ineliminable residue of all articulation, the foreclosed element" (x).

37. Slavoj Zizek uses this Lacanian story to explain the function of ideology: "not to offer us a point of escape from our reality but to offer us the social reality itself as an escape from some traumatic, real kernel." It brings to mind for him the "hippy" slogan of the 1960s: "reality is for those who cannot support the dream" (*The Sublime Object of Ideology* [London: Verso, 1989], 45).

Performing Histories

Chapter 6

Unspeakable Practices, Unnatural Acts:
The Taboo Art of Karen Finley

C. Carr

A raw quaking id takes the stage, but at first you don't notice since she's wearing an over-the-hill Sunday school dress or a Sandra Dee cocktail party outfit and she's stepping shyly to the mike looking nervous. But then her pupils contract as if she's disappeared inside herself. She's slipped into that personalized primeval ooze now, and the floodgates fly open in a loud declamation: *"No, Herr Schmidt, I will not shit in your mouth, even if I do get to know you. . . ."* Or, *"I go down on that ass with my mouth, my penis still kinda high and hard and I suck suck suck my own cum outta your butt juice with a little bit of yum yum yum yum yum baby liquid shit mixed up with that cum, baby. You can jerk off on my pancakes anytime."* She might be stealing the male voice like that. Might be spitting on the stage. Tearing at her taffetas. Smearing food on herself. She might say or do anything up there. Onstage Karen Finley represents a frightening and rare presence—an unsocialized woman.

Finley performs on the club circuit, wafting on to the stage in her polyester good-girl getup at one or two in the morning to wail like some degenerate apparition about incest, priests' assholes, the cum on the bedpost, bulimics upchucking in their stilettos. The fuck-and-shit vocabulary draws shrieks, back-talk, occasional hysteria from the rowdy drunk crowds. But Finley says, "I'm really never interested in the sexual point in my work. I'm really interested in the pathos." In fact, her monologues are obscenity in its purest form— never just a litany of four-letter expletives but an attempt to express

141

emotions for which there are perhaps no words. An attempt to approach the unspeakable.

Finley began performing in 1979 after her father's suicide. She'd been exclusively a visual artist before that, but, she said, "I had difficulty being alone and doing static work when I was feeling such active emotion." She's still working out of the emotional range she discovered in her rage, the skinless panorama of taboo. She says the charge she gets from performing balances the pain she feels about his death.

Deathcakes and Autism was an early performance piece based on the events of her father's funeral, where everyone became preoccupied with the food brought to the bereaved. "People were actually having arguments over which ham to eat. Or saying, 'Was it much of a mess? Did you clean it up?' while they were bringing in two dozen Tollhouse cookies." In that disconnection between custom and emotion, Finley felt she'd become autistic. When she returned to college, the San Francisco Art Institute, she felt an "incredible yearning" to spill it, to get up and tell the awfullest truth in front of people.

The result is both fascinating and horrifying to behold, because audiences can't help but recognize their own most mortifying obsessions in the fast-flowing bile. Finley rivets, but she doesn't entertain. There's no nonsense here about taking an audience out of itself and into the performer's world. Even an artist like Spalding Gray—whose work tells the ongoing story of his own life—uses an I'm-not-acting persona, removed at some level from a "real" self. Finley doesn't offer such wholeness; she presents a persona that has shattered, a self unable to put a face on things.

Finley told me once that she thought some women performance artists were getting more hard-edged, less subtle, while men were learning to be quiet, more contained and passive. Certainly women have no tradition of foul-mouthed visionaries, as men do—Céline, Genet, Lenny Bruce et al. But at least women now have a sort of rude girl network that provides a context for outrageous work. Think of Lydia Lunch and that baby-faced dominatrix image so startling in the late 1970s or the obscene and sexually demanding narrator in any Kathy Acker story or the oddball menace of Dancenoise (Lucy Sexton, Anne Iobst) onstage at 8BC swigging "blood" from coffee cans, tearing dolls limb from limb, shouting, "Give me liberty or give me head!"

Finley, age thirty, grew up in the Chicago suburb of Evanston, the oldest of six children in a somewhat bohemian family dominated by strong and troubled personalities. Her father was a jazz drummer who would quit music periodically to sell vacuum cleaners. Her mother ran a sewing business out of their house and would involve the whole family in her obsession of the moment, which might be Wagner or Jungian psychology or health food. There was never much income.

There *were* lots of people passing through—musicians, customers, and people with problems whom her mother would "adopt." For a number of years a deranged aunt would call them "60 times a day. . . . So whatever was going on, the phone would be ringing, and she would come over to the house with bird crosses and she once tried to kill me with chairs. . . . We would have the police over at our house all the time." One of Finley's grandmothers believed Martians were sending radiation beams to the house, and, when the family visited her, she sometimes had them wear little rubber hats for protection.

Finley began to "perform" as a teenager. Her favorite routine was to stage an epileptic seizure in front of a restaurant—or pretend to vomit—to see whether or not people would keep eating. Mostly, they would. Then, because she and her high school friends had read about Happenings, they created some of their own—again, hardly more than pranks, but like the traditional avant-garde, aimed at interrupting the decorum of everyday life. For example, they covered hallway entrances at school with aluminum foil and waited for people to burst through them. This was the early 1970s, "the time of do-your-own-thing," as Finley put it, "so I just pushed it as far as possible."

No one ever discouraged these playful shock tactics. Today her mother is one of Finley's biggest fans. "She gives me pointers. If I'm in Chicago, she always helps me with my stage work. Actually she usually tells me she thinks I should go farther." In one of Finley's more shocking routines, she pulls her pants down and smears canned yams up her ass and talks—in male persona—about sticking yams "*up my granny's butt but I never touch her twat, baby.*" Even Finley's grandmother has seen this. "I'm really open. I tell people what I do." She showed me a "review" her grandmother had then written on some flowered stationery. "She thinks I'm talented but a toiletmouth."

One night last April at Danceteria, Finley suddenly appeared onstage around 1 A.M. in a tatty satin prom gown. For hours the stoned punky crowd had been juicing up on liquor, hard rock, and the tape loop of slash-and-gore film highlights playing on all the monitors. In her usual confrontational stance Finley shouted, "You leather kind of folk with your spiked hair, I love to think about you masturbating!"

She told them how she was gonna put some peaches up her cunt, then get one of "you mo'fo's" under her party dress and tell him *"Baby, eat those peaches and cream,"* and then how she'd make a visit to the nuns' house because *"I can't go to sleep unless I hear the sound of pussy,"* which she followed with a fierce declamation on the mung juice torture—pregnant Eskimo women with corks in their vaginas and men beating on their bellies—and then the liquid shit number (*"What I do is I suck, baby"*). She punctuated the moment by spilling a can of Hershey's syrup down her dress front.

A powerful charge of hysteria ran through the crowd. Two young guys next to me were twitching and squealing and bent double. Finley then hiked up her gown and turned her naked butt to the audience. "This is 'Yams Up My Granny's Ass,'" she announced. "OH GOD!" one of the men next to me screamed. He and his buddy began throwing lit cigarettes at her. They were out of control. Finley cut the performance off abruptly a few minutes later and had the guys bounced.

But the incident depressed her. It wasn't a first. Last New Year's Eve at Danceteria, men in the audience began yelling "Whore!" (She told them, "Go back to New Jersey and stop coming to our nightclubs to get laid.") And one night at 8BC three men dropped their pants to their ankles during her monologue. (They pulled them back up when she declared their dicks too small to interest her.)

Obviously, a man doing the same routine wouldn't be confronted like this—nor would the act have the same meaning. A filthy woman (in any sense of the word) has stepped further outside social mores than a man can possibly get. Hard-working men get dirty. They're a common sight in soap commercials, taking their showers. But that kind of dirt on a woman signifies "crazy" or "victim." No positive meaning is possible. Just as obscenity coming from a man asserts a tough manliness, in a woman's mouth it signals a threatening femininity, a banshee.

It's hardly surprising, though, that Finley felt an affinity for the work of two men who had made of themselves monstrous Others—the Kipper Kids. The Kippers became infamous in the 1970s for performances that deconstructed every learned nicety into the raw human behavior observable in infants. Dressed in jockstraps and swimming caps, pouring food over each other, the Kippers burped, snarled, and grunted their way toward a state of transcendent gross-out. *LAICA Journal* described a rather typical piece in 1975 as "a Freudian nightmare-comedy of oral and anal obsession."

One of the Harry Kippers, Brian Routh, was Finley's graduate advisor at the San Francisco Art Institute. They developed a personal and artistic relationship and eventually married. "We have a real similar philosophy and both push our work to the limit, so we were very good for each other," says Finley. (They've now separated but remain friends.)

The Kipper Kids were scheduled to tour Europe in 1981, when Martin von Haselberg (the other Harry Kipper) couldn't go. Finley replaced him. She and Routh then touched off a near riot in Cologne at the Theater for the World Festival, when they appeared as Eva Braun and Adolf Hitler.

According to an account in *Unsound* magazine, corroborated by Finley, she and Kipper/Routh had installed several rotting carcasses of beef in the space, where it was SRO—over eight hundred people—on each of their four nights. Kipper goose-stepped and saluted, naked from the waist down. Finley wore a corset and garter belt, and, because she had diarrhea, periodically took a dump on one side of the stage. On one of the nights Kipper sang a Johnny Mathis hit, then went to the bowl where Finley had been relieving herself and lapped up the shit. (Like Hitler used to do, myth has it.)

The audience became increasingly agitated. Finley stuffed toy sharks with hot dogs and sauerkraut and hung them from her body for Kipper to eat. They began reporting anti-Semitic incidents they had witnessed in Cologne, then began to rub chocolate pudding on each other's asses. Spectators started arguing among themselves. "Get off!" "No, she's right . . ." "We don't need to hear this about Hitler," and so on. Kipper and Finley crawled around drinking beer out of bowls. One faction in the audience protested that this gesture said Germans were dogs. Finally, a Spanish woman, a Nazi sympathizer, ran to the stage and attacked Finley with a mop. Kipper threw her off, but then a couple hundred others got up and rushed the stage. The performers made their exit.

One group in the audience had found it all wildly funny—among them the filmmaker Rainer Werner Fassbinder. Fascinated by the crowd's hysteria, he came back the next night to film the show. Fassbinder died soon afterward, however, and the film has never been shown.

Earlier this year, Finley got a letter from *Playboy*, asking to film one of her sexy performances for their video magazine. They hadn't as yet seen one. A couple months later, she got a second letter announcing that they'd changed their minds: this was not mainstream sexuality.

Finley offered to read me the letter but couldn't find it. Perhaps she'd thrown it away. She doesn't like to "harbor badness." As she remembered it, *"Playboy* thought I wouldn't be appreciated by mass culture, which to me says I'm not like a blond sex kitten who deals with passivity and the typical heterosexual way. . . . My work is basically exposing that we as a people really don't deal with that *[Playboy]* type of sexuality."

Then last month Finley was interviewed by someone from *Chic,* a porn magazine. "He asked me these questions like 'Does your lover ever feel you're talking about him?' I mean—really—sometimes I would have to set him straight. I don't feel that my work is pornography at all." As Finley sees it, she's just telling it like it is.

But you can still get censored for that. Police stopped a couple of her performances in San Francisco. Her reputation began to precede her so that, when a Los Angeles club booked her, they told her "no four-letter words and don't show your body." She cancelled. Then last summer, this performer who once told *Soho Arts Weekly* that "if I wasn't avant-garde maybe I'd have my own TV show or be on *Cagney and Lacy,*" was part of the *Mike's Talent Show* that Michael Smith had pulled together for a cable TV taping. But then she wouldn't tone it down for the tube. "I'm an Ass Man" hit the cutting room floor.

Finley plays the club circuit—Palladium, Limelight, The Cat Club—and she's been booked next year for a run at The Kitchen. But right now her only regular venue is the monthly No Entiendes cabaret at Danceteria, hosted by Haoui Montaug and Anita Sarko.

No Entiendes revels in the bad. All kinds of bad. In fact, the acts in this mutant Gong Show are *so* bad that Finley thinks its devoted followers must be "a cult of sadists and masochists." She's been a regular there since last August and also works at Danceteria as a bartender.

Given what Finley puts out in performance, you might expect her to be a tough cookie offstage. But that's hardly the case. She has a sensitive, if blunt, manner, and a definite sense of propriety. When she got some clippings together for me about her work, she mentioned that the review that obviously had a piece missing had praised her but had been uncomplimentary to another, better-known performer. She'd cut off that bit, she said, because giving it out to people would be rude.

When Finley watches videotapes of herself, she says, "I have to close my eyes. I don't know who that person is." She performs in a trance and has never rehearsed a piece. She doesn't even like going to sound checks, because it interferes with spontaneity. "I want the audience to see what I'm going through. I want to demystify this process you go through when you're trying to expose yourself. Also, these issues can't be packaged and polished. It's not like a talk about having a nice day. So it's important to have the rawness to it." Not that she's improvising, either. But if you've seen her do "I'm an Ass Man" eight times, you've seen it eight different ways.

She writes material out of what's floating in the cultural ether, stimulated by books and TV. One day at her apartment—neat, "airy," decorated with her paintings of people throwing up and shitting—Finley pulled some books from her shelf to show me how she might work. Take, say, *Psychoanalysis and Women* and *The Function of the Orgasm* and cross it in your mind with *Citizen Hughes* or *My Life with Jacqueline Kennedy*. She read from a random page in the *Psychoanalysis* book: "'Under optimal arousal conditions, women's orgasmic potential may be similar to that of the primates described.' Now *that* sentence I can do a lot with." She also uses autobiographical material, like the bit on that nice, nice man who was *so* nice that before he put the gun to his brain he laid down some cardboard to soak up the blood.

She also studies TV for women's fashions and roles. "The way they like to team the chicks up" on *Kate and Ally, Cagney and Lacey.*

The women with power who won't really use it—"and they're good women *because* they don't use it"—on *I Dream of Jeannie* and *Bewitched*. Television is the world of kitsch emotion. *The Dating Game, The Partridge Family, Dynasty*—to Finley these are deeply embarrassing shows, but all the more fascinating for that. "I feel personal humiliation for those people. Whenever I see Linda Evans walk in a room, I cannot watch the screen. Or Tony Danza. They're trying to humiliate themselves even more to get at something that deals with emotion."

Finley prefers to dive into the horror, of course. Years ago she even tried out for a *Dating Game* spot but was rejected. As if to finally exorcise the obsession, she staged her own version of the show at 8BC. Now she hosts *Bad Music Videos* for cable TV, along with art critic Carlo McCormick. "When I see The Captain and Tenille, I get really upset. Some people are like that when they see Ronald Reagan's face. They break out in a cold sweat. Some people are like that with their own parents. It's like an allergic reaction."

One night *Bad Music Videos* taped a religious show at The Limelight—Elvis Presley and others turning spirituality into a Lawrence Welk moment. Finley encouraged us to remember Presley's mother fixation, and to "think about what drugs he might be on." Just as she does in performance, she goes straight to the real dirt beneath the banal.

Finley told me she hoped she could do a cable TV special in the fall featuring women performers. She wouldn't label it a women's thing. She'd just exclude those others. "You know, the way men do it," she said.

Finley considers herself a feminist but is obviously working that red light area where feminists are known to disagree with one another. It isn't every feminist who idolizes Carol Doda, a burlesque dancer and one of the first women to get silicone implants. Finley loves burlesque—"the greatest theater in the world" and, to her, a female art form. "If I had a lot of money, I would open up a burlesque house—a really good one. It would be great, with the piano and women walking around in negligees."

Finley put herself through school working at strip joints in both Chicago and San Francisco. She was a hustler, getting the men to buy drinks at "two bucks a guy." Her career as a stripper had been brief, because she made the customers laugh. She considers herself lucky. Never had one bad experience. Says the men she serves now as a bartender at Danceteria are often harder to deal with.

She did not have the conventional feminist reaction to Judy Chicago's *Dinner Party* project, either. She thought it disgusting—memorializing women's achievements by sculpting their vaginas on plates. "Men would never have a show with, like, Abraham Lincoln's dick on a plate." She organized a party outside the Modern (with Bruce Pollack), to which people were asked to bring plates painted "with their favorite man's prick."

A few months back at a conference held by the Women's Caucus for the Arts, Finley's scheduled appearance on the "Hot and Nasty Humor Works" panel created political controversy when she told organizers she'd be doing "I Like the Dwarf on the Table When I Give Him Head." She considers this a pro-woman piece—a woman taking sexual control right there in the title. Caucus organizers asked her to change the title. Get rid of the word "dwarf." Call it "I Like the Person of Shorter Stature on the Table When I Give Him Head." It seems a feminist of shorter stature had complained about *dwarf,* deeply offended. Finley said she thought *dwarf* a beautiful word and wouldn't change it. The panel's moderator, Jerri Allyn, refused to drop Finley but agreed to let the feminist of shorter stature present her case—which Finley never heard because she got sick that day. A painful experience all round. But feminists fight like this over language because they know it controls the world.

Whatever might spew from the wound in the psyche Finley describes in the language of pornography. But she renders the pornography impotent. In this id-speak, shitting and vomiting and fucking are all equal. Desire attaches to disgust. Finley's work moves beyond rage to the trigger for that rage. To damage and longing, the desperate want for something, the hole in all of us that nothing ever fills. The unfulfillable yearning produces an orgy of rage: *"You take your salami and put it up the wrong alley boy, make it all brown and gooey like I wanna take a big brown hot smelly shit. . . ."*

Finley's characters have no boundaries. They flow into each other over the course of a monologue as it moves from one emotional peak to the next, the dislocated genders and narratives held together by a feverish dreamlike logic. The very boundaries of the body collapse. What's inside and what's out when the food is smeared on, not ingested?

It's a big bulimic landscape of consumption and expulsion out there. The constant fetishization of food makes Finley that monster of orality, the devouring woman. *"You aren't throwing up on my tuna casserole, honey; you throwin' up on your own tuna"* becomes the lyrical prelude to sex: *"I mean whenever my child says 'fuck you' I fuck him in the ass. I turn him over and fuck him in the ass. I mean like when I make my husband ooh when I make him his steak sandwich the way he likes it, he turns me over in the kitchen and lets me have it in the ass. He says that's the way you deserve it, baby."* This is penetration as both the desire to connect and the desire to punish. Here sex and rage are virtually the same impulse. And the gender difference based on possession or lack of a dick has disappeared.

Finley often appropriates the male point of view and male desire in her language. Or some woman character starts fucking whoever up the ass, magically acquiring the power of men. Her work returns again and again to oral or anal sex, usually associating them with power, as in the appalling, hilarious passage above (a pecking order of ass-fuckers). Or the story of Mr. Horse confronting his young daughter's friend in the bathroom one night (*"I need your strong mouth to suck the piss out of my dick or I'm gonna die"*).

Only this girl's gonna tell. She's gonna knock the self-censor down and tell on Mr. Horse, her father, the culture. The tired old vocabulary of abuse has never sounded so sad. It's as if we've never quite heard it before, because we've heard it mostly from men. When it *is* abuse. Finley played me a still untitled song she's recorded with Mark Kamins (who produced Madonna's first album). Here were the usual unholy urges chanted over a downbeat disco track: *"You are fuckin' your granny / you're fuckin' your sister too . . . suck the dick, bastard bitch . . . I want your wiener in my mouth . . . get me off!"* The music gave it a yearning quality as it blurted out the true language of love.

One night at the Cat Club, Finley followed Lydia Lunch on the bill. Lunch works the sex/anger territory herself. Stalking around the stage in her tight leather dress, she railed at the men in the crowd: "Stick your dick back in your fuckin' pants, you jellybelly looselip absolute fuckin'. . . . Look I know what you want. You are united in your search for that perfect piece of meat, the one that cooks, cleans, fucks, and sucks. . . ." The drunks around me responded with both adoration and abuse. Lunch even singled some out for special put-downs, but her anger was abstract, an idea of rage.

Finley appeared after her in a yellow 1950s party dress, carrying a can of sauerkraut ("foetus juice," she said), and launched into a bizarre impassioned fantasy of fucking paralyzed boys. *"And after I had that boy he starts crying cuz it's the first time he ever felt anything . . . ooh baby he says to me all I want is to suck some tit with sauerkraut. . . ."* And here she ripped open her dress, dumped the sauerkraut on her breasts in her push-up bra, raised her arms joyously before the screaming crowd, levitating on the energy of some taboo destroyed.

June 1986

Chapter 7

"Telling the Awfullest Truth": An Interview with Karen Finley

C. Carr

Before Rowland Evans and Robert Novak labeled her a "chocolate-smeared woman" in their nationally syndicated newspaper column, and before National Endowment for the Arts (NEA) chairman John Frohnmayer made her one of the "Defunded Four," Karen Finley had won both notoriety and respect in the performance world for her scabrous monologues and her unique brand of rude feminism.

Six years ago Finley was playing the Lower Manhattan club circuit—Danceteria, the Pyramid—doing ten- or fifteen-minutes in the wee hours before crowds of drunken rowdies. She'd walk out in some godforsaken prom dress or polyester gladrag, presenting herself first as the shy and vulnerable good girl. And, then, the deluge. The words were heartstopping in their sexual explicitness, but heartbreaking as well. Finley's territory was abuse, desire, rage—their conflation. She could take a subject like incest and push it to surreal extremes, but above all she would address it without euphemism. She would tell the awfullest truth. This was obscenity in its purest form—never a litany of four-letter expletives but an attempt to express emotions for which there are perhaps no words. She would expose the victimizer's monstrous impulses; she would validate feelings the victim could barely talk about.

Finley's work has always been less about sex than about what she calls "the pathos"—the damage and longing in everyone that triggers both desire and rage. Over the past two years she's begun working outside the monologue form, with installations like *A Woman's Life Isn't Worth Much* at New York's Franklin Furnace, a public sculpture on Manhattan's Lower East Side featuring her beloved *Black Sheep* monologue, and a play called *The Theory of Total Blame* about the holiday travails of a ridiculously dysfunctional family.

The right wing attacked her last year for a much acclaimed solo piece, *We Keep Our Victims Ready*, which is probably the least sexually graphic and most overtly political performance she's ever done. Of course, she did address her favorite unsafe subjects, like abortion and AIDS. Of course, Evans and Novak and their ilk never saw the show themselves. What Finley actually did with the chocolate was use it ritualistically, smearing it on as she talked about the degradation of women—because women are treated like shit. Then she recreated herself, applying sprouts and red candies and tinsel, till she appeared to be wearing a strange and beautiful costume. That is the heart of Finley's work: taking some horror on, then turning it over.

Shock Treatment, published in 1990 by City Lights, collects her major monologues like *We Keep Our Victims Ready* and *The Constant State of Desire,* along with some of Finley's early club work.

This interview was conducted in early summer, 1991.

It's been a little over a year since Evans and Novak first wrote about you and Frohnmayer defunded you. What effect did all the controversy have on you?

Well, first, since this is going to a North Carolina audience, I'd like to begin by saying that I really do detest Jesse Helms. I believe that he's Satan. Could you make those all capital letters, please? S-A-T-A-N. I hope they make that a pull quote. And I really hope that he suffers or that there can be some transformation in him.

The way I've been really affected in this past year is that I used to be more naive. I kind of believed more in the American way—that, if you worked or applied your talents, something would come back from it. I was very angry when I felt that I wouldn't be able to take rewards from hard work. Most recently, there's a performance series at the Kennedy Center which some people at another Washington arts organization are booking, and they wanted to include me. But the people at the Kennedy Center said, "No, we can't do Karen. She's too controversial, too political, because of the NEA situation." I feel that I still do not have the same access as straight white men—even though I'm well known. This isn't the way that I should have become well known. So I'm denied crossover, denied the same opportunities as straight men.

In terms of just getting gigs?

Yes. I get more than most people, but I don't get the same as certain artists who haven't given what I've given to the field. My feminist message is a lot more threatening than a straight man's message. I have had a lot of acclaim with my last work, and if I'd been a straight man I would have had opportunities with movies, galleries, TV shows, other opportunities, and I haven't been given any of those. I probably would have turned them down, but still I would have liked to have that pleasure. The other thing, the whole legal situation is such a waste of time and energy, in terms of suing the government. I feel pretty guilty about it.

You mean your lawsuit against the NEA? [The "Defunded Four"—Finley, John Fleck, Holly Hughes, and Tim Miller—charged that the NEA denied them their grants because of political content, thus violating their First Amendment rights.]

Yes. Even this interview. The interest for it is coming from what's wrong with me rather than what's right with me, and that's disturbing. I've done so many interviews, and all because of this controversy. Americans really like that kind of thing. I think too that I'd really like to perform in North Carolina. Instead of this interview, I think that this paper should get a space and put me down there.

But why did you say you felt guilty about the lawsuit?

We're working with the American Civil Liberties Union (ACLU) and the Center for Constitutional Rights and the National Campaign for Freedom of Expression, and it costs a lot of money. When people are actually physically suffering, that has a higher priority than my problem. Also, it seems like a fight that's already been fought and won, so why should we have to win it again?

Could you talk about your new play, Lamb of God Hotel?

One thing it deals with is abortion. It's about a woman who can't get an abortion even though her life is at risk. Her father turns out to be the father of her baby, and, in this particular state, even if your life is in danger, you have to get both parents to sign. So she can't go to her father to do that. The other story line is about a person who decides he's going to take his own life after he finds out he has AIDS. It goes back and forth between the two stories. I'm trying to make an analogy between the abuse in someone's personal life and the abuse happening in our country's political life. Once you're abused in your own life, that gets translated and comes back to you in the political world. That's what I'm trying to do, but it's very surreal. I think I'd like to make it as a video, and I'm trying to see if I can get it produced as a play. I'm not going to be in this production. So that's exciting for me. I don't really have the energy or time to do everything myself. And I don't have the money. I haven't gotten any grants this year, so I have to think differently.

Have you applied for any more NEA grants?

I've stopped applying because of the restrictive language about "general standards of decency," which is still part of the process. I feel it's unconstitutional.

Lamb of God Hotel *will be the first piece you've done that you haven't appeared in. I wonder if that has something to do with all the weird attention you got during the NEA debates?*

If I'm in there, I lose out. If I'm in there, immediately they'll say "chocolate-smeared woman." I'm really damaged from that. I don't want one character to be looked at more than the others. By removing me, they'll see the message. Also, more people can see it if it's a video or a play. I'd love it if maybe the community colleges in North Carolina would like to put it on. Also, I don't feel its transgressive. If I was in it, I'd be an actress.

You don't think the play is transgressive?

It isn't personally transgressive for me. I don't need to be in it. I just felt there'd be other actresses, other performers, that could do a better job.

Where did the title Lamb of God Hotel *come from?*

Lambs are sacrificial. This is about a place where people live where either they're the sacrifice or they have to have sacrifice in their life.

You've done a lot of visual work over the past year which also seems like a reaction to that scrutiny, like wanting to. . . .

Hide.

You wanted to hide?

I think I did. I've been very defensive. It's taken something away from me.

What else have you been working on?

I'd like to do a piece called *Momento Mori*. Maybe the Jesse Helms Museum would want to do it. It will be an installation dealing with abortion, censorship, homosexuality and really dealing with dying, but it will have performance aspects. People will be able to come in to the gallery for like two hours at night. They'll actually be seeing people suffering in these tableaux vivants, almost like images from a dream state. I'm doing this because I've been to so many memorial services for people who've died of AIDS, and those services aren't doing anything for me. For one of the tableaux I'm going to have a deathbed, and there will be people just naked, waiting in line, waiting to enter the deathbed. They each take turns going in it. There'll be three beds, and people might be praying at them, might be washing the person's face, or something. To me that signifies that it doesn't end and that we're all going to be at that state. There'll be another tableau where a woman is in a corner suffering from an illegal abortion, and there'll be a caged bird above her. I'm going to have a pile of rusted hangers and then some dead birds, chickens, on this pile.

I'm going to have someone coming up to her every five minutes and then turning and saying, "Don't worry she's already dead." It's going to be dark, and I'll have things for the audience to do—little rituals. I'll have a gate with ribbons, and people can write messages on them. I don't want to describe them all, but there will be things that are pretty racy too. Some of the performers will be naked, I'm sure, though there probably won't be much language. The audience will move through these scenes. I'm doing that because I'm sick of the proscenium stage. I always used the proscenium stage because I was appropriating it, almost making fun of it. And I really feel it's important to bring back installation.

Is that what you're doing on Long Island in August?

The Long Island show is more feminist. I have pieces in it like a painting of the Virgin Mary that says, "The Virgin Mary is pro-choice." I have a woman in a bed and underneath it says "Please don't ever beat your wife." I'll take traditional elements of looking at a female from men's perspective, but underneath I'll have a sentence that contradicts that—things like "God is a woman."

And you're going to perform out there also, aren't you?

Yes, and that's going to be a lot about the war. I'm going to be wiping my butt with yellow ribbons basically. I have yards and yards of it. I think that's important to do. I've been fantasizing it for a long time.

Where on Long Island are you doing this?

This is East Hampton, where there's a lot of rich people. And I think that's something they need to see.

Actually, it's probably rich art world people.

It is. There's a whole lot of these guys up there from the 1950s and 1960s who used to make form sculpture—you know, get some big beams, put 'em in a spiral, and paint it red.

So you don't plan to stop performing.

No, I just can't do as much on the road. I have to concentrate on doing stuff here in New York. I will be doing a new solo piece, but I'm not going to tour it around like before. It isn't that easy to do. It's very hard on my body. I can't do runs. That isn't what my goals were, anyway. The people that I look up to are more like Vito Acconci, Chris Burden. I'll probably always be doing performance, because I think I'm like—a ham. An extrovert. Performance will always be the center, and other things are like the little petals around it.

Have you found that certain presenters in the art world are afraid to book you now?

Yes, I've had cancellations. For this year coming up, I haven't had any alternative spaces calling me up at all. Except Sushi. And I'm supposed to be considered one of the top in the field. That's why I also am doing the diversifying with the paintings. The performance work is more confrontational. Painting is never going to be that confrontational. I like doing performances because it does something for me personally, and I like doing the paintings because they're sort of documentation of my existence. And they're harder to misinterpret. Or maybe I should say "misrepresent."

No one who's a performance artist ever imagines they're going to end up on "Good Morning America." That's not what people think of when they choose this as their life's work.

Especially when I'm supposed to be defending pornography. My work is not pornography, and I don't think as an artist that that's really supposed to be one of my jobs. The thing is, I *will* defend pornography, but I'm not really a political activist.

That's what they asked you to do on "Good Morning America"?

They didn't tell me they were going to, but that's what it turned out to be.

Well, I hope you kept a diary of your adventures while you were dealing with all this nonsense.

I was too depressed. Emotionally, what it did for me was make me depressed. And I've had bad things happen to me in my life, I'll tell ya. This got to me more than anything else because it was taking away a part of my soul. Everything else is something that's physical, or it's other people's actions. This was me, my individuality, and America is only defined by individuality. America is not defined by communities. My individuality was threatened, was stopped. Actually, for a year I did not sleep well. I had anxiety, palpitations. I always thought people were looking me over. I was totally afraid that the venues where I performed would get in trouble. I was afraid people would be coming to my house. It isn't like I'm Helen Hayes or someone where you have a brick wall, and you can say, "Hey, let's order a quart of martinis." Or Cher: "Let's take three months off and go to Aspen." It was hard.

Fall 1991

Chapter 8

Resisting Thatcherism: The Monstrous Regiment and the School of Hard Knox

Janelle Reinelt

... of necessitie it is that this monstriferouse empire of Women (which amongest all enormities that this day do abound upon the face of the whole earth, is most detestable and damnable) be openlie reveled and plainlie declared to the world

—John Knox

It has been over twenty years since a group of young female theater professionals decided to form a company dedicated to women's writing, to women's artistic production, and to rethinking women's role in relationship to history. Taking their company name from John Knox's 1558 pamphlet and turning an insult into a banner, this company has become one of the most durable and long-lasting of Britain's fringe theaters. Joint Stock has not fared as well (the company closed its doors in 1989), nor has any other political theater group, not even 7:84, John McGrath's Scotland-based touring company. As for feminist theaters, the Women's Theatre Group preceded the formation of Monstrous Regiment by a year but has not been nearly as consistent nor as successful. These observations are not intended to set up ill-advised comparisons between groups that are all too often placed in competition for funds but, rather, to point out that, in spite of the various difficulties often besetting the company, Monstrous Regiment has made an important and lasting contribution to feminism and to the British theater in general.[1]

This contribution is even more commendable in light of the steadily deteriorating subsidies and the privatization of the arts occurring during the Thatcher years. When the company was first formed, in the comparatively "fat" years of the mid-1970s, it was able to employ eleven people full-time as the core of what was then considered—by the company—to be a collective.[2] Michelene Wandor has documented that, at the time of the formation of Monstrous Regiment, the Arts Council had already begun the series of attacks and adjustments, which have had dire consequences for alternative theater since.[3] As this book goes to press, Monstrous Regiment's personnel number four, only one of whom is employed full-time, and a radical reorganization of the company is underway, one that maintains some of its traditional goals and commitments while adapting to the fiscal pressures of the present historical moment of post-Thatcher crisis.

Mary McCusker and Gillian Hanna are the originary members of Monstrous Regiment; they are both primarily performers. Chris Bowler has been a writer/director with the group off and on since its inception and is counted among the four permanent members as is general manager Rose Sharp. Monstrous Regiment has always been dedicated to developing new work: over the years various well-known writers such as Caryl Churchill, Claire Luckham, Bryony Lavery, and Michelene Wandor have worked on projects for the company. A number of the plays produced by the "monsters" over the years have appeared in print (*Vinegar Tom, Origin of the Species,* and *Teendreams,* for example).[4] Equally important are the productions that, while not quite requiring the label "performance art," have been based on improvisation and imaginative visual and aural work in conjunction with a developing text. Chris Bowler has devised two of these, *Enslaved by Dreams* and *Point of Convergence.* Another aspect of the company's work is the translation and performance of "foreign" material. Gillian Hanna is a gifted translator, allowing the company to introduce French and Italian work by Théâtre de l'Aquarium and Franca Rame and Dario Fo. During this past year the company produced Hanna's translation of Pierre Carlet de Chamblain de Marivaux's *The Colony.*

In the short space of this essay it is impossible to do justice to the range of feminist theater practice displayed in the history of the Monstrous Regiment. The early years of the company have been discussed and documented by Michelene Wandor and Catherine Itzin and also by American scholars Sue-Ellen Case and Helen Keyssar.[5] My purpose here is to examine some of the contradictions facing the Monstrous Regiment by very reason of their longevity and success and thereby to understand what is required to maintain a materialist feminist theater practice in an inhospitable sociopolitical climate over the inevitable changes of fifteen years. In the last part of the essay I will document and discuss some of the specific projects of the Monstrous Regiment from the last decade.

As Loren Kruger has observed in a perceptive essay, "the marginalization of women and the *legitimation* of that marginalization is central to the question of subsidy."[6] Kruger's argument is that subsidy traditionally shows preferment to those "stable" institutions, such as the National Theatre or the Royal Shakespeare Company (RSC), whose permanent buildings combine with middle-class subscriber audiences and literary playscripts to ensure their legitimacy. Touring groups, performing for various local audiences in scattered spaces, often featuring plays that are neither fully "literary" nor fully performance art, are assumed to be unstable and their quality inferior. Of course, lack of adequate subsidy helps to produce the very conditions being faulted in Arts Council thinking.

The impact of the realities of subsidy politics can be seen graphically in the case of the Monstrous Regiment. The monsters are a touring group, usually performing on the road throughout England and Scotland and also in various London venues, as available. Since they are committed to developing new writing, their "scripts" often go through extensive workshop and preparation stages, taking several years to progress from first idea to finished production. Much of their work consists of playwrights' first plays or else pieces that have evolved, through improvisation and directorial experimentation, into scripts that are partly performance pieces and partly traditional literary playscripts. And, although they have achieved a good deal of critical acclaim, even among traditional critics, they are definitely perceived as being politically suspect, linked (correctly enough) to the identity politics of feminism, and therefore "marginal." Sometimes the language of male theater reviewers belies just how little progress beyond misogyny has been made: "Bryony Lavery's latest farce is a complete confusion. Miss Lavery belongs to that modern breed of bellyaching feminists who protest the role of women in what is believed to be a male-dominated world, which is nonsense. The plays are naturally propagandist material."[7]

The results of dwindling subsidies and the general inflationary

Left to right: Sally Cranfield, Celia Gore-Booth, and Tamsun Heatley in
Enslaved by Dreams by Monstrous Regiment. Photo by Roger Perry,
© Impact Photos.

Marcia Tucker as Kate and Joanna Field as Sophia in *Island Life*, by Jenny McLeod, directed by Jane Collins, designed by Iona McLeish. Photo by Mary Tisserand.

spiral, especially with respect to touring costs, have inevitably made
an impact on the company. Salaries for fewer permanent members
have resulted in less continuity in the overall direction of the company. Similarly, diminished support has meant fewer projects undertaken, smaller casts, less time for development of the material. Out
on the road touring venues have also been affected as Thatcher policies have caused some borough councillors to cut subsidies to their
small theaters. When these theaters consider bookings, they too often
make first choice of RSC or repertory company offerings, rather than
booking new, "untested" material from a women's group, which,
while noted for its solid work, may or may not have Mary McCusker
or Gillian Hanna featured in its current offering, may or may not
have a "name" playwright or director or other cast members, may
or may not stimulate reviewers' hostility because of its feminist slant.

A critical example of the way these aspects of producing under
Thatcherism affect the future of the company is the 1990 production
of *More than One Antoinette*.[8] This project began as an idea of director
Debbie Shewell's, stimulated by *Jane Eyre* and Jean Rhys's novel about
the first Mrs. Rochester, *Wide Sargasso Sea*. Antoinette is a Creole
woman growing up in the West Indies just after the Emancipation
Act, while Jane is the poor relation of a northern English family. In
1988 Monstrous Regiment used part of their Arts Council Revenue
Grant, originally earmarked for commissions, to enable preliminary
workshops for three possible projects. Of the three only Shewell's
has been produced, although Chris Bowler's Cruelty/Isolation Workshop is still being developed toward a possible script.[9] In 1990 *Antoinette* was produced at the Young Vic Studio but did not go out on
tour because it had an unknown author and play, and the cast of five
was cost prohibitive. The revenue from touring, however, was, consequently, also not forthcoming. From one perspective the company's
objectives were well served by the project: feminist material about
historical matters, with a multicultural slant, developed into the work
of a new writer. The "costs" of the show, however, included contributing to a financial crisis of significant proportions. The Arts Council,
unhappy at the level of income being produced by the company,
announced that it would not guarantee funding beyond September
1991. This act precipitated the extensive self-study and reorganization
undertaken by the Regiment in recent months and ultimately, the
decision to engage an artistic director for the company. It is certainly

not the case that *Antoinette* was the project that "caused" this crisis; it merely contributed, and illustrates through its combined circumstances both the necessary financial risks attendant upon Monstrous Regiment's work and also the possible results.

These various financial constraints entail dire political, or, more precisely, *ideological* consequences beyond pinching the scope and level of productions. Three of the most serious involve casting, the notion of the "collective," and the content of "feminism."

When finances determine casting one, two, or three actors, the tendency is to produce small-cast shows. (Although one alternative is to double, usually shows that use doubling have larger, not smaller, casts.) During the later part of the 1980s most of the Monstrous Regiment's shows have featured between one and three performers. Especially successful have been the 1989 one-woman shows, Ian Brown's *Beatrice* and Fo and Ramc's *A Common Woman,* in which McCusker and Hanna, respectively, have appeared. Under these circumstances, however, McCusker and Hanna become ever more defined as constituting the company, which contradicts the notion of plurality and collectivity associated with the group. Furthermore, small-cast shows tend to throw the emphasis on individual experience, at the expense of the social group.[10] This happenstance cannot be completely otherwise, not even when the playwright is particularly concerned to represent social positions in the context of the flux of history, such as the highly political Chilean play *My Song Is Free* (1986). The presence on stage of a small number of characters tends, under most circumstances, to highlight internal psychological experiences and unique aspects of personality, rather than the social scope of a community or the dialectical nature of social life among diverse groups. Early Regiment plays such as *Vinegar Tom* and *Scum* were especially notable for these features—what Brecht called historicizing the narrative—and, while some recent work, including especially *Origin of the Species,* partially achieves these effects without the scope of a large cast, there is an unmistakable theatrical relationship between the size of the cast and the politics of representation.

Monstrous Regiment had continued to operate as a collective over the past fifteen years, if this means that the various decisions have been taken in common and the tasks shared among the permanent company members. But, like casting, that permanent company shrunk, and for much of the time McCusker and Hanna have been the company, with some other women contributing to several projects over the years. Only Chris Bowler has maintained a relationship from the beginning, which still gives her company status, and even she has taken various breaks from active involvement from time to time. A number of others, such as Bryony Lavery, Susan Todd, and Nona Shepphard, have worked on multiple projects but cannot be said to be part of the collective. In choosing to hire an artistic director the company is acknowledging that, given the artistic/financial climate of the 1990s, it needs to have an identifiable person who sets the company's artistic agenda and who can be consistently accountable for its work. This change is not necessarily a bad thing nor a hands-down political loss for feminism, but it is a necessity directly tied to the arts management policies of the Thatcher era, which make it difficult if not impossible to continue alternative nonhierarchal modes of theatrical organization, which used to be a significant part, if always contested, of the feminist agenda.

Feminism itself has always been a contested terrain—definition and practice alike. As the Monstrous Regiment moved away from employing anything like a permanent company of women committed to the same goals and values, however, it is understandable that what the company's feminism means has become somewhat blurred. Not all actresses or directors, employed for one show, have explicitly feminist ideas. Younger women who have grown up after the second-wave struggle of feminism have a different relationship to it as a movement.

An example of the contradictions that emerge can be seen in the case of *Island Life* (1988). Author Jenny Mcleod is a young black woman who came to the Monstrous Regiment's attention when she won a prize with her first play, produced at Nottingham Playhouse in the mid-1980s. In interviews she makes it clear that she does not want to be expected to write plays about blacks nor about women. She does, however, have a point of view: "I think that what gets me going is that people should get on with their lives and not sit back and hope for the best. Make a go of the things that they've got, try their best. I'm trying. I want to be able to write the best play I possibly can one day, but I'm not in a position to write it yet."[11] On one hand, this is not the language of a committed identity politics person. On the other hand, Mcleod is twenty-five and has grown up under a different set of historical circumstances than the generation of McCusker and Hanna. Her play, *Island Life,* is an intriguing drama of four older women, who are struggling with their personal histories and with the realities of aging and includes representation of black experience. The play is a clear demonstration that the personal is political. Yet the identity of the company blurs out of focus when the people who create the work do not share a specific feminist agenda. Comparing the loss of collectivity under an artistic director to the previous methods of employing free-lance directors for Monstrous Regiment's productions, McCusker commented: "If we still were a real collective, it would be a handing over of power to an artistic director, but it might even be seen as an enhancement since you hand over a great deal of power to individual directors, and it can be far more distressing with them. In a way they are responsible to you, but in a way they are out the door once the production is on."[12]

If the past decade has seen the Monstrous Regiment maintain the structure and goals of its original materialist feminist project, but also suffer some erosion in terms of the three issues noted above, the reorganization of the company under an artistic director may actually provide some positive trade-offs, of which continuity of vision is one. McCusker and Hanna will not hire someone who differs strongly in values and views from their own politics. And, while wanting to encourage and support the work of new younger women, they are also especially committed to representing the problems and situations of middle-aged women.

Since McCusker and Hanna are "middle-aged," part of their commitment reflects their own desires for challenging roles, as they readily point out. But, of course, this age group is also traditionally underrepresented, and, thus, encouraging work in this area is part of a larger feminist goal: "This is a definite preoccupation that we have and that we'd like to see reflected in the work and we don't always want to choose some new young writers. New exciting young writers come up, and must be discovered and nurtured, and we shouldn't ignore them, but we can also make a conscious choice to encourage older women."[13] In the past year the Regiment held workshops for which it explicitly encouraged older and disabled women to send in scripts. In a related move it offered public workshops on "writing plays with a socio-political agenda without writing polemic," "moving theatre out of the kitchen"—on writing in an epic form in order to broach "greater historical themes."[14] Thus, the political work of the company has continued in spite of Tory restraints and will continue beyond reorganization.

The situation of the Monstrous Regiment in the context of a hostile government is exemplary of the situation of diverse groups struggling to resist the ruling hegemony. Gillian Hanna provides the long view of this predicament: "During the last thirty years, there has been a tradition of public support, which has allowed 'alternative' work to develop. But capitalism pushes everything into a commodity—water is a commodity, so why should art be treated any differently? For Thatcher, it has been terribly important to cut subsidies, important from a philosophical-political point of view. So socialists have to resist; we have to put up an articulate defense of the 'commodities' that should not be put up on the market place."[15]

In the remaining pages of this essay I will discuss several productions that embody various aspects of the work of Monstrous Regiment. In the first part of this piece the emphasis has been on the difficulties of producing materialist feminist theater during an era of repression; in this second part I would like to pay tribute to the achievements of Monstrous Regiment in the face of formidable constraints.

My Song Is Free (1986) is perhaps the most overtly political play Monstrous Regiment has produced in recent years, if "political" is understood as an explicit protest against the injustice of a specific contemporary situation. Set in Chile just after the coup, which replaced Salvador Allende with military dictatorship, the play was written by Jorge Diaz, from the personal accounts of four women who were "desaparicida," disappeared. The front of the playscript carries the notation: "The play is based on events which happened in Santiago, Chile, in the autumn of 1974 inside a secret detention centre belonging to the D.I.N.A. (today C.N.I., Chilean political police)."[16] When the play was performed, both in London and on tour, the company carried Amnesty International information on conditions in South America and led discussions after the play. Thus, the production itself participated in Solidarity work in a direct way. McCusker says they felt that "must do this play" and that, through "integrated casting," they were able to include South American women whose cultural experiences as women and as South Americans contributed to the research necessary for the production.

The play is, on the surface, a realistic thriller, which has some superficial resemblance to *Kiss of the Spider Woman,* insofar as both plays are set in prisons where prisoners of different political and class backgrounds struggle with issues of trust, friendship, and love. *My Song Is Free,* however, concerns itself only with heterosexual women and involves four, not two, prisoners in a complex web of interrelationships. One of the women, Rosario, works for the underground and has been told to expect a contact in the prison. Olga, the most likely contact, is also the most suspicious since she claims to be a double agent and has a mysterious history of being arrested and released repeatedly. Aurora is a famous actress who has apparently been picked up because of her casual association with Olga, and Jimena is a pregnant women who, coming from the middle classes, claims to have no politics at all.

The play sketches the differences in "positionalities" that these women represent. While Olga has lived the most actively committed political life, her ambiguous status as double agent leaves her the most alienated and alone of the group, her existential experience at odds with her political work. "You don't trust me. They don't trust me . . . but I have to go on . . . Knowing all the time that you despise me . . . Strange the way things turn out: I always looked for love amongst companeros—And I have ended up alone."[17] Aurora, on the other hand, is a famous actress, who seems to the others pampered and spoiled. Afraid of torture, focused only on getting released, she seems an unlikely one to be the center of the secret plan to free "an important person," yet she is revealed to be the contact. Rosario, the politically shrewd and experienced *companera,* pronounces her view of artists and intellectuals: "They help popularize the ideas of the movement. . . . Usually political events leave them behind and they end up getting in the way."[18] Aurora, however, is important because she has been the conduit for money coming into the country from exiled comrades. Jimena is a middle-class woman whose political education takes place in the prison as she comes to respect and admire the commitment she sees, even while fearing for herself and her unborn child. Ironically, she is the one taken out and tortured until she dies. Her prematurely born daughter is left in the care of Rosario at the play's end. *My Song Is Free* represents these four women and their differences, brought together in intense crisis. The politicosocial aspects of the script are enhanced by lyrical and communal effects of music and sound. The theme song of the play, repeated several times, is a lullaby and a rallying song:

> Like a free bird
> flying free
> like a free bird
> is how I dream you

One of the most successful productions of Monstrous Regiment during the 1980s was *Origin of the Species,* written by Bryony Lavery for Hanna and McCusker. Its "origins" began in a three-week workshop with the two actresses, Lavery, and director Nona Shepphard, a typical beginning for Regiment productions. It was, Hanna quips, "intended to be a history of the world for two characters."[19] For source material they read widely, ranging from Capra's *The Turning Point* to various classical accounts of evolution to Susan Griffin's *Woman and Nature* to the work of Jane Goodall. Their workshop strategies included mask work and improvisations, wide ranging and without preliminary assumptions about character, plot, or setting. After the workshop Lavery went away and sketched in the script; three more weeks of rehearsals consolidated the project.

In its final form *Origin of the Species* represents the encounter between Molly, a Yorkshire archaeologist, and her four-million-year-old ancestor, whom she uncovers while on a dig with Louis and Mary Leakey at Olduvai Gorge. Molly smuggles her "baby" home and "raises" her, learning in exchange a great deal about human development as Victoria comes into her own. On New Year's Eve, 1984, the present time of the play, Molly sends Victoria out in the world, aware that she cannot keep her at home anymore.

The play works to both insinuate women into natural history and to critique patriarchal history. Digging up the ancient skeleton of originary "man," Molly gets "the shock of her life when this creature, whom she expects to be a man, is in fact a woman."[20] What if historical narrative were told with a woman as the first protagonist instead of a man? As for received stories, gender critique formulates them in a different light: at one point Molly tells Victoria "the clock story," which is an account of scientific investigation and appropriation of the earth by men who treat it as a clock (with suitable resonances to

Enlightenment Deism). A curious boy, called variously "Plato Aristotle Copernicus Galileo Bacon Descartes Newton," took the clocks
apart and assembled new clocks until

> finally he made a clock which could
> make
> everything vanish
> this is my best clock he said
> my vanishing clock
> I must take this and show it to my mother
> and he ran with his vanishing clock
> hither and thither
> but his mother had vanished
> and he looked at his exploding clock
> and saw that he had very little time
> left[21]

To "discover" Victoria is thus to embark on an exploration of seeing
the world and our accounts of it from the perspective of the female
gaze. This is the working premise of the play.

McCusker, whose early training included three years at the
Glasgow Academy of Speech and Drama, had a special acting challenge in creating a representation of the creature Victoria. "I had to
try for a character who was child-like but not childish, who had an
innocence because she didn't know or understand this world she'd
been projected into, and who gradually through friendship leapfrogs
into the 20th century."[22] McCusker did research on the physical development of her creature, especially on gorillas and on the native
languages of the Olduvai Gorge, in order to help find physical attributes of movement and speech for Victoria. Her physical movement,
created with the help of director Shepphard, featured bent legs but a
straight back—"rather like a ballet dancer doing a plié"—which enabled her to move at high speed. She wore a hairy body suit for the
part, from which some of the hair could be removed for the second
act, as Victoria assimilates to modern life. Her vocal work started
with basic words, which approximated the words of people from the
regions where Victoria originated, and McCusker altered her sound
production to create a new voice: "I couldn't alter my own physical
being, but I could try to alter the physical energy in the mouth for

making sentences out of sounds." Reasoning that people who live in the open air must communicate across large distances, McCusker used her diaphragm, creating a "voice for fear which was earsplitting in the auditorium, giving some people quite a fright."[23]

This production is representative of the imagination and collaboration of the Monstrous Regiment at its best. For Hanna and McCusker the opportunity to work together is always a great satisfaction. Gillian Hanna on McCusker: "I think Mary's a terrific actor and it's lovely to be on stage with an actor that you know terribly well, have worked with a lot, and really trust."[24] The production was generally well received on tour and in London at the Drill Hall. Ron Asquith wrote of it: "it has much of the fascination of good science fiction, the moral resonance of a parable, a beautiful set that combines domestic bliss with the call of the wild and confirms Jenny Carey as one of the most innovative designers around, and marvelously funny performances from Gillian Hanna (Molly) and Mary McCusker (Victoria)."[25]

The Monstrous Regiment productions frequently involve staging nonliterary aspects that come from workshop and collaboration among the various artistic contributors. Sometimes their productions border on performance art. Chris Bowler, who has been a founding member and associated with the company throughout its existence, has fashioned several pieces for the company that illustrate this aspect of their work. During the 1980s she devised *Enslaved by Dreams* and *Point of Convergence* and during the last two years has been working on a new project, provisionally called *Isolation and Cruelty*. These theater pieces share an emphasis on spectacle, a fragmented and non-Aristotelian script, and various musical and aural affects. *Enslaved by Dreams* will serve as a concrete example of this style.

The original impulse for the play came from a workshop held in the 1970s at the Institute for Contemporary Art (ICA), in which the company was working with Caryl Churchill on the notion of "a bunch of women in history meeting in a kind of no man's land" (possibly the genesis for the first part of *Top Girls*). Chris read a biography of Florence Nightingale, which was "lying about the office" and which affected her greatly: "I was very taken with her, her sense of not being able to get at what she wanted to do, being prevented by all sorts of things." She proposed it as a show and was designated producer/director, a new challenge for someone who had primarily seen herself as an actress: "I had very strong ideas about the script, and I looked for a while for a writer, but I didn't want a well-made play." In the end she devised it herself. *Enslaved by Dreams* never names Florence Nightingale but, rather, presents three Florences, named in the program by the colors of their dresses but within the text established as sisters with names of Sally, Celia, and Tamsin.

Although set in Victorian times, the set combined various modern elements with the old ones—thus, a modern filing cabinet next to a nineteenth-century chaise; computer print-outs but old-fashioned pens. The floor of the set was covered with papers and writing then shellacked. The play is heavily dependent on music and special choreography for its tone, using a waltz motif to stitch together the scenic and monologic fragments of the women's experiences. In the "Tea Cup Waltz" actresses danced and did cartwheels while passing cups and saucers. Not every aspect of the mise-en-scène was immediately recognizable. Tubs with prop turds representing the lack of sanitation in Victorian hospitals sometimes went unacknowledged: "People didn't always know what they were seeing—some of it worked on an emotional but not on an intellectual level."[26]

The simultaneous portrayal of aspects of Nightingale separates out the young girl who loves to dance but yearns for permission to become a nurse, the hard-working matter-of-fact organizer, and the sickly, bedridden woman who beseeches for medical reforms by letter from her bedside. At times the script establishes concrete historical conditions:

> *Tamsin:* I am witnessing a calamity unparalleled in the history of calamities. The British Army has 11,000 men laying siege to Sebastopol, and 12,000 men in hospital. It is being destroyed. Not by losses in battle, but by sickness—and most of it avoidable.[27]

At other points the personal struggles of the characters are in focus:

> *Sally:* My God what is to become of me. My present life is suicide. Slowly I have opened my eyes to the fact that I cannot now deliver myself from the habit of dreaming, which like

> gin-drinking is eating out my vital strength. . . . I shall never
> do anything and am worse than dust and nothing. Oh for
> some strong thing to sweep this loathsome life into the past.[28]

The gist of the play deconstructs the myth of the historical
Florence, while creating an experience, mood, and feeling of longing
and frustration. It both distances and draws in; the nonverbal aspects
of the production ensure the emotional intertext. Bowler characterizes it negatively as "not quite a movement piece but not quite a
play."[29] This kind of production marks out the theatrical territory for
collaborative, improvisatory work that rests on other-than-literary
creation.

Bowler's next work, *Point of Convergence,* was a fantasy built
around two groups of women, the Wild Girls and the Fighters, who
encounter each other in an unspecified place. Bowler was interested
in representing two generations of women, the older intellectual
feminists, who have engaged in certain "battles" and survived, and
younger women, who have other ways of doing things and take
some of the goals of feminism for granted. This show was very
physical—the Wild Girls trained to do acrobatics, tumbling, rolling,
and wrestling because Bowler was interested in young bodies and the
way they can move physically.

Starting in 1988, and still developing, an idea for a new project
occurred to Bowler. After the birth of her own child, she read in the
newspaper about a three-year-old child who starved to death, locked
in a room for months while the people who were responsible lived
just a few feet away. She began to want to explore the relationship
between cruelty and morality and the way the country neglects its
people—"the post-Thatcher climate of greed." Describing the relationship between the personal and the public, Bowler writes, "At
home, we have the Conservative government consistently attacking
and weakening those least able to protect themselves. I think their
policies profoundly immoral. They make the sort of areas I'm concerned with (e.g., child-abuse) much more likely through the pressure of unemployment, and cuts in living standards. But I think they
also give a model for . . . a degree of personal and domestic cruelty.
The idea of the survival of the fittest has invaded both public and
private life."[30] Her production ideas combine realistic material and
characters—perhaps a child, an old woman living alone, and a social

worker or policewoman—with nonrealistic devices such as sound-taped interior monologue, jagged time-shifts, and even telepathic contact between living and dead characters. Bowler was able, with a seed money grant, to run a week's workshop with four actors in 1988. While the piece had not been produced as of 1991 it still remains on the Regiment planning boards. This project indicates that the style of production that Bowler represents continues to be an important part of the aesthetics of the Monstrous Regiment.

Postscript

Clare Venables, who had been a resident director at the Sheffield Crucible, was appointed as the new artistic director of Monstrous Regiment in April 1991. She had worked on such recent Regiment productions as *Beatrice* and *Love Story of the Century,* working closely with both Hanna and McCusker. In May the Arts Council conducted a major review of the company and its proposed new changes. An interim report, prepared by McCusker and submitted in April, outlined the major changes the company proposes to make over the next three years. These have been discussed above and include the switch to a management style employing an artistic director, a management advisory board, and an executive management team. The pattern of work for the company changed to emphasize nontouring work produced in a "Home Season" at such London venues as The Gate or the Soho Poly. One tour each season was to be offered, to be selected from the previous year's Home Season, in order to ensure its quality. New work continued to be developed through public readings, workshops, and commissions, including a slot for a writer-in-residence. In addition, a marketing consultant was engaged by the company to help create a coherent marketing strategy to accompany the new artistic identity of the Monstrous Regiment.

At the end of 1992, however, the Arts Council cut the revenue grant of Monstrous Regiment and changed their status to project client. This means that they can apply for money for single projects but not to maintain a staff of artistic director, administrative director, or other monies with which to run the company. The Monsters had expected at least three years of revenue funding under Claire Venables's direction but were cut off after two. Venables is no longer the artistic director of Monstrous Regiment. Her last production was

I've Got Nothing To Wear, a comic cabaret on the issue of clothes, which played in London till the end of the year (1992). She would probably not have stayed on anyway, since she wanted to change the name of the company, something the Board, composed of original members Hanna, McCusker, and Bowler, opposed.

However, with the revenue cut, not only Venables but the entire status of the company is severely endangered. The total funds allocated for 1993 represent half of what they requested; Mary McCusker thinks that they may lose their permanent offices. The future is bleak and McCusker acknowledges that their next project, planned for early in 1994, "might be the last thing that we do." The play will be called *More Light,* by Bryony Lavery, who has of course worked with the Monstrous Regiment over the years. It is about Chinese concubines who are buried alive when their emperors die. The women eat the cadavers of the men and acquire their knowledge. According to McCusker, it has a cast of fifteen women, three male corpses, and one live man. If it is truly to be their last production, at least it sounds like they'll go out with a bang. But then this group of women would never leave with a whimper.

NOTES

Epigraph from "The First Blast of the Trumpet against the Monstrous Regiment of Women," in *The Works of John Knox,* ed. David Laing (New York: AMS Press, 1966), 4:368.

1. When the Monstrous Regiment was touring the United States in 1987 the Boston Globe proclaimed that "Monstrous Regiment is one of the leading political theatre companies in the English-speaking world." Considering the difficulty of sustaining political theater practice, this comment does not seem hyperbolic.

2. "Fat" only in the sense that more new playwrights and companies were able to flourish during that period than since that time—not "fat" in any sense of being over or even adequately funded.

3. *Carry on Understudies* (London: Routledge and Kegan Paul, 1986), 34.

4. Caryl Churchill's *Vinegar Tom* and Bryony Lavery's *Origin of the Species* have been published in Methuen's *Plays by Women* series, and Susan Todd's and David Edgar's *Teendreams* has been published as a Methuen playscript.

5. In addition to *Carry on Understudies,* see Catherine Itzin, *Stages in the Revolution* (London: Methuen, 1980); Sue-Ellen Case, *Feminism and Theatre* (New York: Methuen, 1988); Helene Keyssar, *Feminist Theatre* (London: Macmillan, 1984).

6. "The Dis-Play's the Thing: Gender and Public Sphere in Contemporary British Theater," *Theatre Journal* 42, no. 1 (1990): 30.

7. Richard Edmonds, *Birmingham Post*, 23 November 1984.

8. While I am well aware of the ascendancy of John Majors in place of Margaret Thatcher, I still consider these "Thatcher years" in much the same way that we in the United States were still living the "Reagan Era" throughout the Bush presidency.

9. See my comments about this project later in this essay.

10. Production costs and practices in the United States have contributed, I contend, to ensuring that the traditional models of domestic psychological drama continue to enjoy hegemony on American stages.

11. Interview in the *Guardian*, 11 October 1988.

12. Interview with Mary McCusker, 16 January 1991.

13. Ibid.

14. Quotes from the advertising pamphlet announcing the workshops and the Autumn season for 1990.

15. Interview with Gillian Hanna, 14 June 1989.

16. Jorge Diaz, unpub. MS, *My Song Is Free (All This Long Night);* English adaptation by Niger Geanly.

17. Ibid., 50.

18. Ibid., 45.

19. Interview with Gillian Hanna, 22 June 1989.

20. Ibid.

21. Bryony Lavery, "Origin of the Species," *Plays by Women,* ed. Mary Remnant (London: Methuen, 1987), 6:81.

22. Interview with Mary McCusker, 13 July 1989.

23. Ibid.

24. Interview with Hanna, 22 June 1989.

25. *Observer*, 31 March 1985.

26. Interview with Chris Bowler, 22 June 1989.

27. Unpub. MS, *Enslaved by Dreams*, 22.

28. Ibid., 14.

29. Interview with Bowler, 22 June 1989.

30. Chris Bowler, unpub. working notes.

31. Interview with McCusker, 12 February 1993.

Chapter 9

Siren Theatre Company: Politics in Performance

Joyce Devlin

Siren Theatre Company is the longest-running lesbian theater collective in Britain today. In its total of ten touring theatrical productions Siren reflects particular aspects of women's position in society and explores techniques for opposing the institutions of oppression. Its productions raise feminist issues such as heterosexism, violence against women, and lesbian desire as well as women's oppression and draw from numerous political events including the Falklands War, the capture and trial of Peter Sutcliffe (the "Yorkshire Ripper"), women's right to abortion, the miners' strike, the nuclear debate, and freedom of information. Employing a variety of theatrical techniques—agitprop, live music, ventriloquism, visual humor, serious narrative, camp, farce, surrealism, and satire—Siren's productions reflect the evolution of political theater in the late 1970s and the 1980s. The group is internationally known, having toured in the United Kingdom, Holland, the United States, Germany, and Switzerland, playing in theaters, art centers, universities, community centers, schools, and outdoor festivals. Reviews of its performances can be found in the *Tribune, Stage and Television Today, The Scotsman, Spare Rib, Time Out, City Limits,* and *Gay News.*

In 1970 both the women's liberation movement (WLM) and the Gay Liberation Front (GLF) were formed. The two movements grew out of a British social and cultural revolution that was supported by earlier legislative acts.[1] Michelene Wandor describes similarities between the WLM and the GLF both in their aim, "transforming the social structures which oppress people on the grounds of sexual difference or preference," and in their focus, "the entrenched ideology which underpins the sexual division of labor within the family, in which woman is assumed to be confined by her biological role, and in which the heterosexual imperative is held to be the norm."[2]

Siren Theatre Company was formed in this political climate and was influenced by the WLM, the GLF, and the late-1970s punk explosion in the music scene. According to Noelle Janaczewska, the director of Siren's fourth production, "From the late 1970's onwards, the number of feminist companies grew and grew. The punk rock scene of the late 1970's played a large part in this expansion by providing new and strong role models. . . . Some of these women filtered into the theatre industry and injected a mass of energy, humor, outrageousness and new skills into a young and receptive feminist theatre movement. . . . The feminist theatre groups of this time were as varied as their names suggest, and so were their productions: . . . Siren['s] . . . shows were a powerful fusion of complex intellectual argument, sharp humor and rock music."[3]

Tash Fairbanks and Jane Boston, two of the founding members of the company, began in Brighton, in 1978, by organizing a punk rock band called Devil's Dykes. Jude Winter, the third member, joined the band somewhat later. The women bought instruments, perfected their musical skills, and began performing in this male-dominated field while actively involved in the Brighton women's movement. During a particular pro-abortion campaign they created a mixed theater group, which eventually became Siren Theatre Company. The name Siren represents the dual image of loud and luring: "We really liked the idea of a siren being something loud and making an impact. And sirens are those beautiful women who brought about the destruction of men by luring them onto the rocks. In quite a humorous way, we liked the double meaning."[4]

Siren members were very much in the vanguard of "rad/les" (radical lesbian) feminism in their early days. "When we first started in '78-'79," says Tash Fairbanks, "there was a vigorous radical lesbian feminist movement in Brighton."[5] Some of the members were involved in direct action: gluing locks and smashing windows in porn shops, destroying pornographic displays in lingerie shops, demonstrating their disapproval of sexist films, and writing graffiti on sexist advertisements. Uncomfortable with certain direct action tactics, Jane Boston was more interested in studying feminist theory and feminist literature and representing these ideas in theater and music. Even though the founders of Siren came from different social classes, held different political views, and had formed their identities as lesbians at different times and for different reasons, they were all committed to radical social change and to the creation of innovative political theater.

Tash Fairbanks explains Siren's feminisms: "Siren went through a whole gamut of feminisms. We went through a very separatist stage in the beginning. We went through a radical feminism, a revolutionary feminism. In a way, our plays responded to the different kinds of feminisms of the time."[6] Siren Theatre Company's first five productions reflect many of the changes that occurred in British feminism and in the women's liberation movement. Their performance scripts embody ideologies of radical feminism, separatism, revolutionary feminism, socialist feminism, lesbianism and lesbian desire and are always placed within the framework of the larger political context. Never simply the expression of one particular ideology, each play reveals pluralistic influences and always represents a lesbian theme. Nevertheless, particular feminisms can be identified with each production.

Siren's first script, *Mama's Gone A-Hunting* (1980), was influenced by radical feminism and separatism and is an assessment of the divisions between women and men. Set in a courtroom at some time in the future, the opening scene reveals an androgynous intergalactic judge appraising Woman as she argues for her right to leave Man and the planet and establish an all-female civilization elsewhere. But Man claims he needs Woman to maintain his life-support systems.

The ensuing court proceedings included sketches, readings, song and dance, contemporary rock music, mime, and slapstick, revealing Man's oppression of Woman. Taking up the tradition of the WLM and political theater, Siren used agitprop techniques to inform their audience. (Tash Fairbanks played the role of Man by assuming male privilege and power through her characterization and by subverting this power through humor.) Blatantly exposing sexism in domestic matters, religion, science, art, and culture, this polemical piece covered a wide range of issues over a long period of history. This low-budget production was both entertaining and political.

In discussing the link between politics and art and the differences

Left to right: Jane Boston, Tash Fairbanks, and Jude Winter in *From the Divine* by Siren Theatre Company. Photo by Anita Corbin.

in form, ideologies, and aims of alternative theater companies, Michelene Wandor declares, "but they share one common intention: in different ways they have sought to democratise the social division of labor in the theatre by developing flexible and collaborative work methods, by introducing theatre to new audiences, and by representing the experiences and interests of groups of oppressed and exploited people."[7] This description fits Siren Theatre Company exactly.

Mama's Gone A-Hunting was devised by the company. The performers read Mary Daly's *Gyn-Ecology* together, argued over each point, and scripted the play from these discussions: "For the first show, every comma was agreed on by us. It was a clarifying process and a strengthening process apart from producing texts. It was a gathering together, and discovering our shared oppression."[8] The same process was used to create the music and lyrics for the production.

In addition to creating and performing the play the Siren members shared the administrative work. Together they secured grants,

Jude Winter and Tash Fairbanks in *Now Wash Your Hands, Please*
by Siren Theatre Company. Photo by Anita Corbin.

developed publicity, and booked tours. They worked as a collective in the most democratic sense.

Siren had a simple design concept for their first show. They would arrive at a community center, push the chairs out of the way, place three lights on the floor, and perform. Working simply and inexpensively, Siren wore costumes constructed from dyed sheets.

The production dramatized many of men's violations against women as described in Mary Daly's *Gyn/Ecology*. After calling a number of witnesses, including the Virgin Mary, who reveals that the immaculate conception took place without her consent—that is, through a gang rape by the Holy Trinity—the judge asks Woman if she would like to cross-examine a female witness.

> *Woman:* How can I? She's been silenced, like every other woman who said something he didn't want to hear.[9]

The production was radical for its time and received positive reviews in many papers and journals.

> The fast-moving sketches elucidate, deflate and positively devastate. *Mama's Gone A-Hunting* will provoke all manner of reactions, but certainly no one can leave it with a settled mind.[10]

> A string of witnesses (The Virgin Mary, the Perfect Wife), songs and readings combine to provide an intelligent, fiercely partial and very exhilarating feminist show, although it's also in need of editing and hard work in terms of presentation and technique. But then money buys time for such niceties, and Siren's finances would compare favorably to those of church mice.[11]

Lacking support from the national government, Siren raised money from regional arts associations as guarantees against loss from tours.[12] But this did not cover their expenses while writing and rehearsing the production. (Funded only once by the Arts Council, Siren has worked with minimal financial support throughout their production history.) "We worked for next to nothing out of a devotion and a commitment to the politics," says Debra Trethewey, Siren's designer/technician. "The rewards were the expression of who we were and what we believed in."[13]

Influenced by their own direct action as revolutionary feminists, Siren's second play focused on the subject of male violence: *"Curfew* (1981–82) is a play about male violence against women—the ways in which we experience it, the ways we respond to it and are fighting it. Areas of violence examined in the play include pornography, rape and men's control of women's sexuality."[14] Set in the near future, the play focuses on three women's struggle to survive in a nightmare world in which the powerful and controlling "Menace" maintains a mysterious source of strength in the "powerhouses." According to Tash Fairbanks, "the play reflects different aspects of the Women's Movement."[15] One character, Charlene, is a lifetime lesbian, who abhors sexual politics and whose life centers around a lesbian club that has been shut down. Unwilling to fight the Menace, she finally becomes activated at the end of the play when her lover is captured by a powerhouse guard. Tracey, Charlene's lover, is a "rad/rev" lesbian feminist, actively involved in the underground resistance movement. The third character, Fi, is both a socialist feminist and a "manned" woman whose dedication to the resistance and to her male lover produces an irreconcilable conflict resulting in an emotional breakdown. Homophobic, she gradually comes to an understanding and acceptance of many of the issues of lesbianism.

This issue of lesbianism versus heterosexuality caused an enormous split in the women's movement. According to Lynn Alderson, editor and cofounder of the radical feminist journal *Trouble and Strife,* "The tragedy is that one of the main things that divided women was our own debate of political lesbianism versus heterosexuality as a choice. It was at its height at the last national women's liberation conference in 78/79."[16] Siren differentiated itself from the wider movement with its members' identification as lesbians. As Jane Boston puts it: "We were more or less saying, 'come on, this is the solution against male oppression. Forget your men and come with us.'"[17] This differentiation resulted in a homophobic response from many heterosexual feminists. Siren represented this response in its second production.

Siren devised *Curfew* in much the same way as *Mama's Gone A-Hunting,* although in this instance Tash Fairbanks wrote some of the script on her own. The music was composed by Jane Boston and Jude Winter. Described by the company as "a stylistic theatrical counterpart to the cinematic 'film noir' of the 1940's and 1950's,"[18] the production was performed on a silver dome-shaped climbing frame to further define the space, and, dressed in black leotards and silver and black trousers, the performers employed karate, choreography, songs, and live music in this surrealistic theater piece. Limited financially, they created a menacing atmosphere with lighting and unusual sound effects. At this time Debra Trethewey joined the company as technician. In addition to designing sets and lights and running the performances, Debra was the percussionist and the sound designer. This additional member greatly improved the technical aspects of the production in spite of the meager funds available.

Curfew reflected the climate of the times in a very specific way. Peter Sutcliffe, known as the Yorkshire Ripper, was still on the loose and murdering women, although he was caught and tried in 1981, when Siren was invited to a women's conference in Leeds, organized by Women Against Violence Against Women (WAVAW). Sutcliffe was ultimately declared guilty of murdering thirteen women and attempting to murder another seven. His first victim was a prostitute, and Sutcliffe claimed that "God encouraged me to kill people called scum who cannot justify themselves to society." In fact, Sutcliffe maintained that he was able to tell if a woman was a prostitute by the way she walked. If she was a prostitute, he had the right to kill her. During the trial a distinction was drawn between prostitutes and "respectable women," which had the all-too-familiar effect of blaming the victim for the crime.[19]

On the night of Siren's performance a determined group of women marched through the streets of Leeds with banners and torches to "reclaim the night," ending their demonstration at the *Curfew* performance. "I always felt in my bones, if there was any time we were speaking for a movement that was tangible this was the time," says Jane Boston. "I don't know that it was ever quite the same."[20] The topic of violence against women and even the title of their play seemed to capture this historical moment. Unfortunately, this script is still timely: "from the first Reclaim the Night March in Leeds—when women were under *curfew* with the murderous threat of Peter Sutcliffe—we as women still live with the *curfew*."[21]

The music and lyrics to the title song, "Curfew," provide an excellent example of the style of this production. Performed on synthesizer, saxophone, bass guitar, and drums, this soft rock music begins with ominous, sustained sounds played over a driving beat. The lyrics warn women to hear the curfew bell and hide away:

> Out of sight, she is out of mind
> Woman at home
> Behind a drawn blind.[22]

The effect is both alarming and entertaining.

In the first scene the character Fi reveals her homophobia: Charlene and Tracey exchange a kiss, and Fi responds, first naturalistically then surrealistically:

> FI: Oh. I never realized you were weirdo, twisted, queer, maladjusted, neurotic, man-hating, inadequate, lonely, lesser beings.[23]

This is immediately followed by the song "Two Women." With two distinctly different melodic themes and a combination of spoken and sung lyrics this easy rock song provides a foot-tapping response to Fi's ignorance.

The entire production was well received by the press, with particular mention of the music and Siren's clever lyrics addressing women's struggle against tyrannical male dominance.

Siren's next script, *From the Divine* (1983), was inspired by the Falklands War. The company wanted to demonstrate how militarism, machoism, ad patriotism work together. Beginning with the hatred of man for himself, they go on to show how this hatred is directed toward women. "We wanted to look at the State in *From the Divine* because the Falklands War was a real shock to us," says Jane Boston. "It was a disgrace. The type of propaganda that was whipped up in order to summon patriotic fervor was gender related and sexuality and pornography all seemed to come into play."[24]

By this time the company was beginning to discover that collective writing was too time consuming and too difficult. Now the members talked through the politics, the issues, the characters, and the situations, then Tash wrote the script based on the discussions.

According to Hugo Young, a political columnist for the *Guardian*, "The war to reclaim the Falkland Islands from Argentinean occupation was the result of a great failure in the conduct of government: arguably the most disastrous lapse by any British government since 1945."[25] Not recognizing the danger of the Falklands situation until it was too late, Margaret Thatcher ultimately secured an electoral victory through the outcome of this two-month crisis.

From the Divine is set in an army camp in the early 1940s. A cabaret troupe is performing for a group of British soldiers when a working-class angel appears and tells them she is fed up with man's warmongering and the extra cleaning up it creates. She decides to send the world a message through the "show." Under the angel's influence the performers change words in skits and in songs to deliver her message.

In addition to the angel there are four other principal roles in the script: Harry, the troop's manager, writer, and star performer, is played by both an actor and a dummy with the aid of a ventriloquist. Effie, an almost middle-aged woman, trebles as Harry's mistress, a performer, and his righthand helper. Lily is the "ingenue," who represents the "good girl back home," and Ruby is the "tart," who provides the object for male sexual desire. Playing these stereotypes to the extreme in Harry's show, the performers' true natures are revealed during their backstage scenes. We discover, for example, that Effie is obsessed with keeping Harry, even though he is abusive, and Lily and Ruby ultimately decide to form a double act and probably a sexual liaison. Totally consistent both on- and offstage, Harry remains a womanizer.

From the Divine was a tour de force for Tash Fairbanks. Playing multiple roles—the angel, Harry, and Effie (who performed as a ventriloquist with the puppet version of Harry)—she was also responsible for writing the script. A brilliant, self-taught ventriloquist, an experienced actor in cross-dressing, Tash's performance was truly versatile.

The production received rave reviews from the *Tribune* and *Stage and Television Today*. Barney Bardsley from the *Tribune* began her review with the following statement:

> Siren Theatre Company is currently on tour with one of the most imaginative exposés of male-war mentality that I have seen for a long time.[26]

And Tracy Frazer reported:

> Wars are a male pastime and women are only incidental: they are
> whores (to entertain the troops), sweethearts/wives (to keep the
> "home fires burning") or slaves (to clean up after them). This is
> the message of *From the Divine*.[27]

Siren's politics were beginning to change with the times. Lesbians first and foremost, their separatist radical and revolutionary feminisms had not allowed for sufficient inclusion of class issues. When
Debra Trethewey joined the company for *Curfew* the class balance
changed. Now they were evenly divided: two middle-class and two
working-class women. "When we started working together," says
Jude Winter, "we were very close and very similar in our politics.
We agreed on certain fundamentals as women and as lesbians. And
then the differences started showing up. And I think a lot of them had
to do with class. . . . I think what happened was these small differences began to show up in our lives and we had to start talking about
them. . . . We insisted that it was important to talk about class oppression alongside gay oppression, whereas before it was one versus the
other."[28] Siren looked at socialist feminist ideas as they applied to the
members' own lives and the ways in which class differences impacted
their working relationships. *From the Divine* included a working-class
angel. Siren's next play was concerned with working-class issues.

The title of the next play, *Now Wash Your Hands, Please* (1984),
comes from a slogan that is printed on government-issued toilet paper. (Sometimes the words also appear on mirrors or on the backs
of toilet bowls in public places.) The entire play takes place on a
British Rail Inter-city train that is carrying both passengers and nuclear waste. Two strangers—Phyllis, a middle-class physicist, and
Polly, a working-class revolutionary—meet on the train. According
to Siren publicity, "The physicist has the vocabulary and grasp of
Quantum physics, but no political or social consciousness. The revolutionary has gut feelings, visions and dreams, but without the language to communicate them." As the play progresses, these two
women ultimately cooperate and rally the passengers to take action
against those in power. Polly, the revolutionary, also represents the
nuclear family with puppets and ventriloquism. In fact, Polly and her
family (the puppets) have been invited to take a ride on the train for

British Rail promotional purposes. Two other characters, P. R., the middle-class British Rail Agent, and Bert, the working-class conductor, are cross-dressed. An additional twist is that Bert is really a woman who had to change her gender in order to find a job.

Margaret Thatcher's Britain is severely criticized in this farcical script. Issues of classism, unemployment, the nuclear family, nuclear waste, and numerous other topics are examined with razor-sharp wit. The program introduces *Now Wash Your Hands, Please* in this way:

> the fast-moving plot reels from one episode to another of comedy, pathos and biting, savage satire on Tory Britain. Nothing is what it seems, and nothing is quite as it should be—in a play which focuses on the hypocrisies of those in power, the viciousness of their policies and the complexities involved in a struggle to challenge and defeat them. This latter includes the dilemma of how to really communicate a broad conceptual framework of ideas, and to question our very perspectives on the structure of society.

In one scene Phyllis, the scientist, is concerned about discrimination against the second-class passengers. The British Rail employee, P. R., describes the class differences in a witty patter song. He says that there are two groups, us and them.

> Skimmed milk and the creme de la creme
> The trick's not to put it quite that way,
> Or when you say "heel," they'll not obey.[29]

Continuing to express classist views, P. R. makes it clear that the "superior" class need only create the illusion of equality and mobility and the "other" will be satisfied.

A new actor, Hilary Ramsden, joined Siren for this production and became a permanent member. An invigorating force, Hilary's physical and humorous approach was, and continues to be, a valuable addition to the company.

Lyn Gardner praised the production in her review for *City Limits:*

> *Now Wash Your Hands, Please* may pick on obvious targets (nuclear families, nuclear waste and unemployment amongst many)

but it does so with a stunning display of subversive Stoppardian wit, a brilliantly anarchic scenario and music and lyrics that provide a sobering counterpoint to the satire.[30]

In a later edition of *City Limits* Siren was given additional credit for its fine work:

> But the major contributions of the year, and surely the phenomenon that will leave the greatest long term mark upon British theatre was the remarkable upsurge in writing by women. Not that they haven't always been there but 1984 was the year that women really made their voices heard [in production's such as] Siren's witty expose of Tory Britain *Now Wash Your Hands, Please*.[31]

Siren explored various kinds of oppression against women and the ways in which the state contributed to this oppression in its first plays. In its next play, *Pulp* (1985–86), directed by Noelle Janaczewska, Siren wanted to look at lesbian desire. According to Susan Ardill and Sue O'Sullivan: "In Britain, the struggle around lesbian sexuality has been muted and spasmodic, though accompanied by often violently intense reactions. This struggle to retrieve eroticism in the face of, among other things, the political desexualization of lesbianism, has been characterized here by an almost complete absence of talking or writing about sex."[32]

Siren wanted to explore the lesbian culture in this production, representing lesbians as both "good girls and bad girls." "I think we did this play because of and in relation to the changes in the Women's Movement," says Debra Trethewey. "We were going to Women's Liberation Conferences when we were doing *Mama*... and *Curfew* and the discussions revolved around abortion, violence against women, lesbianism and pornography, and so on. At a later date the discussions were about [lesbian] monogamy and long-term relationships."[33]

"I think it became imperative that we look at ourselves," says Jane Boston. "We asked ourselves what are we doing with our own power, our own relationships? Where is the lesbian continuum? One got subsumed into the wider [women's] movement and yet there are enormous differences. Some lesbian theorists argue that there is an entirely separate lesbian continuum that comes through. There is a culture, there are sensibilities, emotions that are often underground, covert, but they are there to be discovered."[34]

Siren used the word *lesbian* in its publicity material for the first time for *Pulp*. Although its identity as a lesbian company was clearly established and its politics were firmly grounded in this identification, *Pulp* was the first script to examine the theme of personal relationships among women. Engaged in the usual lengthy personal and political discussions prior to scripting, the members investigated this subject through their own varied experiences as lesbians, focusing on questions of lesbian identity and desire. "But the message, if there was a message," says Jude Winter, "was that every individual choice that you take as a lesbian has political ramifications. To be out as a lesbian is difficult, and can ruin an individual's career and family relations, but it is a necessary political choice. . . . A big part of that play was about the choices we make."[35]

Pulp, a lesbian thriller, is set in two different time zones: New York, McCarthyite 1950s and London in 1985. And, because one of the characters was a guard in Hitler's extermination camps, philosophically, the play covers three time periods. Influenced by detective novels, Ann Bannon books, and Humphrey Bogart films, this is a seedy tale of crime, double dealing, and desire. The characters on the American side include a blacklisted movie star who sings in a shabby club, a tough newspaper reporter, a waitress-groupie, and a bungling detective. The London scenes revolve around two British government undercover spies, who keep their lesbianism closeted, and a German neighbor. For the first time all the characters are women, and all the women are lesbians. The actors are double cast, except for the detective, who crosses the time zone, providing the physical connection between the two "plays." Politically, numerous parallels are drawn between the two countries in the two different time periods. The issues of personal choice, "coming out," honesty, and fear of failure are examined in the text.

In many ways *Pulp* is Siren's best work to date. The script is more tightly constructed than the scripts of earlier plays, and the interweaving of two time periods is brilliant. The songs are well placed, although less melodic than some of Siren's earlier music, and the performers move comfortably from the scenes to the music and the songs. Noelle Janaczewska showed greater artistry than any of the previous Siren directors. Her high camp style, her use of long, slow takes, tight blocking, butch-femme characterizations, and multiple role playing were well executed by this talented company.

In addition to creating a powerful piece of theater the company gained a new member, Rose Sharp, during the run of *Pulp*. An experienced administrator, Rose came to the company with an excellent theater background and provided much needed assistance with organization, publicity, and booking tours.

Two reviewers from *City Lights* praised the production:

> If you're looking for a show that's daft, daffy and deliciously dizzy, see *Pulp*. If you're looking for a show that's serious, sinister and sad, see *Pulp*. This ambitious new play from the multi-talented Siren Theatre Company is two plays in one, successfully cutting across two time zones.[36]

> Siren have always been mesmerised by the idea of time travel, they move their performances through both past and future and around a central theme of DANGER: the danger of lesbian sexuality (and of any kind of "otherness") to straight society. They're always funny; always full of life; and often very dramatic about what happens when the powers-that-be turn nasty.[37]

Since *Pulp* Siren has performed five additional shows: *Chic to Chic* (1984–87), a cabaret employing stand-up political satire, ventriloquism, and rock music; *Bubbles* (1987), a nonlinear experimental play concerned with the nature and construction of reality; *Hotel Destiny* (1987–88), a British Western look at women performers in the country western music genre; *Les Les* (1988–), a two-character play on the subject of lesbian relationships performed by Jane Boston and Jude Winter; and *Swamp* (1989), a play about the destiny of three Greek mythological Fates—Clotho, Atropos, and Lachesis—directed by Clare M. Brennan from Théâtre de Complicité. Although these next five productions continue to represent women within British society, the earlier period reflects the more rapid transformations in British feminism.

Siren's first five productions reflect political events and changes in the women's liberation movement and lesbianism through a variety of theatrical forms and acting techniques. Examining war from a

historical perspective (World War II) and its relationship to the present (the Falklands War) in *From the Divine,* looking into the future in
Mama's Gone A-Hunting and in *Curfew,* and combining two different
time zones (the 1950s and the present) in two different countries in
Pulp, Siren has examined woman's international oppression in the
past, in the present, and in the future.

Mama's Gone A-Hunting revealed a radical feminist perspective.
Woman was fed up with Man and decided to separate from him by
leaving the planet and constructing a woman-only society. Using
revolutionary feminist ideology in *Curfew,* the women took direct
action against the male powerhouses. Socialist feminism took the
stage when the message in *From the Divine* came from a working-class
angel. And *Now Wash Your Hands, Please* revealed classism in the
disputes between the middle-class and the working-class British Rail
employees and passengers. Lesbian identity, desire, and culture were
fully revealed in *Pulp.* But, whatever particular feminism was explored in these plays, they all came from a lesbian perspective.

These historical events and political ideologies were represented
through the use of nonrealistic acting styles. Using agitprop techniques and cartoonish characterizations in *Mama's Gone A-Hunting,* a
"larger-than-life" reality and surrealism in *Curfew* and in *From the
Divine,* adding elements of farce to an "over the top" reality in *Now
Wash Your Hands, Please,* and camping butch/femme roles in *Pulp,*
Siren's work represented woman in the subject position and always
included a lesbian perspective and the theme of woman's love for
woman. Drawing from the male-dominated punk music scene, Siren
further disrupted reality through the placement of music, songs, and
dance. Cross-dressing in three of the plays empowered the women
playing men, subverted male power through humor, and allowed the
audience to examine the nature of the male prerogative as it exists in
the dominant culture. The use of ventriloquism created multiple levels of meaning in man's relationship to himself in *From the Divine* and
in the nuclear family in *Now Wash Your Hands, Please.*

What is the state of the women's liberation movement and
feminism now? Current British feminism also reflects pluralisms of
ideology, race, class, ableness, and sexual preference. For a variety
of possible reasons—the end of a decade; the last national conference
in 1980; the disappearance of the national newsletter, *Wires,* and
numerous other feminist publications—the need to understand their

history as both an educational tool and as a means of focusing future action—"Feminists are now, particularly, being driven to try to understand ourselves within a historical context."[38] Books such as *'68, '78, '88: From Women's Liberation to Feminism,* edited by Amanda Sebestyen; *The Past before Us: Feminism in Action since the 1960's,* by Shelia Rowbotham; and *Once a Feminist: Stories of a Generation,* by Michelene Wandor; and periodicals such as *Trouble and Strife* and *Spare Rib* are recording a portion of the history of the women's movement from the late 1960s to the present.

A recent article written by the Spare Rib Collective views the lack of hegemony and the diversity of representation as potential strength for the women's movement.

> In trying to understand what is the modern day women's movement—there is no specific theoretical work to turn to, and no central organising committee to contact for a definitive blueprint. . . . this is one of the most potentially dynamic and exciting aspects of the women's movement, affording it a flexibility, and a possibility for a unity with diversity, that is liberating in itself. . . . It has de-emphasised theory and dogma and rules and text book politics . . . and this has led to an emphasis on "process" and "practice."[39]

The Siren Theatre Company reflects this statement. Although they engaged in endless hours of theorizing, ultimately the process of shaping their ideologies was put into practice through the rehearsals and performances of their scripts. The *Spare Rib* article goes on to quote Gita Sen and Caren Grown's global view of feminism (from their book, *Development, Crises and Alternative Visions: Third World Women's Perspectives*):

> Beneath this diversity, feminism has as its unshakable core a commitment to breaking down the structures of gender subordination, and a vision for women as full and equal participants with men at all levels of societal life. . . . But a political movement that is potentially global in scope, needs greater flexibility, openness, and sensitivity to issues and methods as defined by different groups of women for themselves."[40]

Jill Davis represents a different lesbian perspective on the late
1980s in her introduction to *Lesbian Plays:*

> Lesbian women, then, often feel that neither the Women's move-
> ment, in its "pro-family" phase, nor the Gay movement, which
> is inevitably preoccupied by campaigns around AIDS . . . is ap-
> propriately representing their interests. This feeling is voiced in
> the editorial collective's introduction to the first issue of *Gossip*
> [a lesbian radical feminist journal] in 1986: "Many of us have felt
> silenced in the last few years as the Women's Liberation Move-
> ment drifts further and further away from feminism and lesbian-
> ism towards humanism, socialism and liberalism."[41]

In fact, lesbian and gay rights are being eroded under section 28
of the Local Government Act, passed on 24 May 1988: "Section 28
outlaws the 'intentional promotion of homosexuality' by local
authorities, and forbids the teaching of the 'acceptability' of homosexuality as a pretended family relationship."[42] Although there have
been no court cases involving this discriminatory legislation, it has
been intimidating and effective in local government self-censorship.
The lesbian and gay communities have responded to this discriminatory legislation in a number of ways, including marches and
campaigns organized by the Organization for Lesbian and Gay
Action (OLGA). Unfortunately, section 28 is only one of a number
of measures taken by the Thatcher government to erode civil
liberties.

What does the future hold for Siren Theatre Company? Even
though its members are living under a repressive government, the
restrictions of section 28, and an arts funding system that makes it
increasingly more difficult to obtain support, Siren plans to produce
new work.

The atmosphere in England continues to be repressive. The resignation of Luke Rittner, the secretary-general of the Arts Council,
the release of Richard Wilding's report in September 1989—*Supporting the Arts: A Review of the Structure of Arts Funding*—will affect the
policies of the Arts Council and the Regional Arts associations. Political theater, as it existed in the 1980s, will continue to suffer as a result
of these changes.

NOTES

1. 1967—Sexual Offences Act (liberating for male homosexuals), 1968—Theatre Censorship abolished, 1969—Divorce Reform Act, 1970—Equal Pay Act. For a discussion of the ramifications of these acts, see Michelene Wandor, *Carry On, Understudies: Theatre and Sexual Politics* (London: Routledge and Kegan Paul, 1986), 1–18; and Philip Osment, ed., *Gay Sweatshop: Four Plays and a Company* (London: Methuen, 1989), xi–xiii.

2. Michelene Wandor, *Strike while the Iron Is Hot* (London: Journeyman Press, 1980), 7–8.

3. Noelle Janaczewska, "'Do We Want a Piece of the Cake, or Do We Want to Bake a Whole New One?' Feminist Theatre in Britain," *Hecate* 8, no. 1 (1987): 109.

4. Jude Winter, interview with author, London, 21 March 1989.

5. Interview with author, London, 20 March 1989.

6. Ibid.

7. Michelene Wandor, *Carry On, Understudies*, xix.

8. Jane Boston, interview with author, London, 17 April 1989.

9. Tash Fairbanks. "Mama's Gone A-Hunting," Audiocassette, London, 1980.

10. Jim Gilchrist, "Mama's Gone A-Hunting," *Scotsman*, 26 August 1980.

11. Ros Asquith, "Mama's Gone A-Hunting," *Time Out*, 17 October 1980.

12. South East Arts Association, Eastern Arts Association, Greater London Arts Association, and North West Arts Association.

13. Interview with author, London, 21 March 1989.

14. Siren Theatre Company, *Curfew* program, 1981.

15. Interview with author, London, 20 March 1989.

16. Interview with author, London, 11 July 1989.

17. Interview with author, London, 17 April 1989.

18. Ibid.

19. Wendy Hollway, "'I Just Wanted to Kill a Woman' Why? The Ripper and Male Sexuality," in *Sexuality: A Reader,* ed. Feminist Review (London: Virago Press, 1987), 123–33.

20. Interview with author, London, 17 April 1989.

21. Spare Rib Collective, eds., "Reclaiming the Night," *Spare Rib* 208 (December 1989–January 1990): 87.

22. Siren Theatre Company, "Siren Plays," audiocassette, 1983.

23. Tash Fairbanks, *Curfew,* 1981; photocopy, 1981.

24. Interview with author, London, 17 April 1989.

25. Hugo Young, *One of Us* (London: Macmillan, 1989), 258.

26. Barney Bardsley, "War and Marriage," *Tribune,* 8 July 1983.

27. "From the Divine," *The Stage and Television Today,* 16 June 1983.

28. Interview with author, London, 21 March 1989.

29. Tash Fairbanks, *Now Wash Your Hands, Please,* 1984; photocopy.

30. "Now Wash Your Hands, Please," *City Limits* 168 (21–27 December).

31. "Theatre: News and Reviews," *City Limits* 170 (4–10 January).

32. "Upsetting an Applecart: Difference, Desire and Lesbian Sadomasochism," in Feminist Review, *Sexuality*, 288.

33. Interview with author, London, 21 March 1989.

34. Interview with author, London, 17 April 1989.

35. Interview with author, London, 21 March 1989.

36. Lyn Gardner, "Pulp," *City Limits*, 15–21 November 1985.

37. Barney Bardsley, "Theatre," *City Limits*, 8–14 November 1985.

38. Sophie Laws, "'68 '78 '88," *Trouble and Strife* 16 (Summer 1989): 31.

39. Editorial Collective, "Spare Rib Replies," *Spare Rib* 209 (February 1990): 6.

40. Ibid.

41. Jill Davis, *Lesbian Plays* (London: Methuen, 1987), 10.

42. Spare Rib Collective, "Section 28 Local Government Act," *Spare Rib* 197 (December 1988–January 1989): 7.

Chapter 10

The Women's Experimental Theatre: Transforming Family Stories into Feminist Questions

Julie Malnig and Judy C. Rosenthal

I am a separate person
This is my body
These are my thoughts
This is my mouth
My voice
These are my words
I speak for myself

—from *Electra Speaks*

The Women's Experimental Theatre, founded by Clare Coss, Sondra Segal, and Roberta Sklar was one of the foremost women's theatrical collaboratives of the 1970s. Its earliest and best-known work, *The Daughters Cycle* trilogy (1977–81), was a trenchant, often deeply disturbing theatrical exploration of women within the Western, patriarchal family. Each of the three plays, *Daughters, Sister/Sister,* and *Electra Speaks,* reflects an ongoing journey of the women protagonists, as they grow from childhood, adolescence, through adulthood, until Electra finally finds her voice and moves out of the confines of the house. Segal and Sklar's last work, *Feast or Famine* (1985), continued where *The Daughters Cycle* ended, exploring women's negotiation with the world through their relationship to food and their bodies.

The work of the Women's Experimental Theatre (W.E.T.) was emblematic of the revolutionary and culturally creative years of the

201

1960s and early 1970s. It clearly bears the mark of the politics of the period, when the roles of the artist and the social activist merged. Abbie Hoffman faced the House un-American Activities Committee in an Uncle Sam costume; R. Crumb produced dope-smoking comic book characters; and rock groups performed songs of liberation and revolution. New York City's experimental theater, too, reflected this moment of expressive cultural politics in the work of companies such as the Performing Garage, the Open Theatre, and the Living Theatre.

During the late 1960s women who had been working in the counterculture with male New Leftists began to question their own subordinate roles in that supposedly egalitarian world. After unsuccessful attempts to change sexist attitudes many women decided to leave the male-dominated venues altogether. They were, of course, bolstered by a nascent feminist movement, which exposed previously unexpressed desires and needs. In the arts as well as in the theater, there was a renaissance of creative activity, as women discovered latent talent as artists, writers, and producers. Roberta Sklar, one of W.E.T.'s founders, was one such woman. During the early 1970s Sklar had been a codirector with Joseph Chaikin of the Open Theatre. Although Sklar acknowledges the pivotal influence of the Open Theatre on her own directorial and creative work, her reason for leaving the troupe had to do with her inability to develop fully as an artist and a feminist. She saw the men in the company confronting their own racism and the horrors of the Vietnam War yet unable to recognize their own sexism.

In 1971 Sklar attended a performance of It's Alright to be Woman Theatre, an all-female company performing only for women. Sklar was fascinated by this grass-roots theater and the unique rapport established between the players and their audience.[1] During the following two years she taught acting and directing from a feminist viewpoint, shaping her ideas both at the Womanrite Theatre Ensemble and at the Woman's Unit of Bard College. There she was particularly attracted to the work of Sondra Segal (a founder of Womanrite) and writer Clare Coss, with whom, in 1976, she founded the Women's Experimental Theatre.

W.E.T.'s early explorations deepened their own understanding of the possibilities of feminist/political theater. Their primary concern was not simply to reflect women's experiences, but to explore the explicit ways in which gender roles are reinforced and embedded in cultural institutions. They sought to identify those universals that could be traced to female experience as differentiated from previously accepted universals derived from the male perspective.[2] W.E.T.'s work stemmed from the then revolutionary belief that "women are neither flawed, nor self-hating nor inadequate" and that staging moments of their lives could constitute entertaining and instructive theater.[3] Deborah Margolin, a member of the Split Britches Company, recalls the transformative experience of seeing W.E.T.'s *Electra Speaks* for the first time: "I never saw theatre like this. I never saw women that weren't perfect little blonds singing arpeggios. These were skinny women, large women, of different ethnic backgrounds. They affirmed that women's lives have theatrically viable images."[4]

As Coss, Segal, and Sklar shaped the work that would eventually evolve into *The Daughters Cycle,* Margot Lewitin, artistic director of New York City's Interart Theatre, invited the company to use part of her space as their artistic home. For the rest of their producing life they were in residence at the Interart's Fifty-third Street Annex, where they had enormous creative freedom. W.E.T. often worked up to a year on one piece, continually exploring themes and ideas. Without the donated space and support provided by Lewitin and Ronnie Geist, director of programs, it is questionable whether this alternative theater company would have been able to develop and continue.

The history of the Women's Experimental Theatre is instructive since its development reflected the growth of the women's movement in the United States during the 1970s and early 1980s. One of the tools employed by Coss, Segal, and Sklar was that of consciousness raising, a technique being used in living rooms, dining rooms, and kitchens around the country. Women were attempting to construct a politics based on their experiences and concerns—as literary historian Susie Tharu describes, "by challenging and recasting a dominant ideology's characterizations."[5] Members of W.E.T. held workshops (sometimes consisting of groups of over one hundred women) employing a combination of consciousness-raising methods and research to express theatrically the issues being explored. Although Coss, Segal, and Sklar reached out to others for ideas and inspiration, perceiving their audiences as "sister feminists," W.E.T. "was never a participatory democracy."[6] The artistic directors were responsible for developing and shaping the theatrical product.

The first major work of the Women's Experimental Theatre, *The Daughters Cycle,* proceeded to "look at the mother, the daughter, the sister, the woman-self, the corridor of roles implicit in daughter-hood" to facilitate an analysis of women in the patriarchal family.[7] *Daughters,* the first piece of the trilogy, looked closely at the psychic bonds between mothers and daughters. W.E.T. began to explore and deconstruct the "deeply held desire to merge, and the urgent struggle to separate."[8] *Daughters* suggests that in the traditional family, a gendered system that devalues female experience, mutually healthy and satisfying relationships between mother and daughter are impossible.

In its nonlinear, episodic structure *Daughters* enabled the performers to probe the inner lives of the characters, to explore what goes unsaid between parent and child. As Sklar says, "Women knew all along that feelings don't happen in logical sequence."[9] The play comprised a series of vignettes from domestic life, actors shifting back and forth between scenes of adulthood and childhood. The complexity of the relationship between mother and daughter, the way each, at times, absorbs the feelings of the other, was reflected, for instance, in the mother/daughter "totem," in which two women, portraying mother and daughter, perform side by side throughout the production.

Company members consciously performed for an imagined feminist spectator, perceiving each audience member as an "acting partner."[10] W.E.T.'s intent was both to enable women to identify with the characters and to make them aware of women's historical position within culture and within the family. Analogous to the Brechtian theatrical stance, performers in the company saw themselves as engaged in the "simultaneous presentation of self as well as social role and character."[11] The techniques used by W.E.T. served to interrupt and intensify the spectator's emotional involvement, such as the use of a chorus, whose words are spoken over the dialogue between mother and daughter. In a repetitive chant the chorus repeated phrases such as "the mother said to the daughter; the daughter said to the mother." The use of raucous laughter after particularly poignant moments further distanced the audience from the action, allowing its members to become, as feminist theorist Elin Diamond has noted of the Brechtian spectator, "passionately and pleasurably engaged in observation and analysis."[12]

Defining a feminist subject position was a principal goal of the company. One way to challenge objectification was for performers to publicly identify their familial heritage. All performances began with "The Matrilineage," a ritual form in which each actor recites her name, recalling her female ancestry. The Matrilineage names mothers, grandmothers, and great grandmothers, giving tribute to those who may not have been recognized during their lifetime:

> I am Sondra
> daughter of Lille
> daughter of Sarah Rebecca
> daughter of Tzivia
> daughter of a woman from Austria
> whose name I don't know
>
> . . . .
> I am Mary
> daughter of Chew Kwong Ping
> daughter of Nok Yip Lee
> daughter of a peasant woman from my ancestral
> village of Sun Wei in Guangdong, China. . . . [13]

The revitalizing of the mother/daughter connection is forcefully presented in a poetic sequence describing the birth process:

> *Mother:*   Close your eyes. Spread your legs.
> Feel the heat between your legs,
> Imagine yourself becoming wet,
> The muscles of your legs and pelvis
> pulling back, becoming tighter and
> tighter as you open . . .
> You are splitting open
> You are looking down.
> And feel.
> And see.
> A hard round head
> emerging
> Emerging from your body. . . . [14]

Although this graphic image of the mother's experience seems to some performance scholars to foreground a disturbing essentialist position, the crucial, final utterance in this scene,

> Do you wonder why you feel so connected
> to your mother?

brings the spectator back to the analysis of daughterhood and undercuts the valorization of the biological mother and the birthing experience.[15] Although the anatomical ability to bear a child is employed effectively as a theatrical image, the eventual focus of the scene is, in fact, on generational bonding. A constant desire for a healing of the physical and cultural severing of the mother/daughter connective cord is echoed throughout the text. Stage imagery reflects these feelings of grief and desire, culminating in scene 3's stage direction:

> Freeze. An icon of connection.
> separation, and loss [16]

In the second play of the cycle, *Sister/Sister,* W.E.T. confronted the relationships between the female siblings in the family dynamic, looking at the "shifting patterns of alliance and betrayal" among biological sisters.[17] With humor and pathos, the first act illuminates the pain experienced by adult women as they attempt to define their positions in the family. The older, middle, and younger siblings express the complexities of their relationships:

> What do I want from you?
> closeness without sameness
> support without competition
> loyalty without betrayal
> an ending to those ancient dualities
> an ending to living in comparison. . . . [18]

In act 2 of *Sister/Sister* the text focuses on the situation Coss, Segal, and Sklar believe to be a "metaphoric rite of passage" for every woman—"the death of the Mother."[19] In the Quadrologue, for instance, four siblings poignantly describe their relationship to their mother after she dies and openly express their confused feelings toward one another. They blame each other for feelings of loss while at the same time hoping to resolve their differences. This examination of ambivalent emotions among sisters was a continuation of W.E.T.'s effort to unite women through theater. The Quadrologue implies that, by confronting the pain and possibility within each household, women could both achieve reconciliation with their families and activate a larger vision of sisterhood.

Electra Speaks, the culmination of the trilogy, reflected most closely the exciting work being undertaken by feminist critics and theorists of the time, of excavating the lost, untold stories of women, in literature, history, and art. In *Electra Speaks* W.E.T. set out to reexamine the Greek myth of the House of Atreus, attempting, in theorist Teresa de Lauretis's words, to "retell well-known stories in order to destabilize the literary myths of origin."[20] The piece opens with a voice-over of Electra, repeating "the old story." The accompanying performers "go through a series of transforming physical and vocal images,"[21] depicting the horrors of the myth—Agamemnon's sacrifice of his daughter Iphigenia to promote his success at war; Clytemnestra's murder of her husband and his lover, Cassandra, in revenge; and the resulting death of Clytemnestra and her lover, at the hands of her enraged son, Orestes. Of this powerful legend the artistic directors asked themselves, "what was the feminist question"[22] that needed exploring: What were the actions of the women during Agamemnon's years of war, and how does a contemporary Electra move from reactive object to actively realized subject?

As in *Daughters, Electra Speaks* is structured through a series of short scenic compositions using techniques of direct address, commentary, and repetition. More than in the previous parts of the trilogy, *Electra Speaks* questioned the notion of fixed gender, as the actors continually exchanged roles of father, mother, brother, and sister. As the women embodied both sexes, theorist Judith Butler's concept of gender as a "performative accomplishment" becomes clear.[23] The cast members, all female, could easily enact the masculine personae of Agamemnon or Orestes, illustrating the malleability of sex-role construction. Each performer at one point also assumes the identity of Electra herself, symbolizing a kind of Electra everywoman, or "everydaughter."

Unlike *Daughters,* or *Sister/Sister, Electra Speaks* is filled with the violence of fathers and sons, husbands and lovers, often embodied in

the male characters of the House of Agamemnon. While the earlier
plays of the trilogy focused on healing mother–daughter rifts and
locating one's feelings of powerlessness and low self-esteem as deriving from the family, in *Electra Speaks* the characters react against the
men in the story to break free from patriarchal authority and control.

Before Electra can begin to assert her independence, however,
she must understand how role assignments are culturally embedded
and how they work to thwart women's selfhood. In a discussion of
the dynamics of the institutionalized family psychoanalytic feminist
Jessica Benjamin notes, "In every case, the male side of the pole,
particularly the emphatic autonomy that denies interdependence and
mutuality [between mother and children] has been idealized."[24] What
Electra Speaks brings into sharper focus is the fact that within the
traditional family autonomy is embodied in the male, involving rejection and devaluation of the mother. Electra eventually realizes, however, that autonomy does not have to mean denial of the mother.
Coss, Segal, and Sklar use the image of Orestes to illustrate the dangers of excessive valorization of male autonomy, which can result in
the abuse of power and repressive, deadly political systems:

> her milk kept him alive
> his mother became his food
> his mother was his nurturance
> food, nurturance, warmth
> his mother, her breast, were his
>
> . . . .
>
> he's turned her into a tit,
> a jug   a tit   a boob
>
> . . . .
>
> this baby, this infant, this boy
> has colonized her body
>
> . . . .
>
> he creates his institutions
> religion   family law
> philosophy   education
> at night he sucks her titty
> by day he wreaks his vengeance

(30)

In its feminist revisioning of the Agamemnon legend *Electra Speaks* also illuminates the divisions among the women members of the family. The suspicions women have of one another are painfully demonstrated in Electra's plea to her mother. Agamemnon had demanded that Clytemnestra send him their eldest daughter, Iphigenia, promising to have her wed to a war hero. How, Electra asks, could Clytemnestra have permitted Iphigenia to be sacrificed for the sake of victory and the "favorable winds of war"?

> *Electra:* Suppose the winds hadn't come. Suppose after he killed her the winds hadn't come. Suppose he had said Electra, I need Electra too, send me Electra. What would you have done. . . . Or you, suppose he had sent for you. Suppose he had decided that only your life, your blood running cold on his knife would have brought him his precious winds. Then what would you have done. Would you have pretended not to know. Would you have pretended to believe he was just missing you. What would you have done. I hate you. I hate you for this. You would have sent me too.
>
> *Clytemnestra:* Yes, Electra. I would have sent you too. I would have had to send you too. I would have had to believe your father.
>
> (85)

When Electra finally begins to speak as a contemporary woman she begins haltingly, in the third person, obviously fighting societal and familial forces, which threaten to silence her:

> She is biting her lip
> she is picking her fingernails
> she is clearing her throat
>
> . . . .
> she laughs
> she laughs at herself
> she's making a joke
> she's laughing
> she's laughing and giggling
> and sputtering and chuckling
> she's guffawing. . . .
>
> (48)

In this initial attempt at self-definition the audience witnesses an Electra trying to recreate herself after years of indoctrination and stereotyped behavior. Electra has come to understand her previous obedience to an essentially idealized, absent father. During the play's final sequence Electra addresses her real father, no longer desiring to conform to his expectations yet still unsure of her path:

> I don't know how to be any more. I can either be your daughter or my self. I don't know how to act any more. I used to pass. I used to pass very well. I can't pass any more. I don't know how to talk any more. I don't know how to act. . . . (124)

Finally, Electra musters the will to leave and enters the threshold of a new life:

> She tugs
> she lugs
> she lurches
> she heaves
> she hauls
>
> . . . . .
>
> She stands firm.
>
> (127)

Electra will use the confrontations with the mother and father figures to propel herself into possibility and begin to fulfill Teresa de Lauretis's vision of a "feminist subject," this newly formed being who "can find self-determination, can change."[25]

Part of the power of Electra's closing monologue in *Electra Speaks* is conveyed through Sondra Segal's riveting performance. She is, in many ways, a perfect Brechtian-feminist actor, inviting the spectator "to look beyond representation."[26] As she spews out her words, in a flow of "fast talk," her mobile face registers one emotion after another—pain, hatred, shyness, tenderness, confusion, tentativeness.[27] Rather than dwelling on any one emotion, the audience reacts to the total effect of these transformations, recognizing them as a series of protective masks women wear throughout their lives.

In their next major project, Segal and Sklar continued the work of the Women's Experimental Theatre, while Clare Coss resigned to work on her own play writing. The two remaining directors asked in *Women's Body and Other Natural Resources* (1980–85), what happens to Electra when she moves out of the family into the world? Another trilogy, this work specifically explored the issue of food as a "paradigm for the way women relate to the world and the world relates to women."[28] The first two works, *Food* and *Food Talk,* were improvisational pieces in which women audience members shared feelings, earliest memories, and attitudes toward food. Both pieces served as foundational research for their final and most technically complicated work, *Feast or Famine.*

This two-character play, which contained filmed scenes, slide projections, and sculptural representations, dramatized women in domestic and workplace settings as they struggle with their food obsessions. The family dinner hour, for instance, is seen as a locus of control and power for Dad (played by Segal) as he criticizes and manipulates his wife and children. The supporting players in the piece were what Sklar and Segal identified as the "icons of the dilemma," an oversized refrigerator on wheels and a scale, which assume mythic proportions as the play progresses. The refrigerator literally follows Segal around the kitchen, beckoning to her, an unnerving reminder of the obsessions that dominate her life.

Women's warped body images and their complicity in the culture's devaluation of women's status is best illustrated in the devastating nightclub sequences. Segal portrays a stand-up comedian, encased in an oversized body mold, which both distorts and shields her body. She rapidly delivers a series of stinging sexual and ethnic one-liners until, by the end of her monologue, when her jokes pair women and garbage, she apologizes to her audience and breaks down.

Feast or Famine, written by Segal and directed by Sklar, attempted to make much needed connections between women's relationship with food and global politics. As Segal's performer/character declares in a jazz riff:

> What if I didn't lose weight
> What would happen if I didn't lose weight?
> If I weren't obsessed with my body size so
> Well, where on earth would all my energy go?
>
> . . . .
> This economy needs

Me to starve
You to binge
And the third world to bleed[29]

In several scenes oversized slide images of women and children in unidentified Third World countries are projected against Segal and the back wall of the theater. This image suggests "the association with food as nurturance and power is not merely a white, middle-class, western women's issue."[30] Food, like women's bodies, is used as a medium of exchange in an international economy.

By 1985 Segal and Sklar decided to stop producing theater. The group found they could not depend on the bond that had existed a decade earlier between the company and its audience members. Feminists had entered a period of self-reflection and criticism and were grappling with issues of sexual, class, and racial differences within their own community. Sklar, in fact, acknowledges that "things were going on in the women's movement we may not have been aware of."[31] In addition to changes within the women's movement, societal problems were impinging on all alternative enterprises. With a constricting economy, for instance, resources previously available for women's theater and culture were no longer as readily accessible. Women's Experimental Theatre's extant body of work is still, however, an expansive reflection of feminist politics illuminating issues of importance to the early women's movement. The group's staged deconstruction of the family represents a critical step in the ongoing development of feminist theory and theater.

NOTES

1. Cornelia Brunner, "Roberta Sklar: Toward Creating a Women's Theatre," *Drama Review* 24, no. 2 (June 1980): 35.

2. Roberta Sklar and Sondra Segal, interview by Julie Malnig and Judy Rosenthal, 1 February 1991.

3. Ibid.

4. Deborah Margolin, interview by Julie Malnig, 12 May 1991.

5. Susie Tharu and K. Lalita, *Women Writing in India: 600 B.C. to Present,* (New York: The Feminist Press at The City University of New York, 1991): 1:29.

6. Roberta Sklar and Sondra Segal, interview with Julie Malnig and Judy Rosenthal, 30 January 1991.

7. Clare Coss, Sondra Segal, and Roberta Sklar, *Daughters*, pt. 1 of *The Daughters Cycle, Massachusetts Review* 24, no. 1 (Spring 1983): 142.

8. Ibid.

9. Brunner, "Roberta Sklar: Toward Creating a Women's Theatre," 27.

10. Sondra Segal, interview, 1 February 1991.

11. Clare Coss, Sondra Segal, and Roberta Sklar, "Why Do We Need a Feminist Theatre?" *Women & Performance* 1, no. 1 (Spring-Summer 1983): 60.

12. Elin Diamond, "Brechtian Theory/Feminist Theory: Toward a Gestic Feminist Criticism," *Drama Review* 32, no. 1 (Spring 1988): 83.

13. Coss, Segal, and Sklar, *Daughters*, 143.

14. Ibid., 146–47.

15. Performance critic Jill Dolan, for instance, views the birth sequence as a glorification of motherhood and believes that the scene "implies that a woman's self-fulfillment can best be attained by fulfilling her biological capabilities." See Dolan, *The Feminist Spectator as Critic* (1988; reprint, Ann Arbor: University of Michigan Press, 1991), 90.

16. Coss, Segal, and Sklar, *Daughters*, 151.

17. Roberta Sklar, "*Sisters* or Never Trust Anyone outside the Family," *Women & Performance* 1, no. 1 (Spring-Summer 1983): 61.

18. Clare Coss, Sondra Segal, and Roberta Sklar, *Sister/Sister*, in *The Future of Difference*, ed. Hester Eisenstein and Alice Jardine (Boston: G. K. Hall, 1980), 197.

19. Sklar, "*Sisters*," 62.

20. Teresa de Lauretis, ed., *Feminist Studies/Critical Studies* (Bloomington: Indiana University Press, 1986), 11.

21. Clare Coss, Sondra Segal, and Roberta Sklar, *Electra Speaks* (unpub. MS, private collection, 1980), 10.

22. Segal and Sklar, interview, 1 February 1991.

23. Judith Butler, "Performative Acts and Gender Constitution: An Essay in Phenomenology and Feminist Theory," in *Performing Feminisms: Feminist Critical Theory and Theatre*, ed. Sue-Ellen Case (Baltimore: Johns Hopkins University Press, 1990), 271.

24. Jessica Benjamin, "A Desire of One's Own: Psychoanalytic Feminism and Intersubjective Space," in de Lauretis, *Feminist Studies*, 91.

25. Sue-Ellen Case, "Toward a Butch-Femme Aesthetic," in *Making a Spectacle: Feminist Essays on Contemporary Women's Theatre*, ed. Lynda Hart (Ann Arbor: University of Michigan Press, 1989), 282–83. Case is expanding on de Lauretis's concept of the feminist subject

26. Diamond, "Brechtian Theory," 86.

27. "Fast talk" was an acting technique employed by the Women's Experimental Theatre. It expressed what W.E.T. considered the obsessional nature of women's internal experience and enabled performers to articulate feelings and desires previously suppressed and silenced.

28. Sklar and Segal, interview, 1 February 1991.

29. *Feast or Famine*, unpublished manuscript, p. 69.

30. Lisa Merrill, review of *Feast or Famine, Women & Performance* 3, no. 1 (1986): 105.

31. Sklar, interview, 1 February 1991.

Chapter 11

Split Britches in *Split Britches*: Performing History, Vaudeville, and the Everyday

Vivian M. Patraka

Production History

The Split Britches Company is an eleven-year-old, three-woman theater company whose members, Peggy Shaw, Lois Weaver, and Deborah Margolin, have written and directed *Split Britches* (1981), *Beauty and the Beast* (1982), *Unpwardly Mobile Home* (1984), *Little Women* (1988), and *Anniversary Waltz* (1989). In addition to producing original scripts, this experimental feminist group has also presented an adaptation of Isabel Miller's *Patience and Sarah* (1984). Most recently, Shaw and Weaver collaborated with members of the group Bloolips on *Belle Reprieve* (1991), a piece loosely based on Tennessee Williams's *A Streetcar Named Desire*. Their current work, written by Margolin, is entitled *Lesbians Who Kill*.

Split Britches was the company's initial collaboration. Directed by Lois Weaver, it was conceived while both she and Peggy Shaw were performing in Spiderwoman Theater's "An Evening of Disgusting Songs & Pukey Images." This theatrical event was notable for two reasons: it was the first time the group had presented a piece containing lesbian content, and it introduced Shaw as a Spiderwoman performer.

Weaver wanted to memorialize two aunts and one great-aunt, who lived together in the Blue Ridge Mountains of Virginia where Weaver was born. In the summer of 1980, using Spiderwoman people, with Shaw as Della and without Lois Weaver performing, they developed the piece. Tapes of the heavily accented voices of Weaver's relatives were eventually deleted because they were difficult for the audience to understand. When *Split Britches* was presented at the first WOW Festival in 1980,[1] Weaver appeared only as the "folk historian narrator"—a role used to give a frame and cohesion to the workshop material. In the winter of 1981 *Split Britches* became a part of a series of pieces conceptualized as "Blood Roots," a group of works concerned with sisters and family. In this performance Weaver played Cora, while Shaw continued as Della. As a result of this 1981 run, Weaver and Shaw felt they had developed a piece for themselves, and they left Spiderwoman Theater. Pam Verge, however, no longer wanted to continue in the production, so Weaver and Shaw approached Deborah Margolin. She, in turn, created additional monologues and scenic materials, personalizing the role of Emma by including her memories of a great-aunt who lived into her nineties, was hard of hearing, and was an unconventional, unmarried woman "of great intellectual curiosity," regarded as a family scandal.

At that point the piece was structurally set. Moreover, when Deborah Margolin was added the idea of a continuing performance group took shape—a group I see as departing from both the universalizing rituals of cultural feminism and the documentary realism of representative women's experience, which so often was the core of earlier feminist collective performance. This new group then performed *Split Britches* at the Boston Women's Festival in the spring of 1981 and went on to perform the piece that fall at the second WOW Festival. By the next spring the group had produced its second collaborative piece, *Beauty and the Beast,* and had performed *Split Britches* at the Copenhagen Fool's Festival. Subsequent performances were done in the Netherlands, Great Britain, Italy, Germany, and Scotland, before returning to the United States for a 1983 off-Broadway run at the Nat Horne Theatre. It was during that year that I first saw *Split Britches;* it electrified the participants of the Women and Theatre Program preconference in Minneapolis. *Split Britches* premiered on public television in 1988. It was directed by Mathew Geller and produced by him in association with WGBH/WNET New Television and the New York Foundation for the Arts "Artists New Works Program."

Retracing History and Retracking Oral Narrative

In a conversation with the members of Split Britches in January 1989, they told me that they wanted to concentrate on the history of marginalized women, specifically of three women living in a world without men, women who, in this isolated setting, constructed their own reality. This commitment to dramatizing "forgettable" people who others perceive as "unforgivable," "embarrassing," and "eccentric," along with the group's mapping of the unseen communities these women create, "set the tone" for all their work. These forgettable characters, this marginalized *majority*, are the future. When you create the past you create the future by enlarging the circle of who one can associate with and the vision of what people can create and act upon. This includes characters outside the public (male) gaze of history who challenge its standard determinants of class, age, gender, and sexual preference: *Split Britches* is about women too old, too poor, too dumb, too lesbian, or too insistent on controlling their own lives to be visible. One metaphor for this process of undoing and redoing history occurs in the piece itself, when Cora describes erasing a man's tracks in the snow with her own footprints.

An important aspect of this retracking is that of enacting women's sexuality, most especially a lesbian sexuality, just as erased as the material aspects of their lives. Since, according to Shaw, "most history assumes everyone is heterosexual, we assumed Della was homosexual" and the "inner part" of Shaw's character was based on her own experiences and perceptions. In Rhonda Blair's unpublished 1986 interview with Shaw and Weaver, Shaw told her, "It's very new, being a lesbian. The word and the people being out in the world is very new. . . . So we're trying to find out what a lesbian is. Or what I am. We're trying to find out without all these other constrictions or rules . . . trying to find out about all these lives that have been written *around* for so many [hundreds of] years." Weaver continues: "When we worked on *Split Britches,* we wanted to create characters that people would identify with and like, and then realize that '. . . Oh, my God, I like a lesbian!' "[2]

In the character of Della, Split Britches uses clothes as a metaphor for embodying a personal history of sexuality. In one powerful scene

Della/Shaw defiantly peels off pieces of clothing that embody layers
of protection against the oppression and rejection directed at her because of her lesbianism. Clothes also serve as a metaphor for the free
expression of sexual desire when she recalls masquerading at a social
as a man. The spectator is positioned to understand that, for Della,
her current "women's" clothing is more of a permanent masquerade
of resignation, while in the "men's" clothing she was herself for
herself, if in masquerade for others. Fantasy also historicizes desire
for all three characters. The blues song "Bull Dyke Women," which,
having removed all but her underwear, Della sings, explores an ideal
that should be the norm but isn't, especially for Della: "BD women
know where to go" to find women. Both Cora and Emma express
their desire through animal imagery. Cora/Lois, who makes the
mooing noises like a sick cow throughout the piece, at one point
insists that the cow's moo is one of sexual pleasure "in the dark,"
rather than illness. Emma fantasizes an old turkey whose exposed
innards reveal a bed "with the feathers of two hundred ducks," a
huge feast, and two hundred girls in attendance "swattin' the bugs."
As Shaw has noted in talking about this piece of feminist Americana,
"It's not the Waltons," suggesting the avoidance of sentimentalizing
and idealizing.

Moreover, the way the piece embodies the desire of the women
in metaphor and fantasy reveals how *Split Britches* provides more than
a standard alternate history for the Gearhart women. *Split Britches*
enlarges the scope of historical representation. It also challenges the
standard modes of representing historical narrative onstage, including
the conventions of oral narrative as they are sometimes used in feminist dramas seeking to remember women. Techniques of oral narrative, often used to grant authority and authenticity to the marginal
and those too "ordinary" to have a voice in making History, creates
characters within a supplemental reality. These are bodied forth in
realistic terms and controlled, shaped, by the interviewer/playwright.
The goal is to recreate women as individual, coherent social subjects
parallel to representations of men. *Split Britches,* by contrast, plays
with these conventions. Lois Weaver's opening narrative focusing
on the Gearhart family history is an ironic treatment of the folk
historian—not a parody but, instead, a putting into quotation marks
that notes the constructedness of any family narrative. This is especially apt since Weaver could only interview other family members

about Cora, Della, and Emma. Those responses, shaped by a gendered ideology based on the local boundaries of feminine behavior—of domesticity, marriage, children—marginalize the women within the family as well, relegating them to the pathetic and the eccentric. Weaver's performance of the piece's beginning has a kind of suppressed laughter and a deliberate gestural naïveté that intersects with her commitment to presenting needed information about the Gearharts and even offering the play to us. That the spectator must engage with, rather than simply consume, this text is underscored by the deliberate blurring in the opening of the boundaries between person, writer, narrator, and character that will occur with all three women throughout the piece. Even if spectators, in Shaw's words, are "paying to see the fat lady in the circus, there for people to look at," the deliberate ambiguities of the script and performance prevent the comforting distance of the freak show.

Split Britches' subtitle, "A True Story," is not meant to be facetious. Its "trueness" lies in its collaborative composition—the use of other women's stories, such as those of Peggy Shaw's mother, to thicken and multiply the presentations—and in its refusal to slot the characters in a standard documentary form that accedes to the official family narrative. Truth also resides in the commitment to theatricalize the lived experience of these women outside the conventions of realism, outside the selected details of "verisimilitude" that foreclose repetition and routine. Split Britches stages the everyday as history conceived in the labor, gestures, and improvisations of the characters. More pointedly, the group's conception of trueness lies in its playing with narrativity, in its insistent theatricalizing and shifts in perspective, which locate these invisible women in an unstable space of representation revealed in a flickering way onstage. In *Technologies of Gender,* Teresa de Lauretis characterizes the "subject of feminism" as

the movement in and out of gender as ideological representation, . . . the movement back and forth between what representation leaves out or, more pointedly, makes unrepresentable. It is a movement between the (represented) discursive space of the positions made available by hegemonic discourses and the "space-off," the elsewhere, of those discourses: those other spaces, both discursive and social, that exist, since feminist practices have (re)constructed them, in the margins (or "between the lines" or "against the grain") of hegemonic discourses and in the interstices of institutions, in counterpractices and new forms of community. These two kinds of spaces are neither in opposition to one another nor strung along a chain of signification, but they coexist concurrently and in contradiction . . .[3]

and are not either "reconciled or integrated," as they are in master narratives. *Split Britches* is an interplay, always in tension, never reconciled, between the (re)constructed elsewhere, the space-off outside the frame, inhabited by Cora, Emma, and Della, and the texts made out of them by the narrative fragments. These fragments are tied in performance to the "freeze-frames" of the slide tableaux, which temporarily fix and circumscribe their experience within the frames of traditional history, realistic photography, oral narrative, documentary, and linear time. Within a simultaneous space they freeze in the family narrative/slide, speak out at us from their frozen positions, then perform outside the frame as it dissolves. The fragments of narrative overlay, spoken by the performer/characters in deadpan, speculative, or intense voices, create an interplay, coexisting "concurrently and in contradiction" with what we see staged beyond the frame. This oscillation between the various constructions of their reality does not, then, lead to two simultaneous static spaces. It isn't as if there's a fixed place of female culture that they and we can inhabit as an alternative to patriarchy, the place that fixes us in these representations. Instead, Split Britches shows the instability and fragility of their space (in living, in representation) in a movement that underscores the difficult process of oscillating in and out of gender ideology and so is part of the subversiveness of the work, part of its importance.

Thus, the subject of feminism, as de Lauretis has delineated it, is the theatrical subject of this piece, as expressed in its oscillation between the various spaces that are represented and the framing and dissolving, the undoing of those spaces. The unstable space on stage is made up of a series of impulses and moments that keep shifting, not only in performance, blurring the boundaries between performer and character, but also in the improvisations of the characters themselves. In this the characters as well as the performers function in a mode of transformational acting. In the round-robin of "Hey Diddle Diddle" near the end of the piece, for example, the trio parodies the fixed narrative their relatives made of them as well as giving parodic versions of one another. Thus, the song conveys their self-conscious performance as characters, destabilizing these identities.

They also perform monologues and duologues that sustain them, that are the locus of a kind of freedom within their community despite the obvious impoverishment and claustrophobia of their situation. The model of subjectivity used in representing these characters is a fluid, performative interplay, even as the characters' material position within the house is fixed. Cora's obsessive and detailed monologue about going to the store to sell eggs, buy tobacco, and collect coupons creates a routine where none exists and foregrounds her intense desire for self-determination in the details of the everyday. In the departing soldier/flier routine Cora and Della act out a soldier's farewell to his/her girl, creating a physical and emotional intimacy between the two played out with a passion that blurs the lines between sisters and lovers.

The instability of the boundaries between these routines, their reconfigurability in response to each performing character's needs, is exemplified by the way Cora refigures this departure into her departure image of going to the store (just as, earlier, Emma refigured Cora's chicken into her own turkey image). Then, too, the actual "not going" of the characters (despite their departure performances) is framed theatrically by dissolution, as Lois/Cora or Deborah/Emma simply wander out of the frame of the performance space, fictionalizing the portrayal of these characters' confinement in a way that the video version of the piece, with its more elaborate, walled set, could not.

This staging of routines relates directly to *Split Britches'* use of popular forms of entertainment. In the interview with Rhonda Blair, Lois Weaver told her of Split Britches' continuing interest in vaudeville: "[It was] popular entertainment that took some risks. At the same time, they honed the performances, [and] some people worked on *the same bit* for forty years." Vaudeville, itself a marginalized form, is an apt one for exploring the everyday through the body, through repetition and the recognizable. The characters of *Split Britches* stage their own unstable vaudeville show in their everyday interactions, improvising in the "elsewhere" to create community, relieve tension, find pleasure, and create rituals that will channel their desires and staunch the flow of powerful emotions—hunger, despair, fear, rage—

that hover close to the surface, always threatening to erupt. Some of the "honed performances" are broadly gestural, as in the humphing/ stamping stand-off between Cora and Della, where Cora manages to wear the powerful Della down or when Cora echoes, from a hiding place, everything Della threateningly addresses to her.

The idea of "the same bit" especially relates to the repeating trio of the sick cow, which punctuates the play as a kind of refrain: Cora moos, Della announces that the cow is sick, and they all work through a routine of who will leave and who will stay that marks their ambivalence, in this tightly knit community of three, over leaving, staying, and others leaving. It is staged as a repeating event, a kind of daily emergency portrayed so that the spectator is unsure if it is being repeated by the performers within the context of the playscript or if it repeatedly occurred to the characters, thereby blurring the distinction between a simultaneous present and chronological time.

The "bits" also refer to the gestures made in the silences among the three women: how a woman lights and smokes her pipe (Emma), takes a drink of liquor (Della), and holds her teacup or chews and spits tobacco (Cora) are repeating actions that operate as a signature for each of the characters. These signatures become recognizable to the spectator during the performance and belie popularly conceived images of appropriate feminine behavior. The idea of using recognizable bits modeled on vaudeville is a technique that, in Weaver's words, "plays tricks with" rather than simply undercuts the familiar routines of popular entertainment. In choosing this technique, they make the invisible visible by hinging it to and so changing our conception of the popularly recognizable visible. The trio sings, for example, first calmly, then intensely, a blatantly heterosexual song about the world needing to stop because a lover has abandoned them. Their performance of the song reconfigures it into a tight, ritualized expression of rapport among the three women, which oscillates with the song's actual words.

But the word *routine* also suggests the characters' physical labor as well as the labor of performing and improvising. The Gearhart women are immersed in physical labor based in repetition: getting wood, tending the fire, making biscuits, and sewing quilt pieces all inform the material reality of their situation. Even the title of the play itself, expressed visually by their clothing, signifies labor. Having britches that are split enables women to urinate while standing up in the field. If only women who are hard at work in the rural outdoors and have no time to urinate leisurely have been given this dispensation traditionally, the group Split Britches, in the choice of its name, suggests the way it has appropriated this freedom for labor of its own choosing. The words *split britches* draw attention to the the mentioned "unmentionables": women's otherwise invisible physicality, their urinary and sexual organs, and the garments that simultaneously cover and expose them. And it's not *split petticoats* but *britches,* the *split* suggesting female genitalia, and the *britches,* the traditionally male garb, denoting the power that these performers don. The group has said that this piece "set the tone" for pieces to follow. In fact, retaining the title of the playscript as the title of the group does so as well, marking the way women's labor in making theater, their sexuality and physicality, and their survival could be reconfigured again and again. Thus, the feminist subject of Split Britches' theater is in play in the elsewhere outside hegemonic discourse, most specifically in *Split Britches,* recreating the past in order to point ahead to a kind of future space, to space off a space for new possibilities.

NOTES

I would like to thank Deborah Margolin, Peggy Shaw, and Lois Weaver for taking time out from rehearsing *Little Women* to talk with me about *Split Britches.* I would also like to thank Rhonda Blair for making her 1986 unpublished interview with Shaw and Weaver available to me.

Another version of this chapter appeared in *Women & Performance* 4, no. 2, issue 8 (1989): 58–67. This issue also contains the complete text of *Split Britches.*

1. Peggy Shaw and Lois Weaver are also cofounders of the WOW Cafe which was an outgrowth of the WOW International Theater Festivals held in New York City in 1980 and 1981. Begun in 1982, the WOW Cafe is a performance space dedicated to producing works by and for women, including lesbian theater. For a discussion of WOW and Shaw's and Weaver's crucial role in it, see Alyssa Solomon's article "The WOW Cafe" in *Drama Review* T105, 29, no. 1 (1985): 92–101.

2. For theoretical discussions of lesbian representation that include analyses of Split Britches, see Sue-Ellen Case, "Toward a Butch-Femme Aesthetic," *Making a Spectacle: Feminist Essays on Contemporary Women's Theater,* ed. Lynda Hart (Ann Arbor: University of Michigan Press, 1989), 282–99; and "From Split Subject to Split Britches," *Feminine Focus: The New Women Playwrights,* ed. Enoch Brater (New York: Oxford University Press, 1989), 126–46; Kate Davy,

"Constructing the Spectator: Reception, Context, and Address in Lesbian Performance," *Performing Arts Journal* 10, no. 2 (1986): 43–52; Teresa de Lauretis, "Sexual Indifference and Lesbian Representation," *Theatre Journal* 40, no. 2 (1988): 155–77; and Jill Dolan, "The Dynamics of Desire: Sexuality and Gender in Pornography and Performance," *Theatre Journal* 39, no. 2 (1987): 156–74.

3. Teresa de Lauretis, *Technologies of Gender: Essays on Theory, Film, and Fiction* (Bloomington: Indiana University Press, 1987), 26.

The Reproduction of Visibility

Chapter 12

See the Big Show: Spiderwoman
Theater Doubling Back

Rebecca Schneider

It's coming! It's coming! I hear it! It's coming! I'm scared! I'm not ready
yet! I know something is there— . . . oh . . . oh . . . It's going! It's going. . . . I didn't see it. I didn't see it! Coyote saw it. The Birds saw it.
The trees whispered. . . . I didn't see it.
— from *Reverb-ber-ber-rations*

Spiderwoman has a show called *Reverb-ber-ber-rations*[1] in which the
three Native American sisters who make up the company—Lisa
Mayo, Gloria Miguel, and Muriel Miguel—drum memories and
countermemories onto the stage, layered and folded over upon one
another, repetitive, hysterical, rich. Stories are interwoven from before birth to after death, from an experience at a Taos corn dance to
the time Muriel was possessed by Uncle George. Now the sisters are
in Panama City surveying a military parade after the U.S. invasion
(their Cuna father was born in the San Blas Islands). Now they sit at
a table having tea and discussing their shows. Now they are in a
backyard in Brooklyn. Now they are mothers, now they are children, now they are grandmothers, now tea again, now a backyard,
now a Sun Dance, now Panama among the dead and wounded.
Gloria listens to a tape of Indian singing and coyote calling. "I hear it!
It's coming! . . ." Muriel tells about the time she was possessed by her
grandmother. They sing Cole Porter: "Like the beat beat beat of the
tom tom . . . Night and Day." And they talk, again, about their
shows: "Just what did you tell those people?"

First, a Story about Doubt That Includes a Reverberation

> The search for descent is not the erecting of foundations: on the contrary, it disturbs what was previously considered immobile; it fragments what was thought unified; it shows the heterogeneity of what was imagined consistent with itself. What convictions and, far more decisively, what knowledge can resist it? . . . Descent attaches itself to the body. It inscribes itself in the nervous system. (Michel Foucault)[2]

> No matter how narrativized, and progress-oriented the portrayal of history, in reality there is always a point in relation to our own circumstances in history when the steps in the story crack open. . . . Like the Nervous System, this seismological method of Benjamin's and the hope it contains is based on the notion that History forms no structural whole but is made to appear as if it does, and as such is empowered. (Michael Taussig)[3]

> > And my grandmother stepped into my head
> > And my grandmother stepped into my head
> > Behind my eyes
> > Behind my eyes
> > My grandmother was stepping into my head
> >   (from *Reverb-ber-ber-rations*)

In attempting to explore Spiderwoman's work in terms of a notion of the "appropriate body," playing on the double meaning of the word appropriate, I encountered again the problem of *thinking* the body at all. It seemed that, inevitably, "the body" that emerged in my reading, thinking, and writing became bogusly separated from details and markings, hues and shades, of particular bodies. Once articulated "the body" was made appropriate, congealed, accessible, and therefore safe—immediately removed from the "appropriate" body, a body resisting boundaries and definitives, which my feminism told me to champion. Working and thinking about "the body" too easily located it, somehow, outside over there—an object at safe distance from a subject, giving form to and therefore shrouding the abyss of the abject, the fear that informed my queries in the first place.[4] Perhaps, I told myself, my work on gender and representation had simply become awkwardly split from my own body. Perhaps I had lost an intimacy with my own work.

But there was no returning to "my body" as a safe place. As though through a crack in the steps, doubt had seeped into my inquiry, staining the space between a theory of the body and a more literal, perhaps inappropriate experience. And that doubt, I realized, was visceral—felt in my belly, bones, and nerves as much as in my head. One thing the doubt repeated upon me was an old question: How could a white woman begin to write about a Native American performance group in a way that grapples honestly and productively with the tangle of issues involved across difference? Yes, she could ante up in the realm of identity politics and proclaim her whiteness from the start, acknowledging and underscoring her social privilege. But is there something beyond the acknowledgment of that gulf? Should she look for and can she find an intimacy with the work despite or even *because* of the breach of race? And how to write that intimacy of difference? Is an intimacy of difference radically different from the intimacy of same, which so often informs academic feminist associations with women artists? "The failure of the academic feminists to recognize difference as a crucial strength. . . ."[5] The beat of Audre Lorde's words in my mind. *The failure of academic feminists to recognize difference...the failure . . . the failure.* Shut up, I said to my doubt. But its silence was more petrifying than its voice.

So I went to bed. The following story is about a sensual memory, perhaps a bodily memory, which is to say, I remembered something I had never known. I remembered something differently, something that started me thinking about difference in a more conflicted and intimate way. Because of the following experience I began to think more rigorously about history in bodies, inscribed, not only across visible markings but also as accessible in the invisible or disguised traces, in visceral (inappropriate) countermemories of gender, race, and class. Thinking of history in bodies, I thought about the past as tactile, differently accessible in the material senses of a body, in reverberations across viscera—not only across bloodlines but also across nervous systems, the networks of synapses between social structures and the experiences those structures often serve to veil.

A story: As I lay in bed, I was visited by an apparition.

I didn't think of it at the time of the visitation, but I later remembered that Foucault uses the word *apparition* while arguing for another way of apprehending the past, one less patriarchally linear, one that includes ruptures and breaks, one situated in bodies.[6] Walter Benjamin, too, writes of another history retained in physical "flashes."[7] My ghost, however, was making no academic claims. In fact, there was no body to be situated. Absent, invisible, she stood quietly by my computer. She stood beside a Spiderwoman poster I had hung on my wall.

An invisible body makes a strange impression. I had no idea who this absent presence was. I had no idea what she wanted. I felt I must be overtired, stressed out. I tried to ignore her, ignore my fear, and sleep. By then, as suddenly as I'd become aware of her presence, I became aware of her identity: she was my mother's father's mother. Now, as my inquiry trips and falls into personal narrative, I ask my reader to bear with my attempt to steer a critical course through personal experience. First, it's important to know that no one in my family knew anything about my mother's father or his side of the family; a divorce had completely wiped them out of the lineage. We only knew that they were Ozark mountain people—"hillbillies"—a major reason they had disappeared from the map of family memory. For the sake of class purity in narrative line, family history had conveniently erased the details of genealogy. Visibly but not viscerally erased, I thought, because here was this presence in my bedroom. Unable to deal with the invisible body, I decided to go downstairs, watch TV, and get real.

What appeared on the screen was a PBS documentary about Ozark mountain women.

I went back to bed. What do you want?

The ghost told me to keep working. Then she was gone.

The next day I called my mother on the phone, wanting any information she might have on this grandmother. Surprised, she told me that she, too, had been visited in a dream. But, she said, her dream was more farfetched than my encounter. In her dream the woman had appeared as a Native American and had spoken of certain Indian diseases. Isn't that strange, she said. And we silently agreed to forget about it.

Perhaps you have guessed where this is headed. The visitation occurred in February 1990. In March 1990 I saw *Reverb- ber-ber-rations*. In July 1990, my mother did some genealogical investigation and uncovered an aunt in Missouri. "Did you know," the newfound aunt asked, "that your grandmother was an American Indian. Her name was Elvina, but she signed her name with an X."

For me something profound had occurred: I had remembered something differently. I felt elated at first. I felt I had overcome a kind of social erasure—tapped a kind of countermemory. I even felt hopeful: perhaps Difference can become a personal geography, experienced intimately, and fear can be glimpsed as inscribed, palimpsestuous, across the veiled face of the Same.

> I urge each one of us here to reach down into that deep place of knowledge inside herself and touch that terror and loathing of any difference that lives there. See whose face it wears.[8]

And yet other specters soon raised themselves when I considered how to incorporate this visceral memory—or even the idea of bodily experience—into a materialist-informed inquiry into the body in white male patriarchy.

The notion of knowledge *in* a body smacks of essentialism. The absurd idea that I might understand Spiderwoman because of some buried bloodline smacks of colonial nostalgia. Though interrupting my space of doubt, the invisible body had simultaneously immensely complicated my project; I had allowed myself (my story) to become awkwardly and even perhaps indulgently tangled in the complexities of desire and fear surrounding difference. I knew that for many Native Americans, including Spiderwoman, a "Cherokee grandmother" is a problematic symbol of white nostalgia, a symbol of the general unwillingness of whites to acknowledge difference as strength without appropriating some part of it.

> Two weeks ago that woman was nothing but a plain old white woman. After taking one swig of our Yataholay Indian snake oil, she now has a Cherokee grandmother![9]

Still, my experience with the invisible body sat relentlessly in the middle of my efforts to write about Spiderwoman. What to do with that visit? What to do with the reverberations? With the counter-memories of miscegenations forgotten, buried in bodies and cultures—miscegenations that knock on the neat door marked difference?

Left to right: Gloria Miguel, Muriel Miguel, Hortensia Colorado, and Lisa Mayo in *Winnetou's Snake Oil Show From Wigwam City* (1989) by Spiderwoman Theater Inc. Photo by Festival 2000.

I returned to my familiar body of theory as a way of apprehending the strange disembodiment of my great-grandmother, invisible in my space and invisible in my white skin. Following Nietzsche, Foucault proposed a methodology, a practice based upon attention to details, accidents, and errors—to bodies erased by history. As against the sweeping narrative tradition of historical analysis, he suggested the posture of critical retrospection that Nietzsche called genealogy, not only because, opposed to the search for origins, genealogy finds "something altogether different" from dominant practice, but also because it approaches bodies as landscapes of countermemory situated in and affected by that narrative.[10]

> The body manifests the stigmata of past experience and so gives rise to desires, failings, and errors. . . . Genealogy, as an analysis

Spiderwoman in *The Lysistrata Numbah*, with (*left to right*) Lisa Mayo, Pam Verge, and Lois Weaver. Photo courtesy Antonio Sferlazzo/Françoise Lucchese.

of descent, is thus situated within the articulation of the body and history. Its task is to expose a body totally imprinted by history and the process of history's destruction of the body.[11]

Of course, one of history's destructions of the specific, the particular body, is the active forgetting, the disavowal of exchanges and the fear of recognitions across difference.[12] In place of the body erased, disavowed, forgotten, a body of "authenticity" is constructed, which diverts attention from the fraught terrain of exchange.[13] The presence of the absence of my forgotten grandparent underscored for me the notion that implicit in the visibility of my "whiteness" and Spiderwoman's color are a host of invisible bodies—a host of counter-memories that reverberate between us. And yet it is very important

to emphasize that those countermemories could reverberate *regardless
of a Cherokee grandmother*. Aporias in the dominant narratives of colonialism, oppression, and exchange belong to all of us, caught nerv-
ously in the synapses of our shared social Nervous System, surging
intimately if invisibly between and through our differences regardless
of bloodlines like a public secret.[14] Acknowledged or unacknowledged, a social genealogy continues to reverberate in the tangled
spaces between our race, gender, age, and class identities—available
at any moment to be, to quote Lorde again quoting Mary Daly,
"re-membered" differently.[15]

Re-membering is precisely what Spiderwoman does, though not
in a way that fixates upon the past as outside over there. Rather, the
sisters flash their memories across the present like boomerangs slicing
though the myriad fears and desires that surround the issue of neo-
colonial identity. Spiderwoman's theatrical re-membering is a bold
counterpractice, aimed at the creation of the "authentic" Native
American and doubling back upon that creation with a technique that
could be called "countermimicry"—a technique I will explicate later
in this essay.

White Nostalgia, Authenticity, and the Split Subject

> Today, planned authenticity is rife; as a product of hegemony
> and a remarkable counterpart of hegemony and universal stan-
> dardization, it constitutes an efficacious means of silencing the
> cry of racial oppression. . . . On the one hand, i play into the
> Savior's hands by concentrating on authenticity, for my atten-
> tion is numbed by it and diverted from other, important issues;
> on the other hand, i do feel the necessity to return to my so-called
> roots, since they are the fount of my strength, the guiding arrow
> to which i constantly refer before heading for a new direction.
> —Trinh T. Minh-Ha, "Difference"

"I used to be a white woman," says Muriel Miguel. She pulls a
coquettish, somehow WASP-like smile at the audience as though she
were doing an ad for weight watchers or the Daughters of the American Revolution (DAR). Muriel is spinning a parody on the increasing
numbers of whites who think they can simply become native by

uncovering long lost relatives or being bequeathed an Indian name. In *Winnetou's Snake Oil Show from Wigwam City* Spiderwoman enact a mock weekend workshop in which, for three thousand dollars a head, they turn white people into Indians with their amazing "Yataholay Indian Snake Oil." They are spoofing the New Age trend they call "plastic shamanism."

As part of the gimmick to sell their oil, Spiderwoman present a series of mimed Indian rope, knife, and horse tricks in a sendup of Wild West sideshows. At moments between the acts they occasionally pause to intimate another experience—an experience of cultural identity that resists the spoof and touches sometimes on a notion of grace, even sanctity, and often pain. I will return to these interludes later, but the acts themselves are gloriously banal. Mother Moon Face, played by Hortensia Colorado,[16] is "an equestrian from the Ponderosa" who dares to "change horses mid-gallop!" The horses are two mops Colorado rides around the stage, simply crossing them over each other as she "gallops." Lisa Mayo, Princess Pissy Willow of the Mish Mash Tribe, makes an elaborate show of shooting balloons out of an audience member's hands. When she says "pow" the balloon is popped with a tack. Muriel Miguel is Ethel Christian Christianson. She uses a rope "so fine that it can't be seen by the naked eye." After lassoing Gloria Hortensia with the invisible rope she has herself tied up for a "psychic" rope trick. She goes into a trance to deliver a "message from the other side." The message, which she speaks in a low and laboriously slow trance voice, is: "I have hemorrhoids." The solution, of course: "Buy Snake Oil."

While exposing the complicated collusion of "Indian" identity with commodity culture, Spiderwoman repeatedly and purposefully foul their material with allusions to base bodily function, provocatively resisting the more common attempt to counter commodification by alluding to an "essential spirituality" of natives or native experience. At one point in the *Winnetou* show the women all stand around a cauldron, mixing their Yataholay brew. The lights dim, as they dim for more serious moments in the interludes in which the company invokes ancestors, leaving the audience somewhat unsure of the line between satire and sanctity:

What shall this concoction be?
Pure white cat, daughter of a pure white mother

Porcupine piss
Velvet antlers of a well-hung moose (find a left hind leg and suck
    out the marrow)
Bull turd
Bat shit
Yum yum from a bum
Toenails of a lounge lizard
Skunk cum
What shall this concoction cure?
Running asshole
Constipation
Half-breeditis . . .

The banality of the recipe is obvious, but nonetheless the presentation
is somehow ambiguous, leaving unclear the fine line between the
sacred and the profane and making the audience suddenly unsure of
the appropriateness of laughter. When the lights come back up one
can no longer be secure in the conviction that Spiderwoman's spoof
is unqualifiedly funny. Having mixed their brew, the sisters are now
raucously in the business of *making* natives. One "swig" of their oil
and a member of the audience, picked by Gloria—anyone who buys
a ticket for the "show" is susceptible—inherits a tribe and picks a
name from a list that includes "Olddogeyedick" and "Two Dogs
Fucking." The audience member, a white male both times I saw the
show, is then given a xeroxed photo of a "real" Indian's face circa
1900 and told to hold it in front of his face for the rest of his life. He
is sent back to his seat—transformed.

Such moments of bogus transformation stand in strange relation
to the interludes in which the spoof is dropped. In one such moment
a member of the company holds a large bone up into the light of a
movie projector, which is casting a silent black and white image of
natives dancing in full-feathered regalia onto a screen at the back of
the stage. The silence is prolonged as the image flickers over the bone
and across the back of the woman. Then come words, slowly articulated: "This is the bone of our ancestors. This is the bone of our
relations. Digging, digging, digging for bones . . . ." It is in relation
to such moments that Spiderwoman's parody gathers the kind of
punch that knocks the wind out of a spectator.

Laughing, Spiderwoman is sending up something extremely serious. Who are the "Indians" that have been created by white nostalgia? Much of Spiderwoman's work is related to the issue of "Indianness," adroitly played in the painful space between the need to claim an authentic native identity and their awareness of the historical commodification of the signs of that authenticity. Their material falls in the interstices where their autobiographies meet popular constructions of the American Indian. In fact, Spiderwoman Theater shows up the split subjectivity that ensues from the encounter between the two—the doubled image that creates the terrain of their senses of self. Restaging antic Snake Oil sideshows, they explore and explode the business of being exotic. Showing the Indian Other as Show, they display as much about white man's Indian ("the beat beat beat of the tom tom") as about native identity, until the two are seen as impossibly intertwined.

This sense of split subjectivity is poignantly expressed in *Sun, Moon, Feather,* a performance piece woven from childhood memories, which deals explicitly with multiple layers of identity. Cuna on their father's side and Rappahannock on their mother's, the sisters are also Brooklynites who played "Indian Love Call" in their backyard as kids, acting out the parts from the 1938 MGM musical *Girl from the Golden West* and fighting over who got to be Jeannette MacDonald and who had to settle for Nelson Eddy. First performed at the Newfoundland Theater on West 18th Street in 1981 and later made into a film, *Sun, Moon, Feather* combines storytelling with silent filmclips of family outings and snake oil shows as well as clips from *Girl of the Golden West.*

> *Gloria:* Every once in a while our family would go to a pow wow or a snake oil show.
> *Lisa:* Brooklyn.
> *Gloria:* We were part of the circus.
> *Lisa:* And one of the sideshows was my family's snake oil show
> *Gloria:* Here we had an Indian village with teepees and children running around and people eating and so forth.
> *Lisa:* I looked up one day and I saw this whole bunch of people, you know, tourists. And they said "Hey—come here, come here, come here, come here! Look! Look at the Indian's eating!"
> *[A slide is projected of an Indian with a hot dog]*

Gloria: My father and a man named Sam Blowsnake—
Lisa: —the Winnebago guy—
Gloria: —were the two big chiefs there and they would go out
   in the street and around the circus there—
Lisa: To get the people in—Ballyhoo. We'd go outside: "OK—
   all the Indians out." We'd all be dressed up.
Gloria: Screaming Cheedebeecho! Cheedebeecho! Cheede-
   beecho!
Lisa: And we'd give them a little taste of what the show would
   be like on the inside, you see.
*[Silent film clip of many Indians on an outdoor platform dancing to-
gether]*
Gloria: Well, years later I met this Winnebago woman and we
   were talking and I said "You know, I know some words in
   Winnebago." And she said, "Yeah? What are they?"
   "Cheedebeecho."
   She said, "Cheedebeecho? That's not Winnebago."
   I said, "It isn't?"
   And she said, "No, I never heard Cheedebeecho. Uh-uh,
   that's not Winnebago."
   I said, "Sure, Sam and my father used to ballyhoo and they'd
   go out front and call people in and say *Cheedebeecho!*"
   She said, "That's not Winnebago."
   You know, this is like after many many years. I say this over
   to myself slowly: Cheedebeecho . . . Cheedebeecho . . . Chee de
   bee cho . . . Seedebeeshow . . . See the big show! See the big
   show!
   That's what they were calling out! See the big show!

The embattled search for the authentic Indian frequently uncovers, for Spiderwoman, the symbolic order of the white colonial. Too
often, behind the painted face of the authentic is the "wanna-bee."[17]
Too often the authentic Indian becomes the one stuck, stuffed for a
museum, not allowed to step beyond the boundaries of a tradition
frozen in a moment of colonization. As Lisa Mayo put it, the authentic Indian is a dead Indian around which white nostalgia for "better
days" can congeal: "What the white search for the shaman misses is
the reality of the Native American here and now. They're not interested in that. Really for them it would be a lot easier if we would

disappear, all die of alcoholism, and then they could take over and talk about what we had been."[18] This attitude can be insidious. For example, *Taxi,* a popular fashion magazine, recently featured an article entitled "Keeping the Faith" about native performers and "art built on the balance of old and new."[19] While the article was hip to Spiderwoman's message, nevertheless the photographs the magazine published to accompany the text were treated to resemble faded tintypes, tattered at the edges, stained, and weathered—as though the subjects pictured, including the Spiderwoman company, all belonged to a dead generation, circa 1900.

Determined to break beyond the boundaries of a potentially crippling authenticity, Spiderwoman "doubles back" upon white culture the problem of its own authentification—showing the show, spoofing the gaze of the white. Thus, their stories are counter-memories, and, though often humorous, their work is painful. They stand defiantly where a white tintypifying gaze meets Spiderwoman's own desire for the authentic—to express their experience free from the pressure of a commodity culture repeatedly fueled by modernist nostalgia for the "noble savage." Lisa talks of technique, of sending up the authentic only to double back and insist upon the reality of the effects of that authentification: "People are laughing. Then—POW!—we get them with the real stuff."[20]

Spiderwoman—The Early Days

> For our types in the mainstream there was the maid and the mother or there was the mother and the maid—or you could paste on an accent and be Mrs. Sanchez. In our own theater we could do anything we wanted: be skinny, do Juliet—anything.
> —Muriel Miguel, June 1990

These are big, strong women. These are grandmothers, dressed in outrageous filigree and wielding a sharp reflexivity. There may be a feather in someone's hair, but there is also loud lamé, glitter, and, especially in *Winnetou,* a purposeful polyester sheen. Working against the expectations that surround "native performance," they enter the stage fully aware of the complexities in the identifications they are weaving. They are also studiously amateur in their style, their work intricately and consummately flawed: Spider Grandmother Woman, their namesake, always wove an error into her designs to allow her spirit to find its way out and be free.

The sisters began working together in New York in 1976.[21] Muriel was the one to start it. Youngest of the three, she had been a member of Joseph Chaikin's Open Theater in the early 1970s. She had worked with Megan Terry, Sam Shepard, and Alwin Nikolai but had gotten tired of being endlessly typecast as "the Indian." When a woman director, Gilda Russo, cast Muriel in a successful piece called *The Three Marias,* only to bump her for an "uptown actress" when the show moved closer to Broadway, telling her she was just too fat, Muriel discovered that "you can be just as disappointed in a female director." It was this disappointment that made her realize that if she didn't address the appropriate-body problem herself, nothing would change. As she says, "If you don't shake it yourself, nothing will shake."[22]

Muriel Miguel started Womanspace with two white women, Carol Grossberg and Laura Foner, and soon found herself involved in something that was as much a consciousness-raising (CR) group as a theater. She had never felt that her opinions were worth much at the Open Theater, but Womanspace gave her confidence. At first she was not at all sure that she wanted to "disclose herself" to white women, but eventually talking with other women and answering questions about herself felt like the "sun shining in on a new interior." Out of the CR Womanspace created *Cycles,* an autobiographical piece in which Laura Foner came out as a lesbian. The group won a CAPS fellowship but was already breaking up under the stress of internal competition.

Muriel started another group—this time with "lots of women." Awarded a grant to do a piece on violence, Muriel felt that she needed both her sisters to work with her. At this point, however, her sisters would have "nothing to do with her." Gloria was living in Oberlin, Ohio, the wife of a faculty member. But it was Lisa, an accomplished singer studying "serious" acting at HB studio, who was the most reluctant:

> I liked her work, but it was too scroungy. They did everything on the floor [she laughs]. I just couldn't see myself doing it that way. I was an actress; I had a very good technique; working with

Uta Hagen. I was also a classical singer, a mezzo soprano. . . . And she asked me to lay on the floor, and do all these
scroungy things and talk about orgasms. "Oh God," I thought.[23]

But Muriel was persistent and eventually brought Lisa and Gloria
together with Lois Weaver (white), Pam Verge (white), Nadia Bay
(black), and Brandy Pen ("part Asian and part WASP"). They named
themselves Spiderwoman after Spider Grandmother Woman, a familiar household god of the Hopi who was the first to create designs
and teach her people to weave.

Developing a working technique called "storyweaving," the
group kept to a no-holds-barred philosophy. The only thing set at
the beginning of any project was the performance date. But no-holds-
barred was relatively easy; because their racial mix and body types
were already outside the bounds of normative theater, the group
found itself automatically free from the pressure of expectation. Even
within most feminist theater at that time the notion of the appropriate
body held firm: "You still had to be blond and blue-eyed—or you
could be black and thin." Spiderwoman found this a priori freedom
from the appropriate exhilarating and built upon that freedom as the
cornerstone of the group's identity:

CHALLENGING THE "ONE-SIZE-FITS-ALL" VIEW OF FEMINISM, THIS
SEVEN WOMAN COMPANY USES THEIR DIVERSE EXPERIENCES AS
WOMEN, AS AMERICAN INDIAN WOMEN, AS LESBIANS, AS SCOR-
PIOS, AS WOMEN OVER FIFTY AND WOMEN UNDER TWENTY-FIVE,
AS SISTERS AND MOTHERS AND GRANDMOTHERS TO DEFY SUCH
OLD GENERALIZATIONS AS: "ALL BLONDES HAVE MORE FUN," AND
"ALL WOMEN'S THEATER IS THE SAME."[24]

Women and Violence, their first piece, performed in 1976 at the
Washington Square Methodist Church, wove stories from members'
own lives around a central story of a well-known revolutionary
leader in the 1970s American Indian movement who saw no discrepancy between his fight for native rights and his own brutality toward
women. Already the slapstick style and hysterical behavior around
extremely serious topics was in full swing. Vigilantly battling at the
gadfly of the "appropriate," the show closed with the women throwing popcorn and pies at each other. In-jokes were there as well: Lisa

had joined the troupe but disguised herself as a white woman. She was de-wigged and exposed at the finale, when, says Lisa, "they insisted that I throw the pie in my own face because I was such a perfect lady."[25]

After *Woman and Violence* came other shows—*Trilogy, Cabaret: An Evening of Disgusting Songs & Pukey Images, Lysistrata Numbah,* and *The Fittin' Room*—but the stress of special interests within the group began to take a toll. Difference, once of the group's original strong points, began to present difficulties. "White ways" began to class with "native ways," lesbian issues with heterosexual ones. I asked the sisters about the 1981 breakup of the original Spiderwoman into two separate performing troupes—Spiderwoman and Split Britches:

> *Gloria:* Some of the women who were lesbian wanted to make Spiderwoman an all lesbian group . . . and—over our dead bodies.
>
> *Lisa:* Well, you can't become a lesbian if you're not a lesbian. I mean, do we all have to be the same?
>
> *Muriel:* That was the exciting thing about Spiderwoman at that time. We were young, we were old, we were black, we were Indian, we were gay, we were straight, fat, skinny, short. It was really exciting. It was really sad when it broke up. My feeling was that the pressure of the white women in the group got too much for me. The pressure was: you do things this way, you don't do things this way. You know—
>
> *Gloria:* —"this is the white way"—
>
> *Muriel, Lisa, and Gloria (laughing):* —but they didn't say that.
>
> *Muriel:* And involved in all that was the getting grants and everything. And there was always the "right" way to do these things. Also, in the beginning we had wanted it to be that there would be more nonwhite than white women in the group, but a lot of white women ended up coming in, somehow. The stage managers, the costumers, the business manager—they all came and they were white. And there was also the feeling that "the sisters get a lot of attention because they're Indians." It wasn't easy then. There were hard feelings.
>
> *Lisa:* Well that was a long time ago and now everyone's doing well. In 1981 we got a grant which we split between *Sun, Moon, Feather*—our show—and Split Britches with Lois

Weaver, Peggy Shaw, and Deborah Margolin.[26] After that Split Britches became their own company, we stayed on as Spiderwoman, and the amazing thing is—
Lisa, Gloria, and Muriel: —we're all still here![27]

Vigilant Repetitions, the Comic Turn, and Countermimicry

1990. Theater for the New City. We sit in the dark waiting for *Reverb-ber-ber-rations* to begin. A loud, very loud, drumming assaults us and continues in the dark for some time. There is also a scuffling of feet. When the lights come up we see that the drum is a garbage can. Spiderwoman had been clumsily stumbling around in the dark. "I gotta pee!" says Muriel. The sisters Broadway belt Cole Porter: "Like the beat beat beat of the tom tom when the jungle shadows fall. . . ." What stands between the drum, the tom-tom, and the trash can? Does the space between them generate a countermemory?

Natalie Zemon Davis and Peter Starn define countermemory as the "residual or resistant strains that withstand official versions of historical continuity."[28] Foucault's translator defines countermemory as the name of an "action that defines itself, that recognizes itself in words—in the multiplication of meaning through the practice of vigilant repetitions."[29] Can countermemory be an action that defines itself not only in words but in the vigilant repetitions of a body or an object, as in the visceral "words" of a performer's gesture or the violent vibrations of a drum that repeats itself, doubling as both trash can and tom-tom?

Vigilant repetitions. The dark drumming and the trash can scene is repeated later in the show. So are the jokes and ribald humor. So are the knife-in-the-heart stories of loss. So are the reflexive tea scenes. So are the women themselves as the features of one sister can be seen, almost the same but not quite, on the body of another sister. "Just what did you tell those people?" they ask each other again.

Since 1981 Lisa Mayo, Gloria Miguel, and Muriel Miguel have been the core of Spiderwoman. Theater for the New City and the American Indian Community House, both on the Lower East Side of Manhattan, generally host Spiderwoman's work before they tour.[30] *Sun, Moon, Feather* (1981) was followed by *The Three Sisters from Here to There* (1982)—a takeoff on Chekhov; *3 Up, 3 Down* (1987); *Winnetou's Snake Oil Show from Wigwam City* (1988); and

Reverb-ber-ber-rations (1990). Surprisingly, however, the differences celebrated in the original Spiderwoman have not disappeared but have grown in complexity. There is a depth to Spiderwoman's exploration of identity; the differences they explore, like the realities they explore, are rarely limited to the strictly visible ones. In fact, things that "ought" to be different—such as a trash can and a tomtom—are constantly bombarded against each other and against audience expectations. More often than not, it is the "appropriate" that is challenged.

In a segment of *Reverb-ber-ber-rations* titled "Vincent" Lisa Mayo enters the stage chanting: "Hey, hey dooten day, dooten day, hey, hey, dooten day, dooten day." Suddenly she weaves into her chant a pop tune—"Starry, Starry Night"—and her words become impossibly intertwined, miscegenated, with the popular Don Maclean lyrics about Van Gogh:

> The world of the five senses is the world of illusion. Reality cannot be seen with the physical eye. With the eyes that watch the world and can't forget strangers that they've met.
>
> Starry, starry night. The responsibility of creators; people who make things, build, mold, and shape things, is to interpenetrate the layers, bring information between the layers. Starry, starry night! Going back into the before to use for the future.
>
> Starry, starry night. Portraits hung in empty halls. Ragged men in ragged clothes. How you tried to set them free. They would not—. They did not know how. Perhaps they'll listen now.
>
> Starry, starry night. Hey, hey, dooten day dooten day.[31]

What to make of such syncretism, such hybrid perspective in which categories of difference lose their clean edges, their appropriate delineations? Cultivating "details and accidents," countermemory, closely linked to the notion of genealogy, always already "attaches itself to the body."[32] But *the* body? Here problems proliferate like blemishes, grammatical errors, slips of the tongue. What is "the" body to which the details and accidents of countermemory attach—especially when redoubled in such a tumult of blatant and insistant syncretism? The beat of Audre Lorde's words: *See whose face it wears.* In the blindspots of the abluted body of the appropriate, the inappropriate reverberates in a concatenation of resemblances, a circle of "almost the same but not quite,"[33] always, it seems, just beyond the field of appropriation. And yet the challenge demands a recognition of terror: *See whose face it wears. See whose face it wears. See whose face it wears.*

Spiderwoman practices double vision. "Turning" a white into a native, they turn upon a mimicry that has colonized, fixed, and natural-historified Indian identity. They turn upon historical representation of the native, or colonial mimicry, with what might be called countermimicry. Exploring the historical mechanisms of colonial power, Homi Bhabha uncovered what he called a "comic turn." The colonizers constructed their colonial subject through representation, which presented the colonial project as noble by presenting the native as ignoble, or, more to the point, as deficient, partial, or incomplete. The "nobility" of the civilizing mission was erected through the "primitivizing" of the Other, and that primitive was produced through mimicry—textual effects that split that subject into both "human and not wholly human," into almost the same but not quite. Thus, the self-proclaimed noble intentions of the colonizer's construction of the colonial subject ironically hinged upon the ignoble literary effects of repetition, mimicry, and farce to create the colonial subject's deficiency. This literary flip, which creates nobility through creating deficiency, is what Bhabha calls the comic turn of colonialism.[34] As Bhabha notes, historically white recognition of a member of another race as human was always already insidiously coupled with a disavowal of that other as "wholly human." Through the coupling of recognition with disavowal that other emerged as a split subject, a "partial subject," not wholly human in the eyes of colonizers—"almost the same but not white." The other exists, then, in a strange space of ambiguity, oddly doubled with him- or herself: both the same *and* different, subject and object at once. Bhabha defines mimicry as a complex strategy of representation, repeating or doubling the image of the other in a shroud of the authentic, continually producing and delimiting difference through a strategy that "'appropriates' the Other as it visualizes power."[35]

But mimicry has an edge. If mimicry can be articulated as the disciplining gaze that doubles its subjects, then the menace of mimicry is in fact the potential return, or ricochet, of that gaze. As Bhabha puts it, "The menace of mimicry is its double vision which in disclos-

ing the ambivalence of colonial discourse also disrupts its authority."
Thus, "the reforming, civilizing mission is threatened by the displacing gaze of its disciplinary double."[36] In this displacing gaze the tables
are turned on the appropriate, showing the mimicry inherent in its
construction. Under the stress of double vision the body becomes a
scrim, throwing into relief the concealment of other bodies—specific,
detailed, and multiple.

Countermimicry. In *Sun, Moon, Feather* Gloria and Lisa play
"Indian Love Call" in their living room. But they don't act out the
Indian parts—the virulent, near-naked, dancing brave or the dark
Indian Princess—they fight over who gets to be be-ringleted, vase-
line-over-the-lenz Jeannette MacDonald and who has to play stal-
wart, straight-backed Canadian Mounty Nelson Eddy. They are not
re-playing, re-membering, or re-claiming native images but appropriating the appropriate. They sing beautifully: "When I'm calling
you-ooo-ooo." Lisa is Nelson. She wears a low-cut slip and a wide-
brimmed hat. Gloria stands on a chair as Jeanette. They gaze into each
other's eyes as they sing. Silent clips from the movie are interwoven
with their scene so that the mouths of MacDonald and Eddy seem
to lip-sync the lilting voices of Lisa and Gloria, whose bodies repeat
upon the Hollywood lovers, doubling back.

Doubling back, myriad appropriates are recognized as they are
disrupted.[37] The inappropriate bodies of Lisa and Gloria appropriate
the bodies of Jeanette and Nelson and expose a hotbed of error. First,
the lovers Nelson and Jeanette are supposed to be male and female,
not female and female. Nelson isn't supposed to wear a slip that
exposes a healthy cleavage. Second, in a Wild West fantasy whites
aren't supposed to be nonwhites (though Native Americans have
been played by whites in ruddy makeup, one doesn't find "real"
natives playing whites in pancake). Third, and importantly, heavy
women aren't supposed to be so clearly free and comfortable with
their bodies. And, fourth, a native performance troupe isn't supposed
to mirror "mainstream" performance traditions, though the mainstream can mimic native traditions (the native dances in *Girl from the
Golden West* itself a case in point).

Another example of countermimicry occurs in *Winnetou's Snake
Oil Show from Wigwam City*. The show opens with a skit about a
German explorer's "discovery" of Indian ways circa 1860. Hortensia
Colorado plays a scurvy guide. Lisa plays Gunther, a German ex-

plorer visiting the Wild West for the first time. Gloria plays a vicious bear killed by Gunther with a toy hatchet—the dime store variety that squeaks on impact. When the bear is dead (after a drawn-out Swan Lake-type death), Gloria reappears as an ugly, smelly "Injun" who looks like "a horse walked all over his face." Seeing the dead bear, the Injun raises his arms and begins to chant. At this moment Muriel enters as Great Chief Winnetou, wise and noble savage, brilliant and strong. At Winnetou's entrance the skit becomes a full-fledged opera. Winnetou introduces himself in Wagnerian splendor singing: "I am Winnetou." An operatic medley follows in which Winnetou invites the German to become his blood brother and smoke the peace pipe. The sisters bellow operatically and bump into one another while dancing a circle dance with token "Indian" gestures. The point here is that the German meets Winnetou through the medium of grand opera, making explicit the European construction of the "noble savage" and countermimicking the high ideals of European form.

Yet, if the colonial project turned from "high ideals" to its "low mimetic literary effect," as Bhabha would have it, Spiderwoman conversely turns from the low mimetic effect to a searing critique. "People are laughing. Then—POW!—we get them with the real stuff." In fact, if Spiderwoman did not incorporate the turn (in their case away from the mimetic effect), the bite of their critique would be absent and their enterprise would become a repetition of colonial, patriarchal mimesis, reenacted without commentary upon their own bodies. The seemingly endless concatenation of resemblances, in which mimesis repeats again and again and again, is interrupted. Here the redoubling of representation does not erect a Baudrillardian hall of mirrors in which others mimic others mimicking others till the Different supposedly collapses with the Same under the label "representation is all." Instead, Spiderwoman insist upon an interruption: "POW!—we get them with the real stuff."

But what is the "real stuff" that interrupts? Gloria and Lisa are not mimicking Jeanette and Nelson to lose themselves in an endlessly image-seeking whirlpool. In fact, something more strikingly heretical is occurring: they are telling a story about real effects on real lives, and they have an agenda pitched toward change. They are "going back into the before to use for the future."[38] Their doubling back, in fact, has a double meaning. On the one hand, it is a repeating of the technique of their doubling upon the dominant culture (as if to say, you've doubled me, now I'll double you back). But, on the other hand, it is a significant historical counteranalysis, a doubling back as in a retracing of steps as though to find something lost, erased, silenced along the way. The audience laughs with the sisters at their antic re-membering of the double but in the next instant find that we rub up against the silenced side of the double—the real stuff of the everyday. Stories of their father's alcoholism, his violence and his death, sober stories of their mother's embattled Christianity, and stories of their deep, deep anger repeat upon the spoof of the authentic. In one moment the authentic is distanced, exposed as corrupted by colonialist nostalgia, but in the next it (painfully) becomes a detail, a vital memory, a reality—their mother, themselves, their grandmother—very much alive in reverberations across their daily experience.

Reverb-ber-ber-rations closes with a straightforward statement. Muriel Miguel faces her audience in dim light and speaks simply and quietly. Her words echo against all that went before:

> I am an Indian woman.
> I am proud of the women that came before me.
> I am a woman with two daughters.
> I am a woman with a woman lover.
> A woman that is claiming the wisdom
> of the women in my family.
> I am here now.
> I am saying this now because to deny these events
> about me and my life
> would be denying my children.[39]

Parody, Feminism, and the Stubborn Irruption of "Real Stuff"

Muriel Miguel: You know, sometimes I look at *Winnetou's Snake Oil Show* and I say: Is this feminism?

Schneider: But does feminism only have to deal with "women's issues"? And what does that mean? With sex? Some people would be happy if feminism did stick to sex because then it would be kept in a box, so to speak.

Muriel Miguel: Yes, it's the same thing: It would be better for

them if Indians were dead. Or if we were stuck in tradition. I
mean, hah! We're all playing men! Men in gold lamé!
Gloria Miguel: Well, I could be a female bear.
Muriel Miguel: . . . That is true.[40]

Countermimicry, vigilant repetitions, and the painful interruption
of real stuff. All of this tremors and repeats with feminism in obvious
and fundamental ways. Elin Diamond, writing toward a "feminist
mimesis," proposes a reexamination of the complicity between real
ism and hysteria.[41] She suggests a potential hysterical realism in
which a performer's body speaks but escapes signification, a strategy
that reverberates with Spiderwoman's reexamination of the authentic. Imbricating Irigaray's hysterical mimicry (in which woman, positioned as mirror to man, rejects "imposed mimesis" and, instead of
reflecting male virility, mirrors patriarchal oppression) with a historical-materialist perspective, Diamond articulates the need for a feminist mimesis that functions as an alienation effect, framing gender
behavior and exposing its reality effects.[42]

Reminding her readers that feminism "has a stake in truth"[43] and
determined to articulate a mimesis with a clear and conscious access
to that stake, Diamond explores linking Julia Kristeva's notion of the
"true-real" with Irigaray's irreverent mimicry. A politic of the literal
that sidesteps signification, the true-real (the concretization of the
signifier) could be said to reverberate in syncopated time with the
Symbolic Order and to be imbricated in bodily detail. It is stable
referentiality—such as the authentic or the appropriate—which is potentially troubled by any eruption of the true-real.[44] As Diamond
points out, in the language of hysterics details are not displacements
or sublimations of a generality, but, rather, the signified is taken for
the real, "side-stepping the sign-referent model."[45] Diamond implies
that this side-stepping which might also be articulated as a standing
beside and thus as a redoubling, holds a potential for performative
resistance that is productively "parasitic" on patriarchal mimesis—
problematizing Truth by showing the show but not categorically
dismissing the truth of its effects:

Traditional mimesis is precisely what is repressed in the true-real,
for the verisimilar copy is always already inferior to its "real"
model. Kristeva does not celebrate the true-real of hysteria (its

medical label is psychosis), but her concept suggests another way
of retheorizing mimesis. Can the body's true-real destabilize mimetic truth, or, put another way, can the body signify but escape
signification?[46]

It is this question that feminist performers like Spiderwoman are
addressing by theatrically tapping the tension between the authenti-
cated body constructed by the mimetic truth of the colonizing patriarchy and the irruptive true-real of the subject experiencing the effects
of that realism, that authentification.

Karen Finley's work similarly exemplifies a theater of countermimicry. Finley's performance practice could be read as a politic of
the literal that countermimics, or, to use Diamond's phrase, destabilizes mimetic truth.

> The feminine situation is only established, however, if the wish
> for a penis is replaced by one for a baby, if that is, a baby takes
> the place of a penis in accordance with ancient symbolic equiva-
> lence. (Sigmund Freud: "Femininity")[47]

> I take that mama and I push her against that washer. And I take
> her baby, a bald-headed baby, and put Downy fabric softener
> on baby's head. Then I strap that baby around my waist till its a
> baby dildo. Then I take that baby, that dildo, and fuck its own
> mama. . . . AND THEN I BLACK OUT / AND IT'S TWENTY LATER.
> /AND I'm in my mama's house. (Karen Finley *Constant State of
> Desire*)[48]

In literalizing such figurative details upon her own body in performance
Finley unleashes a countermimesis that steps outside the bounds of
the appropriate (and thus loses her funding and often her acceptance
by feminists).[49] As a performance of literalization, Finley's is also a
performance of spatialization. That is, Finley *maps* the violence of
genderization upon her body but, more specifically, upon her bodily
parts. Destabilizing the mimetic truth of the authentic, the "ancient
symbolic equivalence," she simultaneously insists upon its real effects.

This insistence upon real effects is integral to and powerful in
Spiderwoman's work. At times, in fact, Spiderwoman's real stuff
extends not only to the too often dismissed social details of alcohol-

ism and abuse intimated earlier but into a realm more dangerous for a materialist theorist—a "reverberating" realm of sacrality. By doubling their parodies with interludes that beckon toward another experience, by folding their own criticisms of nostalgia over upon their own desires for the sacred, Spiderwoman unleashes multiple and often conflicting reverberations into the space between performer and spectator. While deftly parodying the invention of identity, the commodity-driven co-optation of sacrality, and while bravely exposing the space of syncretism between "Cheedebeecho" and "See the Big Show," Spiderwoman nonetheless insists, ironically, on a firm declaration of identity and a resolute respect for the sacred. Their parody, their doubling back, is clearly political in its overtones, but their simultaneous insistence on an experience of the sacred *despite* the historical corruption and compromise of identities is, though less blatant, also political.

In considering the politic of the sacred in Spiderwoman's work it is important to note that Spiderwoman's invocation of the sacred functions not as independent doctrine but as theatrical interruption, tightly woven into the fabric of the parodic.[50] As interruptions, such moments of serious invocation present a confusing challenge to the audience and function as strangely inverted Brechtian distancing devices. These "sacred" moments interrupt the profanity of parody as if to cast cracks into the criticism (or weave error into the fabric) through which another vision, another experience, might breathe. Brecht used interruptions in order to distance, to point to or underscore the social gest of a situation. Spiderwoman's interruptions similarly point to a broader gest and hint at the depth of their resolve.[51] Here the strange beauty of the interludes invoking ancestors—"digging, digging, digging for bones"—provide the audience with a moment's recognition of the layer upon layer of sediment (and sentiment) stirred by the whitewater of Spiderwoman's own parodic critique.

Exploring Spiderwoman's work, I found myself grappling not with safe residue or traces of history but with a vital, visceral plumb line of historical ghostings questioning the neatly marked categories of said traces. In Spiderwoman's dangerous space between satire and sanctity ancestors are re-membered differently, and *other* histories, shared across the present pulse of a social nervous system as across the darkened space between performer and spectator, are thrown into sudden and violent relief. As for my own experience with the "inappropriate" bodiless body of a ghost casting her shadow over my attempts to deal neatly with the tangle of issues across race, after doubling that shadow with critical inquiry I can only step back and wonder not what answers have been provided but what further questions, like further ghosts, can be raised.

> What is old is new Again.
> We all have the same gift.
> Every person has the gift
> but may not always listen to the messages.
>
> *Reverb-ber-ber-rations*

NOTES

I would like to thank Nicole Ridgway for her careful reading and insightful suggestions at several points during the writing of this essay.

1. The above passage was taken from a March 1990 performance of *Reverb-ber-ber-rations* in a section called "Trail Song," which does not appear in the printed text of the show, in *Women & Performance* 5, no. 2 10 (1992) 184–212. Unless otherwise indicated, all other quotes from *Reverb-ber-ber-rations* appearing in this article do appear in the printed text.

2. Michel Foucault, *Language, Counter-Memory, Practice,* ed. Donald F. Bouchard (Ithaca, N.Y.: Cornell University Press, 1977), 147.

3. Michael Taussig, "The Nervous System: Homesickness and Dada," *Stanford Humanities Review* 1, no. 1 (1989): 59; rptd. in *The Nervous System* (New York: Routledge, 1992).

4. My use of the term *abject* is meant to reverberate with Julia Kristeva's use in *Powers of Horror: An Essay on Abjection* (New York: Columbia University Press, 1982).

5. Audre Lorde, "The Master's Tools Will Never Dismantle the Master's House," in *This Bridge Called My Back,* ed. Cherríe Moraga and Gloria Anzaldúa (New York: Kitchen Table/Women of Color Press, 1981), 100.

6. Foucault, *Language.*

7. A fragment of Walter Benjamin's resonates interestingly with the project of this essay and bears repeating: "To articulate the past historically does not mean to recognize it 'the way it really was' (Ranke). It means to seize hold of a memory as it flashes up at a moment of danger. Historical materialism wishes to retain that image of the past which unexpectedly appears to man [sic] singled out by history at a moment of danger. The danger affects both the content of the tradition and its receivers. The same threat hangs over both: that of becom-

ing a tool of the ruling classes. In every era the attempt must be made anew to wrest tradition away from a conformism that is about to overpower it. . . . Only that historian will have the gift of fanning the spark of hope in the past who is firmly convinced that even the dead will not be safe from the enemy if he wins. And this enemy has not ceased to be victorious." From "'Theses on the Philosophy of History," *Illuminations* (New York: Schocken Books, 1969), 255.

8. Audre Lorde, "The Master's Tools," 101.

9. From *Winnetou's Snake Oil Show from Wigwam City*. All quotes from this play are taken from a videotape of the show. The text is forthcoming in *Canadian Theater Review* in a special issue on native performance.

10. Foucault, *Language,* 142.

11. Ibid., 148.

12. See Homi Bhabha, "Of Mimicry and Man: The Ambivalence of Colonial Discourse," *October* 28 (1984): 125–33.

13. See Trinh T. Minh-Ha, "Difference: A Special Third World Women Issue," *Discourse* 8 (Fall-Winter 1986–87): 11–38.

14. See Taussig, *Nervous System.*

15. Audre Lorde, "An Open Letter to Mary Daly," in Moraga and Anzaldúa, *This Bridge,* 96.

16. Hortensia Colorado appears with Spiderwoman in *Winnetou's Snake Oil Show*. Together with her sister, Vira Colorado, Hortensia Colorado also performs in her own company, The Colorado Sisters, based at Theater for the New City in New York.

17. An article by Dirk Johnson on the front page of the *New York Times* on 5 March 1991 carried the headline: "Census Finds Many Claiming New Identity: Indian." According to the article, this shift is often motivated by the growing realization that an Indian heritage can mean special financial breaks and benefits. Other whites, believing it is fashionable to be Indian or else motivated by spiritual reasons, "stretch the truth about ancestry." Many Native Americans call such people "wanna-bees." The usual wanna-be story is, "My grandmother was a Cherokee princess."

18. Interview with Lisa Mayo, Gloria Miguel, Muriel Miguel, and Hortensia Colorado, December 1989.

19. Pamela Bloom, "Keeping the Faith: Native Americans Transform Tradition on Stage," *Taxi,* January 1990, 104–9.

20. Judy Burns and Jerri Hurlbutt, "Secrets: A Conversation with Lisa Mayo of Spiderwoman Theater," in *Women & Performance* 5, no. 1 (1992) 166–83.

21. Interview with Muriel Miguel, June 1990.

22. The quotes in the following section are, unless otherwise specified, from an interview with Muriel Miguel, June 1990.

23. Burns and Hurlbutt, *Secrets.*

24. Spiderwoman press flyer, ca. 1981.

25. Interview with Mayo, G. Miguel, M. Miguel, and Colorado, December 1989.

26. The problems of identity politics in terms of theater affiliations are complicated. Split Britches is widely heralded as "lesbian theater," but, as Deborah

Margolin pointed out to me in a May 1991 interview, it is important to note that one of the founding members of the company, Margolin herself, is heterosexual.

27. Excerpted from an interview with Mayo, G. Miguel, and M. Miguel, December 1989.

28. Natalie Davis and Peter Starn, "Introduction," Special Issue on Memory and Counter-Memory, *Representations,* no. 26 (Spring 1989): 2.

29. Donald F. Bouchard, in Foucault, *Language,* 9.

30. Theater for the New City (TNC) is the country's leading presenter of new professional theater productions by Native American artists and playwrights. TNC presents an annual Pow-Wow by the Thunderbird American Indian Dancers and has been the dramatic home for Native American performance groups including Spiderwoman Theater, Off the Beaten Path, and Vira and Hortensia Colorado.

31. From the text of *Reverb-ber-ber-rations* forthcoming in *Women & Performance.* The inclusion of "Hey, hey, dooten day dooten day" at the end of the monologue does not appear in the text but was included in the performance I saw both at Theater for the New City in March 1990 and in a solo performance of this section by Lisa Mayo at a rally against the Gulf War at Theater for the New City in February 1991. See also Mayo's discussion of this section of the play in Burns and Hurlbutt, *Secrets.*

32. Foucault, *Language,* 148–49.

33. Bhabha, "Of Mimicry and Man," 126.

34. "In this comic turn from the high ideals of the colonial imagination to its low mimetic literary effect, mimicry emerges as one of the most elusive and effective strategies of colonial power and knowledge" (ibid., 126).

35. Ibid.

36. Ibid., 128.

37. The performance technique I am trying to articulate here under the rubric "doubling back," or countermimicry, can be thought of in terms of French ethnographer Michel Leiris's notion of "writing back," first articulated in the early 1950s in relation to the work of Aimé Césaire. See James Clifford, *The Predicament of Culture: Twentieth-Century Ethnography, Literature, and Art* (Cambridge, Mass.: Harvard University Press, 1988), 255–56.

38. From the text of *Reverb-ber-ber-rations,* forthcoming in *Women & Performance.*

39. Ibid.

40. Excerpted from an interview with Mayo, G. Miguel, M. Miguel, and Colorado, December 1989.

41. See in this volume Elin Diamond, "Mimesis, Mimicry, and the 'True-Real,'" (orig. in *Modern Drama* 32, no. 1 [1989]: 58–72); and "Realism and Hysteria: Toward a Feminist Mimesis," *Discourse* 13, no. 1 (Fall-Winter 1990–91): 59–92.

42. Diamond, "Mimesis," 66.

43. Ibid., 59.

44. Ibid., 69.

45. Ibid., 68.

46. Ibid.

47. Sigmund Freud, "Femininity," in *New Introductory Lectures on Psychoanalysis,* ed. and trans. James Strachey (New York: W. W. Norton, 1965), 113.

48. Karen Finley, "The Constant State of Desire," *Drama Review* 32, no. 1 (1988): 139–51.

49. It is important to note here that Finley makes no allusion to this specific Freud quote in her performance text. Thus, Finley's transgression is not explained by a clear connection to that which she transgresses—to provide such a connection might make her work more understandable or palatable but, ironically, less transgressive. Some feminist scholars have difficulty with Finley's unwillingness to make the inappropriate appropriate by way of explanation.

50. In *Winnetou's Snake Oil Show* this interruptive quality of the sacred is certainly present. In *Reverb-ber-ber-rations,* on the other hand, moments of serious invocation are more broadly interwoven into the fabric of the piece, balancing the parodic and the sincere to the degree that it is sometimes difficult to determine where an interruption begins and ends.

51. See Elin Diamond, "Brechtian Theory/Feminist Theory: Toward a Gestic Feminist Criticism," *Drama Review* 32, no. 1 (1988): 82–94.

Chapter 13

Toward a Lesbian Theory of Performance: Refunctioning Gender

Hilary Harris

Dressed for a straight friend's wedding, lesbian/feminist stand-up comic Kate Clinton passes a plate glass window, catches her wedding outfit moving to the rhythm of a dyke walk, breaks into a grin and concludes, "Nice try."

In the mid-1970s, writing as a feminist, Gayle Rubin charted the neologistic "sex/gender system."[1] Not only did Rubin thus hypostatize the "set of arrangements by which the biological raw material of human sex and procreation is shaped by human, social intervention" from Lévi-Strauss's naturalized notion of kingship systems (Rubin 1975, 165), but, by embodying the distance between those two systems in a notion of gender (that is, woman as social construct, not biological imperative), Rubin provided the theoretical frame for Simone de Beauvoir's "one is not born a woman" to function as both the defining and emancipatory critical epistemology of feminist theory. In the mid-1980s, writing as a sexual transgressive (alienated from both heterosexual feminism and lesbian feminism by virtue of her experiential and theoretical privileging of S/M practices), Rubin deliberately shifted her field of inquiry away from (hetero)gendering to heterogeneous sexuality.[2] My project in this essay is to suggest that this seemingly dis/continuous movement from gender to sexuality by Rubin, and others, marks the moment of production of what, in a signal departure from Rubin, I will call a "lesbian/feminist" theory of (sexual/gender) performance.

The slash makes the position: lesbian/feminism is distinct from lesbian feminism. Lesbian is no longer a postscripted modifier of a liberal, or cultural feminist, project. Lesbian is not woman first (nor is lesbian "not-woman" period, but I will return to that). Rather the sign of lesbians slashing feminism is an enactment of the micro-moment-to-micro-moment resistance to woman, the paring down (or, as I shall suggest, the trading up) of that construct that lesbians must perform to walk, talk, think, speak, fuck like lesbians. Lesbian/feminism discursively "acts out" the geodiscursive/performative site of Saturday night at a girls' bar, where sexuality and gender circulate the room, sometimes alone, sometimes in tandem, occasionally in packs, but *always* in relation . . . cruising and getting cruised to the expropriated rhythm of someone else's beat.[3] Lesbian/feminism performs this sociosymbolic site of sex in academic discourse, but to turn up the heat on the radical potential of this performance, to push at the outer limits of the spectrum of the visible (which this term embodies) toward the white heat of transgression (which this term promises), I must now invoke a sexual narrative and perform it in one of the languages of the lesbian bar itself, where the relation of lesbian to feminist, of sex to gender, might sound like this: while Rubin and others can get excited by the renegade promise of sexuality, sexual performance, sex talk only outside of that bourgeois marriage of institutional respectability, the historically vanilla relationship between (feminist) theorist and gender, I am aroused by the thought of what the tough new baby dyke—(lesbian) sexual theory—might learn under the oh, so demanding tutelage of the much older, wiser (I did not say kinder and gentler) dominatrix (and theoretical matrix)—gender. The public service announcement hanging by thumbtacks in the girls' room of the 1990s, the writing on the wall, says that lesbian and feminist *must* go together hand-in-glove (you know the riff, no glove, no love). But here's the hottest scenario going down in the girls' room: Student/Teacher—a contemporary lesbian classic—sexual theory tears the straightjacket off gender, straps her in a leather dyke's harness and leaves her hanging, makes gender slave to and unbound by the (lesbian's) sexual apparatus, makes gender move through and constituted by a new kind of performance. Makes gender.

Unhappily, though, in theory, sex is a selfish lover. Theories of sexuality got all they thought gender has to offer and rolled over. But because you always hurt the one you love, theories of sexuality suffer the most from the snub. (And here the language must shift again to be precise:) Theories of sexuality constructed at the expense of a refunctioning of a theory of gender cannot make good on their radical potential because they overlook the powerful (and, I will contend, historically necessary) theoretical and sexual—that is, performative—tools (or toys, depending again upon one's language and inclination) available in a refunctioned notion of gender. Further, these theories of sexuality may serve unwittingly and paradoxically to drop at least one sexually renegade (when not retrograde) group, lesbians, preemptively from a cultural address they have yet to successfully inhabit.

Of course, the force of these theories of sexuality is their status as historically specific responses. They are emerging at this specific historical moment—a time of increased homophobia in the form of violent crimes against homosexuals as individuals and New Right attacks against homosexuals as a class. Neither the theories of gender nor the concomitant social agendas of (predominantly heterosexual, not explicitly antihomophobic) feminism seem equal to the task of challenging, or even critiquing, the social relations precipitating this historic crisis. In addition, the theorists engaged in this work recognize its historical particularity, or, more appropriately, its historical imperative. Rubin carefully positions her work as an argument for "theoretical as well as sexual pluralism" ("Thinking Sex," 309). Eve Kosofsky Sedgwick painstakingly charts hers in the field of antihomophobic theory.[4] Together both Rubin's and Sedgwick's writings can be plotted in a single matrix of social theory, one graphing radical sexual acts, politics, and theories intended to resist the erasure and similar punitive measures enacted by hegemonic culture against its other(s).

The result of this historical consciousness is the intertextual production of a kind of theoretical fiction. Sedgwick, for example, explicitly agrees with Rubin on two points: first, that the "question of gender and the question of sexuality" are "inextricable from one another . . . in that each can be expressed only in the terms of the other" (*Epistemology*, 30); second, that they are

nonetheless *not* the same question, that in twentieth-century Western culture gender and sexuality represent two analytic axes that may productively be imagined as being as distinct from one

another as, say, gender and class, or class and race. Distinct, that
is to say, no more than minimally, but nonetheless usefully. (30;
my emphasis)

I call this a theoretical fiction not to undermine the position but to
foreground the fact that both its construction and its usefulness are
determined by a particular sense of the relationship between two
historical narratives: the history of discourse on gender and the history of persecution against consensual sexual activity.[5] A wedge of
critical distance is being placed between gender and sexuality at precisely that site where a progressive discourse of gender is thought to
collapse in the face of a hegemonic discourse of sexual persecution.
That site is the body of heterosexuality's other(s).

Defining the other's body has, of course, proven to be *the* problematic in lesbian/feminist projects. In that body's first incarnation
in feminist representation, we must remember, she was universalized
as Anglo-American, heterosexual, able-bodied, and middle class.
Under the sway of poststructuralism and unflagging identity politics
that singular body has been displaced by multiple and diverse bodies
that are knowable only in the context of their particularized and contingent positions. bell hooks theorizes one such position for an African-American subject as "that counter-hegemonic marginal space
where radical black subjectivity is *seen,* not overseen by any authoritative Other claiming to know us better than we know ourselves."[6]
hooks accomplishes a deft rhetorical sleight of hand in this image by
positing "nonblack" as "Other." Sedgwick, taking to heart her analogy that gender and sexuality are as distinct as "gender and class, or
class and race," attempts an analogous legerdemain. She writes:

> a great deal depends—for all women, for lesbians, for gay men,
> and possibly for all men—on the fostering of our ability to arrive
> at understandings of sexuality that will respect a certain irreduci-
> bility in it to the terms and relations of gender. (16)

Sedgwick assumes here an antihomophobic position from which she
can then posit the disparate subject positions of "women," "lesbians,"
"gay men," and "possibly all men" as others to heterosexuality. With
the critical mass on the side of antihomophobia, heterosexuality thus
becomes the other. But hooks, through the lens of postcolonial the-

ory, offers a reminder of the intimate relation between gender and sexuality that serves to circumscribe Sedgwick's project by prohibiting any easy separation of gender and sexuality. hook writes:

> Sexuality has always provided gendered metaphors for colonization. Free countries equated with free men, domination with castration, the loss of manhood, and rape—the terrorist act re-enacting the drama of conquest, as men of the dominating group sexually violate the bodies of women who are among the dominated. The intent of this act was to continually remind dominated men of their loss of power; rape was a gesture of symbolic castration. Dominated men are made powerless (i.e., impotent) over and over again as the women they would have had the right to possess, to control, to assert power over, to dominate, to fuck, are fucked and fucked over by the dominating victorious male group. (*Yearning*, 57)

Sexuality may be about fucking, but getting fucked is still about gender, even if "only" metaphorically.

Rubin might seem to warn against the gender logic I employ here when she declares that "feminism is the theory of gender oppression" ("Thinking Sex," 307); and that it is, therefore, an insufficient tool with which to analyze sexual oppression (309). I agree with Rubin at the point where she determines that a discourse of emancipation will never arise from a discourse of victimization. Further, I appreciate the political motivation behind Rubin's attempt to inscribe lesbians in a coalition of oppressed sexualities. I disagree, however, with the ahistorical conclusion I believe she draws at the end of her otherwise historical narrative:

> lesbians are also oppressed as queers and perverts, by the operation of sexual, not gender, stratification . . . the fact is that lesbians have shared many of the sociological features and suffered from many of the same social penalties as have gay men, sado-masochists, transvestites, and prostitutes. (308)

What hooks's postcolonial analysis graphically suggests is that, although Rubin's group of "deviants" assuredly share a marginality (and consequent persecution) in direct ratio to their distance from what Rubin labels "good sex" (heterosexual, married, monogamous, reproductive, at home [282]), what actually defines that distance, what measures it, is its proximity to the heterosexual, white, male subject position: aka, Man. Neither gender nor sexuality alone can adequately critique or displace the complex intersection of the two concepts in social organization. But a refunctioned notion of gender, coupled with a race- and class-inflected theory of sexuality, may come closer to dismantling that configuration of (hetero)gendering and (hetero)sexuality that is narrativized in Western political economies as the social contract.

Monique Wittig's conception of the social contract as, at base, structurally coextensive with, if not synonymous to, heterosexuality has circulated with sustained currency for over a decade in lesbian/feminist discourse. Wittig's various articulations of the social contract as the heterosexual contract, or, paradigmatically, the straight mind, represent a discourse in which heterosexuality functions as the organizing principle, the foundational social arrangement for (at least) Western societies. This is not to say, however, that heterosexual social relations "reflect" an "originary" social contract. The materialist Wittig holds no truck in tales of origin, nor in their ontologic relation to current social arrangements. Rather Wittig founds her notion of the heterosexual social contract in a reading of dominant discourses and their systems of representation, namely those "discourses which take for granted that what founds society, any society, is heterosexuality."[7]

From this reading Wittig constructs a notion of "straight society" (that is, hegemonic Western culture) that both produces and is produced by "the necessity of the different/other at every level" (108). This heterosexual imperative of difference between the sexes (which "ontologically constitutes women into different/others" [108]) structures all hegemonic ways of knowing and seeing, not just those manifestly concerning sexual identity. Like hooks, Wittig thus reads seemingly diverse power imbalances as endless reproductions of the foundational asymmetrical difference of heterosexuality. Wittig observes:

> Men are not different, whites are not different, nor are the masters. But the blacks, as well as the slaves, are. (108)

As problematized, then, by both Wittig's lesbian and hooks's more specifically race- and class-inflected postcolonial analyses, a critique of (hetero)gendering cannot be separated out from social theory as solely, or simply, the study of a gender's oppression. Rather, to engage in that critique is to engage in a struggle over the meaning of the central hierarchizing metaphor in a society organized through domination and subordination.

In the context of nascent theories of sexuality Rubin's cautionary note might sound again here:

> Feminist conceptual tools were developed to detect and analyze gender-based hierarchies. To the extent that these overlap with erotic stratifications, feminist theory has some explanatory power. But as issues become less those of gender and more those of sexuality, feminist analysis becomes irrelevant and often misleading. ("Thinking Sex," n. 309)

A lesbian/feminist analysis functions as a corrective by always already reading through the always already doubled perspective of sexuality/gender. Thus, hooks's construction of a "radical black" critical position provides a timely analogy for lesbian/feminism. Through hooks's paradigm we can identify a theoretical position configured as lesbian:feminist::sexuality:gender. Like hooks's example, this equation suggests a synchronic relation between its first term(s), *lesbian* and *sexuality,* which speak from a "counter-hegemonic marginal space," and its second term(s), *feminist* and *gender*—which, by virtue of their ideologically defined surfaces, resist but remain susceptible to reinscription by "any authoritative Other claiming to know us better than we know ourselves."[8] This critical position privileges a theory of (homo)sexual space while simultaneously imagining that space's critical relation to (hetero)gender. It thus fulfills Rubin's penultimate directive that "feminism's critique of gender hierarchy must be incorporated into a radical theory of sex" (309).

Ironically, to meet that challenge in Rubin's theory one must trespass on her primary injunction against encoding "sexual oppression" as "reducible to, or understandable in terms of, class, race, ethnicity, or gender" (292). While all oppression is certainly not "reducible" to gender, most oppression is "understandable" (given the structural hegemony of heterosexuality via the social contract) in gendered terms. Even Sedgwick gestures toward this reading of social contract when she observes:

the extreme intimacy with which all these available analytic axes
do after all mutually constitute one another: to assume the
distinctiveness of the *intimacy* between sexuality and gender
might well risk assuming too much about the definitional *separability* of either of them from determinations of, say, class or race.
(*Epistemology,* 31)

Pushing at the borders of that "definitional separability," Rubin constructs a narrative of race, class, gender, and sexual "deviance" that
privileges sexuality as the defining "vector of oppression":

A rich, white male pervert will generally be less affected than a
poor, black, female pervert. But even the most privileged are
not immune to sexual oppression. Some of the consequences of
the system of sexual hierarchy are mere nuisances. Others are
quite grave. ("Thinking Sex," 293)

Rubin's syntax belies her narrative's putative trajectory:

rich + white + male = oppression as nuisance
poor + black + female = oppression as "grave" (literal or metaphoric?)[9]

The systems of representation engaged by Rubin's narrative *must*
thwart that narrative's desired movement. Wittig and hooks have
demonstrated the gendered metaphors of "color." Common and
government wisdom alike know the gender coding of poverty. Rubin's two bodies are not only gendered along the axis of "biological
sex," or even that of sexual perversion (as I suggested earlier), but
along the related axes of race and economic status as well. The spaces
these two subjects occupy in representation and the differential reception they receive are, consequently, in many ways *only* "understandable" in terms of gender, at least insofar as their relative positions
vis-à-vis what Teresa de Lauretis identifies as the traditional structure
of Western narratives: "male-hero-human, on the side of the subject;
and female-obstacle-boundary-space, on the other."[10]

Central to a disruptive strategy for lesbian/feminist textual structuring is this necessary doubling back of gender on sexuality—and
gender and sexuality on class and race—all as "mutually constituted"

axes of the heterosexual social contract. If, as de Lauretis elsewhere determines, the project of lesbian/feminist representation is to "alter the standard of vision, the frame of reference of visibility, of *what can be seen*,"[11] if, in other words, it is to destabilize the heterosexual imperative of Western narrative, then, properly understood, the project is to interrogate and manipulate the two nominally discrete discourses of sexuality and gender, not one and then the other, but both at the same time. Otherwise, the promise of lesbian/feminist representation remains sorely unfulfilled.

While Wittig's lesbian analysis of the heterosexual contract understands (hetero)gender as the organizing metaphor for all hegemonic social relations, it ignores that metaphor's function in some, but (significantly) not all, *counter*hegemonic relations. That is, in a discourse of racial oppression, Wittig provides for no racialized discursive space distinct from its gendered metaphor. Yet in a discourse of sexual emancipation, Wittig unproblematically places *lesbian* completely outside gender and its metaphorized discourses. In the formulation of *lesbian* as "beyond the categories of sex (woman and man)" and as *"not* a woman," Wittig both assumes the hegemony of a heterosexual gender binary and denies lesbian inscription in it at any level—"either economically, or politically, or ideologically."[12] This articulation of a lesbian sociotheoretical position resonates with Luce Irigaray's query:

> *what if the "goods" refused to go to market?* What if they maintained among themselves "another" kind of trade?[13]

Irigaray posits the site of this refusal as a space "protected from masculine transactions" (110). Similarly, Wittig's lesbian refuses circulation under the mark of "woman," that "specific social relation to a man, a relation that we have previously called servitude" ("One Is Not Born," 53). Certainly, as an imaginative possibility, the sociosexual position constructed by these two theorists, and others, continues to be of inestimable worth to lesbian/feminism. It creates lesbian/feminist value out of the old heterosexual saw that woman acquires agency only in relation to man: for these theorists, lesbians have no such relation, and that lack is precisely their value. But what tools are lesbian/feminists given in this paradigm when they are *not* "protected from masculine transactions"? That is, in representation, can the lesbian be "imaged" (literalized, physicalized, embodied) in relation to the heterogender binary unless she is, in some way, constructed in gendered terms? Wittig concludes that the lesbian cannot, finally, intersect with the social contract as it is currently configured:

> only by running away from their class can women enter the social contract (that is a new one). . . . Lesbians are runaways . . . and they exist in all countries because the political regime of heterosexuality represents all cultures. So that breaking off the heterosexual social contract is a necessity for those who do not consent to it ("On the Social Contract," 248–49)

Of course, Wittig's lesbian, to be read as a lesbian, *must* perform that subjectivity in a cultural space uninflected by the representational "regime of heterosexuality." With her address constituted from outside of gender, Wittig's lesbian is rendered invisible, *as a dyke,* to (hetero)reception: she is received (contained) as woman. Exiled to an unchartable representational economy, Wittig's lesbian is thus more a gender refugee than a sexual terrorist. Likewise, Irigaray's lesbian constructs a homosocial contract that, even *if* (and it is a question for Irigaray) it *has* intersected with the heterobinary and *has,* unlike Wittig's, "undermined the order of trade," it "simply has *not* been recognized" ("When the Goods Get Together," 110; not my emphasis). In sum, neither of these theories of a lesbian sexuality outside of gender provides for a sociosexual position capable of disrupting the heterosexual representational compact, that is, of altering "the standard of vision, the frame of reference of visibility, of *what can be seen.*"

The notion that gender *is* heterosexual woman (and is, thus, unrecuperable as such) functions as the theoretical "negative space" around which these lesbian/feminist theories of sexualities uninflected by gender are being structured. Instructive as a counterpoint, then, is a current heterosexual feminist "take" on gender. Contract theorist Carole Pateman constructs an idea of the social contract that is virtually synonymous with Wittig's yet reaches vastly dissimilar conclusions. Like Wittig, Pateman determines that the social contract is a "sexual-social pact":[14]

> The social contract is a story of freedom; the sexual contract is a story of subjection. The original contract constitutes both free-

dom and domination. Men's freedom and women's subjection are created. . . . (2)

In her project to problematize the feminist appropriation of contract theory, Pateman finds that the seemingly sex-neutral "individual" constructed through and presumed by contract ideology is, in fact, always already masculine. Further, she determines that the lack of anatomical specificity in contract semiotics functions not to mark an assumption of universal human agency undifferentiated by sexual difference but, rather, to signal a screen discourse, one that represses "the missing half of the [social contract] story that reveals how men's patriarchal right over women is established through contract" (2). The notion of gender is unrecuperable for Pateman, then, not because, in Wittig's terms, it marks woman as a class, but because it works to dismantle that class by highlighting its social construction and ignoring, or denying, its biological base (225).

In this context, reformulating woman as either "individual" or "gender" serves only to reinscribe her in a contractual paradigm founded on the pretense, the "legal fiction" of her "free agency." "Woman-as-individual" is not, for Pateman, a new or emancipatory taxonomy. Rather, it perpetuates the historical and oppressive fiction of woman as (man's equal in being a) free agent. This fiction is evident, for example, in the marriage contract, where, in order for a contract to be effected, woman must temporarily be represented as man's equal. Once the contract is engaged, however, that momentary hint of transgression is (re)contained in a relationship predicated on male-sex right (although the fact of male "domination is hidden by the claim that marriage allows equal, consensual sexual enjoyment to both spouses" [159]). "Woman-as-gender" is likewise suspect on the grounds that it denies the biological base of these asymmetrical sociosexual relations. Indeed, Pateman contends that:

> For feminists to argue for the elimination of nature, biology, sex in favor of the "individual" is to play the modern patriarchal game and to join in a much wider onslaught on nature within and beyond the boundaries of civil society. (226)

Whether or not "feminists" *are* actually arguing for the "elimination" of "nature," and so forth, is beyond the purview of this essay (espe-

cially where nature is conflated, as it is in Pateman's text, with
"women . . . land, indigenous peoples, the descendants of the
slaves . . . and animals" [226]). I will address, however, why Pateman
must, first, read such a threat and, second, position her own writing
against it.

Pateman privileges certain nineteenth-century feminists who
"demanded juridical equality and recognition *as woman*": they "grappled with the political problem of expressing sexual difference; they
did not attempt to deny political significance to womanhood" (227).
This particular political nostalgia coupled with the desire to preserve
a sense of "nature" in social theory locates Pateman's notion of
woman in an ontological register. Historical (and contemporary) relations of domination/subordination are unfortunate but rooted, after
all, in the "real" division between the sexes. Further, the wall divid-
ing those two sexes is solid, not porous; there is no question where
one begins and the other ends. If (hetero)gender is superfluous to
Wittig's notion of a new social contract on the sexual frontier, (an/
other) sexuality is unimaginable to Pateman's woman. That woman
is defined only through, what Wittig calls, a "specific social relation
to a man." Indeed, Pateman's reformulation of that relation varies
but slightly from Wittig's original: in the final sentence of her penultimate paragraph, Pateman urges the "creation of free relations in
which *manhood* is reflected back from autonomous *femininity*" (233;
my emphasis). Locked inside a historical heterosexuality, Pateman's
woman remains, ironically, the Lacanian mirror through which man
alone can represent a self.

Missing, finally, from both Wittig's and Pateman's analyses is
the question of performance. What constitutes performance in/of the
new social contract? Where gender is not ontology, or, to put it thus,
where gender is its performance,[15] and the "construction of gender
is the product and the process of both representation and self-representation,"[16] how do we perform/construct differently (if not non-)
gendered subjectivities. For de Lauretis the answer begins in a refusal
to read heterogender as totalizing:

> the terms of a different construction of gender also exist, in the
> margins of hegemonic discourses. Posed from outside the
> heterosexual social contract, and inscribed in micropolitical prac-
> tices, these terms can also have a part in the construction of

gender, and their effects are rather at the "local" level of resistances, in subjectivity and self-representation. (18)

Donna Haraway puts the matter thus: "Cyborg gender is a local possibility taking a global vengeance."[17]

Recognizing the tensions embodied in Haraway's cyborg is central to my project of locating a site at which a radical theory of sexuality can profitably intersect with a (refunctioned) notion of gender. Initially, Haraway posits the cyborg as a "creature in a postgender world," a contribution to the "utopian tradition of imagining a world without gender." Haraway privileges the undecidability of such a world: it is "perhaps a world without genesis, but maybe also a world without end" (192). On the final page of the essay, however, Haraway relocates cyborg within gender, or, perhaps, gender within cyborg. Why does she bother? This movement in Haraway's piece is emblematic of a necessary circularity in current lesbian/feminist discourse. There is at once the sense, provocatively articulated by Audre Lorde, that the "master's tools will never dismantle the master's house."[18] Yet there is also, layered onto the first, a second conviction, voiced by Judith Butler:

> There is no self that is prior to the convergence or who maintains "integrity" prior to its entrance into this conflicted cultural field. There is only a taking up of the tools where they lie, where the very "taking up" is enabled by the tool lying there. (*Gender Trouble*, 145)

There is, in short, no cyborg (or other) self prior to its emergence into hegemonic fields of representation—that is, prior to a performance of gender. Gender functions, then, not only as the tool with which to construct an/other (or outside of) gender but the very possibility of that construction as well.

The cyborg subject position is knowable by its resolute commitment to "partiality, irony, intimacy, and perversity" (192). It is thus strikingly similar to the lesbian/feminist subject position identified by Sue-Ellen Case in "the lesbian roles of butch and femme."[19] Drawing on a history shared with gay male camp, these lesbian performances employ "artifice, wit, irony, and the distancing of straight reality" (287):

In other words, a strategy of appearances replaces a claim to truth. . . . These roles are played in signs themselves and not in ontologies. Seduction, as a dramatic action, transforms all of these seeming realities into semiotic play. . . . butch-femme roles offer a hypersimulation of woman as she is defined by the Freudian system and the phallocracy that institutes its social rule.(297)

Butch/femme role playing thus constitutes what Butler might call a "dissonant and denaturalized performance that reveals the performative status of the natural itself." Butler continues:

there is a subversive laughter in the pastiche-effect of parodic practices in which the original, the authentic, and the real are themselves constituted as effects. The loss of gender norms would have the effect of proliferating gender configurations, destabilizing substantive identity, and depriving the naturalizing narratives of compulsory heterosexuality of their central protagonists: "man" and "woman." The parodic repetition of gender exposes as well the illusion of gender identity as an intractable depth and inner substance. As the effects of a subtle and politically enforced performativity, gender is an "act," as it were, that is open to splittings, self-parody, self-criticism, and those hyperbolic exhibitions of "the natural" that, in their very exaggeration, reveal its fundamentally phantasmatic status. (*Gender Trouble*, 146–47)

Some would argue that butch and femme performances are not, finally, exhibitions of gender, parodic or not. In that context butch and femme become performances of lesbian sexuality, period. No gender. I do not disagree that butch and femme do indeed constitute sexual performances, but I do content that the sexual semiotics of butch and femme are readable primarily through the lens of gender. The lesbian can perform sexually until the first light of dawn, but it's an autoerotic night if sexuality and gender don't meet up first. That is, lesbian as a *socio*sexuality cannot be read (even in bed) without the illumination of gender.

I support this contention by pointing to a telling lapse in recent theorizing of lesbian history. At least one other player was on the scene in the lesbian bar culture of the 1950s now being narrativized in both lesbian/feminist theory and lesbian literature. She was the kiki (or ky-ky), and she faces discursive erasure. Katie King explains that *kiki* is "the stigmatized term for lesbians who don't adopt the identities of butch or femme in a bar scene dependent upon these meanings."[20] I am suggesting that a kiki subject position was stigmatized in the 1950s and is largely untheorized in the 1990s because in it the relationship of homosexuality and heterogender remains ambiguous.[21] Of course, that relationship is marked by ambiguity in the butch/femme subject positions as well; however, there equivocality is privileged by design. Indeed, in butch/femme role playing lesbian (homo)sexuality becomes the very site at which (hetero)gender is demonstrated as always already ambiguous. Kate Davy explains:

> In butch/femme iconography, attributes which in dominant culture are associated with strict gender roles are not sex-class specific. Worn by lesbians, these attributes have meanings for lesbians in a same-sex, lesbian culture that do not necessarily symbolize conformity to rules of gender behavior and the oppositional dynamics of polarized gender roles.[22]

Butler suggests a frame in which butch/femme roles may be read as not, finally, about heterogendering at all. Rather, their particular melding of sexuality and sex/gender manipulation signifies the "product and process" of what might be called *homo*gendering. Butler's strategic heterocentrism thus collapses under the burden of its own construction:

> The replication of heterosexual constructs in non-heterosexual frames brings into relief the utterly constructed status of the so-called heterosexual original. Thus, gay [lesbian] is to straight *not* as copy is to original, but, rather, as copy is to copy. (*Gender Trouble*, 31)

By contrast, the kiki subject position does not appear to perform any critical relation to heterosexuality's sex/gender ontology. Kiki "performs" gender only to the extent that gender is always a performance. Her exhibition of woman, unlike the femme's, is not parodic; it casts no eye toward its own constructedness, its contingency. Consequently, as a performance of lesbian sexuality unmarked by a conscious, or critical, relation to hegemonic gender, kiki seems unable to do the work now required of lesbian (self-)representation. Sexual acts alone do not distance her from the sex-based gender position reserved in her name in hegemonic representation.

The ease with which kiki is contained within heterosexual representation, and the difficulty with which it is theorized as a performance of disruptive sexuality, makes clear the need for explicitly hetero-resistant gendering (or, at least, the attempt) in lesbian/feminist representations, including theories of sexuality. The question is, as de Lauretis formulates it:

> If the deconstruction of gender inevitably effects its (re)construction... in which terms and in whose interest is the de-re-construction being effected? (*Technologies of Gender*, 24)

In an era of coalition building the answer is tricky—so tricky, in fact, that much current lesbian/feminist theory intends to ignore it by focusing instead on "sexuality." Theories such as "queer theory" hope to sidestep the days of gender reckoning implied by de Lauretis in the scramble for a new world order. In fact, queer theory, as Case articulates it, "works not at the site of gender, but at the site of ontology, to shift the ground of being itself, thus challenging the Platonic parameters of Being—the borders of life and death."[23] The same circularity present in Haraway's "cyborg" emerges, however, in Case's queer. Queer does not work "at the site of gender"; rather, "queer desire" works at the site of the "Platonic construction of a life/death binary opposition at the base, with its attendant gender opposition above... producing a slippage at the ontological base and seducing through a gender inversion above" (3). Case further underscores the necessary relation of gender to a queer project in her enthusiastic reading of John of the Cross, in whose works "ontology shifts through gender inversion and is expressed as same-sex desire. This is queer, indeed" (5). Case, like Haraway, is, finally, offering a re-functioned theory of gender, not (hetero)gender, as Case early on defines it as "the very notion that reinscribes sexual difference in a way that makes it problematic for the lesbian, as de Lauretis configures it, 'to be seen'" (3), but *homo*gender (or "queer" gender, as Case might allow) as the very possibility of a sexually disruptive performance.

The problem with theories of sexuality that do not explicitly engage both the problematics and the promise of gender in their own emancipatory projects is, it seems to me, the same problem embodied in my reading of kiki as well as in Pateman's reading of "individual." Unless otherwise marked to encourage a rereading, the female body is gendered (historical, heterosexual) woman, a taxonomy from which lesbians defined by sex acts alone are clearly not exempt. What, then, in queer theory will prevent the lesbian (woman) from being subsumed in the gay (man)? Even supportive, antihomophobic, and feminist theorists such as Butler and Sedgwick do not avoid that containing move. In fact, Butler does not even recognize the distinction between gay and lesbian (see Butler's *Gender Trouble*, qtd. above). And Sedgwick is unclear:

> I sometimes use "gay and lesbian" but more often simply "gay," the latter in the *oddly precise* sense of a phenomenon of same-sex desire that is being treated as indicatively but not exclusively male. (*Epistemology*, 18; my emphasis)

Understanding that "same-sex desire appears as gay male" Case actually privileges lesbian invisibility in the form of the lesbian vampire who exists

> outside of the mirror, collapsing subject/object relations into the proximate of a double occupancy of the sign; abandoning the category of woman as heterosexist, and entering representation only in a guise that proscribes her. You still can only see her, in horror and fear, when you don't. ("Tracking the Vampire," 16–17)

Like Wittig's "not-woman," the lesbian vampire appears to offer another utopic "outside of" dominant representation. Unlike Wittig's lesbian, however, Case's vampire is not only invisible in dominant representation but in her own mirror as well (15). My intention, finally, is to problematize such a representational strategy, to mark its abandonment of the imaging apparati of homogender, to suggest the incompleteness of theories of sexuality that refuse to mark their own engagements with gender. A lesbian/feminist theory of performance, on the other hand, can work *toward* a lesbian (or queer) theory of performance—that is, can move toward a radically (or non-) gendered performance of female sexuality. Indeed, by refusing the ontological base of gender, lesbian/feminist theory may already be performing queerly.

Like many such narratives, mine must defer closure by reasserting its beginning, the experience of this historical moment in which the lesbians I know *do* see their reflections in the mirror and resent and resist their enforced invisibility in the mirrors of both hegemonic *and* counterhegemonic representation: lesbian/feminist stand-up comic Lea Delaria tells the story of walking down a Bay Area sidewalk with an arm around her girlfriend. A carload of "straight boys" drives by; one leans out the window and yells, "You fucking fag!" Mad as hell, Delaria stops, turns fully to face the car, and screams: "I'm not a *fag!* I'm a *fucking DYKE!*"[24] Because Delaria's homogendered performance of lesbian sexuality has disrupted her heteroreception, straight boys might be pardoned the confusion. Queer theory must not.

NOTES

The epigraph is quoted from Clinton's performance, which I attended at Calamity's in Little Rock, Arkansas, 15 February 1985. See Clinton's comedy albums: *Kate Clinton: Making Light* (1984); *Kate Clinton: Live at Great American Music Hall* (1985); *Kate Clinton: Babes in Joyland* (n.d., ca. 1991).

1. Gayle Rubin, "The Traffic in Women: Notes on the 'Political Economy' of Sex," in *Toward an Anthropology of Women,* ed. Rayna R. Reiter (New York: Monthly Review Press, 1975), 157–210.

2. Gayle Rubin, "Thinking Sex: Notes for a Radical Theory of the Politics of Sexuality," in *Pleasure and Danger: Exploring Female Sexuality,* ed. Carole S. Vance (Boston: Routledge and Kegan Paul, 1984), 267–319.

3. The paradox of suggesting that "sexuality and gender" circulate "sometimes alone" but *"always* in relation" does not escape me. It is this paradox that this essay hopes both to explore and exploit.

4. Eve Kosofsky Sedgwick, *Epistemology of the Closet* (Berkeley: University of California Press, 1990).

5. The issue of consensus is, of course, central to the social contract theory, which I engage later in this essay. Consensus is the mise-en-scène of exchange between two free agents; consequently, which subjects are constructed as free and precisely what is allowable, even through consensus, are matters central to questions of sexuality as well. Rubin's "Thinking Sex" is particularly helpful in historicizing these issues.

6. bell hooks, *Yearning: Race, Gender, and Cultural Politics* (Boston: South End Press, 1990), 22.

7. Monique Wittig, "The Straight Mind," *Feminist Issues* 1, no. 1 (Summer 1980): 105. See also Wittig's "On the Social Contract," in *Homosexuality, Which Homosexuality? International Conference on Gay and Lesbian Studies,* ed. Dennis Altman, Carole Vance, Martha Vicinus, Jeffrey Weeks (London: GMP Publishers, 1989), 239–49.

8. Joan Nestle provides a further gloss on the relations among these sets of terms when she writes: "I suggest that the term *Lesbian-feminist* is a butch-femme relationship, as it has been judged, not as it was, with *Lesbian* bearing the emotional weight the butch does in modern judgment and *feminist* becoming the emotional equivalent of the stereotyped femme, the image that can stand the light of day." See Joan Nestle, *A Restricted Country* (Ithaca, N.Y.: Firebrand Books, 1987), 106–7. In my reading both *feminist* and *gender* produce images that can "stand the light of day," which is to say they are both not only potentially assimilable but also imaginable. The importance of the representability of *feminist/gender* will become apparent in its intersection with *lesbian/sexuality*.

9. This reading in no way ignores the reality of AIDS, both as disease and metaphor, in the lives (and deaths) of, especially, gay men. It is, however, to suggest that the body/site/sight of woman continues to function as disease in dominant systems of representation.

10. Teresa de Lauretis, *Alice Doesn't: Feminism, Semiotics, Cinema* (Bloomington: Indiana University Press, 1984), 121.

11. Teresa de Lauretis, "Sexual Indifference and Lesbian Representation," in *Performing Feminisms,* ed. Sue-Ellen Case (Baltimore: Johns Hopkins University Press, 1990), 33.

12. Monique Wittig, "One Is Not Born a Woman," *Feminist Issues* 1, no. 2 (Winter 1981): 53.

13. Luce Irigaray, "When the Goods Get Together," in *New French Feminisms: An Anthology,* ed. Elaine Marks and Isabelle de Courtivron (New York: Schocken Books, 1981), 110.

14. Carole Pateman, *The Sexual Contract* (Stanford, Calif.: Stanford University Press, 1988), 1.

15. See Judith Butler, *Gender Trouble: Feminism and the Subversion of Identity* (New York: Routledge, 1990).

16. Teresa de Lauretis, *Technologies of Gender: Essays on Theory, Film, and Fiction* (Bloomington: Indiana University Press, 1987), 9.

17. Donna Haraway, "A Manifesto for Cyborgs: Science, Technology, and Socialist Feminism in the 1980s," in *Feminism/Postmodernism,* ed. Linda J. Nicholson (New York: Routledge, 1990), 223.

18. See Audre Lorde, *Sister/Outsider: Essays and Speeches* (Freedom, Calif.: Crossing Press, 1984).

19. Sue-Ellen Case, "Toward a Butch-Femme Aesthetic," in *Making a Spectacle: Feminist Essays on Contemporary Women's Theatre,* ed. Lynda Hart (Ann Arbor: University of Michigan Press, 1989), 283.

20. Katie King, "Audre Lorde's Lacquered Layerings: The Lesbian Bar as a Site of Literary Production," *Cultural Studies* 2, no. 3 (October 1988): 325.

21. To state that kiki is currently untheorized is not, of course, to suggest that

she has fallen out of the discourse altogether. But it is to mark her representation as seemingly incomplete, tangential. As a result, the kiki's precise function in the 1950s bar culture is still indeterminate. Nestle, for example, offers a contradictory reading than that employed by King. Unlike King's kiki, who refuses either butch or femme identification, Nestle's performs both at once, for her, "feeling kiki" is "going both ways" (103). Clearly, this model of a kiki subject position would prompt a reading of kiki's relation to gender and sexuality vastly dissimilar, if not mutually exclusive, to the one I deploy here.

22. Kate Davy, "Reading Past the Heterosexual Imperative: *Dress Suits to Hire,*" *Drama Review* 33, no. 1 (Spring 1989): 156.

23. Sue-Ellen Case, "Tracking the Vampire," *differences* 3, no. 2 (Summer 1991): 3.

24. I am quoting from Delaria's main stage performance, which I attended at the *Southern Women's Music and Comedy Festival 1986* (Robin Tyler Productions).

Chapter 14

Robbie McCauley: Speaking History Other-Wise

Raewyn Whyte

For writer/performer/director Robbie McCauley the space of performance is a political arena in which to contest the images of African-American men and women determined in and through dominant discourses: art is both a means by which to explore the issues and contradictions of her life and her weapon against racism. In 1985 she abandoned a well-established acting career to pursue solo and collaborative work with a political edge, and she has continued since then to perform in the galleries, clubs, and alternative spaces that have become the arena of activist artists whose work targets homophobia, racism, and sexism. She is a member of the group Thought Music and has collaborated in such diverse projects as Dave Soldier's opera *The Apotheosis of John Brown,* Urban Bushwoman's *Heat* and *Praise House,* and Fred Holland's *What I Like about Us.* As a free-lance director, McCauley is currently involved in an ongoing series of local black history projects in Buffalo, Boston, and West Mississippi.

In her projects McCauley claims the body as her medium of articulation. This is at once a body saturated with memories of sensual experience, and a text written by racism and bounded by family, history, and gender. In performance she emphasizes the physicality of the experiences she enacts, and at the same time, through her narration, she makes explicit the social implication of such bodily experiences. In *Sally's Rape,* the third and current installment of her ongoing serial performance *Confessions of a Black Working Class Woman,* for example, McCauley strips naked and stands on a bench that serves as a slave auction block. Her partner, a white woman,

Jeannie Hutchins, tells the audience that there needs to be the atmosphere of the slave market here. She exhorts them to be active onlookers in this scene, to chant "Bid em in, bid em in, bid em in," and
prods them to continue their chanting throughout the scene that follows.

Accompanied by the chanting, McCauley replicates the experience shared by her great-great-grandmother Sally and thousands of
other African-American women made chattels under slavery.

> They take off my sack dress
> and order me onto the block with my socks rolled down.
> On the auction block, they put
> their hands all down yr body
> the men smell ya, feel ya
>
> That's what they brought us here for

As she speaks, she flinches at the invisible, probing fingers, which
assess her soundness for childbearing. She crosses her arms across her
breasts as, chin forced upward, she opens her mouth wide for her
teeth to be checked.

> I stand very still, hold myself very tight
>
> That's how you have to be on the block
> til they finish with you
>
> very still, very tight.[1]

For the onlooker there is an awe-ful fascination in this representation
of the slave auction, this scene of victimage. The pleasure of looking
at the naked body of the black woman caught in the spotlight is made
guilty by the awareness of being inescapably positioned as a potential
buyer in the slave market, yet the urge to look away is countered by
the seductive intensity of the scene. Similarly, whether or not you
join the chanting you are trapped by the sympathetic magic of sound,
which reanimates the past, and, no matter how much you tell yourself you had nothing to do with this scene, you are made vicariously
complicit in the auction system that McCauley's staging represents.

The chanting drops off as McCauley's "holding tight" becomes another experience of endurance central to the lives of women slaves—rape. "Sally keeps coming to me in nightmares," she says.

In the dream I be Sally
being done it to down on the ground
The men git their anger on the plantation
they come down to the quarters and do it to us
in the chickens

There's the tightness between her thighs
wouldn't let her go

               she screamed

               it was terrible

Then the tightness again
thighs locking everything up in the body

               had to keep tight . . .

On the plantation we had to stay tough and tight
you dint know how many times
they'll come down there

They comes down there
they pulls us out in the dirt and does it

               Stay tight til they do it
               down on the ground

Sally stayed tight

One would do it
the others would watch
sometimes they would do it too.[2]

McCauley's body quakes, jerks, tries to escape, her voice raw as she tells what is happening, her breathing ragged, her words garbled,

Jeannie Hutchins and Robbie McCauley in McCauley's *Sally's Rape*. Photo by Joyce George.

phrases intercut, cadences elided as the pace of her speaking speeds up, her shoulders hunching, her body somehow shrinking as she embodies her narration of Sally's rape, of Sally's bitter resignation to the domestic power relations of life under slavery.

The rape and the slave auction are only two of the scenes in *Sally's Rape: The Whole Story—The Past Becomes the Present in This Portrait of Survival within Today's Plantation Culture.* In this work Mc-Cauley makes evident the power relations that shaped the life of her great-great-grandmother Sally, a slave on the Monticello estate of Thomas Jefferson.[3]

Sally was "both house and yard" while in slavery at Monticello. She was Jefferson's mistress and bore him several children and had special privileges as a house servant, yet in the slave quarters she was a slave like all the others, a woman caught between the codings of patriarchy, black and white. Being the master's mistress was no protection from maltreatment; the slaveholder's mistress was usually held in contempt by her fellow slaves as the worst kind of collabora-

Jeannie Hutchins and Robbie McCauley in McCauley's *Sally's Rape*. Photo by Joyce George.

tor.[4] Like other female slaves, house servant and fieldhand alike, Sally was subjected to rape and enforced childbearing. Her life stories are the central thread in McCauley's examination of slavery.

Through the layering of her words, her body's actions, the staging of scenes, the positioning of onlookers, and the commentary and exchanges between the black woman and the white woman in *Sally's Rape*, McCauley demonstrates the connections between her great-great-grandmother's everyday experience, the domestic domination of women by men on the plantation, and slavery as a system of economic, racial, and gender domination. These themes are taken up in other sections of the work, as the two women reflect on their own positioning and life experiences in late-twentieth-century urban America. Situations recur, and incidents many years apart are shown to be connected, along with the attitudes and values they have engendered. There's "staying tough and tight," being in therapy, and turning one's rage to good use; there's charm school rules for "proper" poise, assertiveness training, and speaking out against oppression;

there's black women's history and white women's ignorance about it, and Jeannie and Robbie, exploring the contradictions of their friendship and the misunderstandings between them.

In the telling, the social conditions in which personal experiences are situated are made explicit, and the prevalence of white racism in American society is called into account. McCauley intends that her onlookers, whatever their race or gender, in witnessing the experiences she invokes in her performances, will begin to understand their own implication in the situations that she presents, will understand that we all share the same history, albeit from differing positions.

History is very much at issue in her work. "History," she says,

> is who's telling it. It's political, rhetorical, and personal, all at once. The way you tell it is important, and the way you see it and hear it is as important as the story is. . . . if we can really hear each other's stories then we can participate in them, understand them. Nothing will change until we do so—listening to history is the hardest thing we must do.[5]

The composition and telling of official American history is contested in McCauley's performance serial, which has three installments to date. Taken together, these installments offer testimony, bear witness, to the "true" American history lived by her (un)famous ancestors. McCauley meditates on the official narratives found in encyclopedias, textbooks, history books, and state documents throughout her performance serial, responding to these official narratives by posing a "view from beneath" constructed from African-American experiences. Rather than a catalogue of dates of events significant to those in power, she promotes, instead, through her montage of cameos and commentary, history as the concrete experience of the powerless who survive it. Always she draws attention to the ways in which status and identity in America are tied to ancestry, to skin color, to ideologies that serve the interests of dominant political and economic groups.

McCauley's alternative history is a collection of separate but related stories that map a period of time as a process constituted, like bodies and subjects, within a particular social and cultural context. The first installment of her serial, *My Father & The Wars*, explores her father's service in several branches of the American military. It seeks to understand the smoldering anger that accompanied his deeply felt patriotism, and it examines the impact of militarism and racism on black men fighting white America's wars.

By presenting incidents from her father's life, McCauley traces the ways those impacts flow through to African-American military families. Her father's demands for "Reee-Spect," his barked orders to

Make That Bed, Turn That Corner
Everything Shipshape, Shoes with a Spit Shine
Be on Time for Meals And Don't You Eat At Anybody Else's House,[6]

are shown as inversions of his own subjection to military authority; the way he beat his family up "with his words, his thoughts, his fists" are linked to the undermining of his intense patriotism by his inability as a black man to achieve his own ambitions, because of the institutionalized racism of the American armed forces, which has historically limited the rise of black men above certain ranks.

The second installment of her serial, *Indian Blood*, takes much of its material from her grandfather's life. He was a soldier in the all-black 24th Infantry of the 10th Cavalry, fighting under Roosevelt during the Spanish-American War at the end of the nineteenth century. His regiment took an active role in campaigns that seized both Puerto Rico and the Philippines as American colonies. McCauley uses his stories to explore the absence of an African-American perspective in the telling of official American history, and to make evident the connections between military racism and America's imperialist ambitions.

Her grandfather was also married to an Indian woman whose parents had died in an epidemic and who had been raised by church people and placed in service with a colonel in the U.S. army. When grandfather rode through the colonel's backyard on patrol in 1897 he saw her washing the colonel's laundry and fell in love with her. Through incidents in their courtship and marriage, and through her grandfather's role in chasing Indians off their homelands and preventing them from crossing the Canadian border, McCauley examines the historical relationship between blacks and Indians in America, one marked by blood—Indian blood in the veins of blacks, Indian blood on the hands of the black soldiers who killed them on the orders of successive white governments. These blood relationships, like the "costs" of spilled Indian blood, and stolen Indian land, she shows, are seldom written into the official record of American history.

The master-slave relationship, with its dynamics of dominance and subordination, is shown by McCauley to be the paradigm behind all racist power relations between whites and blacks and whites and Indians, whether in historically specific situations or in American life in general, or in institutional or interpersonal relationships. In *Indian Blood* she draws parallels between Roosevelt's command over his black soldiers and the way these black men have been written out of historical accounts of their victory at San Juan Hill, between the religious indoctrination of Indian children in Mormon boarding schools and the Klan's burning of a cross on her grandfather's lawn. In *Sally's Rape* she not only shows the literality of the paradigm in the relationship between Sally and Thomas Jefferson but also shows how it is displaced into the relationship between black men and women on the plantation. The very same dynamic, subtly inverted, structures her relationship with her largely white audience and the relationship between herself and Jeannie—she, Robbie, is the dominant one in their ostensibly equal partnership; Jeannie, the white woman, is learning to speak black English.

But McCauley also demonstrates that resistance is engendered by the dynamic of dominance and subordination in the master-slave relationship. Active resistance is detailed in *Indian Blood*—in her grandmother's refusal to leave her sons in the South where they would be drafted to chain gangs, in the campaigns of the civil rights movement and the Black Panthers—and in all her work we see her own refusal to comply with white racism.

Covert resistance, which is hidden behind a veneer of apparent compliance and enables the survival of the oppressed, is also explored in *Sally's Rape*. Sally endures slavery and all it entails, holding tight until she is freed, some time after Jefferson's death. Determined that her daughters will not be servants, she takes in laundry and does housecleaning until she has enough for a house of her own; later she marries and gives birth to two sons, whom she calls her "only chillun." Similarly, in *Indian Blood* McCauley's father joins the military to provide for his family, and later he takes them on the northern migration shared by so many black families who sought a better life, out of the South, in the 1950s and 1960s.

The way McCauley tells her stories directs attention to the connections she draws between individual experiences and the patterned social relation in which they are embedded. She has said that much of her inspiration is physical,[7] and many of her stories are associated with particular parts of her body, such as the tightness between the thighs in *Sally's Rape* or her father's puffed-out chest as he gives orders to his family in *My Father & The Wars*. In *Indian Blood,* for example, she replays her long expedition into white territory as a ten-year-old driven by her desire for the taste of strawberry bubble gum and palpably transfers to her onlookers the intense triumph she experiences when the white shopkeeper sells her the gum. Another childhood memory, represented with similar intensity, is that of being thrown out of the emergency room in a Catholic hospital in Washington, D.C., when she was in a close-to-diabetic coma, because she was not white.

In McCauley's work there's a fusion of politics, poetry, and music, a combination she draws from jazz poets whose work has influenced her own, such as Thulani Davis, Sekou Sundiata, and Sonia Sanchez, and those with whom she has collaborated, such as Ntozake Shange, Jessica Hagedorn, and Laurie Carlos. In the 1970s and 1980s jazz poetry was the hot new form in New York, San Francisco, and Washington, D.C. It brought a new intensity to performance poetry by combining theatrical presentation of texts and an emphasis on the viscerality of the words.[8] The rhythms and cadences and resonances of McCauley's narratives also owe much to musical forms that arise from black Southern tradition—rap, blues and soul, jazzin on a theme, and call-and-response antiphony.

Her stories are artfully verbal, poetic texts, orally presented with a measure of improvisation and punctuated by the accompanying bodily text. There's no beginning-middle-end to these stories, no narrative closure, no "once upon a time" or happy ending, no stereotyped, familiar characters, no comforting moral messages. Fragments, individual incidents, are pieced together in the course of a performance, becoming part of a bigger picture through repeated images that extend the mininarratives and through repeated phrases that connect the underlying themes. Tags such as "I told y'all about . . . didn't I" and "Somebody said . . . ," and the always ironic "Now there's another part to this story . . ." alert the listener to her metacommentary.

The stories are built from multiple layers, connected by repetitions of situations and relationships or by phrases of text and/or movement. First there's a mininarrative, a story in brief form; then the condensed analysis of the story, the part that's lying in wait; and then the sting in the tail—the critique, the acid aside, the ironic meta-commentary, and the segue into the next story or set of anecdotes or images, often by way of just a few words. A sequence in *Indian Blood,* for example, starts with a chanted song about the way America is always involved in war even when it isn't called that;[9] McCauley telling how her mother always called her The Mouth; the story of how her grandmother got permission from her employer/master, the colonel, to marry her grandfather; and the racism rap song ("Racism is based on class / is classifying us / is caste-based / is class-ifying us").

This is followed by the joint observations that blacks internalize the effects of racism and that the hunger for freedom is eating away inside her; then comes the connection between these stories, one word shouted by all the performers at once: *Food!*—the word that encodes the desire for freedom from racism and carries McCauley's anger about the way that the need to survive has forced the construction of situational ethics that make blacks who have enough to eat complicit with racism.

She passes slices of apple and fig newton biscuits through the audience, observing as she does that lemon juice is supposed to help apples keep their color, and she goes on to tell how food is central to everything:

> I mean
> they tell us that you gotta EAT
> YOU GOTTA TAKE THE JOB
> Cause You Gotta eat
> you gotta JOIN THE ARMY
> cause you gotta EAT
>
> I mean food is at the CENTER of everything
>
> Daddy was a mess sergeant once
> and for him having enough to eat and being on time for
> meals
> was a matter of Ree-spect

You see daddy and his family had been hungry between
wars
but mother and us and them
we had not

You know there never was a war
that We was not in
fighting for Them.[10]

From here she returns to her grandfather and his regiment, fighting
in the Spanish-American War, drawing her listeners back into their
hunger for the completion of her stories.

She draws on African-American ways of speaking and telling the
things that are important and on the narrative forms of Southern
black storytelling to link an individual incident to its historical conditions, to give it a shared meaning for the temporary community of
witnesses to the events she narrates. Brief form is particularly important here,[11] with its emphasis on the teller being at one with the
narrative and the listener, as in the auction and rape scenes in *Sally's
Rape,* and specifying,[12] the serialization of references, is what helps
audiences to piece the stories together.

The black English and Southern colloquialisms she employs vividly make present the aunts and cousins and grandparents who
peopled McCauley's childhood in the South. There are flashes of
impersonation—the aunts who tried to make her "say the right
thing," to copy "their soprano Southern Belle voices" because they
believed that magical protection from all harm was offered by talking
in certain ways. They were "good people who believed in God and
the government / in talking nice and being polite," she says, with
heavy irony. She gives a ghostly presence to her parents, too—to her
mother, who spoke *in italics* in indignant response to her outrageous
daughter, and to her father, the tough sergeant with his military bark,
who spoke In Capitals.

Always, too, there's McCauley's own trenchant sass, at times
roughened with rage:

My people didn't jump off the slave ships
so now I have to bear witness.

Well Thomas Jefferson slept with Sally
my great great grandmother

She was a slave on his estate
Monticello
And she had his chillun

Evrybody says like that was somethin special

As if she had a choice

Thomas wouldn't marry her
when he'd mourned Martha's death

His liberty was hegemonic[13]

As much as this is black storytelling it is also an avant-garde /
performance art kind of storytelling. Taking autobiographical material as its starting point, as does much activist art, the narrative is
made up of interwoven fragments, personal anecdotes, incidents, and
aspects of African-American history, organized by montage and col-
lage structures; there are multiple story lines and multiple points of
view, and several historical time zones often overlap in the same
space.[14] *Sally's Rape,* for example, switches backward and forward
between the present day and the first third of the nineteenth century,
counterposing McCauley's ironic metacommentaries about the social
conditions of the 1990s against the details of life on the plantation,
setting the views of George Bush beside those of Thomas Jefferson
and Andrew Jackson, countering the contemporary rhetoric and
methods of rape crisis centers with Sally's curt "ain't no rape crisis
centers on the plantation."

McCauley's stories are dramatically presented, disjunctively col-
laged and, in the case of *Indian Blood* and *My Father & The Wars,*
embedded in an intermedia environment composed of slide projections and video images, with music from the jazz/blues Sedition Ensemble. The "story" gets passed around, shared, among these different media, with the different story lines initiated, carried, or held for
the moment by her body and/or voice, the music, video clips, pro-

jected images, a singer, or another performer, or by various combinations of them.

The other media and other performers at times stand in for McCauley, enabling doubled versions of the same narrative fragment or a splitting of the narrating subject. In *Indian Blood,* for example, the story of her father's encounter with a racist gas station owner is narrated on the monitor, while she reenacts the terror of being the eight-year-old witnessing this event from the backseat of his car. At first denial, wishing to not be seeing this happening; then confusion at seeing her daddy taking his fists to a white man, embarrassment. Hiding her eyes, refusing to look until the car is driven away, then bursting with pride when her father recounts his victory over the bigot.

In *Indian Blood* the narrative is carried at times by slide projections that cover the walls—photographs of her grandfather, her father, the Black Panthers and the Chicago Seven, antiwar and antiracism protests, the Declaration of Independence, the Bill of Rights, and diagrams of the slave ships with their cargoes of kidnapped Africans. These projections envelop the performance space, and they spill over onto the audience, writing black history larger than life. Most of the images are accompanied by instrumental and sung solos and at times are supplemented by McCauley's identification of who is in the photos and why their names are known.

There is, however, no high-tech environment enveloping the audience in *Sally's Rape.* Instead, there are efforts to actively involve audience members in dialogue with the performers at moments when particular hand signals are made by them. Audience members have the option to express agreement or disagreement and to offer commentary on the issue under consideration. At times this results in a vocal involvement similar to that of a black church congregation responding to a sermon.

The stories that provide the text for any production are reworked in successive versions of the work. Sections of the text may stay substantially the same, or relatively so, given the improvisatory nature of McCauley's performance style, while aspects of the performance may change considerably as McCauley experiments with the sequencing and framing and juxtaposition of individual fragments and explores the relative impacts of the various strategies of address on audience response. The early versions of *Sally's Rape,* for example, included much about slavery—narratives of capture and the Middle Passage, statistics, and quotes from the *Congressional Record* and the Monticello logbook—that have been dropped from later versions.

The stories of Sally and Grandfather Key are central to McCauley's critique of American history as an unacknowledged history of black subjection to white racism. The story of the all-black 24th Infantry of the 10th Cavalry who were at the top of San Juan Hill well before the all-white Rough Riders, and who planted Old Glory in victory to mark the taking of Puerto Rico for America, was unacknowledged in official American history until very recently. McCauley's narration shows that the battle for San Juan Hill was not the act of heroism which it has long been claimed to be—that, rather, it was the act of mercenaries, black soldiers paid to fight a vanity war financed by Randolph Hearst in a campaign to boost Roosevelt's chances of winning the upcoming election. By resurrecting the "true" story McCauley writes her grandfather's regiment back into the public record.

By contesting history through her stories, through what she has called "content as aesthetic,"[15] McCauley offers an aesthetic practice that constructs an adversarial critique and which demonstrates that the taken-for-granted explanations of how race relations came to be the way they are in America, can no longer be taken at face value. She seeks in this way to destabilize and alter the meanings of the representations on which American history has been built. Her strategic choices, however, are subject to the particular limits of the cultural situation in which she works; activist performance has largely white, middle-class audiences with no particular investment in facing up to their own racism. If her stories are to intervene in the taken-for-granted assumptions of these audience members, she must assist them to make the connections between the particular, personal body that she stages in her work and the collective black body that she presents, represents, speaks through her stories.

Her stories offer a body always already inscribed as Other within dominant American discourses of power—the black body, which has been treated by white masters as a blank text to be used according to the needs of their dominant order.[16] Accordingly, she presents particular constructions of the African-American body that remain present in social memory today—the slave body and the soldier body, black bodies that were similarly exploited to the point of death—used to service white America's economic and imperialist objectives.

McCauley's stories reclaim the particular identities, subjectivities, and motivations of her ancestors, using them to open up a space for her contestation of racism. In her commentary she reminds her audience that long past events continue to shape the bodies and memories and attitudes that she brings into the performance and that these events have contributed not only to the constitution of her own subjectivity but also to theirs. These influences need to be acknowledged, she reminds them, if they are to understand their own histories more fully.

She places her own body on the stage as a register of history, a means by which Others can share the connections that she has made between skin color and slavery, servitude and survival, resistance and redemption. Her words, her actions, testify to things experienced by Sally and her father and grandfather, survivors all; they attest also to those things she has experienced herself, as a woman who seeks to intervene in the social order. McCauley's own body thus becomes the means by which she makes connections between the stereotypes and the particular, the means by which she brings the past into the present, where it can be interrogated and revisioned.

By interweaving the stories of her father, grandfather, and great-great-grandmother with her own, McCauley offers a persuasively Other view of material reality, one that is shaped by the undeniable experience of oppression, one that persuasively supports the ethical stand that is at the center of her intervention into racism. By performing her own body, McCauley seeks to implicate, to socially engage, her other Others in her dialogue with history. To those Others, those in dominant social groups and those who taken-for-granted assumptions position blacks as subordinate, she offers an invitation to consider their involvement in the history, the construction, the subjection, of the African-American bodies of which she speaks.

McCauley seeks, by means of her socially engaged narratives, to persuade her audiences to contend with her understanding, her body on the block. She stages her body in order to contest the official narratives of slavery, of racism, in order to intervene in the present by means of bodies of the past. At the same time she inverts the power relations of the prevailing social order, placing herself, a black female social subject, in the position of power, a position whereby she controls the flow of information, where she decides what is important, which history should be told. And always she tells it Otherwise.

NOTES

1. Robbie McCauley, *Sally's Rape: A Work in Process,* Avery Fisher Fall, Lincoln Center, July 1989; Aaron Davis Hall, New York, May 1991; and *Sally's Rape: The Whole Story,* The Kitchen, New York City, November 1991.

2. Ibid.

3. There is another Sally associated with Thomas Jefferson—the slave Sally Hemings, who bore him several children. Two of these children, sons Madison and Eston, were freed after his death when they turned twenty-one. The story of Jefferson's long liaison with Sally Hemings has been the subject of great interest since it was first made public in 1801, causing considerable scandal. McCauley assumes that at least some of her audience will be familiar with the story of Sally Hemings, and she plays on the similarities between the lives of these two Sallies and those of other women slaves. ("All of 'em," she says, "who bin with the Massa, were Sallies.")

The story of Jefferson and Sally Hemings can be found in Fawn Brodie, *Thomas Jefferson: An Intimate History* (New York: W. W. Norton, 1974); Pearl M. Graham, "Thomas Jefferson and Sally Hemings," *Journal of Negro History* 49, no. 2 (April 1961): 89–103; Jack McLaughlin, *Jefferson and Monticello: The Biography of a Builder* (New York: Henry Holt, 1988); the scandal surrounding the first public release of the story of their liaison is the subject of Virginius Dabney *The Jefferson Scandals: A Rebuttal* (New York: Dodd, Mead, 1981).

4. The realities of slave women's lives are detailed in Deborah Gray White, *Ar'n't I a Woman: Female Slaves in the Plantation South* (New York: W. W. Norton, 1985).

5. Robbie McCauley, "Content as Aesthetic," Plenary Address, Performance Studies International Conference, New York University, 4 October 1990.

6. *Indian Blood* video recording, The Painted Bride, Philadelphia, December 1988. Text from one work often turns up in another. This fragment from *Indian Blood* is also included in *My Father & The Wars* and in the duologue *Persimmon Peel,* performed with Laurie Carlos at the Anchorage, Brooklyn, September 1990.

7. McCauley, "Content as Aesthetic."

8. These and other developments through the late 1960s to early 1980s are documented in Stephen Vincent and Ellen Zweig, eds., *The Poetry Reading: A Contemporary Compendium on Language and Performance* (San Francisco: Momo's Press, 1981).

9. A commentator on National Public Radio during December 1990 surveyed the war-free Christmases in this century and found that U.S. forces had

been involved in war on warlike operations in forty-five of the past ninety Christmases, usually on foreign soil.

10. *Indian Blood.*

11. Susan Willis, *Specifying: Black Women Writing the American Experience* (Madison: University of Wisconsin Press, 1987), 14.

12. Ibid., 15–16.

13. *Sally's Rape: A Work in Process,* Avery Fisher Hall, Lincoln Center, July 1989.

14. See Ann-Sargent Wooster, "Why Don't They Tell Stories Like They Used To?" *Art Journal,* Fall 1985, 204–12.

15. "Content as Aesthetic."

16. Spivak says that the body as the blank text of racism is surrounded by an interpretable text: McCauley's performances seem to offer a portion of that interpretable text. Gayatri Chakravorty Spivak, *The Post-colonial Critic: Interviews, Strategies, Dialogues* (New York and London: Routledge, 1990), 1–2.

Chapter 15

Staging Hurston's Life and Work

Lynda M. Hill

Zora Neale Hurston, who saw the basis for a style of black theater derived from the drama of everyday life in African-American culture, wrote in her 1934 essay "Characteristics of Negro Expression" that black people are expert mimics who are constantly creating new forms of expression by revising social rituals rooted in folk culture.[1] Her ethnographic field research had led her to conclude that, because mimicry and parody permeate all black folk genres, the best way for the world at large to become familiar, if not intimate, with forms of expression indigenous to black culture would be through staged productions, rather than through written texts.

I argue in this essay that current theater productions based on Hurston's life and work have come about because black theater artists are beginning to realize the far-reaching aesthetic implications of Hurston's ideas and are beginning to take her seriously because she exemplifies a style of theater conceived as a bridge between black folk life, black community theater, and mainstream commercial theater produced and attended predominantly by whites.[2] She also represents a pivotal juncture between black female playwrights of the 1930s and 1940s whose work has remained obscure until recently, and current efforts to renegotiate the influence black women artists have had in shaping a black theater movement. Moreover, as I will argue, there is a need to position Hurston as a theater practitioner and performance theorist within the twentieth-century black theater tradition, particularly in light of crucial historical moments in its development, such as the 1930s, when she did most of her theater work; the 1960s and 1970s, when Black Revolutionary Theater seemingly superseded the previous generation's work; and the present, when, as I argue, there is a shift toward restoring the past through a revised aesthetic.

Before examining the productions it is useful to place Hurston alongside her contemporaries to see how her work, then, made her especially suited to the current status she has posthumously achieved as a feminist iconoclast. "A female creator needs to be slotted into the context of male traditions," according to Christine Battersby, "but to understand what the artist is doing, and the merits or demerits of her work, she will also have to be located in a separate female pattern that runs through the first in a kind of contrapuntal way."[3] Battersby's argument rests on the assumption that the female artist, particularly when she is a genius, has to be evaluated first by locating traditional boundaries then by examining the ways her work defines a distinctive pattern in relation to those traditional boundaries. For Hurston the male context is comprised of the American popular and folk theater traditions, broadly defined, and the male-dominated black theater tradition.[4]

Because the terms used to qualify artistic genius have historically been gender biased, as Battersby argues, only one sense of the term *genius* can be applied to a feminist aesthetic. If "the genius is the person whose work (a) marks the boundaries between the old ways and the new within the tradition, and (b) has lasting value and significance," Hurston emerges as a female genius, which is to say, a woman who occupies an intersection between "the matrilineal and patrilineal patterns that make up culture."[5] To define her as a genius within that matrix it is necessary to identify her matrilineal and patrilineal patterns. Clearly, the aspect of her work linking her with a matrilineal inheritance is her role as a tradition bearer within the folk context but also, more broadly, her career as a proponent of traditionality in the sense that a folklorist defines it when presenting folk arts to the public.[6]

On the other hand, Hurston fits into a patrilineal pattern as an interpreter of culture, as a person with a specialized point of view concerning cultural production and as a collaborator in popular, mainstream theater, since these are skills she developed through her formal education and mentorships, not only with the anthropologist Franz Boas, as is well known, but also in her apprenticeships in the theater. As Hurston wrote of her involvement with *Fast and Furious* (1931): "I have learned a lot about the mechanics of the stage, which will do me good in playwrighting. I have received a good deal of publicity which is helpful *and* I did earn a little money."[7] Showing that she was conscious of her role as an intermediary between the black folk life she understood and valued and the popular theater world's attempts to usurp black art forms, she asserted: "John Golden sent for me to be Negro adviser on a play he is to produce soon. It was written by white people and they want to be sure of the atmosphere. I shall insist on program credit along with salary."[8] Her awareness, coupled with her expertise, was augmented by her strong motivation to go beyond the established parameters and to have an impact on aesthetic standards; she wanted to surpass the efforts of her male peers.

In line with Battersby's guidelines for defining a feminist aesthetic, Hurston's theatrical work as both a practitioner and a theorist can be seen as exemplary, even though she is usually excluded from discussions about blacks in theater. Among Hurston's peers only three black women playwrights (Angelina Grimke, May Miller, and Eulalie Spence) can be considered feminist, according to Elizabeth Brown-Guillory, who describes their feminist aesthetics in terms of their female characters' asserting their rights to individuality.[9] Because black women playwrights of Hurston's period generally explored subjects with social and political themes focused on racially inspired conflicts—although some works centered on religious subjects, folk life, and women's concerns—their feminism is tempered by the mores of their generation. For the most part characters in plays by black women contemporaries of Hurston fit into traditional roles, which they sometimes challenged. The actress's role during Hurston's period meant exploring female identity within a traditional framework, while the current productions based on Hurston's life and work explore—in addition to folk life—nontraditional roles for women, not the least of which is the role of the artist, particularly the female writer.

Hurston's aspirations as both a writer and a theater artist epitomize the determination she and her black female peers manifested in pursuing careers in the arts; it would have been improbable for them to have created characters and situations representing their own lives as artists, since there was already a substantial risk involved in their claiming a "place on the stage," to echo Brown-Guillory. Nevertheless, Hurston, rather than her counterparts, now is perceived as a colorful, heroic, even legendary figure of the period, who has inspired current developments in black theater, as indicated by the recent productions to be discussed in this essay.

Hurston's theatrical career, amazingly, has received very little attention, even given the recently intensified critical interest in her work as a fiction writer and folklorist. Two of her plays, *Color Struck* (1925) and *The First One* (1927), appear in *Black Female Playwrights: An Anthology of Plays before 1950*, edited by Kathy Perkins, with a profile of Hurston's work in the field. More notable than her plays are the musical revues and concerts she wrote, produced, and sometimes performed in, because these are the productions that showcased the forms of folk expression she sought to introduce to the larger white public. Although discussions of Hurston's contributions to American musical theater have been scarce, since her work in the theater was considered minor, the style of theater she pursued is significant, particularly in light of efforts throughout the twentieth century to produce an alternative to the strong influence of popular, variety-style entertainment on black performance traditions.

When Hurston's work is viewed in relation to her male peers' she stands in a unique position, as a black woman aspiring to a place on the main stage, where the stakes were commercial as well as aesthetic. In a vivid discussion of black theater history during the 1930s, in particular the Federal Theater era, E. Quita Craig details the major shift toward greater accessibility to mainstream stages for black artists and exposure to white audiences as well as expanded potential for collaborations with white directors and producers. The period, nevertheless, was still dominated by racial segregation and widespread resistance to blacks having a distinctive aesthetic.

"The conditioning of the white American public did not incline towards either understanding or appreciating black American culture," in Craig's view.[10] While, on the one hand, black community theaters largely inspired and supported by W. E. B. Du Bois, where the works of black female playwrights usually appeared, in part filled the need for an independent black theater (if partially supported by white benevolence), on the other, the mainstream theaters were the arena for commercial success and professional recognition—two objectives that strongly motivated Hurston. Along with certain of her black male cohorts, such as Hall Johnson and J. Rosamond Johnson,

Ann Duquesnay as Blues Speak Woman and Danitra Vance as Delia perform an expressionistic interpretation of Zora Neale Hurston's story "Sweat," in the Public Theatre Production of *Spunk*. Photo © 1992 by Martha Swope.

with whom she collaborated, Hurston sought to make inroads in the popular theater not only because it had the potential to be lucrative but because, in her view, it was there where the damage to the integrity of black art forms was being done.

"The most immediate problem of racist expectancy, inherited by the black playwrights of the thirties," according to Craig, "was the derogatory black stereotypes which had been established by the white stage of the nineteenth and early twentieth centuries."[11] Craig argues that not only the white public but also the producers and critics formed a kind of circle, constraining black theater artists of the 1930s, for whom distorted images of black culture represented an affront and an obstacle to free expression. Craig describes the relationship of black theater artists to the main stage as a "war with the Broadway stereotypes," which entailed unreasonable expectations for adherence to stereotypes and to the dominant aesthetic standards. Further, she makes the point that the work by black playwrights during the 1930s historically has not been given its due because whites at the time often thought of black artists' work as "too black," while, later, when a black perspective gained prominence during the Black Revolutionary Theater movement of the 1960s and 1970s work from the Federal Theatre period was dismissed as "not black enough" for advocates of a new Black Aesthetic.

Amid the interstices defined by these ideological and aesthetic positions, Hurston's statements about mimicry and its significance in characterizing the distinctive features of African-American expression establish her, uniquely, as an artist with a theoretical basis for her practical work. Indeed, her productions, as well as Hall Johnson's *Run, Little Chillun'* (1933), drew from her field research for the songs, sermons, characters, stories, and situations she believed would, if presented with loyalty to their context, counter the parodic and diluted renditions of black life commonly seen on mainstream stages. At the same time she was critical of some of her male counterparts' willingness to participate in what she considered "degenerate and self-seeking" creative enterprises, which meant selling black culture at too great an expense to the integrity of the people, because, as she remarked: "I am on fire about my people."[12]

The recent productions inspired by Hurston show that dramaturgical issues now considered urgent can be traced to Hurston's theoretical and descriptive statements on black performance traditions and their significance for understanding the distinctive features of African-American culture generally and "Characteristics of Negro Expression," particularly. Because black artists and critics then and now have spent considerable effort trying to differentiate between "real" and "authentic" forms of black expression, on the one hand, and misrepresentations often seen as derogatory, on the other, it is important that in Hurston's theories neither the forms of expression she describes nor her own words should be taken literally. When she writes that "the Negro's universal mimicry is not so much a thing in itself as evidence of something that permeates his entire self," she calls into question the way that mimicry can be misread as copying when in black culture it is a dynamic way of playing back "reality" in a different register.[13] "Original" drama is that which shows the most inventiveness in molding everyday life behavior into a panoply of vignettes.

Each of the productions I discuss demonstrates specific aesthetic choices, suggesting resolutions or compromises directly arising from the dramaturgical and ideological issues influencing Hurston's theatrical career. *Mule Bone, a Comedy of Negro Life,* coauthored by Hurston and Langston Hughes, before it was produced on Broadway in 1991, inspired a debate at Lincoln Center Theater over whether the play would be too offensive to audiences because of its alleged stereotypes. *Zora Neale Hurston,* written by Laurence Holder, with Hurston being played by Elizabeth Van Dyke, through an autobiographical narrative explores some of the most controversial questions surrounding Hurston's life and poses questions that cut to the very core of what it means to expose oneself, as a black woman, to the public for scrutiny, when isolation may be the reward. *Zora Is My Name,* a video production by Ruby Dee, also adapted in part from Hurston's autobiography, *Dust Tracks on a Road,* and in part from her folklore collection, *Mules and Men,* focuses on Hurston's use of mythic time and sense of character, therefore presenting some striking possibilities for bringing the folk culture to a broader audience in ways that were not feasible during Hurston's lifetime. And *Spunk,* adapted by George Wolfe, concretizes an alternative to realistic staging, forcing a response to accusations about whether folk culture in general and Hurston's work in particular are stereotypical.[14]

"Much of Hurston's work (and life) used conventions of self-parody," according to the late George Houston Bass, former artistic director of Rites and Reason Theater in Providence, Rhode Island, where *Mule Bone* received a workshop and a revision following the 1988 reading of the play and a consequential debate over whether to produce it at Lincoln Center Theater.[15] In an attempt to come to terms with Hurston's theory of mimicry Bass speculated about her conception of its practice in black culture and the consequent implications for the stage. "Hurston's use of self-parody is very complex in that she takes the black comic masks of popular culture and enlarges them through exaggeration," said Bass. The workshop at Rites and Reason was conducted in an attempt to resolve performance-related difficulties discussed at the Lincoln Center reading in 1988. At Rites and Reason the play development process created by Bass emphasizes play writing and directing based on historical and sociological research.

Not unlike Hurston's method of staging productions using material she collected while doing folklore research, the research-to-performance concept at Rites and Reason stems from Bass's awareness that black theater and other ethnic theaters can increase their viability when research on cultural history is integrated into the artistic process. Intrigued by the means through which cultural traditions, particularly performance traditions, are passed on, Bass, as a director, passed on to performers his understanding of traditional forms of expression as they are practiced in their social context. More important, he focused on how the forms of folk expression take on different meanings when staged. Staging Hurston's work places one in the complex situation of reenacting parodic social rituals, such as the "lying sessions" on Joe Clarke's porch vividly recreated in *Mule Bone*. In trying not to create a performance in which literal and naturalistic interpretations of the text lead to realistic staging conventions, Bass sought to avoid turning a parodic play into a parody of itself.

Mule Bone was considered by Bass and Arnold Rampersad, Hughes's biographer, to consist of Hurston's content in its use of stories, characters, and the setting of her folklore and of Hughes's dramatic structure; both authors were relatively new to the craft of play writing when they collaborated on *Mule Bone* in 1931. In part because of an irrational disagreement over who had a rightful claim to the play, when discussions about producing it arose, Hurston and Hughes became irreconcilably embroiled in a clash that caused the play never to be produced in their lifetimes; nor was it ever quite finished, according to Bass. Thus, in an attempt to compensate for there being no production history Bass revised the script based on the workshop and staged reading at Rites and Reason. When the script was turned over to the Lincoln Center producer Greg Mosher, analyzed by dramaturg Anne Cattaneo, and entrusted to director Michael Schultz, the decision was to restore the original text, to add a musical score composed by blues musician Taj Mahal and based on the blues poetry of Hughes, and to stage the play on Broadway at the Ethel Barrymore Theatre.

The Broadway production of *Mule Bone* is a landmark in American theater history because, for the first time, a mainstream theater produced a play by a nonliving major black playwright. In this case two major black writers were involved in an intriguing personal and professional conflict that ended their friendship, all of which has been brought to public attention through the publication of *Mule Bone,* in a volume, edited by Bass and Henry Louis Gates, Jr., including letters documenting the real-life drama. There is no better place to begin establishing Hurston's importance as a challenge to the aesthetic direction of black theater, in particular, and American theater, in general, than with the precedent set by *Mule Bone.* In my view the aesthetic challenges she poses were illuminated rather than resolved in the production.[16]

The main aesthetic issues, as already suggested, center around the contradictions in reproducing literally that which is meant to be parodic. Based on "The Bone of Contention," a folktale Hurston collected, *Mule Bone* has a straightforward plot revolving around a confrontation between two young men that results in one being assaulted. The play's structure, however, is anything but straightforward, constructed as it is out of a cast of thirty-some characters, storytelling sequences, and a long trial scene in the second act. With music and dancing added, the Broadway production was envisioned as a celebration of the play's uniqueness. Although the prevailing concept for the production was to remain close to the script in realistic detail, there was an attempt to historicize the debut of the play, by inviting the public to a series of panels and forums on topics related to the work and lives of the playwrights. These events, ostensibly held to encourage awareness of the cultural history surrounding the play, also worked as a form of audience development.

The aesthetic issues took form in the rehearsal process as well as in the mixed audience reception, including critical responses. Casting and directing the performers, according to Schultz, depended on their "having a natural affinity with the dialect," on their feeling an emotional and psychological connection with the heritage of the characters. In New York City, locating performers with the range to handle the language of early twentieth-century rural Florida and to perform comic roles without using broad portrayals common in popular, variety entertainment, presented a challenge as well. It points to the need for specialized training, following the model of the workshop and rehearsal process practiced at Rites and Reason. Indeed, Bass's ideas about the need to codify styles and movement, gesture, facial expression, and voice intonation in black performance seem to address the training requirements for a production like *Mule Bone,* drawn from the folk culture of a remote historical period. The objective is to develop dramaturgical methods for black theater that can be transferred from a community context to a major commercial venue. Because such a method has yet to be developed, adapting works for the stage from the canon of early black writers can result in a short run, as happened with *Mule Bone.*

The popular, critical, and commercial success or failure of a production has significance for the current Hurston revival because her work and life are a focal point for the convergence of ideology and aesthetics. While seeking financial benefits as well as broad audiences, Hurston was determined not to compromise her aesthetic preferences. She was conscious of the need for growth and willingly worked on projects she considered merely a means to an end.

Of her contribution to the Broadway production *Fast and Furious* and her revue *Jungle Scandals,* which closed shortly after opening, she wrote: "I do not consider either of the revues great work, but they are making the public know me and come to me, and that is important."[17] According to Laurence Holder, author of *Zora Neale Hurston,* she was misunderstood by most people. Holder's affinity with that form of social and intellectual alienation made him feel capable of writing a convincing character. His play examines some of the threats to Hurston's genius and some of the reasons her being misunderstood also meant being mistreated by the art world.[18]

"At age 49, I am on my way home, I'm broke and am explaining and exploring, asking and answering the question—'How did I get that way?'" This is how Van Dyke, the lead actress, describes the

basic situation, the central action that gives the performance its structure.[19] In creating a play that tries to present the tragic aspects of
Hurston's life, Holder has found a medium that enables a female
performer such as Van Dyke to embody the spirit of the neglected
genius, while reviving the powerful human forces that drove Hurston
to create and to leave a legacy.

Originally a one-character script, the play presented at American
Place Theatre in New York in 1989 included a male actor, Tim
Johnson, playing various men with strong influences on Hurston's
life—Herbert Sheen (her first husband), Langston Hughes, Alain
Locke, and Richard Wright. The male characters seem to encircle
Hurston, encapsulating her in a mold, but no one knows exactly why
the shape of the mold is drawn as it is since it never reproduces a
perfect Hurston, at least not to the men who judge and condemn her.

Juxtaposed with her male peers, Hurston, although surrounded
and entrapped, remains unwilling to submit to their pressures. Lack
of submissiveness seems to cause her demise, according to the trajectory established in the play. In her relationships with men, a difficult
arena in which the stakes are high, Hurston encounters problems,
from her earliest years with her father through a short-lived marriage
and her outstanding career. The play outlines her life, allowing the
autobiographical details to determine the dramatic structure. Because
Hurston's fascinating life, including her unbelievable disappearance
from public attention, propels the drama, the production has demonstrated its power to attract audiences, as it has been touring nationally
in its current form since 1988.

Bursting from the mold imposed by the scrutiny of male characters, Van Dyke exudes Hurston's energy, flamboyance, and style in
a radiating performance. Van Dyke's own exuberance comes across
in the glow of her face and eyes, the spring of her dance steps, in the
range of her voice—from low and throaty to loud and forceful, to
sweet and eloquent. With a red scarf, signifying the brilliance of an
era and a woman who thrived in the limelight, Van Dyke mimes
clothing accessories such as belts, boas, and bandannas, illustrating
Hurston's elegant style and versatility.

Much of the lore about Hurston emphasizes the irrepressible
quality of her character, her capacity to mesmerize, to command the
center of attention, and to confound. Her life has inspired intriguing
dramas also because of her entanglements with socially prominent

people. "When sources said she was bold, brass, or brazen, I incorporated that because it is a clue to her character," said Van Dyke. Hurston's animated storytelling at fashionable parties and her ability to command an audience present challenges for Van Dyke, which she effectively meets by elaborating factual details about Hurston, using her autobiography and Robert Hemenway's biography, embellishing the facts with a subjunctive mood, a sense of what might have been, how Hurston might have looked based on her photos, how she might have walked, posed, gestured.

When Van Dyke tells a tale from Hurston's folklore collection, "Why Women Always Take Advantage of Men," for example, placed within the context of an awards reception at which Hurston decides to entertain everyone by telling a story, the audience watching the play becomes a collective character in the drama and eventually becomes the collective witness of her life's tragedy. Because of the blurred boundaries between past and present, changes occur from one performance to the next. Although the script remains the same, "in some places people had no idea who Zora was and some adjustments were made." said Van Dyke. At a performance at the Billie Holiday Theater in Brooklyn, New York, Van Dyke coaxed her audience by breaking further through the fourth wall than already occurs in the production; she directly addressed people in the audience when reenacting certain scenes such as Hurston's trip to Harlem as an anthropology student of Franz Boas to measure head sizes. Van Dyke pointed and called out to specific people: "Hey, you, there, how would you like to be part of an experiment?" In contrast, at a performance presented by the Paul Robeson Performing Arts Company in Syracuse, New York, Van Dyke was able to build toward the high moments in part through the energy supplied by an audience that laughed at all the jokes and remained hypnotically still during sad moments. The play's flexibility in translating its meaning from one context to another is an example of the kind of bridge building Hurston envisioned for her own theatrical work.

Van Dyke's attunement with audiences has meant not only ensuring a long life for the production but also broadening public awareness of Hurston. The performance generates energy, says Van Dyke, because it is insightful. The relationship between the performer and the audience creates a space for Hurston and for a reevaluation of her life and work, on the one hand, and the dialogue contemporary black artists are having with Hurston's personal history, on the other. The current productions connect Hurston to an ongoing black theater tradition, while making it possible to reassess her value as a woman artist and to bring that assessment to the public for a final gloss.

There is a line of continuity from an individual's culture and gender to her work; defining what that work should be, maintaining control of the work, and having it reach the desired audience are a small part of what Hurston, as an African-American woman, had to manage as she pursued her theatrical career. A difficult childhood, harsh economic circumstances, and complicated personal relationships caused tensions along her journey toward self-fulfillment and recognition. While Holder's play confronts "the lies of enemies and the envious hostility of friends," which clouded Hurston's brilliance during her lifetime, Dee's production *Zora Is My Name,* also biographical, presents another perspective.[20] Here Hurston's genius is explored through a kind of imagery and narrative structure that tests the boundaries of realism, therefore proposing an alternative to the literal interpretations of Hurston's life and work.

Whereas the Hurston of Holder's play reflects upon events that threatened Hurston's independence, Dee's Hurston takes charge of the image being constructed onstage. Whereas Holder's Hurston confronts the spectator—implying that her image was a product of others' perceptions of her and suggesting that the audience as witness is somehow complicit in isolating her from the center of attention she needed to thrive, if not survive—Dee's Hurston never alludes to any tragedy related to her career but only to the devastating effect her mother's death had on her sense of security.

The mother, and other characters depicting women as influences in Hurston's early life and her refiguring of their images in her folklore and fiction, constitutes a central motif in Dee's production "I have memories within me that came out of the material that went to make me" is Dee's opening line. Remembering, collecting, and documenting are actions performed by Hurston as narrator, played by Dee. The Hurston who acts, who listens as a child to storytellers, who experiences the trauma of her mother's death, who leaves home, is a separate character, the Hurston of history, played by Lynn

Whitfield, related through memory to the writer she becomes (Dee). This device, of having two women play Hurston, allows actions in the present to refer mimetically to the past and future, as both characters simultaneously appear in some instances. Hurston, as an adult ethnographer returning to her hometown to collect folklore, enters the world she inhabited as a child. The young Hurston plays games and enacts the other scenes as they are narrated by her Double—Hurston as an adult. At two crucial moments the two Zoras embrace and thereby suggest that narrative chronology is an illusion—past, present, and future coexisting—made concrete through the simultaneous presence of a woman who reminisces and her Double, a woman who experiences, and both, of course, are the selfsame person, each the Double of the other. Conflating the past and the future by having the young and old Hurston appear together in the present concretely represents the ethnographic present used by the narrator; it also demonstrates that the retelling of Hurston's life story, particularly through a dramatic performance, signifies her relationship to herself and to others.

There is realism in the adaptation's fidelity to Hurston's autobiography and to her folklore collection *Mules and Men*. The Eatonville of Hurston's youth and of her fiction and folklore comes to life from tableaux, as if to illustrate Hurston's concept of the way African-Americans interpret the English language in pictorial terms, what she calls hieroglyphics. By this she means that objects, thoughts, and actions are represented in language through visual metaphors. When Dee's Hurston narrates, the scenes pictured in her words are enacted through actors' miming the characters. The spectator sees Hurston controlling her role, her relationship to her past, her reality as represented in her written works.

Hurston's motivation to write and the act of writing are the substance of Dee's adaptation. In contrast with Holder's play, which also examines Hurston's literary career, *Zora Is My Name* celebrates the worldview rendered in her folklore texts and her commitment to her community. It attempts to explain why Hurston worked "so every one would know they had a history and a culture to be proud of"—an objective that has taken on new meaning with the renewed interest in her work. It is an interpretation on Dee's part, in keeping with her role as an actress, that she sees in part as being a tradition bearer and educator, particularly for young black Americans. Whether attributing this objective to Hurston as an overriding motivation can be borne out through all of her actions remains a subject of conjecture.

bell hooks has suggested that, although Hurston was interested in preserving black folk culture, "she never directly states for whom she wished to preserve the culture, whether for black folks, that we may be ever mindful of the rich imaginative folkways that are our tradition and legacy, or for white folks, that they may laugh at the quaint dialect and amusing stories as they voyeuristically peep into the private inner world of poor Southern black people."[21]

In my view avoiding direct statements that would allow her motives or her work itself to be strictly classified was exactly Hurston's point: she opposed the paradigms that rigidly constrain our interpretations of culture to either/or categories, even as she paid respect to the value of the forms she worked against, by appearing to work within the formal conventions of novel writing, ethnography, and drama. Although she realized the patronage that went along with cultivating a white audience, she did not pursue the attention because she condoned the derision that often came with it. Her work, rather, grew from a long view of history, what can be seen as Hurston's vision—indeed, her genius—which has inspired the current movement toward restoring her work and her ideas.

Of the productions discussed in this essay the one that perhaps best captures the complexity of Hurston's vision is *Spunk*, adapted by George Wolfe. His adaptation of Hurston's stories "Sweat," "Story in Harlem Slang," and "The Gilded Six Bits" combines several nonrealistic staging techniques with storytelling, masking, and the blues.[22] Under Wolfe's Obie Award-winning direction the performance strikes a balance between loyalty to Hurston's text and innovative blends of movement, gestures, facial expressions, music, and visual imagery—including tableaux with characters frozen in expressionistic postures.

Wolfe sees himself as translating some principles of Japanese Nōh drama into the context of southern black culture, as when masked figures serving as a chorus, float in and out of scenes.[23] The visual language of the production "moves from a heightened reality into some ritual, abstract world."[24] The language of the stories, part prose narrative and part dialogue, deconstructs the action as characters speak the narrative, sometimes referring to themselves in the third person, sometimes sharing the same narrative with one or more characters in a polyvocal chain linking one moment to the next. While Wolfe rigorously adheres to Hurston's text, short riffs of blues music and lyrics bridge scenes and set the mood.

Hurston's stories provide rich material for Wolfe's Brechtian technique of focusing on the core meanings produced by words, on their sense and the external displays that illustrate a character's feelings. Hurston captures specific emotional landscapes in poetical language, which "excludes the psychological, the subconscious, the metaphysical unless they can be conveyed in concrete terms."[25] Wolfe's decision to stage the stories is ambitious, considering that his understanding was that they were not meant to be performed.

Also innovative is the use of the title *Spunk,* which is the title of a short story by Hurston not included in Wolfe's production. True to her high regard for irony, Hurston named the story after its main character, although Spunk's arrogance becomes the first step toward unraveling a dark tale of betrayal and death. Spunk, in a sense, is unmasked and undone by his name. What is more, Hurston in 1931 had plans for a play of the same title.

"I shall do something good with 'Spunk,'" she wrote to her patron Charlotte Osgood Mason. "I am working on that also [in addition to *Fast and Furious* and *Jungle Scandals,* the revues mentioned previously] and it looks like a very good play can be made from it. Anyway, I like the idea of going from the light and trivial to something better, rather than coming down from a 'Spunk' to 'Fast and Furious.' The public will see growth rather than decline, you see."[26] As the public has seen, perhaps much later than Hurston had hoped, the theater practice she envisioned has a greater resonance now than the French composer George Antheil might have predicted when he told Hurston in 1931 that she "would be the most stolen-from Negro in the world for the next ten years at least": "He said that this sort of thievery is unavoidable. Unpleasant of course but at the bottom a tribute to one's originality."[27]

As an afterword to her paraphrase of Antheil's comment about her position within the performance traditions I have discussed, Hurston's remarks on imitation, mimicry, and parody in black culture reinforce the continuing power of her ideas as dramatic theory: "If you look at a man and mistrust your eyes, do something and see if he will imitate you right away," she wrote, "If he does, that's My People."[28] Thus, as she apparently exalts mimicry, she draws attention to the peculiar contradiction involved in classifying the "essential" quality of a culture and its forms of expression.[29] In her refusal to be categorized she is a progenitor, indeed an archetype, for theater artists who recognize that her life and work has empowered a new generation to be, above all, unrelenting.

NOTES

1. See Zora Neale Hurston, "Characteristics of Negro Expression," in *The Sanctified Church* (Berkeley: Turtle Island Press, 1981), 41–78. All further citations from the essay will be from this edition. Her views on mimicry also appear in "My People! My People!" *Dust Tracks on a Road*, ed. Robert Hemenway (Urbana: University of Illinois Press, 1984), 215–37; and in the appendix of the same edition, 291–306.

2. My sense of the term *aesthetic* as it is being used in this discussion applies to questions concerning the choices artists make in creating their work. I am discussing the aesthetics of black theater within the context of a historical debate over "authenticity," initiated by artists and critics of the early twentieth century, particularly of the 1920s and 1930s. The other aspect of a historical perspective on aesthetics in African-American culture relevant to my argument raises questions about the relationship between political ideology and art. I explore these topics in further detail in "The Authenticity Debate," "Performance Theory, Gender, and Black Culture: The Iconography of Zora Neale Hurston" (Ph.D. diss., New York University, 1993). Some sources in which the issues are raised include: Harold Cruse, *The Crisis of the Negro Intellectual* (New York: William Morrow, 1967); David C. Driskell, "The Evolution of a Black Aesthetic, 1920–1950," *Two Centuries of Black American Art* (New York: Los Angeles County Museum of Art/Alfred A. Knopf, 1976), 59–79; Nathan Irvin Huggins, *Harlem Renaissance* (New York: Oxford University Press, 1971); Larry Neal, "The Black Arts Movement," *Drama Review* 12, no. 4 (Summer 1968): 29–39; Steven C. Tracy, "Folklore and the Harlem Renaissance," *Langston Hughes and the Blues* (Urbana: University of Illinois Press, 1988), 11–58; Michele Wallace, "Who Owns Zora Neale Hurston? Critics Carve up the Legend," *Invisibility Blues* (London: Verso, 1990), 172–86.

3. Christine Battersby, *Gender and Genius: Towards a Feminist Aesthetics* (Bloomington: Indiana University Press, 1989), 152.

4. American popular and folk theater traditions as referred to here are connected with white male playwrights working in the folk drama genre as well as in the musical, including Marc Connelly, Paul Green, Dubose Heyward, Eugene O'Neill, and Ridgely Torrence. The dominant black theater trend will be discussed at greater length.

5. Battersby, *Gender and Genius*, 157.

6. When folk arts are presented for exhibition or folk performances are staged, the folklorist will try to account for the work being outside of the social

context where it would ordinarily be displayed or practiced. This does not necessarily entail interpretation or mediation—although both are hard to avoid— but it does require sensitivity to the possibility that the work might be misinterpreted if not given a coherent frame.

7. Hurston to Charlotte Osgood Mason, 25 September 1931, Alain Locke Papers (ALP), Manuscript Division (MD), Moorland-Spingarn Research Center (MSRC), Howard University.

8. Hurston to Mason, 15 October 1931.

9. See Elizabeth Brown-Guillory, *Their Place on the Stage: Black Women Playwrights in America* (New York: Greenwood Press, 1988), 19.

10. E. Quita Craig, *Black Drama of the Federal Theatre Era: Beyond the Formal Horizons* (Amherst: University of Massachusetts Press, 1980), 10.

11. Ibid., 11.

12. Hurston to Mason, 15 October 1931.

13. Hurston, "Characteristics of Negro Expression," 49.

14. During the course of researching this project, numerous productions based on Hurston's life and work were brought to my attention. Among them are *Jump at the Sun,* adapted by Glenda Dickerson and produced at the Theater Lobby in Washington, D.C. (1972); *The Sanctified Church,* by Ellen Sebastian and Marilyn Waterman, originally performed in San Francisco at Life on the Water Theatre (1988); *Their Eyes Were Watching God,* adapted by Mari Evans, first performed at Karamu House in Cleveland (1982); *Forever Zora* (1987), by Wanda Schell, Theatre for Emily, Providence, R.I.; *A Tale of Madame Zora,* by Aishah Rahman; and *To Gleam It Around, To Show My Shine,* by Bonnie Lee Moss Rattner. For a discussion of the last two productions and other works on Zora for which Olu Dara has composed musical scores, see Celest Bullock, "Olu Dara and the Zora Neale Hurston Blues," *Black Masks,* Summer 1990, 4–5. In addition to these staged performances, a screenplay of *Their Eyes Were Watching God* by Larry Neal played a significant part in my formulation of the dramaturgical issues in this project at an early stage of my research. See the Larry Neal Papers, Schomburg Center for Research on Black Culture, New York Public Library.

15. George Houston Bass, "Editor/Dramaturg's Notes," *Mulebone* (Providence, R.I.: Brown University, Rites and Reason Theatre, July 1989), unpub. MS.

16. Information regarding *Mule Bone*'s production has been compiled through my discussions with Lincoln Center dramaturg Anne Cattaneo, director Michael Schultz, and George Houston Bass. An unpublished transcript of the discussion among producers and literary and estate executors of Hurston and Hughes and prospective directors, following the initial reading of the play at Lincoln Center Theatre in New York, 28 November 1988, supplied some of the background for the discussion of the dramaturgical, directorial, and political issues. See Langston Hughes and Zora Neale Hurston, *Mule Bone: A Comedy of Negro Life,* ed. George Houston Bass and Henry Louis Gates, Jr. (New York: Harper Collins, 1991).

17. Hurston to Mason, 23 July 1931.

18. Interview with Laurence Holder, 8 August 1991.

19. A series of dialogues I had with Elizabeth Van Dyke are the basis for her comments and quoted statements.

20. Alice Walker, "Anything We Love Can Be Saved: The Resurrection of Zora Neale Hurston and Her Work," in *Zora! Zora Neale Hurston, a Woman and Her Community,* comp. and ed. N. Y. Nathiri (Orlando, Fla.: Orlando Sentenial, Sentenial Communications, 1991), 82. *Zora Is My Name* was a 1990 American Playhouse production, which aired on the Public Broadcasting Service.

21. bell hooks, "Saving Black Folk Culture: Zora Neale Hurston as Anthropologist and Writer," *Yearning: Race, Gender, and Cultural Politics* (Boston: South End Press, 1990), 136.

22. The production was initiated at the Mark Taper Forum in Los Angeles in May 1989, premiered at Crossroads Theater in New Brunswick, N.J., on 1 November 1989, and was produced in 1990 at the Public Theater's New York Shakespeare Festival.

23. See Rosemary Bray, "An Unpredictable Playwright Reverses Himself," *New York Times,* 15 April 1990, 7.

24. Program Notes, *Spunk* (New Brunswick, N.J.: Crossroads Theatre Company, 2 November–10 December 1989).

25. John Willett, *The Theatre of Bertolt Brecht: A Study from Eight Aspects* (Norfolk, Conn.: James Laughlin; New Directions, 1959), 175.

26. Hurston to Mason, 23 July 1931.

27. Hurston to Mason, 15 October 1931.

28. Hurston, *Dust Tracks,* 300.

29. For a discussion of Hurston's nonessentialist self-concept, see Barbara Johnson, "Thresholds of Difference: Structures of Address in Zora Neale Hurston," in *"Race," Writing, and Difference,* ed. Henry Louis Gates, Jr. (Chicago: University of Chicago Press, 1985), 317–28; see also Wallace, "Who Owns Zora Neale Hurston?"

Chapter 16

"Brought to You by Fem-Rage": Stand-up Comedy and the Politics of Gender

Philip Auslander

> Culturally speaking, women have wept a great deal, but once the tears are shed, there will be endless laughter instead. Laughter that breaks out, overflows, a humor no one would expect to find in women— which is nonetheless their greatest strength because it's a humor that sees man much farther away than he has ever been seen.
> —Hélène Cixous, "Castration or Decapitation?"

> It is not polite to laugh and point at the penile member.
> —Cynthia Heimel, *Sex Tips for Girls*

One of the cultural legacies of the 1980s is the resurgence of stand-up comedy as a popular genre, evidenced by the appearance of comedy clubs in virtually every American city, the prevalence of stand-up comedy programs on cable and broadcast television, and the number of stand-up comics who have made the transition to film acting or roles in television situation comedies. An important aspect of the phenomenon is the increased access women now have to the stand-up comedy stage.[1] Phyllis Diller recalls that when she entered the field in 1955, there were no other women comics.[2] Today there are a large number of well-known women comics, including several superstars of the genre (e.g., Lily Tomlin, Whoopi Goldberg, Joan Rivers). Estimates suggest that about 10 percent of professional American stand-up comics are female, as are 25 percent of aspiring comics.[3]

The issues I will discuss here relate to the particular circumstances confronted by female comics in a culture that traditionally has suppressed women's humor and denied to women even the right to be funny. Traditional literary theories of humor and comedy, social prejudices against joke making as an aggressive and "unfeminine" behavior, and the processes by which cultural expression is disseminated in a patriarchal culture all create obstacles for the comic woman and the woman comic. A growing strain of feminist literary theory, on the other hand, suggests that humor and comedy may be valuable as empowering "feminist tools," especially when motivated by the anger women need to express at the social and cultural limitations they confront.[4] My objects here are to situate the woman comic culturally and to offer an analysis of a specific cultural text, Roseanne Barr's 1987 cable television special.

The mass-cultural context of stand-up comedy, which is disseminated today chiefly by broadcast and cable television, raises important issues as well. Chief among these is the traditional theoretical opposition of vanguard culture and mass culture, which sees mass culture as necessarily co-opted and only vanguard culture as possessing critical potential. As rock music critic Dave Marsh asserts, today "all culture is made in an industrial context," and therefore all cultural production is politically compromised, "if participating in the only world any of us has to live in represents a compromise."[5] In analyzing a mass-cultural phenomenon one must be alive to the potential for co-optation and recuperation that resides in mass culture, an issue I discuss here. My working assumption, however, is that mass-cultural status in and of itself does not vitiate a genre's or text's potential to do positive political work.

Women's Comedy in the Patriarchal Public Sphere

As the well-worn clichés about women (especially feminists) having no sense of humor attest, women have been excluded from the comic tradition, except as the objects of male humor.[6] Perhaps literary critic Reginald Blyth's 1959 definition of women as "the unlaughing at which men laugh" can stand as the epitome of this tradition (qtd. in Barreca, *Last Laughs*, 4). Humor in women's writing, for example, has often gone unrecognized as such by male critics or has been dismissed as trivial in comparison with the comic efforts of male writers.[7] Comedy writer Anne Beatts suggests that part of the reason for men's failure to acknowledge women's humor is that "there is a women's culture that men just don't know about. So when they say,

'Hey, that joke's not funny,' it's sometimes because they don't understand the vocabulary" (qtd. in Collier and Beckett, *Spare Ribs,* 24–25).

The issue goes beyond the specificity of cultural vocabularies, however, for humor is inextricably linked to social power and dominance. Unsurprisingly, social scientists have uncovered evidence that people generally laugh along with those they perceive as more powerful than themselves and tend not to make jokes at their expense, at least not in their presence.[8] Even women in positions of power are disinclined to make jokes with men present but will laugh at jokes made by men (Pollio and Edgerly, "Comedians," 225). Pollio and Edgerly summarize the social situation succinctly: "men talk and joke; women smile and laugh." They go on to note that

> women just do not attempt to be humorous in a mixed group setting and the reason seems to be that women are neither expected, nor trained, to joke in this culture. It seems reasonable to propose that attempting a witty remark is often an intrusive, disturbing and aggressive act, and within this culture, probably unacceptable for a female.

"Responsive behaviors" such as laughing and smiling, however, are perfectly socially acceptable for a woman in our culture (225).

Beatts's interpretation of these phenomena is that men are afraid of allowing women the access to power represented by humor (or of acknowledging that women in fact have such access) because a humorous woman threatens the central icon of the mythology that supports male dominance: "they unconsciously are afraid that the ultimate joke will be the size of their sexual apparatus."[9] Once women start making jokes, men fear, nothing will be exempt from female comic derision, no matter how sacred to patriarchy. Further evidence for the idea that a humorous woman is perceived as a threat to male sexual dominance is Mahadev Apte's observation that "in many cultures norms of modesty cause women who laugh freely and openly in public to be viewed as loose, sexually promiscuous, and lacking in self-discipline."[10] (At some point in their careers most female comics have experienced similar responses from the men in their audiences, who either treat them with hostility or assume that a female comic is presenting herself as sexually available.)

Beatts's analysis suggests that humor by women may be an effective weapon against male social dominance and phallocentrism. When assessing the political positioning of a performance genre, however, it is not enough simply to evaluate its content; one must also look at the ideology of performance itself.[11] The relationship between women and stand-up comedy as a performance genre is by no means unproblematic. For one thing there is a plausible argument to be made that stand-up comedy is an intrinsically male-centered form. Comic Marjorie Gross has observed, in the context of a discussion of the comic's authority over the audience, that "holding a microphone is like holding a penis," an analogy endorsed by male comedians (as qtd. in Collier and Beckett, *Spare Ribs,* 99).[12] When discussing the dynamic of their work both male and female comedians stress the importance of control over the audience, of mastery of the performance context, in which the phallic microphone plays a significant role. Stand-up comic Jerry Seinfeld summarizes the essential relationship between audience and comic succinctly: "To laugh is to be dominated" (as qtd. in Borns, *Comic Lives,* 20). David Marc goes so far as to propose that the dynamics of stand-up comedy may suggest "totalitarian imagery" or "may even conjure hallucinations of Mussolini working the crowd from a terrace," though he goes on to dismiss such a perception of stand-up comedy as "a bum rap."[13]

A performance genre that apparently depends on the dominance of the audience by the performer through phallic assertion does not seem a promising candidate as a medium for women's expression. Indeed, Lisa Merrill, in an essay on feminist humor, implies that conventional stand-up comedy is less appropriate as a vehicle for feminist concerns than the decentered, multicharacter performances of Lily Tomlin and Whoopi Goldberg.[14] Just as traditional stand-up comedy seems phallocentric from a formal perspective, historically, it has also assumed a heterosexual male audience and a performance presented for the enjoyment of the male gaze. As Merrill points out, "traditionally, women have been expected to identify with comedy which insults us" ("Feminist Humor," 274); such comedy radically disempowers the female spectator by obliging her to participate in her own objectification and victimization as the butt of the joke, if she is to participate at all.

One powerful recuperation of stand-up comedy as a feminist practice is represented by the work of Kate Clinton, the radical-lesbian-feminist-humorist (who has contracted that designation to "fumorist"), who performs primarily for audiences of women and who began her performing career at women's coffeehouses and feminist writing conferences. As Cheryl Kader has suggested, "Clinton's humor implies a spectator who is neither male nor heterosexual"; by constructing her audience as lesbian she creates "a community of spectators . . . which liberates its occupants from uniformity to general norms, however temporarily."[15] Presumably, this construction of the audience as lesbian may also place the heterosexual male (and perhaps the heterosexual female) spectator in something like the uncomfortable position that the woman spectator has occupied relative to traditional stand-up comedy, though Kader interprets this kind of reversal more as a by-product of Clinton's performance practice than as its main point (see Kader, "Kate Clinton," 52).

This kind of practice is extremely valuable politically in that it "open[s] up a space for a restructured history and a reconceptualized subject" (Kader, "Kate Clinton," 42). That it also, however, "succeeds in producing a *separation* from the dominant culture" may be its weakness as much as its strength. Lauren Berlant describes such separating cultural practices as efforts to create a feminist public sphere, "a theatrical space in which women might see, experience, live, and rebel against their oppression *en masse,* freed from the oppressors' forbidding or disapproving gaze."[16] In Berlant's terms these efforts are limited by their inability to engage mainstream culture and perhaps exemplify what she describes as the "imaginary sphere of public-feminist intimacy, which relies on a patriarchal fantasy of woman's sameness to herself to produce an adversarial politics" ("Female Complaint," 240). Berlant sees greater value for feminism in a strategy of "engagement of the female culture industry with the patriarchal public sphere, the place where significant or momentous exchanges of power *are perceived* to take place" (240).

Significantly, Clinton herself has expressed interest in reaching a broader audience and has emerged from the coffeehouse circuit to play at comedy and music clubs and theaters and on television comedy shows. She acknowledges that this has meant "internalizing" her feminism.[17] Women comics who choose to remain within the conventional form and performance contexts of stand-up comedy are essentially appropriating a cultural form traditionally associated with, and still dominated by, male practitioners. Undoubtedly, they are offering themselves to "the oppressors' forbidding or disapproving gaze" and run all the risks attendant on doing so. But those risks may be worth running if they give women greater access to the cultural arena and permit the female culture industry to engage the male public sphere, as Berlant argues they may.[18]

The analysis of stand-up comedy upon which the previous comments are based is in any case incomplete, for it considers only the image of the comic without taking the audience into account. Specifically, it does not fully address the comic's relation to the audience, the dependence and vulnerability that the comic's often aggressive stance and phallic microphone only partly mask (consider, for example, the comic's extreme vulnerability to hecklers). Comics' own perceptions of their audiences may offer evidence that a kind of empowering of female performers and spectators can take place within the context of conventional stand-up comedy. Beatts observes that, whereas a woman in an audience who is with a man tends to wait to see if he will laugh before she will, women in a social setting unaccompanied by men feel much freer to express themselves humorously and to respond to the humorous expression of other women (qtd. in Collier and Beckett, Spare Ribs, 26). As we have seen, her observation accords with social-scientific conclusions.

The experience of stand-up comedians suggests, however, that, while this situation may be normal (in the strict, statistical sense), it is not inevitable. Although Joan Rivers would probably not qualify as a feminist comedian in the minds of many, her observation on this subject is of interest. Rivers vigorously denies that there is any such thing as "women's humor," yet she does see a gender-inflected distinction among audiences. She refuses to perform for all-male audiences, not because she does not want to be objectified for the male gaze but because she feels that men alone do not understand her humor. "You need women to relate to because the men relate to you through the women they are with, and then they go forward" (qtd. in Collier and Beckett, Spare Ribs, 8). This description reverses the social norm, in which the woman looks to her male companion for cues. It is also the case that most women comedians specifically address the women in their audiences during some portions of their acts. For those moments the comedian creates a community with other women based on common experience (frequently of men) but not separate from the patriarchal public sphere. In the hands of the most skilled practitioners this community becomes a strategic community, a moment at which a shared subjectivity that excludes men is created under our very noses, again placing the men in the audience in the position women have traditionally occupied as comedy spectators. These examples suggest that the articulation of the comedian's performance as a cultural text, which occurs through negotiations between comic and audience conditioned by the gender identities of both, can produce circumstances within the context of the performance that run counter to the social norm, circumstances in which women may find a sense of empowerment through a sense of shared subjectivity—or, by identifying with a performer who depends on their presence for the text she produces to have meaning or by being the authority on what is funny to men. Similarly, the female comic can engage the women in her audience in a way that empowers both them and herself, even directly under "the oppressors' forbidding or disapproving gaze."

One clear indication that women's comedy is perceived as genuinely dangerous within "the patriarchal public sphere" is that it is so often subject to strategies of patriarchal recuperation. Women comics face the greatest risk that the challenge they represent will be neutralized by the contexts in which they are presented when their work is disseminated beyond the realm of the club performance, a relatively privileged realm over which the comedian, male or female, has the greatest control. I would like to offer two examples here of recuperative strategies to which female comics are subjected in two different cultural realms deriving from the institution of television: the videocassette market and the network talk show.

The packaging and production of a videotape entitled *Women Tell the Dirtiest Jokes* (High Ridge Productions, 1985) offer instructive examples of how (male) producers attempt to recuperate provocative work by women and make it safe for the male gaze. The label on the front of the videocassette box is an illustration depicting several young, male sailors in the front row at a comedy club performance, blushing conspicuously at the utterances of a female comic onstage.[19] Because the point of view of the illustration is at stage level and from behind the performer, the comic herself is represented only as a pair of shapely legs in stockings. At one level this packaging seems designed to titillate the male viewer with a promise of raunchy women offered up to this gaze and, thus, to objectify the female performer.

At another level the title of the tape and the idea that what the woman is saying could make a sailor blush seem intended to suggest, in effect, that women have beaten men at their own game by telling jokes even dirtier than typical locker-room repartee. This transforms the woman from a threatening Other into just one of the guys; her humor, which could be seen as a challenge to male power, becomes the same as the humor men exchange among themselves. The image undermines women's autonomy in two ways—through straightforward objectification and by denaturing the woman into a foul-mouthed "man without a penis."[20]

This kind of contextualizing is not confined to the tape's packaging. The eight female comedians on the tape, all recorded before a live audience in a clublike setting, are introduced by a disembodied male voice informing us, barker-like, that we are about to see "eight lovely ladies." Another male voice takes over to introduce each of the acts, becoming an invisible and pervasive authority, defining each woman and categorizing her work. In some cases the implications of the categorizing are disturbing, as when the voice refers to LaWanda Page as "the black queen of comedy."

The last thing on the tape is a song written by the program's producer, which is played over the end credits. Entitled "Pain," it seems designed to assuage the male ego after the assaults it has sustained at the hands of female comedians:

> When you shake your hips, girl
> How it drives the boys insane;
> When you wet your pretty lips, girl
> The feeling spreads—I can't explain
> The pain . . .

The song refers to pain inflicted on a man by a woman, but it translates the pain of stinging satire into the pleasurable pain of seduction, reducing the woman from a subject attempting to carve out a piece of discursive space into a male-constructed object whose every move, even if unconsciously motivated, is to be seen as an attempt to attract the male's attention. The final implication, then, is that, even the female comics on the tape, some of whom are quite vigorous in their assault on male privilege, are really only engaging in seduction by unconventional means and need not be taken seriously. The curious end result of this packaging and production is that, whereas many of the comics themselves specifically address the women in their audience in an attempt to stress the commonality of women's experiences with men, the producers seem to assume a male spectator and seem to want to protect him from that unfamiliar entity, the aggressively funny woman, by objectifying her.

Another means by which women comics are frequently threatened with recuperation is mediation by a male talk show host as "kindly father" on network television.[21] Although the comics have relative autonomy during their five minutes on "The Tonight Show" or "Latenight with David Letterman" (though they are always subject to network censorship), the host is in a position to contextualize the comic's performance. Not only does the host mediate between the performer and the home viewer through his introduction and the interview that often follows the comic's performance, but the program's apparatus further mediates the home viewers' response by positing the studio audience, manipulated by applause signs and other cued responses, as the "ideal audience" whose response the home viewer is implicitly asked to emulate.[22] The particular character of current hosts also works to neutralize the performances they present:

> The talk show host . . . is a figure of the ideal viewer. As we watch TV's images, so does he sit and look on at his parade of guests, evincing a boyish wryness . . . especially when he glances our way with a look that says, "Can you believe this?" He is a festive version of the anchorman, with an air of detached superiority that is enabled by his permanent youthfulness, and by his middle-American calm and plainness. Johnny Carson of Iowa, like his heir apparent, that supreme ironist, David Letterman of Indiana, always seems above the excesses of either coast, even as he brings them to us.[23]

Anything is grist for the mill in this parade of performances, none more challenging or meaningful than another. An example of how this effect can neutralize potentially challenging performances is that of Victoria Jackson's appearances on "The Tonight Show." Jackson's peculiar postfeminist performances, which have combined high school gymnastics with songs on subjects one does not expect to hear of on Carson (female anger, suicide) sung poorly in a little-girl voice, are sui generis and difficult to fathom. Carson, however, successfully undermines any challenge Jackson may pose, first by introducing her paternalistically as an oddity he has discovered, then by eliciting mundane personal information from her during subsequent interviews. This trivialization has only been furthered by the "dizzy blonde" characters Jackson usually plays as part of the "Saturday Night Live" company and in films. The result is that Jackson, initially a fascinating, enigmatic performance artist, has become an eminently safe commodity.

Obviously, the same kind of contextualizing can rob a male performer's work of its impact as well, but the fact that the figures of authority on all the major late-night talk shows that serve as launching points for national recognition are men (Carson, Letterman, Hall) confronts women performers with a set of issues their male counterparts do not have to negotiate in the same form. Betsy Borns discusses the fact that talk show hosts like Carson and Letterman prefer to give exposure to new comedians or those they can claim to have discovered. She uses the phrase "TV virginity" to describe the condition of comics before their initial talk show appearance (*Comic Lives,* 199). The implications of this phrase are particularly disturbing in the context of a discussion of female comics in that it implies that the talk show host as "kindly father" also figures as a seducer (or rapist?) whose paternalistic interest extends only to those he has deflowered.

Of necessity, this discussion of the positioning of women's comedy within the patriarchal public sphere must remain open-ended, for comedy's potential for empowering women is always accompanied by the potential for patriarchal recuperation; both can take place simultaneously, in fact. To assume, however, that because recuperative mechanisms are in place recuperation inevitably occurs would be to deny that the audience retains any capacity for independent action. The fact that a representation may appear to be highly compromised, in league with repressive cultural forces, does not determine how an audience will *use* that representation and, possibly, be empowered by it. Lawrence Grossberg argues for the value of the Gramscian concept of "articulation" as a way of understanding the relation between a cultural text and its audience, a concept that suggests that audiences are always actively constructing texts rather than simply "decoding" meanings that are present in them. "[The theory of articulation's] disdain for any assumed historical necessity and its emphasis on the reality of struggle direct the critic toward the complex and contradictory relations of power that intersect and organize an audience's relation to particular cultural texts" and challenges any assumption that the audience and the performer are simply putty in the hands of the hegemonic. "People are never merely passively subordinated, never totally manipulated, never entirely incorporated"; rather, they can often discover sites of empowerment within seemingly co-opted discourses by finding their own ways of using them.[24] Therefore, although the recuperative mechanisms I have discussed here may have the effect of domesticating women comics for male spectators, they may not succeed in inhibiting female spectators from being empowered by the comics' representations.

"Brought to You by Fem-Rage": The Angry Comedy of Roseanne Barr

In her introduction to the collection *Last Laughs: Perspectives on Women and Comedy* Regina Barreca argues that "recent feminist criticism has acknowledged the power of rage in writings by women, but has as yet left unexamined the crucial roles of comedy paired with anger as shaping forces and feminist tools" (5). In the final portion of this essay I shall analyze the interplay of humor and anger in the work of Roseanne Barr and show how that work self-consciously responds to the cultural positioning of the woman comic, especially in relation to the images of women disseminated by television.

In her essay "Situation Comedy, Feminism, and Freud: Discourses of Gracie and Lucy" Patricia Mellencamp points out that women television comedians like Gracie Allen and Lucille Ball challenged male dominance by "unmak[ing] 'meaning' and overturn[ing] patriarchal assumptions" but that, finally, "neither escaped confinement and the tolerance of kindly fathers."[25] In Mellencamp's view the comic and narratological codes of the situation comedy inevitably confined and tamed the woman comedian, despite her challenge to the domestic containment of American women so characteristic of the 1950s and 1960s and her appropriation of typically "male" comic modes (e.g., Ball's skill in physical comedy).

I would like to apply some of the terms of Mellencamp's rich and complex analysis to the work of a current stand-up and television

comedian, Roseanne Barr. The particular work I will examine is
"The Roseanne Barr Show," Barr's HBO television special of 1987
(not to be confused with her current network series, "Roseanne"). I
shall argue that Barr's distinctive hybridization of the situation comedy and stand-up comedy genres and her explicit designation of anger
as the source of her humor enable her to thematize, and thus to resist,
recuperation in a way that Allen and Ball could not.

Barr's hybridization of genres is an important strategy of resistance, for stand-up comedy, Barr's original medium, does not place
the woman comic at the same risk of recuperation and containment
as the situation comedy (though I have already pointed out the risk
of recuperation the woman comic runs in the cultural realm). For one
thing stand-up comedy is not a narrative form; there is no "situation"
to surround and contain the actions of the comic woman. Like so
much postmodern performance, stand-up comedy is monologic—the
comedian stands alone, unmediated by other characters; there is no
George for every Gracie, no Ricky for every Lucy. In his book on the
evolution of the situation comedy David Marc argues vigorously
that, as "an art of the middle" designed to appeal to the widest possible segment of the television audience, situation comedy "rarely
reaches the psychological or political extremes that have been com-
monplace" in stand-up comedy, which remains a realm of idiosyn-
cratic expression (*Comic Visions,* 26).

Despite the performative freedoms offered by stand-up comedy,
the few female stand-up comedians of the 1950s and 1960s tended to
work within self-imposed restrictions that reflected the social stigma
attached to aggressively funny women. The traditional female
comic's chief strategy was to render herself apparently unthreatening
to male dominance by making herself the object of her own comic
derision in what is usually referred to as "self-deprecatory" comedy.
The self-deprecatory mode is the mode of both Phyllis Diller, who
entered comedy in the mid-1950s, and Joan Rivers, who entered the
field in the early 1960s. Both women have created personae who
make their own supposed unattractiveness (to men) and their failure
as housewives the subjects of their humor. (Rivers's notoriety derives
in large part from material in which she ridicules other women celeb-
rities for not meeting the patriarchal standards of beauty and decorum
her own persona also does not meet.) Clearly, whatever anger may
be implicit in the self-deprecatory comedy of Diller and Rivers has

been turned inward onto the female subject herself, rather than out-
ward onto the social conditions that made it necessary for Diller and
Rivers to personify themselves in this way in order to have successful
careers as comics. It seems to me that in "The Roseanne Barr Show"
Barr offers an example of a woman's humor that is explicitly based
in the kind of active anger Barreca sees as an empowering response.

Roseanne Barr belongs to the family tree that produced both
Diller and Rivers; now that she has her own television series, comparison with Allen, Ball, and other domestic situation comedy performers becomes relevant as well. Like Diller's comic persona in
particular, the Barr persona is once again that of a disgruntled housewife (or "domestic goddess," as Barr insists she wants to be called).
But, whereas the personae of earlier comedians such as Diller and
Rivers turn the anger and frustration of a life confined to domesticity
in on themselves in self-deprecation, Barr's housewife persona speaks
out petulantly against husbands, children, and the social expectations
and limitations imposed on women. Whereas the Diller and Rivers
personae make their own supposed physical unattractiveness a source
of humor, Barr insists on her right to be overweight, making those
who are not the objects of her humor. She protests that Californians
are "rude to the fat," implies that slender people are necessarily bulimic, and compares "skinny moms" with "fat moms":

> What do you want when you're really depressed, you know,
> some skinny mom: "Well, why don't you jog around a while and
> that'll release adrenalin in your blood and you'll better cope with
> stress" or some fat mom: "Well, let's have pudding, Oreos, and
> marshmallows."

Her response to the idea that people overeat as a sexual sublimation
is: "I think people just have sex because they can't afford good food."
Her definitive word on the subject is: "If you're fat, just like *be* fat and
shut up. And if you're thin—fuck you!"[26]

In a discussion of Louie Anderson, a young male comedian who
also refers to his own overweight status in his act, Marc comments
that "a modern American fat person demonstrates a powerful mastery over social convention by actively calling attention to his presumably deviant and deficient condition" (*Comic Visions*, 18). While
it is true that Anderson highlights and underlines the fact that the

accepted lore about weight is precisely a matter of convention, and is thus empowered, his humor is essentially self-deprecatory. Barr takes the next step: she rejects self-deprecation, not just by drawing attention to social convention but also by insisting that she is *not* "deviant and deficient." And, of course, the question of body image in general and of weight in particular has special relevance to women in our culture. Whereas a fat *man* like Louie Anderson can still be accepted as jolly—a large elf, if not exactly Santa—a fat woman is not generally granted that latitude. As Carol Munter has pointed out, the body is a political arena for women: "As long as we [women] remain unempowered, we will need our conflicts to disappear through the loss of a pound of flesh because we have no access to other modes of action. . . . We're taught to shape our bodies and not the world."27 Implicit in Barr's resounding "fuck you" to the thin world is a call to action, a refusal to turn her energies upon herself, her resentment literally broadcast as she chews gum or Cheetos directly into the microphone.

In addition to challenging the cultural standards of attractiveness reified in Diller's and Rivers's performances Barr aggressively points up in no uncertain terms the absurdity of men's obsession with our sexual apparatus and the symbolic authority we believe it confers upon us. In a routine on the behavior of men and women while traveling together she refers to men's chastising women for not being able to read maps. Apparently conceding that men are in fact the better map readers, she says, "They are good at that map-reading, aren't they? 'Cause only the male mind could conceive of one inch equalling a hundred miles." She goes on to describe the only other thing that men are better at than women: "peeing out a campfire." In a comic *reductio* of phallogocentrism, she enacts a man "writing [his] name in the snow," strutting and posturing proudly over his accomplishment.

It is worth observing that these subjects and strategies appear regularly in the work of other women comedians. In a routine included on the *Women Tell the Dirtiest Jokes* video Barbara Scott follows a very similar pattern by first criticizing men's concern with the size of their apparatus then apparently praising them for their "writing" ability. "Men—you give them an inch, and they'll add it to their own. Guys are neat, though, 'cause guys can do great things, like write their names in the snow. All I can do is dot 'i's and an occasional colon, you know." She then demonstrates the writing of a colon by hopping. Here, of course, the woman seems to present herself as anatomically inferior to the man; her writing is only subsidiary to male writing, limited to dotting the 'i's made by men or providing their writings with punctuation. She contextualizes this part with the first line, however, poking fun at men's concern with the size of their apparatus. Her examination of the capacities of *her* apparatus thus becomes a parodic version of male behavior. The physical gesture of hopping underlines the ludicrousness of the whole enterprise of writing in the snow, much as Barr's strut deflates male pride in this pointless accomplishment so intimately bound up with men's identification with the penis.

Comedian Carol Leifer applies a similar comic strategy to a different topic. A staple of her stand-up act is a bit that begins with her saying, "What can I tell you about myself? I'm divorced, no children . . . well, none that I *know* about."[28] As she says these last words, she gives the audience a knowing wink and makes other stereotypically "male" gestures. Again, the anatomical comparison underlies the power of the joke, here in an attack against men's assumption that our anatomical differences somehow makes us less responsible than women for the production of children and the assumption that one's worth as a man is measured in potency, promiscuity, and the victimization of women.

Leifer and Barr end their acts on very similar notes. Leifer ends with a comment on birth control, noting that the pill has wrought havoc with her hormones: "I woke up with a beard—on my dick!" Barr ends with a rejoinder to people who accuse her of being unfeminine because of her aggressive comedy. Her response: "Suck my dick!" In both instances these last lines are the most overtly vulgar moments in the comedians' respective performances. At one level these remarks are simply what comedians refer to as "dick jokes," cheap shots whose primary impact derives exclusively from their shock value (Borns, *Comic Lives,* 14–15). In each case, however, the woman comedian turns the dick joke into something more challenging than a jarring instance of locker-room humor. Even though (perhaps because) Leifer's joke apparently posits the woman as the victim of a contraceptive technology invented by a man, which has, in a surreal twist, turned her into a man, the fact that it occurs at the end of her act is highly significant. Because of this placement, her remark

joins Barr's in constituting the comic woman's most overt challenge
to phallocentrism. Anne Beatts posits the image of a man without a
penis as the male recuperation of womanhood; Leifer and Barr insist
that their status as comics makes them self-constructed women *with*
penises. By claiming to possess a metaphoric penis each woman
claims her right to the comic stage and challenges the cultural values
that assert that women are not supposed to be aggressive and funny,
are not supposed to have access to the power that humor represents.

The patriarchalist nightmare Beatts describes has come true:
given access to the comic stage, women have indeed made men's
sexual apparatus one of their ultimate jokes. They have also gone
well beyond such mockery: by claiming to have a penis they are
thematizing the inequity of a politics that equates possession of a
penis with the symbolic authority of the phallus. This is indeed "humor that sees man much farther away than he has ever been seen"
(Cixous), humor that altogether usurps traditional male prerogative.

The form of Barr's television special is as important as its content. By crossing generic boundaries Barr critiques the containment
of the woman within the bounds of domesticity that Mellencamp
sees in situation comedy and thus resists patriarchal recuperation by
thematizing it. Indeed, "The Roseanne Barr Show" can almost be
seen as a direct response to Mellencamp's perceptions of situation
comedy women. Although the centerpiece of "The Roseanne Barr
Show" is her stand-up act, she presents that act within a domestic
context; her stand-up routine even takes place on a set decorated as a
living room rather than the traditional bare stage. It is in this sense
that "The Roseanne Barr Show" is a generic hybrid, combining elements of both stand-up and situation comedy. The Barr persona is
in a sense the fulfillment of Lucy Ricardo's dreams: she is both a
housewife and a professional entertainer. Although her professional
status may be a sign of some sort of "progress" (from the 1950s to
the 1980s? from broadcast to cable?), she remains subject to the same
containing forces Lucy battled.

Far from dismissing the domestic containment implied by the
treatment of the comic woman in traditional situation comedies, Barr
represents and thematizes containment in her work by encasing her
stand-up act in a sort of triple Pirandellian frame. The outmost frame
involves scenes of Barr, the housewife, at home with her "real" family before and after her stand-up performance (her husband in these

scenes is played by Bill Pentland, Barr's husband at the time). The next frame presents Barr in a trailer home behind the theater with her fictional family, ostensibly the one she comments on in her act. The children of this family come onstage during her act, and Barr has to leave the stage to return to the trailer and keep the domestic front running smoothly. Her real family sits in the audience and watches the scenes involving her "stage" family. The third frame is the fiction that her stand-up act is a show sponsored by a product called "Fem-Rage." A male announcer asserts this fact and describes the product at the beginning and the end of Barr's act; a mock commercial for the product appears in between.

The stage family is the housewife's nightmare Barr comments on in her stand-up act: a slovenly husband in an undershirt who does nothing but drink, belch, and watch sports on television; children running amok through the trailer. The real family seems much more supportive, laughing while listening to Barr practice her jokes but also criticizing her relentlessly for her jokes, for the way they, the real family, are represented by the stage family, and so on. Barr overcomes one level of containment: as the show's creative force, she can shape the stage family any ways she likes. At the end of her performance she returns to the trailer to find her husband asleep and transforms him magically from a slob into a tuxedoed beau who literally sweeps her off her feet. Ironically, however, this happy ending only throws her into the arms of her real family, who are harping on her act and their place in it, as always. This family lives in a comfortable-looking house, not a trailer; the opening scene is scored with a doo-wop number by Frankie Lymon and the Teenagers, as if to evoke the "Donna Reed Show" and "Father Knows Best" era, and these family scenes appear to have been shot on the "Happy Days" set. Barr's neighborhood, however, is not the safe, middle-class haven that is the locale for most traditional domestic situation comedies but, rather, the postmodern suburb of slasher films: those monsters from the id, Freddy Krueger and Jason (of the *Nightmare on Elm Street* and *Friday the Thirteenth* movie series, respectively) lurk immediately outside the door. The Barr persona, a woman with considerable power to shape her own reality, is nevertheless entrapped by domestic containment: her life is quite literally in danger except when she is confined in one or another version or representation of a domestic scene.

The third frame, however, proposes a provocative response to that very entrapment. The announcer's references to Fem-Rage, which frame Barr's stand-up act, and the commercial for it within the act, contextualize her performance in a very specific way. The tag line for Fem-Rage is: "For that one time of the month you're allowed to be yourself." Because the announcer clearly speaks *for* Barr, he does not become the pervasive voice of male authority that dominates and domesticates the female comics in *Women Tell the Dirtiest Jokes*. That we *see* him at one point also tends to emphasize that he is a professional announcer in Barr's employ, not an ineffable, transcendent male presence. The commercial reveals that Fem-Rage is a product that gives women the strength to stand up to a male-dominated world. In the commercial Barr plays Doris, a timid nuclear power plant employee whose male boss refuses to listen to her when she tells him that he is causing a meltdown. Shoved aside, she takes solace with some female coworkers who encourage her to try Fem-Rage, telling her: "It's pure encapsulated estrogen which enhances the natural female hormone, and counteracts that learned feminine social response." Thus fortified, Doris returns to the control room, shoves her boss aside, and saves the world.

Barr's stand-up performance can easily be seen as an example of the literary/performance genre Lauren Berlant defines as "the female complaint," a genre "situated precisely in the space between a sexual politics that threatens structures of patriarchal authority and a sentimentality that confirms the inevitability of the speaker's powerlessness" ("Female Complaint," 243–44). Certainly, Barr seems to present herself as the type of woman Berlant identifies as the producer of the complaint, one "who wants to maintain her alignment with men to speak oppositionally but without fear for her position within the heterosexual economy" (243).

I would argue, however, that Barr's version of the complaint finally does not merely "confirm the inevitability of the speaker's powerlessness." Berlant notes that, "as a euphemism for menstruation, 'the female complaint' typifies the banality of female suffering," thus trivializing and dismissing it (243). Through her Fem-Rage commercial Barr undermines this trivialization, turning the female complaint—in both of Berlant's senses—quite literally into a source and sign of power: of comedic power in her stand-up act, of physical power in the mock commercial. Rage, she suggests, is the natural state of women's being, at least in a world that attempts to contain women through the imposition of "that learned feminine social response." And she makes no mystery about the source of her comedy; as the announcer tells us, Barr's humor is quite literally "brought to you by Fem-Rage." Barr presents her persona as a situation comedy housewife who is self-consciously *aware* of the conventions that seek to contain her and *angry* about them. Her role as stand-up comic gives her a platform from which to express that anger. Although she does not escape the domestic constraints that fettered Gracie and Lucy, she resists them: she is not just silently subject to those constraints, as Gracie and Lucy finally turned out to be. Roseanne Barr's voice is that of what Judith Wilt describes as the matriarchal comic who has "given herself to love, marriage, family, community, a hostage to the fortunes of that myth,"[29] but with the difference that this time the matriarch is angry, and she wants us to know it.

NOTES

1. One provocative piece of show business lore is that many young female stand-up comics, including Judy Tenuta and Carrie Snow, got their start in a way that is a mirror image of the traditional avenue followed by male comedians of previous generations—by emceeing at male strip clubs.

2. As quoted by Denise Collier and Kathleen Beckett, *Spare Ribs: Women in the Humor Biz* (New York: St. Martin's Press, 1980), 3. Further citations of this source will appear parenthetically in the text.

3. See Mary Anne Dolan, "Today's Women Comics—Knock-Down Funny, Knock-Down Serious," *Los Angeles Times*, 2 January 1989, sec. 2, 5; and Mary Unterbrink, *Funny Women: American Comediennes, 1860–1985* (Jefferson, N.C.: McFarland, 1987), 197.

4. Regina Barreca, Introduction, *Last Laughs: Perspectives on Women and Comedy*, ed. Regina Barreca (New York: Gordon and Breach, 1988), 5. Further citations of this source will appear parenthetically in the text.

5. Dave Marsh, "It's Like That: Rock & Roll on the Home Front," in *The First Rock & Roll Confidential Report*, ed. Dave Marsh (New York: Pantheon, 1985), 15.

6. An essentialist view of male humor, however, is no more acceptable than an essentialist view of female humor. It is important to note that men do not *necessarily* enjoy humor that reaffirms cultural and social dominance, such as racist or sexist humor. During a recent club visit I saw a black male comic berate his substantially (thought not exclusively) white male audience because it would not laugh at his crudely sexist jokes. His repeated rejoinder was: "What is it—fag night at the club?" A more important case in point is that of Arsenio Hall, a

comic and the host of a late-night television talk show, who has apologized for the poor judgment of a comic who had been on his program. The comic had done a tasteless "date rape" joke; Hall interrupted his own monologue the next night to apologize.

7. Barreca, *Last Laughs*, offers a variety of responses to these critical issues. In addition to the two essays from that collection that I cite specifically here, I found those by Reginia Gagnier, Judy Little, and Nancy Walker particularly illuminating.

8. Howard R. Pollio and John W. Edgerly, "Comedians and Comic Style," in *Humour and Laughter: Theory, Research and Applications*, ed. Antony J. Chapman and Hugh C. Foot (London: John Wiley and Sons, 1976), 221. Further citations of this source will appear parenthetically in the text.

9. Quoted in Collier and Beckett, *Spare Ribs*, 28. Beatts's hypothesis may have some empirical grounding. Melvin Helitzer reports:

> Research on sexual humor indicated that student joke tellers were more likely to select jokes with sexist content discriminating against males regardless of the gender of the performer or the audience. And the most common subjects were those which denigrated bodily parts and sexual performance. It is, therefore, hostility against male sexual inadequacy, more than sexism against women, that appears to be the dominant theme of most sexual humor. (*Comedy Techniques for Writers and Performers* [Athens, Ohio: Lawhead Press, 1984], 25)

Helitzer's finding is suspect because he does not specify the nature of the "research" that produced it. It also seems to be challenged, at least in part, by a study in which different versions of the same jokes were used: "Both males and females appreciated the joke versions in which a male dominated a female significantly more than those in which a female dominated a male" (Dolf Zillman and Joanne R. Cantor, "A Disposition Theory of Humour and Mirth," in Chapman and Foot, *Humour and Laughter*, 97). Nevertheless, Helitzer's finding certainly suggests that, if women's humor implicitly (or explicitly) attacks phallic authority, it aims for a vulnerable target.

10. Mahadev L. Apte, *Humor and Laughter: An Anthropological Approach* (Ithaca, N.Y.: Cornell University Press, 1985), 75.

11. See Herbert Blau, "Ideology and Performance," *Theatre Journal* 35, no. 4 (1983): 441–60.

12. For the male endorsement, see Betsy Borns, *Comic Lives: Inside the World of American Stand-up Comedy* (New York: Simon and Schuster, 1987), 21. Further citations of this source will appear parenthetically in the text.

13. David Marc, *Comic Visions: Television Comedy and American Culture* (Boston: Unwin Hyman, 1989), 17. Further citations of this source will appear parenthetically in the text.

14. Lisa Merrill, "Feminist Humor: Rebellious and Self-Affirming," in Barreca, *Last Laughs*, 275–78. Further citations of this source will appear parenthetically in the text.

15. Cheryl Kader, "Kate Clinton: The Production and Reception of Feminist

Humor," *Sexual Politics and Popular Culture,* ed. Diane Raymond (Bowling Green, Ohio: Popular Press, 1990), 46, 48. Further citations of this source will appear parenthetically in the text.

16. Lauren Berlant, "The Female Complaint," *Socialtext,* nos. 19–20 (1988): 238. Further citations of this source will appear parenthetically in the text.

17. See Russ DeVault, "A Working 'Fumorist': Comic Kate Clinton Brings Feminism to Her Humor," *Atlanta Journal-Constitution Weekend,* 24 September 1988, 25.

18. In January of 1991 an ad appeared in an Atlanta newspaper for a "Girl's Night Out" at a local comedy club, scheduled for Super Bowl Sunday. This was a "for women only" event featuring a woman comic, Jenny Jones, who now hosts a syndicated television talk show. The ad also mentioned a competition: "Tell us in 25 words or less 'Why You Need a Girl's Night Out'" to win free admission to the club. This ad would seem to represent a co-opted version of the "feminist public sphere" Berlant mentions: both the phrase *girl's night out* and the scheduling of the event for Super Bowl Sunday suggest the degree to which it is inscribed within patriarchal culture. At the same time it is possible to see such an event as one that might attract women who do not necessarily identify themselves as feminists in a way that a woman's coffeehouse might not. The significance of the event depends finally on what sort of discourse Jenny Jones engages her audience in.

19. *Women Tell the Dirtiest Jokes* (videotape), prod. Stephen L. Singer; dir. Greg Grosz, High Ridge Productions, 1985.

20. Anne Beatts, qtd. in Collier and Beckett, *Spare Ribs,* 27.

21. I have borrowed the expression "kindly father" from Patricia Mellencamp, who uses it to designate male characters in television situation comedies who keep their "zany" female counterparts in check (e.g., Ricky Ricardo and George Burns). I return to Mellencamp's argument later in the present essay.

22. Robert C. Allen, "Reader-oriented Criticism and Television," in *Channels of Discourse: Television and Contemporary Criticism,* ed. Robert C. Allen (Chapel Hill: University of North Carolina Press, 1987), 94. In moving from a discussion of the possibilities for female empowerment inherent in the comic-audience dynamic to a discussion of the dangers of recuperation inherent in cultural media, I have also moved from the context of "live" performance to that of mediated performance. It would not be valid to conclude, however, that live performance necessarily offers more of a foothold for critical practice and empowerment than mediated performance. It is true that the comic-audience dynamic that informs club performance does not occur when the same performance appears on television, with the studio audience serving as a surrogate for the home viewers and cueing the latter's responses. Nevertheless, as John Fiske points out throughout his *Television Culture* (London and New York: Methuen, 1987), television audiences exercise considerable discretion in how they use and interact with the texts offered to them; the fact of mediation does not in itself determine the "meaning" of the mediated text.

23. Mark Crispin Miller, "Deride and Conquer," in *Watching Television,* ed. Todd Gitlin (New York: Pantheon Books, 1986), 218–19.

24. Lawrence Grossberg, "Putting the Pop Back into Postmodernism," in *Universal Abandon? The Politics of Postmodernism,* ed. Andrew Ross (Minneapolis: University of Minnesota Press, 1988), 169–70.

25. Patricia Mellencamp, "Situation Comedy, Feminism, and Freud: Discourses of Gracie and Lucy," in *Studies in Entertainment: Critical Approaches to Mass Culture,* ed. Tania Modleski (Bloomington: Indiana University Press, 1986), 90.

26. "The Roseanne Barr Show" (videotape); prod. and dir. Rocco Urbisci; written by Roseanne Barr, Bill Pentland, Rocco Urbisci, HBO Video (Comedy Club), 1987. Much has changed since I first formulated these ideas in 1988. Roseanne Barr (now called Roseanne Arnold—I choose to continue to refer to her by the name that appears in the title of the show I discuss) has become an advocate of weight-loss and cosmetic surgery. Following several years of highly negative publicity concerning her divorce, her rowdy relationship with current husband Tom Arnold, her controversial rendition of the national anthem at a baseball game, and her alleged intractability as the star of the highest-rated television show in the country, she seems to be undertaking a specific effort to rehabilitate her public image. In so doing she has sacrificed much of the edge that originally gave her stand-up comedy its pith and power.

27. Carol Munter, "Fat and the Fantasy of Perfection," in *Pleasure and Danger: Exploring Female Sexuality,* ed. Carole S. Vance (Boston: Routledge and Kegan Paul, 1984), 228–29.

28. Carol Leifer, stand-up comedy performance at the Punch Line Comedy Club, Sandy Springs, Ga., 1989.

29. Judith Wilt, "The Laughter of Maidens, the Cackle of Matriarchs: Notes on the Collision between Comedy and Feminism," in *Gender and Literary Voice,* ed. Janet Todd (New York: Holmes and Meier, 1980), 176.

Chapter 17

Is She or Isn't She?: Madonna and the Erotics of Appropriation

Amy Robinson

It's flattering to me that people take the time to analyze me, that I've so infiltrated their psyches that they have to intellectualize my very being. I'd rather be on their minds than off.

—Madonna

Flanked by two indistinguishable ladies in waiting and a court of multicolored (mostly) queer half-dressed gentlemen, Madonna performed "Vogue" via her newest incarnation as Marie Antoinette for the 1990 MTV Video Awards. Flagrantly heterosexualizing her admitted appropriations of black gay culture, Madonna subsidized her televised paean to power inequities with the captivating chorus of liberal humanism: "It doesn't matter if you're black or white, a boy or a girl."[1] But, surely, this must be an example of Madonna's notorious ironic proclivities, for how else in this context is it possible to read her as anything but white, aristocratic, female, and indelibly heterosexual? The woman whom Camille Paglia has solemnly crowned "the future of feminism"[2] enacts the awkward riddle of her popularity as an erotic spectacle of dispossession. Against the backdrop of her dancers, she resubstantiates the very categories she claims to subvert.

My preoccupation with Madonna began in 1986 with the release of her contentious video *Papa Don't Preach*. As a consummate performer, Madonna continues to enchant American consumers, and, even as my ongoing fascination with her places me firmly within that assembly, I will risk here the wrath of Ms. Paglia, who claims that

Madonna's feminist detractors are "hangdog dowdies and parochial prudes . . . stuck in an adolescent whining mode."[3] As such, the first portion of this essay is constructed by, through, and within a discourse of gossip that has enveloped Madonna since she materialized on the music scene in 1983. For I believe her work solicits an active community of spectatorial investment and petitions the viewer to engage in her performance as an exercise in those identities that she stages so unrelentingly in her interviews and videos. In the remaining sections I will pay particular attention to *Papa Don't Preach, Like a Prayer,* and *Justify My Love,*[4] as I argue that Madonna's authorizing strategies prove inextricable from the theater of appropriation which constitutes her as phenomenon.

In a 1989 article published in *Gay Community News* Sydney Pokorny argues that Madonna "adorns herself with the markings of the Other and then sells that look to the masses through the wanna-be phenomenon."[5] Indeed, I would further argue that Madonna peddles such identifications by dramatizing the acts of appropriation that constitute her image—a sure-fire formula for success that in a recent "unauthorized" biography earned her the affectionate title "Our Lady of Perpetual Promotion."[6] Such mercenary tactics have produced vehement reactions from her critics, who alternately praise her as "one of the century's great inventions" or accuse her of fashioning an empty series of superficial images in the name of sheer greed and capitalist exploitation. Her cosmetic makeovers have earned as much attention as her music, prompting her publicist, Liz Rosenberg, to warn prospective interviewers: "Don't ask Madonna questions about her image . . . she hates that word."[7] In fact, the debate often hinges on the issue of whether Madonna *is* a commodity, her frequent mutations not unlike "Ford's yearly production of its 'new' models."[8] In an exchange-based society that has abandoned "natural form" for the "form of appearance of value" Madonna's made-for-MTV persona seems to epitomize the trepidations of those who fear that postmodern culture signals the death knell of authenticity and genuine political virtuosity.

In this essay I will reconsider the commodity debate from the standpoint of the status of privacy as an authorizing discourse of the self. While the discrepancy between use-value and exchange-value has served many scholars as a critical gauge of social appropriation,[9] it is especially relevant once the division between private and public comes to be figured as the very battleground of identity itself. As a particular form of cultural capital, the commodity rehearses a "politics of value"[10] in which a boundary of the "real" insulates certain subjects from the seeming artifice of cultural manipulation. Such discrete boundaries are historically indebted to a gradual shift in the eighteenth century; as the market replaced the household as the center of a commercial economy, commodity exchange became increasingly dependent on what Lauren Berlant has aptly christened the enabling fiction of a "prophylactic private sphere."[11] Such an imagined realm prior to financial and ideological mediation is commensurate with a model of the self defined in the foundational documents of liberal humanism. According to John Locke, "every man [sic] has a property in his own person" and thus is licensed as a legitimate subject precisely to the extent to which "the body" qualifies as a paradigmatic "private" dominion.[12] In this economic framework the legal scholar Patricia Williams contends:

> ... "black," "female," "male" and "white" are every bit as much properties as the buses, private clubs, neighborhoods, and schools that provide the extracorporeal battleground of their expression.[13]

Williams accentuates the illusory ground of purity that certifies a legal "right to privacy." In so doing she insinuates the potential hazards of identity as a construct complicit with the exclusionary premises of the propertied self.

It is in this context that I would like to pose Madonna's proliferation of a series of "public" images as a challenge to an enabling rhetoric of privacy. For her oft-cited propensity to wear her theoretical underwear as outerwear would seem a willful renunciation of the "private" and its attendant claim to an interior "truth" prior to cultural arbitration. Flaunting privacy as a predicament of mimesis, being natural is—in the tradition of Oscar Wilde—a difficult pose for Madonna to keep up.[14] Nonetheless, her publicity continues to stress the sincerity of her manifold presentation. Her 1990 "Blond Ambition" tour book maintains: "Honesty. It's what Madonna has been about from the very beginning."[15] Consequently, I will argue that Madonna embodies the paradox of the "private"; her accumulation of a vast wealth in private property (in 1990 Forbes estimated that she had earned at least \$125 million since 1985)[16] is the direct result of her disavowal of privacy as an authorizing edifice of the self. Despite her overt rejection of mimesis and the purity of the propertied self, Madonna continues to derive the pecuniary benefits of claiming "the real."

Gossip, argues Patricia Mayer Spacks, "demands a process of relatedness among its participants; its *I*'s inevitably turn into a *we*."[17] Circulating "secrets," gossip constitutes insiders and outsiders by violating the discrete boundaries between public and private knowledge. A rhetoric of the "apparent," which rejects truth in favor of interpretation, gossip is uniquely suited to the epistemological event of Madonna. More than almost any other artist whose identity seems patently intelligible, Madonna has provoked immense pleasure in her fans by courting their identities as a component of her own. At various stages in her interviewing career Madonna has claimed to be black, a man, working class, and a lesbian. With the exception of her sexual preference she has courted a seeming ambiguity in the fact of little ambiguity at all. But, rather than merely chastising her for appropriations of Other's identities (I will undertake that task later in the essay), I would like to examine the way in which her persona seems to invite the spectator to speculate on Madonna's membership in his or her community of identity.

Both of Madonna's "unauthorized" biographers claim that the success of her first single release, *Madonna,* depended on the record producer's decision to leave her face off the cover: "They didn't put her face on the album . . . because they didn't want people to know she was white." A former Warner executive is alleged to have said, "Would black radio stations continue to play her records and young black audiences buy them if they were confronted with the fact that Madonna was not one of them?"[18] According to these sources, Warner Studios had assumed that Madonna was black and attributed her popularity in the African American and Latino communities to a similar misconception. Such a pattern of attributing Madonna's success to the commensurate identities of her consumers, speaks to the ambivalence at the center of the wanna-be phenomenon. Interpretive endeavors (is she or isn't she) serve as an eccentric form of advertising in which the spectator petitions the performer in the name of an identity that the performer deploys as persona.

In a 1989 interview in *Rolling Stone* Madonna audaciously claimed that most of her musical "imitators" were black. In a peculiar followup question Bill Zehme inquired, "Do you ever feel black?" She responded at great length:

> Oh, yes, all the time. That's a silly thing to say, though, isn't it? When I was a little girl, I wished I was black. All my girlfriends were black. I was living in Pontiac, Michigan, and I was definitely the minority in the neighborhood. White people were scared there. All of my friends were black and all the music I listened to was black. I was incredibly jealous of all my black girlfriends because they could have braids in their hair that stuck up everywhere. So I would go through this incredible ordeal of putting wire in my hair and braiding it so that I could make my hair stick up. I used to make cornrows and everything. But if being black is synonymous with having soul, then, yes, I feel that I am.[19]

In rapid succession, Madonna juxtaposes her claim to be the "original" with her admitted desire to copy a (hair) style, which she then names (black) as an ontological (soul) substance. As an artist who specifically targets the African-American and Latino communities,[20] Madonna's claim to possess "soul" and therefore "be" black invests blackness with an essence insofar as it enables her to gain notoriety as the "crossover girl."[21] Dedicating "La Isla Bonita" to the "beauty and mystery of the Latin American people,"[22] Madonna identifies ethnicity as a natural resource only to *perform* it as a theatrical event.

Oddly enough, it is hair that transports Madonna from the prototype to the facsimile, testifying to Kobena Mercer's contention that, "where race structures social relations of power, hair—as visible as skin colour, but also the most tangible sign of racial difference—takes on another forcefully symbolic dimension."[23] Exhibited even in the eminent pages of the *New York Times Magazine*, Madonna's sundry tresses have played a crucial role as the trademark of her ongoing self-creation.[24] In this respect it is particularly interesting that the question of Madonna's appropriation of African American expressive culture manifests itself repeatedly around the issue of hair. Perhaps her notorious appearance on the "Arsenio Hall Show" encapsulates this pattern. She charged that Arsenio's hair was "tired" and announced: "If you were one of my dancers you couldn't wear your hair like that." Hall's open reply was published in *Ebony* several months later and highlights the significance of hair in popular articulations of authenticity and originality:

> First, Madonna, I will never have to work for you because I have as much money as you have. . . . Number two, I've seen your dancers and . . . I'm nothing like them. They work *for* you. I work *with* you. Point number three is, you wanted to be Black when you were little but you are not Black, so don't try to understand Blackness. It is not your place to dictate Black hair care or fashion. You have borrowed our sound but not our sensibilities, so don't make an attempt to tell me how I should look.[25]

Arsenio Hall's persuasive rebuttal posits a radical discontinuity between Madonna's persona and the identity of her spectators. Using hair as the corporeal evidence of her exteriority, Hall names himself as *insider* in order to condemn her. But, in rejecting Madonna as a member of the community, Hall nonetheless assists in her singular staging of racial impersonation. That is, Madonna performs her racial impersonation *as* appropriation and, in so doing, subsidizes her claim to "be" black with her manifest whiteness.

One explanation might situate her within the theoretical domain of the Platonic simulacrum, the third order copy that passes for the "real," thereby disengaging the model/copy dichotomy that insures the priority of the "original" or the "model."[26] Positioned in such a way so that they cannot see the sun, the men chained in Socrates' cave believe in the truth of the shadows on the wall. In this sense, the simulacrum (shadow) takes the place of the Ideal (Sun) by rejecting the authority of the Ideal within whose terms the shadows *are* shadows rather than a legitimate source of light. Like Madonna, then, the simulacrum stages the truth as an appropriation, "by means of an aggression, an insinuation, a subversion."[27] In other words, it is precisely because the simulacrum is *not* the truth that it can make its claim to *be* the real. In this context, her mimetic subversions are equivalent to a wholesale *invasion of privacy:* a repudiation of the interior "truth" of identity which would disallow her claim to inhabit the racial identity of another.

But, unlike the simulacrum, Madonna makes no claim to the "real." It is her spectators, on the contrary, who claim to have access to her "true" self. Thus, in a peculiar formulation of the dilemma of authenticity Madonna solicits the spectator to make those truth claims forbidden by her romance with artifice. And, indeed, it is the role of the Platonic simulacrum to position the spectator as the definitive arbiter of epistemological truth.[28] While in Socrates' rendition of Plato's "Allegory of the Cave" both the chained men and the obedient student owe their respective readings of the shadows on the cave's wall to their spatial positioning (literally the ability to *see* the model), only the willful student of the simulacrum refuses to claim the "real" as prior to her perceptual intervention. As Audouard contends, "Simulacra are those constructions that included the angle of the observer, in order that the illusion be produced at the very point where the observer is located."[29] To concede the spectator's role in all model-copy epistemology is to endanger the fundamental tenets of mimesis by placing presumption outside the internal logic of the object and inside the eyes of the subject who looks. Madonna's ongoing drama of appropriation is thus inseparable from the identities of her spectators; her claim to the "real" is necessarily authorized by the interpretive intervention of her fans. *Is she or isn't she,* her prolific interviews seem to compel us to ask, juxtaposing her desire to "be" an/other against the very other whose presence insures her phenomenal success.

Like Peter Pan, who, as Marge Garber notes, must be played by a woman, "because a woman will never grow up to be a man,"[30] Madonna stages her excursions into masculinity with the reassurances of her female body. Claiming "masculine" prerogative and "feminine" charm, she clothes herself in men's suits and grabs her crotch, occasionally reiterating her childhood aspiration to "pee standing up." While she admits craving the freedom "to be both sexes," she most often displays her gender insurrections on the bodies of her male dancers. In fact, she maintains, "Effeminate men intrigue me more than anything in the world. I see them as my alter egos. I feel very drawn to them. I think like a guy, but I'm feminine, so I relate to feminine men."[31] Once again Madonna ascribes an essence to an/other and then appropriates it as performative. Not unlike the exclusive exhibition put on for her by the *House of Xtravaganza,* from which she freely admits her inspiration(!) for "Vogue,"[32] Madonna reveals her models only to claim herself as the impossible original. It is to gay men that she ascribes a compassionate understanding of her genuine character. And, indeed, "the gay world," reports Don Shewey from *The Advocate,* "gets Madonna in a big way."[33]

But, above and beyond her noted work on behalf of AIDS and her status as diva within the gay male community, her flirtation with lesbianism in the person of Sandra Bernhard has focused media attention on the issue of Madonna's sexual identity. On 2 July 1988 she appeared on "David Letterman" with Sandra Bernhard, where the two women, dressed in identical clothes, claimed to have been dancing at a New York lesbian bar. Later in almost every mainstream publication except the national gay magazine, the *Advocate,* Madonna denied having ever been to the Cubby Hole, let alone having slept with Bernhard. In a response to Carrie Fisher's inquiry, "So why don't you go out with women?" Madonna explained: "Because after they give me head I want them to stick it inside me. . . . I've certainly had fantasies of fucking women, but I'm not a lesbian."[34] In spite of this definitive refutation, Madonna suggested in her *Advocate* interview that her assertiveness uniquely suited her to be "a really good mascot or spokesperson or something" for lesbians.[35]

Despite this contrary testimony, many lesbians continue to thrive on the possibility of a kindred spirit in Madonna. For instance, Sydney Pokorny, from *Gay Community News,* who calls Madonna a "double agent who sells out to the other side," also cites Madonna as "my favorite post-Stonewall lesbian sex symbol." But how is a lesbian to reconcile Madonna's ongoing rendition of our identities as a joke? In interview after interview she maintained:

> I've never been to the Cubby Hole. That's the joke of it. Sandra and I were just fucking with people. . . . Then, of course, it got out of hand and I didn't want to do it anymore, because it was more important for me to have a friendship.[36]

In contrast to almost every other act of identity appropriation Madonna has deployed throughout her career, the claim to "be" a lesbian, she insisted, was just "an inside joke."[37] But for whose "inside," one might ask, is Madonna's excursion into lesbianism a joke? Is it here that Madonna invokes a discourse of privacy to protect her from the possible repercussions of an identity whose inhabitation might not reap financial reward?

Always a context-sensitive performer, Madonna changed her tune during her interview at the *Advocate:*

> The fact is, she's a great friend of mine, whether I'm gay or not is irrelevant. Whether I slept with her or not is irrelevant. I'm perfectly willing to have people think that I did. You know, I do not want to protest too much. I don't care. If it makes people feel better to think that I slept with her, then they can think it. And if it makes them feel safer to think that I didn't, then that's fine too.
>
> You know, I'd almost rather that they thought I did. Just so they could know that here was this girl that everyone was buying records of, and she was eating someone's pussy. So there.[38]

In the *Advocate* Madonna deflects the question of "truth" to the interpretive acumen of her spectators. Leaving the stable contours of her "real" identity to her fans, Madonna manages to revel in her heterosexuality while flirting with the identities of her gay and lesbian devotées. But her peculiar formulation of denial in the mainstream press—the joke that is really a joke—suggests her return to a protected sphere of private "real" identity. For, while she grants her gay and lesbian fans the erotic delight of ambiguity, she poses the debate explicitly in terms of what makes a spectator "feel better." In this case *she* provides the gauge of authenticity: the truth, she insists, is that she and Sandra were "just friends." In true Platonic form "copies are second-hand possessors, well-grounded claimants, authorized by resemblance."[39] The role of the spectator in the construction (authorization) of meaning is only to verify the prior truth of heterosexuality.

But if, as Elin Diamond argues, "realism is more than an interpretation of reality passing as reality; it *produces* 'reality' by positioning its spectators to recognize and verify its truths,"[40] then Madonna's courtship of her fans' identities neatly captures the epistemological strategy at the heart of her enormous appeal. Poised on the edge of appropriation and possibility, Madonna foregrounds the act of *making truth* as a crucial component of the performative transaction. Eluding the issue of authenticity, Madonna's persona invites the spectator to acknowledge her own role as interpretive referee. Such a method both avoids responsibility for cultural appropriation and forms the basis of her interest to those communities whose voices and images are often stifled in other mainstream representations. In effect, Madonna raises gossip to the high art of identity: it doesn't matter if she is or she isn't; what matters is that she solicits our opinions.

Such interlocutory address may offer little solace to those subjects whose identities constitute the repertoire of Madonna's personae. Endowing her fans with an elusive interpretive power, this analysis may seem to beg the question of politics by legitimating the deconstructive bliss of her MTV salute to cultural diversity ("It doesn't matter if you're black or white, a boy or a girl"). But identity politics is invited, for the spectator of Madonna, to materialize as a skill of reading. Our answer to her question—*is she or isn't she*—is intimately connected to the complex systems of cultural literacy with which we engage when we read her self-constructions. To imagine identity politics as a skill of reading is to reject the burden of the "real" and replace it with the exigencies of daily vision. For, surely, reading is neither a naive nor essentialist activity; one need not claim the ground of purity to reject another's style of perception. As distinguished drag queen Dorian Corey reminds us in Jennie Livingston's film *Paris is Burning,* the *read* is "the fine art of insults."

If, as Judith Butler has claimed, "the body *is* a historical situation ... and is a manner of doing, dramatizing, and *reproducing* a historical situation,"[41] then Madonna's authorizing strategies are inextricable from the dramas of appropriation that constitute her *as* phenomenon. Locating her body as a stage of identities, Cindy Fuchs argues that each Madonna incarnation "surpasses her own image as a newly constituted type."[42] Situating her most recent "look" as an overdetermined essence, Madonna rewrites herself in what can be seen as the familiar gesture of appropriation she extends to others. But, if in her interviews Madonna deflects the dilemma of authenticity to her spectators, then in her performances she explores the problem of appropriation as a function of her own corporeal command. In this sense her authorizing strategies are the subject of the spectacle and anticipate her rise to fame as the erotic diva of self-creation.

In his essay "The Economics of Linguistic Exchange" Pierre Bourdieu asks what authorizes language usage and rejects pure semiotic explanations of linguistic competence (the ability to endlessly generate grammatically regular discourse) in favor of an analysis of the symbolic market, in which "the power of words is never anything other than the power to mobilize the authority accumulated within a field." Bourdieu argues that:

> We learn that the efficacy of a discourse, its power to convince, depends on the authority of the person who utters it. . . . A person speaks not only to be understood, but also to be believed, obeyed, respected, distinguished.[43]

While Bourdieu's analysis concerns a primarily linguistic contract, his tendency to read strategies instead of truths facilitates a reading of Madonna that does not merely reproduce the "truth" of identity in an attempt to frustrate her parasitic infatuation with the margins. Claiming identity as performative, Madonna confiscates the principal signs of an/other's identity; claiming to own that identity, one can name her performance as theft. But such grounds of resistance merely substitute the perils of exchange value for the dangers of use value, replacing the fluidity of identity with the faithful stability of the propertied self. To claim use-value as an antidote to exchange-value is simply to construct an elaborate "alibi"[44] for an oppositional reclamation of authenticity and "natural" essence. In this section, I hope to avoid such an impasse by reading Madonna's strategies of authorization not as evidence of her private self, but, rather, as testimony to her successful commodification of privacy. If in the terms of mimesis the claim to "the private" is equivalent to a dispensation of authenticity, then perhaps privacy is, for Madonna, the penultimate simulacrum. As Henry Louis Gates, Jr., recently observed, in the marketplace of values "authenticity remains essential: once you can fake that, you've got it made."[45] Madonna's remarkable access to the center stage of American culture is therefore, like the simulacrum, indebted to (rather than in spite of) her unrelenting vision of authority as a necessary version of appropriation.[46]

In 1986 *Papa Don't Preach* became the first of a series of trademark "controversial" videos that would establish Madonna "herself" as the subject of media speculation. Nationally syndicated columnist Ellen Goodman called the video "a commercial for teenage pregnancy," while groups opposed to abortion embraced it as a "pro-life . . . alternative." Madonna resolved the dispute by describing the video as "a message song that everyone [was] going to take the wrong way," but her publicist, Liz Rosenberg, hastened to add, "She's singing a song, not taking a stand."[47] The video itself alternates between two competing representations of Madonna. The first-person lyrics emanate from a dark and empty stage, where a curly blond Madonna is dressed in sleek black pedal pushers and a plain black bustier; the slice of life drama offers a linear realism in which Madonna, dressed in jeans and loosely fitting shirt, enacts the story of a young Italian-American woman pleading with her father to accept her decision to keep her baby. The two visions of Madonna form a bridge between two styles of dramatic address, but, in retrospect, the media controversy ignored the movie star segments and focused exclusively on her rare display of fourth-wall realism. Charging coercion, both sides saw the video as an invitation to a certain way of life, denying *Papa Don't Preach* its stylistic invocation of a rhetoric of self-authorization.

While the slice-of-life portion of the video focuses on the family drama played out between Madonna and her father (played by Danny Aiello), Madonna the star voices the accompanying chorus of domestic conflict:

> Papa don't preach. I'm in trouble deep.
> Papa don't preach. I've been losing sleep.
> But I made up my mind, I'm keeping my baby
> I'm gonna keep my baby, mmm.

Using a rhetoric of "choice" as a license to remain pregnant, the video disintegrates the inviolate binaries of the abortion debate by employing the terms of pro-choice to insist on an antiabortion outcome. But, simultaneously, the video reproduces *the* informing dichotomy of the abortion debate: it poses an optic binary between a "private" domestic sphere and a "public" sphere of negotiated performance. Inviting us into the intimate setting of a domestic household (replete with close shots of mealtimes, bedtimes, and Danny Aiello's tattoos), *Papa Don't Preach* stages the private sphere as the "real" in visual contest with a public space of deliberate theatricality.

For those social subjects who have been made equivalent to the "private," or private property, privacy has often served as an efficacious discourse of social inclusion. What Patricia Williams designates

as legal "alchemy" denotes the necessarily arduous task of transforming a selective barrier into an inviting aperture of institutional representation. For privacy has historically been used as a gauge of cultural
legitimacy, buttressing the legal exclusion of those subjects deemed
unfit for juridical representation. In *Bowers v. Hardwick,* for example,
the Supreme Court upheld a Georgia antisodomy statute, judging
homosexuality a threat to the very notion of privacy itself as a protected sphere. The ruling relied on an earlier case in which Justice
Scalia had defined the scope of the Fourteenth Amendment's "liberty
clause," the clause under which the "right to privacy" has conventionally been enumerated:

> In an attempt to limit and guide interpretation of the Clause, we
> have insisted not merely that the interest denominated as a "lib-
> erty" be "fundamental" (a concept, that, in isolation, is hard to
> objectify), but also that it be an interest traditionally protected
> by our society. As we have put it, the Due Process Clause affords
> only those protections "so rooted in the traditions and conscience
> of our people as to be ranked as fundamental." Our cases reflect
> "continual insistence upon respect for the teachings of history
> [and] solid recognition of the basic values that underlie our soci-
> ety."[48]

In Scalia's formula, the basis for the majority opinion in Bowers,
the "right to privacy" is unabashedly a function of the normative.
As such, it (as well as the court's limitation of abortion rights in
Webster v. Reproductive Services) uncannily echoes the Court's 1896
ruling in *Plessy v. Ferguson:*

> In determining the question of reasonableness [the legislature] is
> at liberty to act with reference to the established usages, customs
> and traditions of the people, and with a view to the promotion
> of their comfort, and the preservation of the public peace and
> good order. Gauged by this standard, we cannot say that the law
> which authorizes or even requires the separation of the two races
> in public conveyances is unreasonable.[49]

In each of these cases the private is a function of the "usages, conventions and customs of the people" and not, as some would claim, a

"real" space prior to political negotiation. Perhaps this is why our efforts to secure gay and lesbian rights, civil rights, and reproductive freedom seem destined to fail, for we inevitably collapse a quest for human rights with a humanist discourse that pretends to offer safe havens of privacy in an effort to naturalize the very "standards of decency" that exclude us.[50]

While this detour into the juridical maze of privacy may seem peripheral to the authorizing strategies of Madonna in *Papa Don't Preach,* her video explicitly addresses the abortion debate in the terms of the private/public divide. From the working-class mechanic who dances with Madonna in the basking approval of an older Italian couple to the tender role inversions played out between father and daughter as he ages and she matures, the narrative would seem to grant corporeal control to the private dominion of the beloved patriarch. And, indeed, the antagonism produced by the video would seem to locate its diegetic command in the realistic segments. The video glorifies parental consent, however, even as it stages the "public" as the authoritative arena of speech and identity. While I would make no claim as to Madonna's intention, the video *as a whole* seems to offer a rhetoric of choice detached from its judicial spouse: the right to privacy.

The discrete opposition between a "real" and "performative" context is abandoned as the first frame of Madonna "herself" appears as the voice-over of the video. The slice-of-life portion becomes incomprehensible without the dramatic intervention of the self-consciously theatrical segments; the "I" of the lyric is commissioned by the "I" that plays to and for the camera. In the "public" sphere Madonna executes a highly controlled and conventional jazz choreography, whose strict rhythms propel her working-class facsimile to stride purposefully throughout the outdoors of the "private" domain. Utilizing a two-dimensional plane of movement and rigid upper body isolation technique, the theatrical sections emphasize a movement vocabulary of self-control mimicked in the interior scenes: shot at close range, they emphasize claustrophobic walls and floors. Posing authority as a contest between two versions of herself, *Papa Don't Preach* denies the possibility of a "right to privacy" that is not always already a function of the public staging of identity. But in so doing, Madonna fortifies the troubling binarism of private and public, even as she performs its constitutive instability. In effect, Madonna offers privacy as a commodity whose marketability derives precisely from its belated posture as the "real." As disingenuous as the "public" itself, the "private" is useful to Madonna as a tactic of predication that allows her to deploy herself as phenomenon.

By assigning the task of representation to the public arena Madonna embraces a performative paradigm of identity. But, as we have seen in her interviews, such a rejection of mimesis often serves as the prerequisite for her attribution of essence to an/other. It is this scenario, rather than a vision of disembodied racial possibility, that informs Madonna's second "controversial" video: *Like a Prayer*. Replete with burning crosses, malevolent white men, a falsely accused black man, a virtuous white woman victim, a desexualized black woman, and a credible sexualized white woman, *Like a Prayer* would seem to redeploy the lynching formula as a prime-time, white, liberal miniseries with a happy ending. Having witnessed a white gang's attack on a white woman and the false arrest of a black man, Madonna portrays herself as tormented white savior whose testimony could (and will) emancipate the black male victim/Christ figure. But this version of the story ignores the iconic sustenance of the video: the red-robed black female gospel singer who literally propels Madonna to "do the right thing." Appearing in both the banned Pepsi advertisement[51] and the Mary Lambert video (unlike the black male victim/Christ figure), the black woman choir leader takes on a crucial authorizing function in *Like a Prayer*. The media erasure of her consequence mimics the structural sequence of the video, which consistently elides her significance by focusing on the more conventional blaspheme of interracial heterosexuality.

As Madonna disappears into a Baptist church to find an answer to her ethical dilemma, she lies down on a pew, and the video moves immediately into a dream sequence. Wearing a maroon, spaghetti-strap full slip, she intones,

I close my eyes
Oh God I think I'm falling
Out of the sky
Heaven help me

and free-falls from a background of blue sky and white clouds to the reassuring arms of a black woman, who is fully clothed in the heavy

robes of a gospel choir. Not only does the choir leader literally cast
Madonna back to heaven and to the moral high ground of the narrative—the decision to testify on behalf of the black male victim—but
in the camera's frame the black woman serves as the horizontal bottom of the screen: her physical body takes the place of the Earth in
the topography of the camera's gaze. In the *New York Times* Madonna gave a play-by-play narration of this section of the video:

> She lies down on a pew and falls into a dream in which she begins
> to tumble in space with no one to break her fall. Suddenly she is
> caught by a woman who represents earth and emotional strength
> and who tosses her back up and tells her to do the right thing.[52]

Figured as material foundation, the black woman is then subject to a
displacement: her authorizing function is visually replaced by an image of Madonna kissing the feet of the black male saint.

In her essay "Black Feminist Theory and the Representation of
the 'Other'" Valerie Smith argues:

> The black woman as critic, and more broadly as the locus where
> gender-, class-, and race-based oppression intersect, is often in-
> voked when Anglo-American feminists and male Afro-Ameri-
> canists begin to rematerialize their discourse. . . . Such a formula-
> tion erases the specificity of the black woman's experience,
> constituting her as the point of intersection between black men's
> and white women's experience.[53]

While Smith's observations are directed at the practice of academic
criticism, her analysis of the routine inscription of the "embodied"
African-American woman proves instructive to the religious theatrics
of *Like a Prayer*. For the black woman who "represents earth and
emotional strength" serves not only as the material ground of Madonna's video but also as the vanishing point of intersection between
a black man and a white woman. In fact, it is only by occluding the
choir leader's authorizing function that Madonna can occupy the role
of redeemer in the narrative. While such an enabling disappearance
invokes the choir leader's symbolic function as an angel, her role in
Madonna's Catholic melodrama seems decisively anchored in a secular politic of racial convention.[54]

As Madonna prepares to enact her ethical decision, she returns to the enervating atmosphere of the gospel church, where a cherubic young black boy clothed in a white robe invites her to join their celebration. As the chorus sings,

> Just like a Prayer
> I'll take you there
> It's like a dream to me,

Madonna dances ecstatically with the same black woman who now sings solo on the line, *"I'll* take you there." Gently pressing Madonna's head down to the floor, the two women dance together, as Madonna, in her own words, "reaches an orgasmic crescendo of sexual fulfillment intertwined with the love of God."[55] It is this erotic dance of spiritual and power *inequity* that launches Madonna out of her dream and back onto the church pew, where the Christ figure lies on top of her and tenderly kisses her awake. In other words, a scene of explicit power disparity is countered with a scene of heterosexual interracial reciprocity. An inverse repetition of the previous sequence, the white woman who has kissed the feet of the black man from below is now the object of his kiss from above.

In both scenes the black woman serves as a conduit for the sacrilegious heterosexual encounter—a scenario that eclipses the foundational character of her role. While I am not suggesting that *Like a Prayer* enacts an interracial lesbian spectacle, I am arguing that the erotics of appropriation (dramatized between the two women) are replaced by a utopian interracial heterosexuality in which the white woman is always already constituted as redemptive savior. In this respect the media proved complicit with the video, for almost no references to the choir leader's role can be found in the ensuing fracas over *Like a Prayer* and its Pepsi commercial cousin. In refusing to confront the exhibition of white prerogative which propels the video, the media enabled Madonna to portray herself as radical subversive.[56] Duplicating the strategy of the video itself, even her most vehement critics licensed her status as embattled patron of the Other.

As in all of Madonna's dramas of appropriation, the video solicits the spectator as the ground of the "real." *Like a Prayer* ends with a company bow and the lowering of a red curtain onto what now becomes visible as a proscenium stage. As THE END appears in white

cursive across the curtain, the video acknowledges its status as performance and petitions the spectator to acknowledge her role as witness.
To this end Cindy Fuchs maintains:

> In turning our attention to the artifice of the production, the
> video also insists on our spectatorship as a source of the text's
> meaning. We have watched Madonna's dream about watching,
> a drama that ends by re-naming that activity as a socially culpable
> performance. (44)

Fuchs's persuasive argument positions the spectator as Other to the
artifice of the text, only to implicate this audience in a self-conscious
"drama about watching." But for what activity has Madonna named
the spectator responsible? It is this question that I would like to examine in the context of Madonna's most recent foray into the controversial. *Justify My Love,* the video that even MTV wouldn't broadcast,
is as explicit in its references to "deviant" sexual practice as it is to its
own theatricality.

During her appearance on "Nightline" following the worldwide
release of *Justify My Love* as the first video single ever, Madonna
claimed that MTV objected to the "whole tone" of the video, that
there was no one scene in particular that disturbed the censors.[57] And
yet the media focused almost exclusively on her steamy tongue kiss
with Amanda Cazelot, the androgynous Parisian model, who is reported to have said: "After seeing it [*Justify My Love*] the first thing
you want to do is make love. She knew exactly what she wanted. She
had this inner power which is extraordinary."[58] The erotic texture of
Justify My Love is accompanied by the equally erotic camera work
that guides the spectator through the narrow halls of a black and
white hotel. Commensurate with the spectator's eye *except* for the
"lesbian" spectacle, the camera revels in the seductive gaze of power
imbalance. *Justify My Love* is less a paean to sadomasochism than it
is a testimony to the power of the voyeur: performing exquisite
pleasures for the privileged eye of the camera, the video relishes the
spectatorial experience as a seductive invasion of a private expanse.

Justify My Love opens with a quick flash of visual clarity, which
is rapidly replaced by the camera's blurry lens. From the outset, then,
Justify My Love installs the apparatus of the camera as a subject of the
spectacle. This self-consciousness is accompanied by the video's only

"colored" presence; clad in a full bodysuit with speckled hair and clawlike fingernails, he recedes into illegibility as the lens clouds. Intelligible only for an instant, this androgynous (read: not-male) and racially ambiguous (read: not-white) dancer is collapsed with the filmic apparatus; like a symptom, he serves as an ongoing reminder of this *theater* of desire. But, as Slavoj Žižek reminds us, the key to the symptom is "not the secret *behind* the form, but the secret of *this form itself*."[59] As such, his alterity assumes the formal character of a hesitation between acts; his sculpted conjure movements form a narrative bridge *between* each room of the video's fantasy. Figured as intermission to an ongoing parade of white leather-clad cohorts, the conjure figure is barred from active participation in the onscreen play, but serves as the literal screen on which it is enacted. Functioning as this fantasy's "limit-text"[60]—the exception against which the unruly norm is defined—he positions the spectator as a vantage point of command in what will be an erotic spectacle of appropriation.

For the majority of the video the spectator is positioned with the camera, consuming a dyadic procession of white "perversion." From a heterosexual couple miming sodomy to a nipple-pierced dominatrix roughly stroking her male bottom's crotch, the video provides an erotic exhibition to the husky accompaniment of Madonna whispering, "Wanting . . . Needing . . . Waiting / For You . . . To Justify My Love." But, as the possibility of a lesbian embrace emerges on the screen, the camera dissolves its sole position as spectator of the boudoir. Instead, the faint stubble of Tony Ward's beard emerges through the bodies on the bed. As the camera confirms the lesbian spectacle by panning the top figure's back and bra, Tony Ward—hot and bothered—keeps an agitated vigil by the bedside. Visibly aroused, he shifts in his chair, as Madonna hungrily kisses the androgynous woman lying on top of her. Rendering the spectator manifest, Ward plays the role as a participatory voyeur. The much heralded lesbian exhibition is thus soldered to an explicit invocation of spectatorship. Like the two women who draw mascara mustaches on each other to the amused background chuckle of Madonna, the scandal of the video is in its impersonation of its audience.

While I am not attributing such acute self-consciousness to the MTV censors, I believe the discomfort produced by *Justify My Love* lies in the sly joke it plays on its viewer. Like *Open Your Heart*, Madonna's most accessible mock tribute to the spectator, the audience is designated as an active consumer of the voyeuristic. But, for those spectators immersed in the vicissitudes of Hollywood romance, Tony Ward also served to safely ensconce the lesbian spectacle in a heterosexual frame of vision. As Madonna's "real-life" lover, he assuages the potential subversion of her lesbian exhibition by functioning as the equivalent of a heterosexual "safe-word" in this racy impersonation of sadomasochistic practice.[61] In tandem with the conjure figure, then, Ward establishes the video as a *performance* of s/m, which, unlike its practice (however performative), requires a third person to license its titillating exhibition. If the conjure figure is indeed a symptom of the camera's gaze, then in the act of seeing, the spectator engages in the erotic power play on the screen as a willful and necessary ocular participant. Such an inscription in the perverse order of *Justify My Love* establishes the spectatorial relationship within the visual terms of s/m performance. Constituted as the *outside* of this paradigmatically *insider* experience, the conjure figure records the fantasy from a position of exclusion, marking a textual bottom to the viewer's top. Implicit in our pleasure in the video, therefore, is its homage to appropriation as erotic play.

Like many of Madonna's videos, *Justify My Love* offers its viewers an invitation to invade a privacy which is always already an illusory space of intimate revelation. But unlike either *Papa Don't Preach* or *Like a Prayer, Justify My Love* acknowledges its own authorizing strategies by taking as its subject the erotics of appropriation. If, as Donna Haraway writes, "Vision requires instruments of vision, an optics is a politics of positioning,"[62] then Madonna's theater of appropriation is, above all, a theater of spectatorial complicity. As we engage with her manifold self-constructions, it is the erotics of decoding[63] that replaces the uncertain pleasures of her relation to the "real." To "read" her, then, is to own our accountability for the texts we laboriously decipher.

Few of Madonna's interviewers fail to mention the exquisite irony of her fabled "privacy pledge," a document that, in effect, prohibits her staff and dancers from corroborating anything but the official version of her multiple selves. For a woman who, as Warren Beatty strategically phrased it in *Truth or Dare*, "doesn't want to live off-camera, much less talk," her imposition of a contractual privacy agreement seems, at the very least, to inhabit the paradox of her relationship to the "real." In fact, if we are to address her popularity as a function of her dedicated audiences, then the "privacy pledge" installs a visible apparatus of access to Madonna that anticipates the wanna-be phenomenon in all of its bilateral manifestations. Deploying privacy like a decoy, she entices her audience with the possibility of a genuine knowledge, which, in return, forms the reservoir of her personae. *Is she or isn't she,* we wonder, as she accumulates millions at the expense of our continued fascination.

NOTES

I would like to thank Elizabeth Alexander, Wendy Bach, Jennifer Brody, Anne Cubilie, Nicole King, and Rona Robinson for their generous wisdom and support.

Epigraph from "White Heat" by Kevin Sessums, *Vanity Fair*, April 1990, 148.

1. "Vogue," as performed at the 1990 MTV Awards, written by Madonna and Patrick Leonard, *Madonna: The Immaculate Collection,* Warner Reprise Video 3–38195.

2. Camille Paglia, "Madonna—Finally a Real Feminist," *New York Times,* 14 December 1990, A29.

3. Ibid.

4. "Papa Don't Preach," written by Brian Elliot, with additional lyrics by Madonna; dir. Jamie Foley. "Like a Prayer," performed by Madonna and the Andrae Crouch Choir; written by Madonna and Patrick Leonard; dir. Mary Lambert. Both these videos are commercially available on *Madonna: The Immaculate Collection.* "Justify My Love," written by Madonna and Lenny Kravitz; dir. Jean-Baptiste Mondino, *Justify My Love.* Warner Reprise Video 3–38224. All further references are cited from this version.

5. Sydney Pokorny, "Obsess Yourself? The Root of My Obsession with Sandra and Madonna Is Unbridled Lust," *Gay Community News,* July–August 1989.

6. Christopher Anderson, *Madonna Unauthorized* (New York: Simon and Schuster, 1991), 334.

7. Becky Johnston, "Confession of a Catholic Girl," *Interview,* May 1989, 55.

8. Susan Willis, *A Primer for Daily Life* (London: Routledge, 1991). In her chapter "I Want the Black One: Is There a Place for Afro-American Culture in Commodity Culture," Willis uses this phrase to describe Michael Jackson, "the consummate expression of the commodity form" (122). While she makes no mention of Madonna, some of her critique of Jackson seems appropriate in this context. In general, Willis's work expresses the position of those who recommend a return to use-value to combat the triumph of exchange value in the commodity age.

9. See in particular: Luce Irigaray, *This Sex Which Is Not One,* trans. Catherine Porter (Ithaca, N.Y.: Cornell University Press, 1985); and Abdul R. JanMo-

hamed, *Manichean Aesthetics: The Politics of Literature in Colonial Africa* (Amherst: University of Massachusetts Press, 1983). Please also see indirect responses: Gayatri Chakravorty Spivak, "Scattered Speculations on the Question of Value," *In Other Worlds: Essays in Cultural Politics* (New York: Methuen, 1987); and Jean Baudrillard, "For a Critique of the Political Economy of the Sign," *Selected Writings,* ed. Mark Poster (Stanford, Calif.: Stanford University Press, 1988).

10. Arjun Appadurai, ed. "Introduction: Commodities and the Politics of Value," *The Social Life of Things: Commodities in Cultural Perspective* (Cambridge: Cambridge University Press, 1986).

11. Lauren Berlant, "National Brands/National Body: *Imitation of Life*," *Comparative American Identities: Race, Sex, and Nationality in the Modern Text,* ed. Hortense Spillers (London: Routledge, 1991), 139. In a vastly different context she claims that there is "no prophylactic private sphere, no space safe from performance or imitation." My thinking on the public/private debate is particularly indebted to: Carol Pateman, "Feminist Critiques of the Public/Private Dichotomy," *Disorder of Women: Democracy, Feminism and Political Theory* (Cambridge, Mass.: Polity Press, 1989), 118–40; Linda Frasier, "Rethinking the Public Sphere: A Contribution to the Critique of Actually Thinking Democracy," *Social Text* (London: Verso, 1985), 56–80; J. A. Pocock, *The Machiavellian Moment: Florentine Political Thought in the Republican Tradition* (Princeton, N.Y.: Princeton University Press, 1975); and *Virtue, Commerce and History: Essays on Political Thought and History* (Cambridge: Cambridge University Press, 1985).

12. John Locke, "Of Property," *Two Treatises of Government,* ed. Thomas I. Cook (New York: Hafner, 1947), 134.

13. Patricia Williams, *The Alchemy of Race and Rights* (Cambridge, Mass.: Harvard University Press, 1991), 124. Williams makes this comment in relationship to a white transsexual student who comes to her in desperation after being barred from every bathroom on campus following her sex change operation.

14. See Oscar Wilde, *The Picture of Dorian Gray* (1891; reprint, London: Penguin Books, 1985).

15. *Madonna: Blond Ambition World Tour* (Boy Toy/Music Tours, 1990).

16. Matthew Schifrin with Peter Newcomb, "A Brain for Sin and a Bod for Business," *Forbes,* 1 October 1990, 162.

17. Patricia Meyer Spacks, *Gossip* (New York: Alfred A. Knopf, 1985), 261. I am indebted to this landmark study.

18. Anderson, *Madonna Unauthorized,* 109–11. See also Douglas Thompson, *Madonna Revealed* (New York: Birch Lane Press, 1991). This is not a rare practice. Artists such as Mariah Carey, Lisa Stansfield, and Tina-Marie have been explicitly marketed as "ambiguous" or black to target black radio stations. In the case of Mariah Carey she was marketed as "tawny" until, confronted with media speculation, she presented her African-American father.

19. Bill Zehme, "Madonna: The *Rolling Stone,* Interview," *Rolling Stone,* 23 May 1989, 58.

20. Schifrin, "A Brain for Sin," 163.

21. Mary Harron, "McRock: Pop as Commodity," *Facing the Music,* ed. Si-

mon Frith (New York: Pantheon Books, 1989), 216. In this same collection see also Steve Perry, "Ain't No Mountain High Enough: The Politics of Cross-over."

22. Anderson, *Madonna Unauthorized,* 210.

23. Kobena Mercer, "Black Hair/Style Politics," *New Formations* 3 (Winter 1987): 35.

24. Stephen Holden, "Madonna Re-Creates Herself—Again," *New York Times Magazine,* 19 March 1989.

25. Laura B. Randolph, "Arsenio Talks about His Feuds with Roseanne and Madonna and the Rumors about Him and Eddie," *Ebony* (December 1990): 58. On a less positive note Arsenio responded to rumors of his homosexuality by saying, "When you challenge a Black man's . . . manhood . . . there are no rules anymore" (56).

26. Please see Plato, "Allegory of the Cave," *Plato's Republic,* trans. Francis MacDonald Cornford (Oxford: Oxford University Press, 1991). Also see Luce Irigaray, *Speculum of the Other Woman,* trans. Gillian G. Gill (Ithaca, N.Y.: Cornell University Press, 1985); Homi Bhabha, "Of Mimicry and Man," *October* 28 (Spring 1984): 124–33; and, in this volume, Elin Diamond, "Mimesis, Mimicry, and the 'True-Real,'" (orig. in *Modern Drama* 32, no. 1 [March 1989]: 58–72).

27. Gilles Deleuze, "Plato and the Simulacrum," *October* 27 (Winter 1983): 48.

28. I develop this idea further in the context of the cultural performance of passing. See my *To Pass//In Drag: Strategies of Entrance into the Visible* (Ph.d. diss., University of Pennsylvania, 1992).

29. As cited in Deleuze, "Plato and the Simulacrum," 49.

30. Marge Garber, *Vested Interests: Cross-Dressing and Cultural Anxiety* (New York: Routledge, 1992), 168.

31. Lynn Hirschberg, "The Misfit," *Vanity Fair,* April 1991, 200. She cites her desire to pee standing up in many interviews. Madonna's gender disruptions have been elegantly documented in the work of E. Ann Kaplan and others.

32. In Don Shewey, "The Saint, the Slut, the Sensation . . . Madonna," *Advocate,* 7 May 1991, 48.

33. Ibid., 44.

34. Carrie Fisher, "True Confessions: The *Rolling Stone* Interview with Madonna," *Rolling Stone,* 13 and 27 June 1991, 40 and 120.

35. Don Shewey, "The Gospel according to St. Madonna," *Advocate,* 21 May 1991, 41.

36. This particular example is from Sessums, "White Heat," 21.

37. Zehme, "Madonna," 182. "Well, yes, we threw that out to confuse people. It was definitely an inside joke for people in New York. I mean, I've never been to the Cubby Hole, I just think its hysterical "

38. Shewey, "Saint," 51.

39. Gilles Deleuze, "Plato and the Simulacrum," 48

40. Diamond, "Mimesis" (orig. p. 60).

41. Judith Butler, "Performative Acts and Gender Constitution: An Essay in Phenomenology and Feminist Theory," *Theatre Journal* (December 1988): 521.

42. Cindy Fuchs, "'I don't want to live out your fantasy': Sex and Subject in Madonna's Performances" (unpub. MS), 7.

43. Pierre Bourdieu, "The Economics of Linguistic Exchange," *Social Science Information* (1977): 649, 653.

44. Please see Jean Baudrillard, "For a Critique of the Political Economy of the Sign."

45. "'Authenticity,' or the Lesson of Little Tree," *New York Times Book Review,* 24 November 1991, 29.

46. This style of self-authorization is reminiscent of Jacques Lacan's work on the mirror stage. In this scenario authority is a necessary function of appropriation as the "I" establishes its fiction of coherence by misrecognizing itself in the Other.

47. Ellen Goodman, "Commercial for Teenage Pregnancy," *Washington Post,* 20 September 1986. Other quotes cited in Georgia Dullea, "Madonna's New Beat Is a Hit, but Song's Message Rankles," *New York Times,* 18 September 1986, B9.

48. Cited in Lawrence H. Tribe, *Abortion: The Clash of Absolutes* (New York: W. W. Norton, 1990), 92.

49. Justice Brown's decision, as cited in Richard Kluger, *Simple Justice: The History of* Brown v. Board of Education *and Black America's Struggle for Equality* (New York: Vintage Books, 1975), 79.

50. Rather than privacy, therefore, many legal scholars suggest that we pursue legal redress under the Fourteenth Amendment's equal protection clause.

51. On 2 March 1989 the National Broadcasting Company showed a ten million dollar Pepsi Cola advertisement starring Madonna and the music from her *Like a Prayer* video, which would be released the following day. The commercial aired only once and a month later was withdrawn due to pressure from fundamentalist groups led by the American Family Association. Pepsi claimed consumer "confusion between the ad and a Madonna music video which depicts the singer kissing a saint and coming away with stigmata" (Peter Waldman, "This Madonna Isn't What the Reverend Really Had in Mind," *The Wall Street Journal,* 7 April 1989.

52. Holden, *New York Times Magazine,* 19 March 1989, 13.

53. Valerie Smith, "Black Feminist Theory and the Representation of the 'Other,'" *Changing Our Own Words,* ed. Cheryl Wall (New Brunswick, N.J.: Rutgers University Press, 1989), 44, 47.

54. I have obviously chosen to focus on the secular dynamics of Madonna's work throughout this essay. For an analysis that takes into account the religious symbolism of her imagery as well as Madonna's reworking of the virgin/whore dichotomy, please see E. Ann Kaplan, *Rocking around the Clock: Music Television, Postmodernism, and Consumer Culture* (New York: Methuen, 1987). John Fiske, "British Cultural Studies and Television," in *Channels of Discourse,* ed. Robert C. Allen (Chapel Hill: University of North Carolina Press, 1987) also deals extensively with Madonna's relation to the image. Also see Susan McClary, "Living to Tell: Madonna's Resurrection of the Fleshly," *Genders* 7 (Spring

1990), for a more optimistic reading of *Like a Prayer,* which takes into account the complex musical significance of Madonna's work.

55. Holden, "Madonna Re-Creates Herself Again."

56. Since this essay was completed for publication, bell hooks's article on Madonna ("Madonna: Plantation Mistress or Soul Sister") has appeared in her book *Black Looks* (Boston: South End Press, 1991). hooks's caustic examination of Madonna's appropriation of black culture, as well as her specific interrogation of *Like a Prayer,* is the rare exception to the media celebration of Madonna's "transgression."

57. "Nightline" interview with Forest Sawyer, 3 December 1990.

58. Thompson, *Madonna Revealed,* 154.

59. Slavoj Žižek, *The Sublime Object of Ideology* (London: Verso, 1989), 15.

60. Homi Bhabha "The Other Question: Difference, Discrimination and the Discourse of Colonialism," in *Literature, Politics and Theory* (Papers from the Essex Conference), ed. Francis Barker, Peter Hulme, Margaret Iversen, and Diana Loxley (London: Methuen, 1986), 151. He writes, "The place of otherness is fixed in the west as a subversion of western metaphysics and is finally appropriated by the west as its limit-text, anti-west."

61. I am indebted to Elizabeth Alexander for pointing out this subtlety of the popular connoisseur.

62. Donna Haraway, "Situated Knowledges: The Science Question in Feminism and the Privilege of Partial Perspective," *Feminist Studies* 14, no. 3 (Fall 1988): 586.

63. In *Vested Interests,* Marge Garber writes, "For decoding itself is an erotics—in fact, one of the most powerful we know" (161).

Chapter 18

Mimesis, Mimicry, and the "True-Real"

Elin Diamond

The question came up in a plenary session in a recent conference on feminist theory and practice: Can there be a feminist mimesis?[1] The question raises perplexing problems for feminists in theater studies, a few of which I want to consider here. Mimesis, from its earliest and varied enunciations, posits a *truthful* relation between world and word, model and copy, nature and image, or, in semiotic terms, referent and sign, in which potential difference is subsumed by sameness. In book 10 of *The Republic* Plato denounces mimesis as a dangerous and illusory model-copy structure; in his triadic hierarchy true Forms, mirrored by second-order visible objects, are in turn mirrored or imitated by third-order copies. Aristotle, on the other hand, focuses his *Poetics* on the more ambiguous "action" as object of mimesis, praising the heuristic benefits of imitation for spectators, who as children learned by imitating and as adults enjoy identifying the models invoked by an artist's "imitations."[2] Renaissance and Neoclassical theories, tied complexly to shifting definitions of Nature, emphasize the artist's distinctive embellishments, not the slavish copying of models,[3] while for Romantics the artist's "soul," emotions, and psyche are the proper source or ground for poetic creation.[4] But, even if we acknowledge a play of ambiguity in Aristotle's "imitation of an action" and recall the Neoclassical preference for creation over copy, or the romantic valorization of subjective temperament, there is in all mimetic representation an implied axiology, the upholding of truth. For feminists this "truth"—usually understood as Truth, a neutral, omnipotent, changeless essence—is inseparable from gender-based and biased epistemologies.[5] That is, the model of imitation may be the Platonic Ideal, or Aristotle's universal type; Truth may be conceived as model-copy adequation, or as an unveiling, "that which shows itself or *appears*";[6] but in all cases the epistemological, morphological, *universal* standard for measuring the true is the masculine, the universal male who stands in for God the Father. "Phallogocentrism" (Derrida's coinage, following Lacan)[7] inflects this embedded hierarchy; in the logos, language itself, the phallic signifier organizes the production of meaning. Luce Irigaray goes further, politicizing this observation in the direction of feminist critique. She links the phallus to (Platonic, model-copy) mimesis: the female, lacking the organ of privilege, unable to symbolize her fantasies and desires in a male symbolic, is positioned as mirror to the male, reflecting back to him—*thereby demonstrating the truth of his centrality*—his own image, his Self-Same. Irigaray calls this specular operation of female erasure "mimesis imposed,"[8] the alternative for which is hysteria, a female miming that has no recognizable referent.

Before turning to Irigaray and her important reconfigurations of mimesis as mimicry, and before considering the hysteric's "true-real," I want to interject another question: Can feminism do without mimesis? Postmodern conceptions of language derived from deconstruction and Lacanian psychoanalysis are polemically antimimetic: signifier is released from signified, sign from referent, signification from intention. In its simplest sense a nonmimetic language means that a speaker can no longer lay claim to a stable system of reference, can no longer rely on language to mirror (express, represent) her entire thought. But feminism, whose empirical, historical project continues to be the recovery of women's texts and activities, has a stake in truth—in contributing to the accumulation and organization of knowledge by which a culture values or forgets its past, attends to the divergences of the present. And this axiological concern, it seems to me, crosses ideological barriers among the feminisms. That is, whether a feminist views the problematic of the signifier and of representational systems through a postmodernist prism or through a historical-materialist lens, the critique of patriarchy carries with it a commitment to the truth value of one's own position, however complex and nuanced one's account of that position might be. To critique the representations of dominant male culture one assumes the correctness of one's own models, whether one defines them as oppositional or, as Sue-Ellen Case and Jill Dolan have more subtly phrased it, "resistant."[9]

Feminism has, I believe, important things to gain from postmodernism. The decentered postmodern subject implies the dismantling of the canonical cogito/self, whose inferior other has been traditionally gendered female. If "difference" seems to have become the theorist's privileged trope,[10] it also has proved a powerful rhetorical lever for prying open any hegemonic binary, even, as Teresa de Lauretis has recently argued, the male-female binary of "sexual difference."[11] Feminists, in our different constituencies, with our different objects of analysis, seek to intervene in the symbolic systems—linguistic, theatrical, political, psychological—and intervention requires assuming a subject position, however provisional, and making truth claims, however flexible, concerning one's own representations.

Theorizing from the site of theater, feminists have a particular interest in the problematic of mimesis. Theater, like feminism, finds it difficult to rid itself of the mimetic structure, not only because the drama was Aristotle's specific object for articulating the rules of mimetic art but also because the discourse of theater, like the discourse of feminism, cannot rid itself of the temptation to refer, to emplot, to remember, to show. The actor's body cannot forget its gender (in the most exciting feminist practice performers remember with a vengeance), cannot shake off the referential frame imposed by text, mode of production, and spectators' narrativity (those trajectories of scopic desire that performer and performance text can only partially control). In fact, certain texts of early realism provoked excitement when middle-class women found, for the first time, mimetic models that sparked and mollified both political and emotional desire. Of Elizabeth Robins's performance, as the first Hedda Gabler on the London stage (1891), an acquaintance commented: "Hedda is all of us."[12] Speaking unabashedly for "all women," this female spectator designates Hedda as the ultimate referent. Insisting on her mimetic relation to Ibsen's fiction, she verifies not only the truth of the representation but also reaffirms the solidity, the correctness of her own ideological position.

Realism, the modern theater's response to mimesis, has been decried, deservedly, for precisely these reactions. Realism's putative object, the truthful representation of social experience, remains a problematic issue for feminism, not least because theatrical realism, rooted historically in domestic melodrama, retains melodrama's oedipal family focus, even as it tries to undermine the scenarios that

Victorian culture had reified—the angelic wife, the lost child, the poor but faithful husband, the fallen woman, among others. In line with Diderot's tragedy for the common man, late-nineteenth-century social realism establishes its authenticity against the "artificiality" of Neoclassical rules, and against Romantic "historical" melodrama, by carving out a "natural" present. The walls of the patriarchal drawing room and later the oedipal family living room—particularly the fourth wall—created a privileged space for breathing what Zola called "the free air of reality."[13] The notion that realism offers, as William Archer put it, "an unexaggerating mirror of real life" follows the curve of Plato's condemnation of mimesis but inverts the valuation.[14] The lifelike stage sign is not only validated by, it also reinforces the epistemology of, an "objective world," for the referent does not simply exist (the historical drawing room on which Hedda Gabler's is modeled); it is reaffirmed in the activity of reception. Realism is more than an interpretation of reality passing as reality; it *produces* "reality" by positioning its spectator to recognize and verify its truths: this escritoire, this spirit lamp, affirms the typicality, the universality of this and all bourgeois drawing rooms. Human signification becomes no less teleological. In realism the actor/signifier, laminated to her character/signified, strenuously seeks admission to the right class of referents.

With Brechtian hindsight we know that realism, more than any other form of theater representation, mystifies the process of theatrical signification. Because it naturalizes the relation between character and actor, setting and world, realism operates in concert with ideology. And because it depends on, insists on a *stability* of reference, an objective world that is the source and guarantor of knowledge, realism surreptitiously reinforces (even if it argues with) the arrangements of that world. Realism's fetishistic attachment to the true referent and the spectator's invitation to rapturous identification with a fictional imago serve the ideological function of mystifying the means of material production, thereby concealing historical contradictions, while reaffirming or mirroring the "truth" of the status quo.

But if, as Derrida highhandedly asserts, mimesis is representation at its most naive,[15] surely realism is mimesis at its most naive—its positivist moment, which, historicized, can be codified, critiqued, even as we acknowledge that its appeal is as strong in Reagan's America as it was in Gladstone's Britain. Mimesis, however, cannot so easily be seen, framed, gotten around. Brechtian theory gives us the means of defusing realism's narrativity, of prying loose actor/signifier from character/signified, of exposing or alienating the illusionistic apparatus, but Brecht never denied referentiality; he aimed rather to expunge the psychologized ahistorical referent. In Brecht's plays the subject's dialectical struggle ceases only in a socialist future, when the capitalist state has been dismantled, but that Brecht's much wished for proletarian spectators could imagine themselves as new referents is imminent in the *Lehrstück* mode of address. In effect, Brecht insisted on more mimesis, not less: "The first thing therefore is to comprehend the new subject-matter; the second to shape the new relations. The reason: *art follows reality*. . . . Can we speak of money in the form of iambics? . . . Petroleum resists the five-act play" (my emphasis).[16] Feminists would add that female experience and desire, and the new relations thereby effected, also resists the five-act play. I have argued elsewhere that Brechtian theory and feminist theory, read intertextually, create the basis for a flexible materialist criticism.[17] As I hope to demonstrate below, Irigaray and Kristeva offer conceptualizations of mimetic theory that contribute to this project. Let me simply note here that Brecht provides a salutary reminder that it is through some manipulation of referentiality that the political may be broached.

Reading (and resisting) in the spirit of Brechtian historicization but through a feminist lens, Sue-Ellen Case links the gender bias across social organizations in ancient Greek culture to Aristotle's prescriptions and proscriptions in the *Poetics,* concluding that just as Aristotle denies women the capacity to exemplify tragic virtues, the erasure of women from social representation means that "mimesis is not possible for [them]."[18] Case notes that Greek culture denied subjectivity to women but elevated or excoriated Woman, whose gender attributes were defined and represented by males.[19] Plato's formulations about mimesis are even more susceptible to feminist critique, for Platonic loathing of imitation—by definition, an imperfect representation of a model—was exacerbated by the implicit link between mimesis and the female. To turn Case's phrase, if mimesis was not possible for women, it was not possible without them. As Froma Zeitlin writes, for the Greeks "Woman is the mimetic creature par excellence, ever since Hesiod's Zeus created her as an imitation with the aid of the other artisan gods and adorned her with a deceptive allure."[20] Plato, anticipating the misogynist antitheatricalism that took root in Patristic writings, considered women (along with children) most susceptible to illusionism and most likely to deceive. But more influential, Zeitlin argues, is the rhetoric of his condemnation: "by a whole series of innuendoes and juxtapositions" poets are compared to male tricksters and branded with the feminine attributes of pandering and corrupting; mimetic experience, especially in *The Republic,* is explicitly feminine: "when heroes are shown to weep and lament their misfortunes, they are not only endorsing a false theology about the justice of other gods but are weakening themselves and others by their indulgence in womanish grief" (*Republic* 387e–388a, 605d–e).[21]

However, unseemly behavior provoked by mimesis pales next to the slippery ontology of mimesis itself. What Plato distrusts (what Aristotle only partially reinstates)[22] is that mimesis implies difference—the copy is not the model; the character not the actor; the excited spectator not the rational male citizen, yet both occupy the same ontological space. Most disturbingly, when male actors impersonate female characters, though they are merely theatricalizing a discrete set of man-made gender gestures, they are, by participating in a mimetic activity, becoming dangerously *like a woman.* Understood this way, mimesis has little to do with the stable mirror reflection that realism inspires, but rather suggests—if we follow Platonic anxiety to its limits—a trick mirror that doubles (makes feminine) in the act of reflection. What I am proposing is that theater is a privileged site for feminist analysis because of, not in spite of, its long association with mimetic practice and theory. This is not to say, however, that centuries of patriarchal humanist larding (increased in our time by the dominance of realism in the media) can be easily stripped away. Perhaps, though, mimesis can be retheorized as a site of, and means of, feminist intervention. My intertexts here are Irigaray's exploration of mimesis as mimicry and Julia Kristeva's notion of the hysterical body's "true-real." My grouping of mimesis, mimicry, and the true-real is not meant as sequential but, rather, as a kind of unstable triangulation. It suggests that, as praxis, the sign-referent model of mimesis can become excessive to itself, spilling into a mimicry that undermines the referent's authority; it also suggests that the interposition of the performer's body signals an interruption of signification itself. Why make this effort to recuperate mimesis? Because it tends, I think, to recuperate us. It is better, perhaps, to acknowledge certain mimetic desires, to militate for the complex, the *different* references we want to see, even as we work to dismantle the mechanisms of patriarchal modeling.

Mimicry: Irigaray's Hystera-Theater

After reading *Speculum* it is difficult to understand the all too convenient labeling of women theorists as the homogenous "French feminists," or, more specifically, to subsume Luce Irigaray in essentialist interpretations of *écriture feminine*. The body writing Irigaray describes has none of the ecstatic alterity that Cixous imagines in "The Laugh of the Medusa."[23] In "The Blind Spot of an Old Dream of Symmetry," a rereading of Freud's "Femininity" through Lacan's mirror stage (although Lacan's name is never mentioned), Irigaray condemns the specular logic by which the female is seen as lack because she lacks what is "like a man." Condemned to the Law of the Same, to reflect back the male's image, she must "abandon her relation to her own primal fantasy so that she can inscribe into those of men"[24]—which will in turn become the "origin" of her desire. In Freud's account of "the phallic phase" the little girl is "a little man," or in Irigaray's words, a normal female is configured as "a man minus the possibility of representing [her]self as a man."[25] In a brilliant move Irigaray accounts for penis envy as an epiphenomenon of Freud's specular logic. It is not enough for women to lack the penis; they must also be envious, driven by the desire to have it, thereby confirming to men that they still possess it. It is her female envy that in effect fills out the mirror reflection, making her look like the male looking at himself.[26] In "Plato's Hystera," coming after "Speculum," ten short but dense meditations on (among other things) feminine desire, female ontology, and the speculum as mirror and tool for probing the secrets of female sexuality, Irigaray transforms the mirror into a political tool: mimetic submission becomes destabilizing mimicry.

Irigaray's intertext is, of course, Plato's Allegory of the Cave in book 10 of *The Republic,* in which the cave wall, with its projected images, serves Plato as a metaphor for the illusory nature of worldly objects that keep man from contemplating true Forms, the unseeable Ideal. Only when forced to leave the dark cave and emerge into the light are the symbolically chained men allowed to see the Truth. Making explicit the birth metaphors that Plato leaves implicit, Iriga- ray exchanges metaphor for metonymy; cave as embedded enclosure becomes the womb, or *hystera,* embedded in the mother's body/ earth. And this hystera—by Plato's own account—is nothing less than a fully operational theater whose illusionistic apparatus is (as in traditional realism) designed to obscure the mode of production; the chained men cannot see the fire or the parade of whispering, image- carrying men behind them, whose voices, melding perceptually with the object projections, are taken for truthful presences. However, we have here something stranger than a proscenium setup. Reimagin- ing Plato's cave as the theater he himself has limned, Irigaray also reconfigures the embedded hystera as a theater. "Chains, lines, per- spectives oriented straight ahead—all maintain the illusion of constant motion in one direction. Forward."[27] But what is ahead (the cave wall) is in fact behind (the opening to the cave). Thus, Irigaray con- cludes: "You will always already have lost your bearings as soon as you set foot in the cave; it will turn your head, set you walking on your hands. . . ."[28] In this ocular funnyhouse (the reference to Adri- enne Kennedy will be taken up later) of thrown images and ventrilo- quized voices, Irigaray gives us a "mimetic system" that completely belies the model-copy, for to the prisoners no origin of the image projections is imaginable; or, to put it another way, what they experi- ence as origin is always already mimicry, a representation of repeti- tion. Hence, mimesis without a true referent—mimesis without truth. With this reconfigured "womb-theater" Irigaray wittily re- trieves and confirms Plato's worst fears about theater, female duplic- ity, and, by implication, maternity. Platonic philosophy wants to place man's origins not in the dark, uncertain cave but, instead, in his recognition of the (Father's) light. The philosopher wants to forget— wants to prove illusory—his female origins. But the anarchic effect of that proof, in Irigaray's playfully serious rereading, is the discov- ery that his mother is a theater.

What might be the effects of this audacious womb-theater for feminist theater theory? To imagine a theater, whose "mimetic sys- tem is not referable to one model, one paradigm. . . . dominated by Truth"[29] is to undermine the ideality of logos as truth, the basis of Western thought and mimesis theory since Plato and Aristotle. At the origin of human existence (the mother) Irigaray situates an irreducible conundrum: the nontruth of truth—reality ("the real" of the prisoners' experience) constructed as a shadow-and-mirror play. And these mirrors are not to be confused with the reflective mirror constructed by and for the male imaginary. Rather the cave hystera "is already a speculum. An inner space of reflection. Polished and polishing, fake offspring. Opening, enlarging, contriving the scene of representation, the world as representation."[30] This last statement, only one thread of the Irigarayan web, has startling implications. In the feminist theater theory many of us have been writing "the scene of representation" is generally understood as a narrativization of male desire, an effect of the castration complex. Representation, we tend to say, *inevitably* transforms female subjects into gendered, fetishized objects whose referent is ideologically bound to dominant (heterosexual) models of masculinity and femininity.[31] After spending most of *Speculum* denouncing the specular reflection imposed on women by the male eye/I, is Irigaray proposing that representation—so invested in the mimesis of an absent present—will suddenly become female?

The answer to this question—indeed, to any question posed to Irigaray's text—is unambivalently double. That is, "Plato's Hystera" posits two mimetic systems that exist simultaneously, one repressed by the other. Patriarchal mimesis, articulated by Plato and Aristotle, is the traditional mimetic system, in which the model, the Form or Ideal, is distinguishable from and transcendently beyond "shadows—images in the mirror—mere copies."[32] Subverting patriarchal mimesis is what we might call mimesis-mimicry, in which the production of objects, shadows, and voices is excessive to the truth/illusion structure of mimesis, spilling into mimicry, multiple "fake offspring." Lest readers think that these two versions redound into gender stereotyping, it is helpful to remember that Irigaray's revisionary hystera-theater lies in the "womb" of Western thought since Plato, and patriarchal Truth cannot tolerate mimicry, the promiscuous and destabilizing generation of fake offspring.

Rewriting Plato's allegory, Irigaray also rewrites the maternal hystera not as passive vessel of male creative seed (Aristotle's assertion in 'De Generatione Animalium") but as site of material production. While Irigaray insists on the mother as forgotten origin, erased from psychic history, she also, through the metonym of materiality, links the illusionistic theater apparatus—its mirrors, fetishes, light, voices, the whole "stage set-up"—to matter, earth, body, and

to the ideological practices that have denied their importance.
"Plato's hystera" in effect forestalls recuperation by essentialist feminists, who valorize maternity and nurturance as the defining elements of female subjectivity. A theatricalized hystera necessarily *de-
essentializes* both female anatomy and maternal experience,[33] for if
mother's womb is a theater, then ideas of essence, truth, and origin
become continually displaced onto questions of material relations
and operations. Nevertheless, this displacement (like all displacements) is slippery. As Meaghan Morris puts it, Irigaray "is very far
from confusing the anatomical and the social, but she works with a
deadly deliberation *on* the point (the site and the purpose) of the
confusion of the anatomical and cultural." *Speculum* thus "resists
definition as feminine; for her the feminine is conditional or future
tense, an interrogative mood. . . . [she] remains the recalcitrant outsider at the festival of feminine specificity—she lounges ironically at
the door."[34]

Women playwrights and feminist performers, in various ways,
have taken up Irigaray's ironic disturbance of the unitary Self-Same,
though perhaps no one has *written* mimesis-mimicry with the excru-
ciating lucidity of Adrienne Kennedy. As Irigaray proposes the ruina-
tion of Truth by multiply mimicking and exceeding the mirror's
content, Kennedy, over two decades ago, displaced the "character"
of her female "Negro" onto fractured "selves." In *Funnyhouse of a
Negro* (1964) the Duchess of Hapsburg, Patrice Lumumba, a hunch-
backed Jesus, and Queen Victoria are each designated "One of Her-
selves," and in *The Owl Answers* (1965) discrete selves are changing
reflections of a single entity: "SHE who is CLARA PASSMORE who is the
VIRGIN MARY who is the OWL." In these and other texts history and
"self" mirror each other in violent contradiction,[35] producing reflections as unthinkable in racist North America as Kennedy's Negro,
who mimics and consequently destabilizes the very models (or identities) she most desires. Kennedy invites, yet resists, postmodern deconstruction. Hallucinatory repetition in her "funnyhouse," as in Irigaray's hystera-theater, subverts the illusion of psychic coherence,
but displacement for a black female subject can never be simply a
theoretical given. "From the trickery of magic [the hystera-cave],"
notes Irigaray, "we move on to the trickery of authority"[36]—and one
of the traditional tricks of authority is making the black woman disappear.

Contemporary women performers, and Irigaray herself, have produced different inflections of mimesis-mimicry. Indeed, in "The Powers of Discourse" (one of many essays written after, and in dialogue with, *Speculum*) Irigaray invokes Plato's loathed mimicry and hands it over to women: "One must assume the feminine role deliberately. Which means already to convert a form of subordination into an affirmation, and thus to begin to thwart it. . . . To play with mimesis is . . . for a woman, to try to recover the place of her exploitation by discourse, without allowing herself to be simply reduced to it."[37] This move from "subordination" to "affirmation," from "play" to "recover[y]," pushes the irony of multiple reflection into dialectical struggle. Mimicry can function, in other words, as an alienation-effect, framing the gender behavior dictated by patriarchal models as a means of "recover[ing] the place of her [the performer's] exploitation." Some brief examples of the political potential of mimesis-mimicry will have to suffice. Lois Weaver's creation/impersonation of Tammy Whynot (in Split Britches's *Upwardly Mobile Home*, 1985)[38] mimics the carefully choreographed gestures and bittersweet seductiveness of a country music star. Through subtle exaggeration, Weaver defuses the obvious fetishization inherent in that role, even as she reroutes Tammy's seductiveness for the spectatorial pleasure of her generally all-woman, generally lesbian audiences at the WOW Cafe in New York's East Village. Weaver foregrounds Tammy's exploitation "without" (as Irigaray puts it) "allowing herself to be simply reduced to it." On the contrary, Weaver, a skilled performer, can explore the desire that drives the fetishizing, exploitative gaze, but in a "stage set-up" that deliberately privileges the female eye.[39]

If, as Jill Dolan observes, Weaver as Tammy uses her dyed-blond hair and heavy makeup to send up the "femme" role of the lesbian couple, Italian performer Franca Rame exploits, more dubiously, her dyed blond hair and heavy makeup to mimic the gender signs of heterosexual femininity. Rame's one-woman series of playlets, *Female Parts* (1977), explores female oppression in a variety of contexts, but I want to focus briefly on her signature monologue with which she greets the audience and which she occasionally performs in a thin, black floor-length wrap, worn over a black lace chemise, black hose, and spike heels. In this overcoded sex-object garb Rame jokes about the assymetry of female and male parts, noting (a comic mimicry of Freud's "Femininity") not the parts but their Italian nomenclature—

Left to right: Jo Ann Schmidman, Hollie McClay, and Sora Kimberlain in *Body Leaks* by Megan Terry, Jo Ann Schmidman, and Sora Kimberlain. Photo © 1992 by Megan Terry.

the glorious *fallo* and *prepuzio* (foreskin) of the male versus the ill-sounding *vulva* and *vagina* of the female. Assuming in appearance the *role* of fantasy fetish, Rame invokes the taboo body parts that drive fetishization. Her body is thus on display—a fetish object—even as the terms of female objectification become available for critique.[40]

In *Rachel's Brain* (1987), a recent piece by performer Rachel Rosenthal, mimesis-mimicry is emphatically grounded in the epistemological discourses of the Self-Same. Emerging bewigged and corseted, an exaggerated parody of a salon aristocrat, Rosenthal eulogizes in mock aria the Cartesian cogito against the Truth of which all matter is measured. Gradually, however, in the course of her song, the performer's body rebels, and in twitches and gasps the crystalline beauty of rational discourse melts into an incoherent ooze of whines, grunts, and stifled hysterical cries. Rosenthal sees the mind-body split as the source—and justification—of man's [*sic*] pollution of the ecosystem, but for our efforts in conceptualizing mimesis-mimicry we

Robert N. Gilmer and Sora Kimberlain in *Body Leaks*. Photo © 1990 by Megan Terry.

might note that Descartes continues the Platonic bias toward rational intellect over against sensory bodily error. Rosenthal's body virtually stages the revolt of the hystera, her convulsive movements signifying the "wandering womb," of early Platonic theory (a woman's uterus, physicians of antiquity believed, tends to wander upward, choking off the breath), but also demonstrating, with Irigarayan clarity, the divisive effects of the patriarchal Self in a body that is not the Same.

In Irigarayan discourse the Self-Same shrinks from maternal fluids, from "the flow of some shameful liquid."[41] As though similarly inspired, *Body Leaks* (1990) by Megan Terry, Jo Ann Schmidman, and Sora Kimberlain explores the metaphorics of leaking as an antidote to psychic repression and social censorship. Long an activist company, Schmidman's and Terry's Omaha Magic The ater typically mocks and demystifies patriarchal sites and practices, but in this multimedia performance piece feminist truths are displaced by materials and language that pun on truth making. The mimetic mirror is contorted by an environment of glass bricks, neon tubes, metal trays, and reflecting sunglasses. Domestic objects mimic their "real" functions becoming extensions of the body's obsessions, yet the body itself is written over by slide projections that capture the performer in illusory grids. And the body leaks. "Welling up with love"[42] or purged by a "cleansing enema"[43] the leaking body blurs the boundaries between inner and outer, depth and surface, truth and falsehood, that consolidates identity for the Western subject. In *Body Leaks* the reflecting glass "is no longer transparent" but, rather, in mimicry of the body, "beaded and sweating"[44]—as Irigaray would put it, one of "the flowing things."[45]

In this too brief review of some contemporary women's work I hope merely to suggest the disruptive potential of Irigaray's concept of mimicry. Whether a funnyhouse concatenation of irreconcilable "selves" is brought into view; whether the effects of gender models are foregrounded by lesbian and heterosexual performers; whether the modes of patriarchal modeling are themselves theatricalized, women's theater writing has been able to decenter ideal Forms with false offspring. Like the mirror-play of Irigaray's effeminate tricksters, this writing dislodges the mimetic referent from its moorings and, thus, women from their prisonhouse of otherness (Kennedy perhaps the exception). It might be worthwhile to reiterate that Irigaray's mimicry has no specific ontology; it is deliberately and productively parasitic on patriarchal mimesis. Similarly, Irigaray's "elsewhere" of female pleasure, even the space where two lips speak softly, cannot be situated as a simple alterity, for it is never *not* interrupted by an unruly, theatrical clamor.

Kristeva's "True-Real" Body

In feminist theory over the last decade the clamoring site of disruption has been the "disease" that, since antiquity, has been associated with the female womb: hysteria. Whether one situates the hysteric empirically, as a historical-medical object, whose unreadable somatic symptoms derive from the material and gender constraints of bourgeois life (particularly the Victorian tendency to channel young women into jobs as governesses or nurses to the dying) or discursively, as a "speaking body," that defies the grammar of the patriarchal symbolic, hysteria in feminist discourse has become meaningful precisely as a disruption of categories and systems of meaning. [46] Julia Kristeva, in her essay "The True-Real," links the Lacanian "Real," that which cannot be symbolized or represented, to axiology—hence the true (*vrai* + *réel* = *vréel*). [47] According to Kristeva, the true-real unites the hysteric to the artist because both take the signifier for the real, thereby sidestepping the sign-referent model. And for both hysteric and artist the real signifier is the body: "In this economy, there are no *images* or *semblances* (any more than in the Eucharist): each element is neither real, nor symbolic, nor imaginary, but true." [48] Traditional mimesis is precisely what is repressed in the true-real, for the verisimilar copy is, as we have seen, always already inferior to its real model. Kristeva does not celebrate the true-real of hysteria (its medical label is psychosis), but her concept suggests another way of retheorizing mimesis. Can the body's true-real destabilize mimetic truth, or, put another way, can the body signify and also escape signification?

It is tempting, in answering this question, to leap to examples of performance art in which, supposedly, the body's texts displace the conventional mimesis of the text-performance structure. [49] But it may be also useful to test the possibilities of the nonmimetic body in plays that, historically, helped establish the importance and notoriety of the most circumscribed of mimetic forms: realism. Interrupting realism with the "true-real" seems a more challenging test of the concept and may suggest ways in which feminist practitioners might avail themselves of realism's referential power without succumbing to its ideological conservatism. What follows is drawn from a long chapter, "Realism and Our Discontents," which resituates Ibsenite realism through an adjacent cultural discourse, psychoanalysis, as represented in, among other texts, Freud and Breuer's *Studies in Hysteria* (1905). [50] In the chapter I argue that realism and psychoanalysis share a parallel object (the hysteric/fallen woman), a common claim to truth (the discovery of her secret), and even a common signifying history. I then propose that, in exploiting the signifiers and medical models of the hysteric, realism catches her disease—that is, produces in others the malady it is supposed to cure. Drawing on both empirical evidence (reviews, prompt-books) and psychoanalytic theories of transference and the imaginary, I consider the possibility of a hysterical realism—a realism without truth.

A key text in this discussion is *Alan's Wife* (1893), co-authored

by Elizabeth Robins and Florence Bell and produced at the same time
as Robins was reviving or creating her great Ibsen roles. However,
Alan's Wife is distinctly un-Ibsenite, ignoring the ubiquitous drawing
room of late-nineteenth-century realism; ignoring, too, the formal
arrangement of retrospective action, the process whereby the past
remembered produces its behavioral aberrations (hysterical symptoms), followed by the obligatory confession, which (as in Freud)
constitutes the disease's cure. Robins and Bell's *Alan's Wife* reads
instead like a Nietzschean morality play based on a dialectic of strong
blond health—the protagonist Jean and her factory worker husband,
Alan—versus sickly Christian conservatism—Jean's mother and the
village curate. In scene 1 Jean is pregnant and sexually radiant, setting
out dinner for her young husband while extolling his beauties to her
mother, who wishes she had married the weaker but wealthier curate.
The scene ends with Alan brought home on a stretcher hacked to
pieces by a new mill saw. In scene 2 Jean sits to the side while her
mother and neighbor attend to her crippled baby boy: she has reproduced the trauma of her husband's mutilated corpse. The women
leave, and, after agonizing (and suspenseful) doubt, Jean smothers the
child so that he won't suffer into adulthood as a cripple. In scene 3
Jean is in jail. She refuses to speak to the magistrate until the end of
the play, when she affirms the logic of the murder and walks off
unrepentant to her death.

What is remarkable is the play's final scene in which Jean scarcely
speaks or moves but the play's stage directions *translate* her body
"language" into sentence form. Here is a typical exchange:

> *Mrs. Holroyd [Jean's mother]:* How could you do it, my lass? Can't
> you remember? If you could have told them all about it and
> asked for mercy you could have got it.
> *Jean (silent—smiles strangely):* I don't want mercy.[51]

It would be impossible to represent Jean's discourse, either as stage
direction—the "strange" smile—or in the translation—"I don't want
mercy." In other words, Robins and Bell have produced a true-real
body: they have given the body axiological (truth-telling) status but
have made it impossible for that body to tell the truth. By wedging
a space between the body and the text of the body Robins and Bell
displace the imaginary wholeness of the actor in realism, making her

truth provisional, contingent. *Alan's Wife* suggests no less than a subversive mimesis, one in which the actor's body speaks not for but before the referent.

While Irigarayan mimicry dismantles the Truth—patriarchal mimesis—through endless repetitions and reflections, the hysteric's true-real dismantles Truth by referring to yet refusing to symbolize its meaning. Reaching back to an obscure text of early realism, written by feminists, allows us to historicize and thus change habits of thinking that have become ossified and which plague even contemporary theorists. Now perhaps we might answer our initial question: can there be a feminist mimesis? Not in the way we have understood mimesis in traditional theater history and theory. However, feminist theory and practice, in all its variety, suggest ways of rethinking theater discourse: we might imagine a mimesis that is undermined (or overcharged) through repetition, or a stable referentiality troubled by the body's true-real. As feminist critics, we are bound to critique Western theater as a cultural site where the gender models against which women and men struggle are systematically and profitably imitated. But theater is also, and in a complex sense, the place of play, and, unlike other media, in the theater the same play—and the "Same" theory—can be played not only again but differently.

NOTES

Except for the addition of material on the Omaha Magic Theater's *Body Leaks,* this essay is a reprint of "Mimesis, Mimicry, and the True-Real," published in *Modern Drama* 32, no. 1 (March 1989): 58–72.

1. The Women and Theater Program of the American Theatre in Higher Education (ATHE) conference in Chicago, Summer 1987. See Sue-Ellen Case's editorial "Comment" to her *Theatre Journal* issue, "Feminist Diversions," 40, no. 2 (1988): 152–53.

2. See Jonas Barish, *The Anti-Theatrical Prejudice* (Berkeley: University of California Press, 1980), 5–37, for a polemical review of early Greek mimesis theory. For a more theoretical approach informed by postmodern strategies, see *Mimesis in Contemporary Theory,* ed. Mihai Spariosu (Philadelphia: J. Benjamins, 1984), esp. "Editor's Introduction," i–xxix.

3. In *The Arte of English Poesie* (1589), Puttenham identifies the poet as "both a maker and a counterfeiter" (cited in Madeleine Doran, *Endeavors of Art* [Madison: University of Wisconsin Press, 1954], 71); and in *Timber: or, Discoveries,* Ben Johnson asserts that "to Nature, Exercise, Imitation, and Studie, *Art* must be added, to make all these perfect" (cited in Timothy Murray, *Theatrical Legiti-*

mation: Allegories of Genius in Seventeenth-Century England and France [Oxford: Oxford University Press, 1987], 27).

4. According to Coleridge, "Images, however beautiful, though faithfully copied from nature, and as accurately represented in words, do not of themselves characterize the poet. They become proofs of original genius only as far as they are modified by a predominant passion, or by associated thoughts of images awakened by that passion . . . or lastly, when a human and intellectual life is transferred to them from the poet's own spirit" (cited in M. H. Abrams, *The Mirror and the Lamp* [New York: Oxford University Press, 1953], 55). See also Joel Black's discussion of the Romantic and earlier theories of mimesis in "Idolology: The Model in Artistic Practice and Critical Theory," in Spariosu, *Mimesis*, 172–200.

5. Perhaps feminist historians and scientists have most eloquently addressed the question of patriarchal models for the discourses of truth. See several recent examples: Linda Gordon, "What's New in Women's History"; Evelyn Fox Keller, "Making Gender Visible in the Pursuit of Nature's Secrets"; Carroll Smith-Rosenberg, "Writing History: Language, Class, and Gender" all in Teresa de Lauretis's excellent anthology *Feminist Studies/Critical Studies* (Bloomington: Indiana University Press, 1986).

6. Spariosu, "Editor's Introduction," xi.

7. In "Question du Style" in *Nietzsche aujourd'hui? I: Intensités* (Paris, 1973), 247–48.

8. Luce Irigaray, *Speculum of the Other Woman,* trans. Gillian C. Gill (Ithaca, N.Y.: Cornell University Press, 1974), 54.

9. See Sue-Ellen Case, *Feminism and Theatre* (New York: Methuen, 1988), 6ff; and Jill Dolan, *The Feminist Spectator as Critic* (1988; reprint, Ann Arbor: University of Michigan Press, 1991), 2ff. The term derives from *The Resisting Reader* (Bloomington: Indiana University Press, 1978), Judith Fetterley's feminist rereading of some canonical texts of American literature. As readers of texts *and* spectacle, Case and Dolan read differently from Fetterley, and their ways of conceptualizing representation are more complex.

10. See Gordon, "What's New," in de Lauretis, *Feminist Studies,* 25–38.

11. See de Lauretis, *Feminist Studies,* 14–15. See also my article, "Brechtian Theory/Feminist Theory: Toward a Gestic Feminist Criticism," *Drama Review* 32 (1988): 85–86.

12. Elizabeth Robins, *Ibsen and the Actress* (London, 1928), 18. See also Joanne E. Gates, "Elizabeth Robins and the 1891 Production of *Hedda Gabler,*" *Modern Drama* 28 (1985): 611–19.

13. Emile Zola, "Naturalism in the Theatre," in *The Theory of Modern Drama,* ed. Eric Bentley (New York, 1968), 351.

14. William Archer, *The Old Drama and the New: An Essay in Revaluation* (Boston, 1923), 286.

15. Jacques Derrida, "The Theatre of Cruelty and the Closure of Representation," *Writing and Difference,* trans. A. Bass (Chicago: University of Chicago Press, 1978), 234.

16. Bertolt Brecht, "On Form and Subject-Matter," in *Brecht on Theatre,* trans. John Willett (New York: Hill and Wang, 1964), 29–30.

17. See Diamond, "Brechtian Theory."

18. Case, *Feminism and Theatre,* 15.

19. Ibid., 11–12.

20. Froma I. Zeitlin, "Playing the Other: Theater, Theatricality, and the Feminine in Greek Drama," *Representations* 11 (1985): 79.

21. Ibid., 85.

22. Spariosu, "Editor's Introduction," ix–x.

23. And this is, of course, early work. Cixous's theater writing and her piece on Winnie Mandela point to other styles of intervention.

24. Irigaray, *Speculum,* 52.

25. Ibid., 27.

26. ". . . through her 'penis-envy,' she will supply anything that might be lacking in this specular(riza)tion" (Irigaray, *Speculum,* 54).

27. Irigaray, *Speculum,* 244.

28. Ibid.

29. Ibid., 292.

30. Ibid., 255.

31. See my "(In)Visible Bodies in Churchill's Theatre," *Theatre Journal* 40 (1988): 190–91; see also Jill Dolan's discussion of representation and the Lacanian mirror stage in *The Feminist Spectator as Critic,* 41–42ff; 86–87. See also Sue-Ellen Case and Jeanie Forte, "From Formalism to Femininism," *Theater* 16 (1986): 62–65.

32. Irigaray, *Speculum,* 289.

33. See Marilyn R. Farwell's recent explication of these turns in feminist thinking in "Toward a Definition of the Lesbian Literary Imagination," *Signs* 14 (1988): 101–2ff.

34. Meaghan Morris, "The Pirate's Fiancee: Feminists and Philosophers, or maybe tonight it'll happen" in *Feminism and Foucault: Reflections on Resistance,* ed. Irene Diamond and Lee Quinby (Boston: Northeastern University Press, 1988), 35.

35. See the new collection of Kennedy's major plays, *In One Act* (Minneapolis: University of Minnesota Press, 1988).

36. Irigaray, *Speculum,* 274.

37. "The Power of Discourse," in *This Sex Which Is Not One,* trans. Catherine Porter with Carolyn Burke (Ithaca, N.Y.: Cornell University Press, 1985), 76.

38. Split Britches's production of *Upwardly Mobile Home* included Peggy Shaw, who played Mother Godam, and Deborah Margolin, who played Madeleine LeVine.

39. See Jill Dolan's account of Lois Weaver's Tammy Whynot and Split Britches in general in *The Feminist Spectator as Critic,* 70–76.

40. See my review of Rame in "Female Parts" in *Theatre Journal* 40 (1988): 102–5.

41. Irigaray, *Speculum,* 237.

42. From an unpublished manuscript of *Body Leaks,* by Megan Terry, Jo Ann Schmidman, and Sora Kimberlain, 33.

43. Ibid., 31.

44. Ibid., 25.

45. Irigaray, *Speculum,* 237.

46. See particularly Hélène Cixous and Catherine Clément's *The Newly Born Woman,* trans. Betsy Wing (Minneapolis: University of Minnesota Press, 1986); and Sarah Kofman, *The Enigma of Woman,* trans. Catherine Porter (Ithaca, N.Y.: Cornell University Press, 1980).

47. Julia Kristeva, "The True-Real," in *The Kristeva Reader,* ed. Toril Moi (New York: Columbia University Press, 1986), 214–37.

48. Kristeva, "True-Real," 236.

49. See Jeanie Forte's summary/analysis of women's performance art, "Women's Performance Art: Feminism and Postmodernism," in *Theatre Journal* 40 (1988): 217–35.

50. This chapter is from *Feminist Stagings: Unmaking Mimesis,* to be published by Routledge.

51. *Alan's Wife: A Dramatic Study in Three Scenes* (London: Henry, 1893), 43.

Chapter 19

White Men and Pregnancy: Discovering the Body to Be Rescued

Peggy Phelan

The antiabortion demonstrations staged at medical clinics under the direction of Operation Rescue are deeply revealing indications of the fraught relation between visibility, invisibility, and reproduction. While feminist theory has been preoccupied   not to say obsessed— with the structure of the gaze within representation, a useful theory explaining the actual political consequences of visibility and invisibility remains underdeveloped. The performances inspired by the abortion debates provide an instructive example with which to begin to explore the psychic and political investments in visibility and invisibility across both the representational and reproductive field.

The protests I discuss here are unusually conscious of the camera and print journalism.[1] The members of Operation Rescue shrewdly understand the necessary requirements of making a spectacle and acting out *for* the sake of publicity. Knowing that the press corps would be in Atlanta for the Democratic National Convention in 1988, they targeted that city for their first national protest. In so doing Operation Rescue simultaneously attacked Democrats who ran on pro-choice platforms, signaled a new political history for civil disobedience, and declared their antipathy to law, order, and the democratic way. They accomplished all of this by diverting the press's attention from the pageantry of the orderly conventional convention toward the drama of clinic blockades, threats of imminent violence, and hundreds of arrests. By capturing the media's attention in Atlanta, Operation Rescue gained an enviable notoriety and revitalized the stagnating abortion debates. Therefore, those who want to launch a counterargument about the politics of reproduction must assess how they relate to the politics of representation. As the debate about reproduction develops, so too does an ideology of representation.

Operation Rescue was established by Randall Terry, a white man from Rochester, New York, in 1987. The membership of the group is very difficult to chart demographically, in part because many participants remain anonymous (protesters are instructed to give their names as John or Jane Doe when they are arrested), and in part because "membership" can mean anything from participating in a single rescue to traveling throughout the country and performing rescues continually. But it seems clear that there are a surprisingly large number of men in the group; in 1989 Frances Wilkinson noted that 56 percent of its members were men, the three highest paid staff members on a fifteen-person payroll were men, and almost all of its members were white.[2]

It's hard to build a critique of a group based on shifting numbers and demographic makeup. There is, however, a coherent ideology, most powerfully articulated by Terry himself, which guides Operation Rescue and which bears close scrutiny. Terry believes: "Most people—men and women included [since women are not necessarily included in the category "most people" they must be marked]—are more comfortable following men into a highly volatile situation. It's human nature. It's history."[3] The "highly volatile situation" Terry refers to here is the "rescue."

The members of Operation Rescue believe that by staging demonstrations outside of abortion clinics they will rescue the unborn. These rescues tend to be emotionally and often physically violent. Like most staged rescues, Operation Rescue's demonstrations generate a feeling of terror and thereby produce the feeling that one needs to be saved. In creating an opportunity for rescuing the unborn, the demonstrations also catalyze the conversion narrative so crucial to Christian nature. Saving the unborn allows those who were "born again" to continue the missionary work that concludes all conversion experiences. The women who walk into clinics often have more to fear from Operation Rescue than from doctors. Fewer than ten of the 1,600,000 women who have abortions each year in the United States die as a result of the procedure.[4] The incidents of violence at Operation Rescue demonstrations exceed this, as we shall see, and the number of actual "babies saved" is nowhere documented.

The rescues, theatrical performances of extraordinary boldness and violence, are largely sex-segregated. Many of them are doubly oppositional because pro-choice groups, composed largely of women, often attempt to stage counterdemonstrations at the same clinics. The Operation Rescue men confront the counterdemonstrators or, on occasion the clinic workers, and form a wall, shoulder to shoulder, often screaming "dyke" or "whore" to any woman who walks across. (The idea underlying these appellations is breathtakingly crude: all feminists are lesbians; all pregnant women contemplating abortion are sexually promiscuous). When a pregnant woman attempts to enter the clinic a male rescuer will yell out in a strange falsetto: "Mother, please don't murder me." Off to the side most of the women from Operation Rescue form what is called a "Prayer Support Column": they chant hymns, stand still, try to maintain an air of "above the fray" about them, and keep their hands open and raised toward heaven. Another group of protesters carry placards with alternating images of the "innocent" and the "mutilated" fetus on them. The spatial separation between the men and the women rescuers mimics the situation often found in mainstream theater—speaking men and observing women—to reinforce the idea that in any drama, including the drama of pregnancy, mainstream theater will do all it can to ensure that the main character remains an (embryonic) man.

Inside the clinic a group of other people lock themselves to chairs in the waiting room and, if possible, to the desks of the clinic workers. While lying there waiting to be removed, they sing Christian hymns. The locks they use are made of cryptonite (as in *Superman*), and they must be sawed off by police officers. While the flames from the electrical saws fire, the rescuer calls on Jesus. In the meantime another group of people sit or stand in the waiting rooms with open Bibles and read Scripture in soft voices. They sit very close to those waiting and try to provoke a conversation. When the police come to saw the locks off their colleagues this group will often sing hymns.

At the heart of the New Right's relation to abortion is a psychic fear about paternity; this fear is repressed and displaced through a series of substitutions and disavowals that make the chain of significations in the demonstrations *productive* of another terror, the terror of absolute alterity, which is displaced onto the body of the pregnant woman trying to enter the abortion clinic. Conveying an ideological and religious belief about abortion, the blockades and demonstrations also frame and define a contested psychic arena between men and women.

Freud describes men's psychic relation to reproduction as an "anxiety" stemming from the inability to prove paternity; what we are witnessing now is a transformation of that psychic field. Paternity is now verifiable by science and thus subject to law. Paternity is newly visible, and the men of the New Right, like most men, are uneasy and ambivalent about that. In an effort to displace the consequences of paternal visibility a new effort has been made to make the fetus visible.

Fetal imagery, a persistent and ubiquitous focus in the abortion debates, is important because it upsets the psychic terrain that formerly located all reproductive visibility exclusively on the body of the pregnant woman. Fetal imagery locates reproductive visibility as a term and an image independent of the woman's body. Once that independence is established the uses of fetal imagery become vulnerable to all the potential manipulations of any sign system. Within the strategy of Operation Rescue two representations of the fetus continually work together in a complex dialogue. On the one hand, the "innocent" fetus is photographed, as Faye Ginsburg observers, "in warm amber tones, suffused with soft light, [and] rendered more mysterious by their separation from the mother's body." This image is juxtaposed with "gruesome, harshly lit, clinical shots of mutilated and bloody fetal remains."[5] The innocent image works to induce sympathy and protection while the mutilated one is a call to outrage and outrageous action.

Making the fetus visible allows Operation Rescue to erase the pregnant woman. Detached from the mother, the image of the fetus is rendered as utterly alone and heartbreakingly innocent. Held aloft on signposts outside of abortion clinics during Operation Rescue's demonstrations, the fetal image functions like a flag, a banner under which protecting rescuers march off to prevent the "slaughter of the innocent." But what happens, as in most wars, is a slaughter of a different order. By the erasure of the woman from the image, the fetal form has become a token in a discourse of and about men.

Cropped out of the picture, the pregnant woman's life and reasoning are rendered both invisible and irrelevant. By focusing on the fetus Operation Rescue manages to ignore the pregnant woman. This literal ignorance of the pregnant woman limits sympathy for her situation and represses ethical uncertainty about her liberty; this same ignorance props up the righteous tone of the demonstrations.

Detached from the pregnant woman, the fetal form has become a sign that is already powerfully implicated in the political economy of capitalism and patriarchy. Take, for example, the recent Volvo television advertisement: a sonogram of a fetus fills the screen, on the soundtrack the steady beating of a fetal heart, and then, as if on the sonogram monitor itself, computer print rolls up the television screen as a male voice-over intones: "Isn't it time for a Volvo?" Many parents experience their first feeling of "bonding" with the fetus when they see its sonogram.[6] Exploiting this feeling of protectiveness, Volvo uses the fetal form to make the same emotional plea as the antiabortionists—protect this helpless, beautiful life. But the means by which protection is assured are dramatically different. The Volvo people want you to buy their safe car; Operation Rescue wants you to help outlaw abortion. In both instances an implied moral threat is operative: not buying a Volvo, like refusing to rescue babies, leaves blood on your hands. Fetal imagery provokes both protectionist sentiment and the potential feeling of guilt in those who "bond" with it.

In a brilliant discussion of fetal imagery Rosalind Petchesky argues:

> "The fetal form" itself has, within the larger culture, acquired a symbolic import that condenses within it a series of losses—from sexual innocence to compliant women to American imperial might. It is not the image of a baby at all but of a tiny man, a homunculus.[7]

In other words, the fetus is always already gendered—and, not surprisingly, gendered male. The identification between fetus and man is accented within the demonstration as he speaks for/as the fetus. The grown man speaks in full sentences—"Mother, please don't murder me"—ventriloquizing for the unborn child a fear of murder. This fetus is not only sentient; he is Noam Chomsky's dream child—within the womb the deep structure of language is up and running. The men who would rescue place their own voices and heroism center stage, while the drama of the pregnant woman remains invisible, unspoken, pushed to the other side of the curtain that opens and closes on their own holy work.

Additionally, by locating "maleness" within the image of the fetus, men displace their new reproductive visibility onto representations of the hitherto unseen "child," further strengthening the identification between the fetus and the men of Operation Rescue. It is this identification that justifies the belief that they must be noble advocates for "the preborn child," a point that also underlines the swift enactment of fetal rights laws—most of which have been used to incarcerate pregnant women, charging those who drink or take drugs with child abuse. In the meantime, however, child abuse outside the womb, often at the hands of male guardians, continues beating its repetitive rhythms.[8] Under the banner of protecting women and children men protect themselves.

In other words, the psychic economy of Operation Rescue's demonstrations enact a series of political displacements whose consequences have not been sufficiently elaborated.[9] The demonstrations aim to produce fear and terror not *because* Operation Rescue is composed of "fanatics," as the Left sometimes too quickly assumes. Rather, the production of terror sets up a more profound psychic theater in which the potential power of pregnancy for women is transported into the province of men's power. The production of terror allows men (and their "female support column") to cast themselves in the role of "nurturing protectors," thereby appropriating for themselves the traditional female role of emotionally sensitive being and of caretaker, while the pregnant woman becomes the murdering, hateful mother. The image of the fetus displaces attention from both the pregnant woman and the father. And the only part of the reproductive triangle in need of rescuing becomes the tiny, innocent fetus. All of these displacements occur under a veil, in a kind of psychic and political theater whose curtains are heavy and whose nameless performers appear only behind scrims. The veil that sheaths the innocent fetus has an uncanny similarity to the veiled paternal phallus, Lacan's ubiquitous caul-baby-who-would-be-king. Unlike the hymen, this veil cannot be broken if patriarchy is to continue to be reproduced. What is required to interfere in its reproduction?

Values about reproduction govern ideas about representation and inflect the negative values associated with the nonreproductive and the unrepresentable.[10] Homophobia, for example, stems partly from cultural discomfort with a nonreproductive sexuality. Sexual activity that leads only to more of the same activity (as against leading to procreation) is unattractive to the ideology of production and reproduction that suffuses late-twentieth-century U.S. culture. While we've long recognized the connection between the fiscal economy of capital and the psychic economy of sexualities, the particular shape of this connection is now changing as we attempt to face the alarming specter of prodigious spending in both spheres. The national response to HIV infection and AIDS has unwittingly made clear the intimacy of the ideological relation between safe sex and safe spending. In a sexually grieving culture conservative politicians exploited rampant homophobia under the guise of fiscal restraint to restrict the National Endowment for th Arts' (NEA) spending. Attacking performance art in part precisely because it cannot be reproduced, the ontological claims of performance dovetailed with the nonreproductive ontology of homosexuality. All four performers "defunded" by the NEA make work that incorporates a sympathetic, if not evangelical, attitude toward homosexuality.[11]

This same distrust and suspicion of the nonreproductive reifies the pregnant woman as the embodiment of "natural" desire, for both men and women within the patriarchal economy. The reification of the pregnant woman (furthered in part by limiting her visibility within representational systems) sets the dialectic between the good mother and the evil mother in motion, a cycle that once again represses the question of paternity within the abortion debates (and makes the woman who is not a mother valueless—or a "failed" woman or a woman soon-to-be-a-mother-we-hope). Patriarchy oscillates between reverence for the "natural" maternal instinct and the haunting specter of the monstrous, forever murdering/castrating mother. It is this dialectic that accounts for: (1) the need for "objective" men to determine the legal and financial parameters within which abortion is legitimate; and (2) the intricate relationship between abortion and racism, which is to say, as well, between abortion and money. Currently, medicaid funds will pay 90 percent of a voluntary sterilization procedure for a woman and will pay nothing for an abortion. While abortion has long existed, its particular relation to legality, funding, and publicity has been a relationship dominated by the agenda of white men and secondarily by white women.[12]

In the United States traditional common law permitted abortions before quickening until 1845, when physicians led a campaign to restrict them. Intent on establishing medicine as a profession, the doctors wanted to outlaw untrained physicians, primarily midwives, from practicing medicine. By the turn of the century almost all states had passed laws restricting abortion.[13] Thus, *Roe v. Wade* (1973) relegalized abortion for the first six months of pregnancy.

In turning back to an earlier "right" Justice Harry Blackmun, writing the opinion of the Supreme Court in *Roe,* declared that the court recognized "a right of personal privacy . . . [which has] some extension to activities relating to marriage; procreation; contraception; family relationships; and child rearing and education." While both Justices Stewart and Renquist agreed that the "liberties" protected by the Fourteenth Amendment (passed in 1868) cover more than those explicitly named in the Bill of Rights, by the time the Court heard *Bowers v. Hardwick* in 1986 it did not believe that "privacy" or "liberty" extended to one's right to engage in nonreproductive sexuality. Thus, although heterosexual activity, and its attendant reproductive consequences, is a private matter protected by the Fourteenth Amendment, homosexual activity, which does not broach a reproductive consequence, is subject to "prevailing moral standards." The threat of homosexuality is that it does not need a larger sociality than the actors who consent, thus the law seeks to make it an illegal activity, a pursuit explicitly regulated by the sociality of law and prevailing moral standards. Heterosexuality, firmly entrenched as the very ground of a reproducible sociality, must be protected from the "constraints" of a surveying law.

The members of Operation Rescue, however, want to resocialize the relation between the law and reproduction. They want to suggest that the "unnaturalness" of women who would abort is much the same unnaturalness as those who would engage in nonreproductive sexuality. (Not surprisingly, Randall Terry wants to outlaw all forms of contraception). Arguing that abortion cannot be private, the members of Operation Rescue seek to make abortion a visible and public problem that cries out for legislative reform. *Bowers* is a serious threat to those seeking to ensure sexual object choice and reproductive choice. It may well be that the new abortion legislation will be crafted around the precedent against sexual (and, by implication, reproductive) privacy established in *Bowers v. Hardwick*. Distracted by the explicit legislative interest in revising the abortion laws, the prochoice people may fail to notice this open door. Conservatives who prefer that the Left remain divided into small and separate constituents benefit from the tendency to see *Bowers* exclusively as a "gay rights case." It has a much wider net than that.

In Wichita, Kansas, in the summer of 1991 Operation Rescue added another act to their drama. The group launched what has come to be called the Wichita Walk. Defying a court order to clear the entrance to three abortion clinics, Operation Rescue protesters crawled and/or took baby steps to the patiently waiting paddy wagon. The police allowed the demonstrators to proceed (legally, if they were "progressing toward the conveyance," the police are enjoined to wait): it took twenty-eight hours to remove all the demonstrators from the clinic entrances. Literally performing the part of sentient and calculating infants, the members of Operation Rescue put the law into a stupor for more than a full day. Encamped in Wichita for three weeks, Operation Rescue took over the city and dominated the air and radio waves with its psychic theater. The "Summer of Mercy" campaign marks a new level of drama in the abortion debates. As the legal battle unfolds, more of these powerful demonstrations are sure to occur. Alisa Solomon points out that Operation Rescue members are "as litigious as they are liturgical."[14] The demonstrations themselves are becoming progressively intense and dramatic as the members of Operation Rescue seek to hold the attention of the media, the public, and the politicians.

Between 1987 and 1990 over twenty-eight thousand rescuers have been arrested; they refuse to give their real names—they call themselves "John Doe" or "Jane Doe"—and with this form of civil disobedience they clog the overcrowded courts and the prisons. Over 267 incidents of violence and disruption have been documented by the National Abortion Federation between 1987 and 1990. In 1989 alone nine clinics were either bombed or set alight; the estimated cost of physical damage to clinics is $375,000.[15]

This visible violence masks the invisible violence of the psychic wrestle raised by the politics of reproduction. It is no accident that it

is a man who mouths the words of the unborn child in Operation
Rescue's demonstrations. For the effort is to make the "male seed"
productive—a speaking seed, however infantilized. He addresses her
repeatedly as "mother," the appellation under which all adult women
in this culture labor. His most urgent adult plea from his deepest
passion is still "Mother, please don't murder me." These men are
not, generally speaking, terrifically empowered.

Susan Faludi, who has written the best mainstream account of
Operation Rescue, points out that these activists

> do not fit the stereotype of grizzled Christian elders. Almost all
> its leaders and nearly half its active participants are in their late
> twenties to mid-thirties. They are men who belong to the second
> half of the baby-boom generation, men who not only missed the
> political engagement of the sixties but were cheated out of that
> era's affluent bounty. They are downwardly mobile sons, con-
> demned by the eighties economy to earning less than their fa-
> thers, unable to buy homes or support families. . . . These are
> men who are losing ground and at the same time see women
> gaining it—and suspect a connection.[16]

In what sense, precisely, are these men losing ground? What are the
anxieties of paternity underlying the abortion debates, and why are
they elevated to this pitch now? The intersection of the legal and
psychic transformation of paternity provides part of the answer.

In *Moses and Monotheism* Freud defined *paternity* as "a hypothesis
based on an inference and a premise."[17] At the origin of the patriarchal order, Freud argues, civilization "advances" because, in honor-
ing the paternal rather than the maternal line, civilization chooses
"intellectuality over sensuality" as the means of establishing power.
Since maternity is visible and "proved by the evidence of the senses"
and paternity is a hypothesis based on an inference and a premise, the
authority of the patriarchy depends on a hierarchical relationship between the visible and the invisible, with the invisible (God and paternity) being the ascendant term in the pair. Abstract thought must be
made to be superior to matter/mater/mother. Law's abstractions,
until recently, have proven to be patriarchy's best friend in the establishment and maintenance of this superiority.

As Foucault and Freud have, in their different ways, shown us:

law needs invisibility to survey the visible; visibility inspires surveil-lance and submits to the gaze of the panoptic authority.[18] Insofar as law involves the delicate negotiation of inferences and premises, the balance between hypothesis and contested evidence, it is aligned with the inferences and premises of paternity. But what we are witnessing right now is perhaps the first serious threat to the shared sympathy between the law and paternity. Paternity too can now be a matter "proved by the evidence of the [scientific/legal] senses." In a newly fascinating way paternity—and male sexual potency and impotency, which underlie it—is both more *and less* than an inference and a prem-ise. By making paternity visible civilization robs it of its complicity with the law; the new visibility of paternity feminizes it and submits it to the decisions and mediations of law. Rather than enjoying the freedom of doubt, paternity has moved into the realm of the verifiable. Verity thy name is Woman—but it is in the realm of fiction and fantasy that freedom and power live.

As paternity becomes as visible as maternity and loses its ascen-dancy in the binary, the pressures brought to bear on it become more intense and more confining. In Prince George's County alone Judge Gary Ross's paternity court processes over 150 paternity cases *a day*. In 1987 his court handled 1,757 cases and made the county second in the amount of money collected for child support in Maryland. In two years Prince George County raised child support by $9,000,000 from $13.5 million in fiscal 1985 to $22.5 million in 1987.[19] How has this happened? In the courtroom itself the medical technicians now con-duct paternity tests.

Rather than seeing paternity's "doubtability" as *only* a source of psychic anxiety, as Freud argued, I am suggesting that, in fact, the unverifiable status of paternity also pleased men, for it justified their role as policemen over women and criminals (who, sexually, are the same) and as "disinterested" arbitrators of law, including reproduc-tion laws. The psychic law of the father is powerful precisely because, while remaining unseen itself, it determines what is and what is not seen, what is and is not subject to visibility and the apparatus of surveillance. Now paternity can itself become a subject of legal scru-tiny and modulation.

Instead of staging themselves as fathers, the men of Operation Rescue stage themselves as speaking fetuses or nurturing rescuers. The men of Operation Rescue understand that their goal in the demonstration is to remain veiled as fathers. While I am not suggesting that we imitate the men of the New Right, I do believe that the power of a finely calibrated invisibility has been too quickly dismissed as a political strategy by the Left. Representational visibility, as *the* goal for progressive, leftist representational politics, may overlook too much when it ignores the real traps within visibility itself. What the Operation Rescue blockades demonstrate is the need for a much more nuanced relation to visibility and invisibility within representation itself.

More than calling for a shrewd analysis of the "terms and structures of representation," I am suggesting that we rethink the entire visibility-power game itself. The relations between visibility and power are never only representational; representation is not a simple abacus adding and subtracting power from visible beads. To employ that much overused Turnerian term visibility and invisibility within representation are always liminal. To watch paternity enter this liminal zone is to see the disadvantages of staking too much on visibility as a means of achieving representational power. Visible to whom? Who is looking, and who is seen?

In the past decade medical technology has made it possible to determine paternity within a range of about 96–98 percent probability. Formerly, a simple blood test (used extensively through the 1970s) could reliably *eliminate* possible fathers, but it could not ascertain the correct father; since there are only six blood types many unrelated people share the same blood type. In the early and mid-1980s a new test, called the human leukocyte antigens test, compared similarities between the child and the alleged father by concentrating on molecules that formed above blood cells. While it is still possible for unrelated people to have the same human leukocyte (HLC) types this was a far more reliable test than a simple blood test (there are many more possible HLC combinations than blood types). And then. in the late 1980s, the DNA test, which compares genetic material itself, became a relatively cheap (about two hundred dollars) method for paternity testing. The chance of two unrelated people having the same DNA pattern has been calculated to be one in thirty billion.[20]

If DNA tests are allowed to be widely admissible, paternity trials will become a thing of the past; the test will make a trial unnecessary. Currently, in the United States 285,000 paternity cases are filed each year; 60,000 of them are disputed.[21] The possibility of bringing a false claim against a putative father as well as the possibility of such a father disputing that claim will be effectively eliminated by the DNA test. (Trials will be heard about the reliability of the test; different labs have different records of accuracy. But this will be a fundamentally different kind of trial than in the past. Perhaps what may emerge as a trial issue is the legality of forcing a man to undergo a paternity test against his will. Precedent may be established by cases in which rape victims are demanding that their alleged rapists undergo HIV tests). However, the Supreme Court has not yet declared DNA tests admissible in paternity trials and, in fact, seems troubled by the test's threat to "the marital family."

In *Michael H. v. Gerald D.* (June 1989) the Supreme Court upheld an 1872 California law stating that the husband of the mother can be "presumed" to be the child's legal father. I want to describe this case at some length because it so dramatically illustrates the vested interests in keeping paternity and potency as "an inference and a premise." The mother, Carole, was married to Gerald in 1981, when she became pregnant and gave birth to her daughter, Victoria. She was, however, estranged from Gerald (but still legally married), and she was living off and on with three different men for the first three years of Victoria's life. One of these three was Michael H. In the case Michael H. argued that he was the child's father—a DNA test demonstrated a 98.07 percent chance that Michael H. is Victoria's father— and that he should be granted visitation rights because he had a "constitutionally protected liberty interest" in maintaining a relationship with his daughter. In 1984 Carole and Gerald were reconciled, and they both opposed Michael H.'s wish to visit Victoria. Gerald argued that, as the husband of Carole when the child was conceived and born, he was "presumed" to be the child's father and thus the law should guarantee protection to the marital family against claims such as Michael H.'s. Michael's argument that he was being denied due process by being unable to prove his paternity was rejected by the majority.[22] The majority of the Court, in other words, preferred to keep paternity "a hypothesis based on an inference and a premise," rather than something that could be proved by medical "senses." To do so they had to uphold a law from 1872, a law written very much in the spirit of Freud's idea about the paternal hypothesis. Not surprisingly, Justice William Brennan (that much missed rational man) in his dissent argued that Justice Antonin Scalia, who wrote the deci-

sion, had a view of the Constitution that "is not the living charter I
have taken to be our Constitution; it is instead a stagnant, archaic,
hidebound document steeped in the prejudices and superstitions of a
time long past."[23] As of this date, no further challenges have been
brought regarding the admissibility of DNA tests.

Michael H. v. Gerald D. is a case about competing claims to
fatherhood; one claim is based on the integrity of biology and the
other on the integrity of the marital family.[24] By giving credence to
the marital over the biological the court implicitly devalues the biological claim of paternity. This is consistent with the pattern of decisions governing competing claims between maternity and paternity.
In the 1976 case of *Planned Parenthood v. Danforth* the Supreme Court
held that it is not necessary for a woman to gain the consent of the
biological father in order to have an abortion. Laurence Tribe summarizes the Court's thinking:

> Of course, it would be ideal if both parties concurred in an abor-
> tion decision, but when the woman is unwilling to continue the
> pregnancy, a requirement of consent from the man would not
> facilitate *consensus*. It would simply transfer the power to decide
> from the woman, who has decided on an abortion, to the man,
> who has decided to stop her. Only one party can prevail in such
> a situation. Since the abortion at issue is one that would be legal
> if the man had no objection, the interest in the life of the fetus
> cannot justify ruling for the man. (198)

In other words, within the legal parameters of reproduction
rights biological paternity comes in second place, and this, I suspect,
is the real outrage that fuels the abortion debates. The only arena of
law that gives "preferential" treatment to women, the abortion decisions give women more legal "potency" than men. On the one hand,
women can use paternity tests to enjoin men to pay child support
against their will, but men cannot enjoin women to bear children
against their will.[25] It is this perceived inequality that accounts for
what seem, at first glance, to be the bizarre affinities Randall Terry
insists on making between the civil rights movement and Operation
Rescue. After being arrested in Atlanta in 1988 Terry spent his time
in prison reading the work of Martin Luther King, Jr. Since then
Terry has repeatedly claimed that he is continuing the civil rights

movement: "In many, many ways, the rescue really is like the civil rights movement. This is a civil rights movement, seeking to restore the civil rights of children, the right to life."[26]

Within the series of substitutions and displacements that align men with the fetus Terry's belief that the rescue is part of the civil rights movement highlights the implicit agenda of Operation Rescue: that men must not be secondary partners in reproductive choices. Defiantly opposed to the law that would give them only secondary rights, Operation Rescue runs up court fines, frustrates the Internal Revenue Service, and clogs the courts with arrests that cannot be processed without the "name of the father."

Revising the ideological claims of the civil rights movement to make themselves heirs to it is a bold move. But even more extraordinary is Operation Rescue's current project of revising the legacy of the women's movement. In a remarkable editorial in the August-September 1990 *Rescue Report,* the newsletter of Operation Rescue, entitled "What Ever Happened to the Women's Movement?" Operation Rescue declares itself the rightful heir to the women's movement:

> What has happened to the women's movement? We have picked it up; we have become the true defenders of women in this generation by allowing women to be what God intended them to be. We are the ones who are intervening for women in the courts. We are the ones helping single women raise their families.

This "we" refers to men and addresses them as the protectors of women. The abortion debates are conversations among men about the bodies of women; when women enter the conversation as speakers they enter a conversation with well-defined parameters and rigid language. (Thus, "pro-life" is countered with the rather weaker motto "pro-choice.") While there is nothing new about men determining the thoughts and actions of women—after all, this is what Virginia Woolf satirized so brilliantly in *A Room of One's Own* in 1929—what is new and startling is the belief that in this gesture Operation Rescue has become the heir to the women's movement itself. In Wichita many women Operation Rescue demonstrators wore T-shirts with a small (baby) women's sign nestled within a bigger women's sign and accompanied by the words "Equal Rights for Unborn Women." The more subversive among us may read this in a very "French" fashion—living women are not yet born or bearable within representation—but, alas, the intention is quite the opposite. The unborn fetus can be part of a sloganeering campaign for the newly emerging "feminist" turn of Operation Rescue.

It would be a mistake to read this turn as part of an ideological shift in the paternalistic thinking of Operation Rescue. It is, rather, part of the group's larger attempt to appropriate the signs of other "popular" movements. For this group the women's movement and the animal rights movements are equally vulnerable to appropriation. One of their other new T-shirts borrows the motto of environmental groups who saved baby seals trapped in fishermen's nets. The shirt has an image of a circle with a line through it (stolen from the movie *Ghostbusters*) and reads: "Save the Baby Humans."

By defining paternity as more and less than an inference and a premise, medicine and the law have rendered paternity feminine. To add insult to injury the law has had the temerity to give "real" women greater legal right to reproductive "freedom" than men. Under the threat of this feminization Operation Rescue has ignored the law, revised the history of the civil rights and women's movements, and, Tootsie-like, has staged performances in which they take on the role of the "good mother" in order to perpetuate fear of the "murdering mother." Disguising the newly visible claims of paternity within the image of the fetal form, Operation Rescue has attempted to hide the fact that the baby they want so desperately to rescue is that mythically innocent white man, still caught in the silent womb of the maternal body.

As performance, Operation Rescue's demonstrations elucidate the political consequences of making the hitherto unseen visible. These consequences are bound up with reproductive visibility, but they are not limited to it. Randall Terry takes every opportunity offered him to explain that reproductive rights are only a small part of his overall plan to control representation and power knowledge: "Ultimately my goal is to reform this culture . . . the arts, the media, the entertainment industries, medicine, sciences, education—to return to right and wrong, a Judeo-Christian base." He wants to ban all birth control, censor sex scenes in films, and eliminate pornography. He wants to influence the direction of scientific research and curricular organization. The object of scrutiny—the fetus, the woman—allows the subject who looks to continue to direct his own play. Becoming the visible father is the real anxiety; controlling maternity offsets it.

While I mentioned that 56 percent of the members of Operation Rescue are men, I have not here considered what motivates the women of Operation Rescue. In focusing on men I do not mean to imply that the complex relationship between patriarchy, paternity, and women is not itself worthy of careful scrutiny. There are real benefits for some women in the current order of things. And many women are complicitous with the system that "protects" their positions. My effort here, however, is to consider in some detail the ways in which what can and cannot be seen in the abortion debates everywhere relates to what can and cannot be seen within reproduction and representation.

NOTES

1. See Faye Ginsburg, "Saving America's Souls: Operation Rescue's Crusade against Abortion," in *Fundamentalisms and the State: Remaking Politics, Economies, and Militants,* ed. Martin Party and R. Scott Applebee (Chicago: University of Chicago Press, forthcoming).

2. Cited in Frances Wilkinson, "The Gospel according to Randall Terry," *Rolling Stone,* 5 October 1989, 85–89.

3. Terry quoted in Wilkinson, "Gospel," 85–89. All quotes from Terry, unless otherwise noted, are from this essay.

4. Laurence Tribe, *Abortion: The Clash of Absolutes* (New York: W. W. Norton, 1990), 207.

5. Faye Ginsburg, *Contested Lives: The Abortion Debate in an American Community* (Berkeley: University of California Press, 1989), 105.

6. See Rosalind Petchesky, "Fetal Images: The Power of Visual Culture in the Politics of Reproduction," *Feminist Studies* 13, no. 2 (1987): 263–92.

7. Petchesky, "Fetal Images," 268.

8. See Tribe, *Abortion,* for a discussion of the Court's reluctance to impose state responsibility for child abuse and its haste to provide fetal protection; hereafter all references to Tribe will be cited in the text.

9. There are, of course, excellent reasons for this insufficiency. Terry will not be "stopped" by my reading of the protests. The urgency of the political squirmish has led people to believe that readings such as mine are beside the point. It is my belief that the long and deep impasse in the reproductive rights campaign in the United States is due in part to the impoverished discourse around the psychic investments catalyzed by reproduction—for men and women. My reading, then, is not meant "instead of" political action; it is of-

fered, rather, as a way of rejecting the "either/or" of theory and practice—and as a probing of the underside of the demonstrations themselves.

10. See my book *Unmarked: The Politics of Performance,* for a full discussion of what it would take to begin to value the nonreproductive (New York: Routledge, 1993).

11. For a detailed discussion of the connection between safe sex, safe spending, and performance, see my essay "Money Talks, Again," in *TDR: A Journal of Performance Studies* 35 (Fall 1991): 131–42.

12. It is worth noting that there are very real historical and political determinants that have fed the idea that abortion can be seen as a form of genocide; both blacks and Jews have reasons for voicing this fear. Just as the New Right has used alternating images of the innocent fetus and the mutilated fetus, the racial politics of the abortion rights campaign has been haunted by the specter of enforced sterilization. For a harrowing account of this history, see Angela Y. Davis, "Racism, Birth Control, and Reproductive Rights," in *Women, Race and Class* (New York: Random House, 1981). The continuing failure to distinguish adequately the difference between being pro-abortion *rights* and pro-abortion has severely undermined the campaign for reproductive freedom. Currently, there is a serious danger that something akin to enforced abortion is occurring with HIV-infected pregnant women, particularly among the poor and nonwhite. For fuller treatment of the racial politics involved in reproductive technologies, see *From Abortion to Reproductive Freedom: Transforming a Movement,* ed. Marlene Gerber Fried (Boston: South End Press, 1990).

13. See *International Handbook on Abortion,* ed. Paul Sachdev (New York: Greenwood Press, 1988), 476.

14. Alisa Solomon, "Oppression Theology," *Village Voice,* 27 August 1991, 35.

15. The National Abortion Federation: 1436 U St., Ste. 103, Washington, DC 20009. It should be noted that 267 is actually fewer incidents than during the previous three years (1984–86), when 413 incidents were reported. But before 1987 there were no "blockades" and, therefore, no subsequent arrests for blockading.

16. Susan Faludi: "Where Did Randy Go Wrong?" *Mother Jones,* November 1989, 25.

17. Sigmund Freud, *Moses and Monotheism, The Standard Edition of the Complete Works of Sigmund Freud,* ed. and trans. James Strachey, 24 vols. (London: Hogarth Press, 1953–66; New York: Macmillan, 1953–74), 23:113–14.

18. See Joan Copjec, "The Orthopsychic Subject: Film Theory and the Reception of Lacan," *October* 49 (Summer 1989): 53–71, for a brilliant discussion of Foucault, Lacan, and the law.

19. Debbie Price, "Pr. George's Paternity Court Delivers Results," *Washington Post,* 11 October 1988, A1.

20. See Lis Wiehl, "DNA Test Dooms Paternity Trials, Lawyers Say," *New York Times,* 21 July 1989, B9.

21. Wiehl, "DNA Test."

22. Ruth Marcus, "States Can 'Presume' Husband Is Child's Father," *Washington Post,* 16 June 1989, A22.

23. Qtd. in Marcus, "States Can 'Presume.'"

24. In the Baby M. case the marital family of the Sterns was valued over the biological claim of Mary Beth Whitehead, the surrogate mother. But, interestingly, the judge did give Whitehead visitation rights. These rights were not extended to Michael H. Thus, the court's thinking seems to go like this: marital family with biological tie to child who wants child has first priority, biological mother second, and biological father third.

25. Spatial limitations make it impossible for me to discuss fully the logic of the "consent" requirement in relation to parents, as against "fathers." In other words, while the biological father's permission to abort is not required, in the case of teenage pregnancy the consent of a parent, or a judicial paterfamilias, is required (see *Hodgson v. Minnesota* and *Ohio v. Akron Center for Reproductive Health* [1990]). In effect, the pregnant woman is still required to enter a public discussion about her reproduction—with the doctor; the teenager is required to enter a discussion with the doctor, a parent, or a judge. The potential interest in the abortifacient known as RU-486 is keen in part because eventually this has great potential to become a medical technology capable of restoring some privacy to the pregnant woman. (It is not yet private, however; the pill must be administered under a doctor's care and requires three visits to the doctor's office). See Tribe, *Abortion,* 215–20, for a full discussion.

26. Randall Terry on videotaped interview with Julie Gustafason, October 1988; qtd. in Ginsburg, "Saving America's Souls," 26.

Contributors

Philip Auslander is Associate Professor in the School of Literature, Communication, and Culture at the Georgia Institute of Technology. He has written extensively on the theory of performance for *Theatre Journal, Drama Review, Performing Arts Journal,* and other publications. He is the author of *The New York School Poets as Playwrights* (1989) and *Presence and Resistance: Postmodernism and Cultural Politics in Contemporary American Performance* (1992).

C. Carr is a staff writer for the *Village Voice*. A collection of her performance pieces will be published next year by Wesleyan University Press.

Kate Davy is Associate Professor of Drama and Women's Studies at the University of California, Irvine. The editorial positions she has held include theater review editor for *Theatre Journal* and associate editor of *Theatre Design and Technology*. She is the author of *Richard Foreman and the Ontological-Hysteric Theatre* and the editor of *Richard Foreman: Plays and Manifestos*. Her work has appeared in *Performing Arts Journal, Theatre Journal, Drama Review, Twentieth-Century Literature, Parachute,* and *Studio International*. She is currently writing a book on the performance work of artists from the W.O.W. Cafe.

Joyce Devlin is chair of the Theatre Department, Mount Holyoke College. A graduate of Columbia University, she spent ten years in the New York professional theater before beginning her academic career. In 1988 she devised and toured a one-woman performance piece entitled *Chrysalis: A Journey of Women,* and her book, *Women's Scenes and Monologues: Annotated Bibliography,* was published in 1989. She is a former president of the New England Theatre Conference, a member of the College of Fellows, and a former chair for the new play division of the American College Theatre Festival. Currently, she is writing a book on the alternative British theater.

Elin Diamond is Associate Professor of English at Rutgers University, New Brunswick. Author of *Pinter's Comic Play* (1985), she writes on feminist and theater theory for *TDR, Modern Drama, Theatre Journal, ELH, Art and Cinema,* and *The Kenyon Review.* Her essays have appeared in such anthologies as *Intersecting Boundaries: The Theatre of Adrienne Kennedy* (1992); *Critical Theory and Performance* (1992); *Performing Feminisms: A Critical Anthology* (1990); and *Making a Spectacle* (1989). Her new book, *Unmaking Mimesis,* will be published by Routledge.

Jill Dolan teaches theater and drama and women's studies at the University of Wisconsin–Madison. She is the author of *The Feminist Spectator as Critic* (1989) and the forthcoming *Presence and Desire: Essays on Gender, Sexuality, Performance,* as well as articles on feminist performance theory, criticism, and practice published in *Theatre Journal, TDR, Modern Drama,* and *Women & Performance.*

Hilary Harris is a Ph.D. candidate in English at the University of California, Irvine. In the mid-1980s, she logged over 100,000 miles and as many one-liners as a stand-up comic on the women's music and comedy circuit.

Lynda Hart is Assistant Professor of English/Theatre Arts at the University of Pennsylvania. She is the author of *Sam Shepard's Metaphorical Stages* (1987) and editor of *Making a Spectacle: Feminist Essays on Contemporary Women's Theatre.* Her most recent articles have appeared in *TDR* and *Genders.* Her book *Between the Body and the Flesh: Performing Lesbian Sado-Masochism* is forthcoming from Columbia University Press. Her current project is *Fatal Women: The Violence of Sexual Difference,* a study of representations of female aggressors, which will be published by Princeton.

Lynda M. Hill recently completed a Ph.D. in Performance Studies at New York University. She has contributed to *American Theatre, Black American Literature Forum,* and other publications, and is now engaged in research on myth and intertextuality in contemporary cultural performances, while teaching American and African-American literature in the English Department at Temple University. She is preparing her dissertation, "Performance Theory, Gender, and Black Culture: The Iconography of Zora Neale Hurston," for publication.

Julie Malnig teaches in the Gallatin Division at New York University and is Associate Director of NYU's Center for Near Eastern Studies. She is on the editorial board of *Women & Performance*.

Vivian M. Patraka, Professor of English at Bowling Green State University, has contributed work to *Theatre Journal, Modern Drama, Discourse,* and *Drama Review,* and to the books *Critical Theory and Performance, Performing Feminisms,* and *Making a Spectacle.* She is now completing *Spectacles of Suffering: Theatrical Representations of the Holocaust and Fascism.*

Peggy Phelan is Associate Chair of the Department of Performance Studies, Tisch School of the Arts, New York University. She is the author of *Unmarked: The Politics of Performance* (1993). Her articles have appeared in such journals and collections as *TDR: A Journal of Performance Studies, Artforum, Lacanian Ink, The Hysterical Male,* and *American Literary History.* Her current project is *Perform/orials: Theatre Architecture, Grief and Writing.*

Janelle Reinelt is co-editor of *Theatre Journal.* Her recent work includes *Performing Power: Politics and Theatrical Representation,* edited with Sue-Ellen Case, and *Critical Theory and Performance,* edited with Joseph Roach. Her book on Brecht and British political drama is forthcoming from the University of Michigan Press.

Sandra L. Richards is an Associate Professor of African American Studies and Theatre at Northwestern University. Her articles on Nigerian and African-American playwrights have appeared in such publications as *Theatre Journal, New Theatre Quarterly, The Brecht Yearbook,* and *Black American Literature Forum,* and in *Critical Theory and Performance,* edited by Janelle Reinelt and Joseph Roach. Richards's association with Anna Deavere Smith goes back to the mid 1970s when both worked with the now-defunct Black Actors Workshop at the American Conservatory Theatre (A.C.T.) in San Francisco.

Amy Robinson is a doctoral student in English at the University of Pennsylvania. She is currently completing a dissertation entitled "To Pass//In Drag: Strategies of Entrance into the Visible," for which she was awarded the 1991 National Women's Studies Association/Naiad Press Graduate Scholarship in Lesbian Studies. Her article "Perversion or Production: Work and Sex in Victorian America" is forthcoming in *Eros and Masturbation,* edited by Vernon Rosario and Paula Bennett.

Judy C. Rosenthal has worked as a dramaturg on productions at the Spectrum Theater, Circle Repertory Company, and Women's Interarts Theater. She is on the editorial board of *Women & Performance,* and is currently completing her dissertation on the evolving American dramaturg at New York University's Department of Performance Studies.

Rebecca Schneider, a Ph.D. candidate in Performance Studies at New York University, teaches at Yale University and is Contributing Editor to the *Drama Review.* She is currently working on a book about feminist performance art tentatively titled *The Explicit Body.*

Raewyn Whyte is Dance and Theater Commentator in New Zealand for *The Listener* and *Dance Australia.* She is a Ph.D. candidate in Performance Studies at New York University. Her dissertation examines the performance of biculturalism in New Zealand.

Yvonne Yarbro-Bejarano is Associate Professor of Romance Languages and Comparative Literature at the University of Washington. She is the author of *Feminism and the Honor Plays of Lope de Vega* (forthcoming in Purdue Studies in Romance Literatures) and is currently writing a book on Cherríe Moraga and Gloria Anzaldúa.